California People

1^{50} (one fifty)

This is a Peregrine Smith Book, first published in 1982
by Gibbs M. Smith, Inc. PO Box 667, Layton, UT 84041

Manufactured in the United States of America

Book Design by Scott Knudsen

Library of Congress Cataloging in Publication Data

Dunlap, Carol, 1943-
  California People

    Includes index.
    1. California—Biography. I. Title
CT225.D86   1982   920'.0794 [B]   82-10495

ISBN 0-87905-091-8

CALIFORNIA PEOPLE

CAROL DUNLAP

Gibbs M. Smith, Inc.
Publisher of
Peregrine Smith Books
Salt Lake City

Introduction

There was rather more serendipity than science in the selection of *California People*. I started by combing the index pages of general works on the state, jotting down names that rang a bell. Some were familiar from the landscape (**Lassen, Blythe, Wilshire**), and I wanted to know who they were. Others are known to us all: **Mark Twain, Robert Louis Stevenson, Eugene O'Neill, Arnold Schoenberg**. I was curious to find out what attracted them to California, the quality of their lives and achievements here, and their effect on the cultural climate.

I decided at the outset to include all of California's governors, who turned out to be an interesting collection of rogues and characters. Otherwise, there are few rules of thumb. I simply began to read, accumulating as I went along the names of people who figured largely in their contemporaries' lives: **George Sterling**, for example, whose acquaintanceship was more interesting than his poetry.

In reading the biographies of Californians, I found some recurring themes: restlessness rather than rootedness, innovation instead of tradition, freedom replacing responsibility, personality and celebrity superseding achievement, and a new morality of self-indulgence.

I also found an obsession with bigness. California people built the biggest bridges and dams, the world's largest clothing manufacturing concern, the most bunyanesque used-car lots and—tempting fate—the biggest bomb.

What about Casey Stengel, a friend insisted—why isn't Casey Stengel in the book? For me, Stengel evokes Kansas City and New York, the cities where he was born, nicknamed, and won baseball immortality. Stengel married a silent screen actress and wintered with her in Glendale, California for the last half of his life. But he arrived in California a fully-developed personality and made his mark elsewhere, leaving no identifiable imprint on the landscape.

Likewise Hollywood stars. You will find Jimmy Cagney and Humphrey Bogart in other biographical sources on California, but not in this one. The only movie personalities in *California People* were born and/or raised here: **Marilyn Monroe, John Wayne, Esther Williams**. (I made an exception of **Rudy Vallee**, for reasons you can read for yourselves.) The movie moguls, on the other hand, are included as builders.

The emphasis here is on the people who made California or were made by it, who left their names on the landscape of our collective experience, who created our institutions, landmarks, myths.

California People is a bookworm's book, an impressionistic view of state history through the unit of biography. In fact, some of my people qualified primarily because they caught the fancy of some biographer: the gentle **Hugo Reid**, who lives in Susanna Bryant Dakin's book, or writer-guru **Ken Kesey**, the central character in Tom Wolfe's classic on the psychedelic era.

In case you might be tempted to try a biography or two, I have planted clues to the great bibliographic treasure hunt in the footnotes accompanying the sketches. (The footnotes are intended solely to suggest further reading; in no case is any sketch based exclusively on the work footnoted.)

Writing *California People* was for me a voyage of personal discovery. I was born and raised in Los Angeles, but never felt any particular sense of belonging—to the land perhaps, but not to any group of people called Californians. Only through reading did I begin to perceive a pattern of roots— my own roots as well as those of other Californians.

Leafing through one of **McGroarty**'s "mug books," I found my great-grandfather, a bush-league robber baron who is described as living a life out of *Treasure Island*. (I must have heard him mentioned, but Californians are not in general ancestor worshipers.) I also discovered that my grandmother helped count the daily take on one of **Tony Cornero**'s outlaw gambling ships, anchored off the Los Angeles coast during the 1930s. (She will be angry with me for telling, but I can't resist.)

I was born in the hospital where Robert Kennedy would die, and raised in Brentwood, which a junior high school teacher had the wit to describe as Ellis Island to Bel Air. As a child the neighborhood seemed perfectly ordinary to me although it now strikes me as insufferably affluent. I was never afraid of earthquakes; in fact, I rather enjoy them. But I conceived an exaggerated notion of tidal waves, which I imagined could roll over the palisades and sweep five miles inland.

In the years when prices were still slightly higher west of the Mississippi, I remember **Earl Warren** and his friendly family radiating a healthy aura from Sacramento. Then I recall being frightened by airplanes overhead during the Korean War, a fear I personally blamed (fairly or not) on **William Knowland**, California's "senator from Formosa."

Adolescence may be the peak California experience for the post-World War II generations, the experience that bonds us just as our forefathers once shared the Gold Rush. At school I was considered a hopeless grind, but still I spent whole summers perfecting my tan at **Will Rogers** State Beach. And I learned the exhilaration of driving in a two-tone convertible with tail fins. I chose to go "back East" to college, to grow up in a world where beaches were remote and cars superfluous. I have spent my adult life going back and forth from coast to coast. (I am convinced I could never live in between; I would get claustrophobia.) When I am in the East, I miss California, and vice versa. Having been in California for over two years now, writing this book, I need to get away. But I shall be back, I'm sure.

I have tried to pay my professional debts as I went along—notably, to Dorland Mountain Colony and to the Los Angeles Public Library. But some debts can never be repaid. This book is therefore dedicated to Paul Dunlap, who provided a room with a view where most of it was written; and to the libraries of America, for a lifetime of free reading.

Carol Dunlap
California, 1982

California People

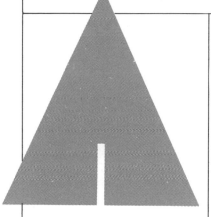

Albert Abrams

(1863-1924). He started out as a successful, respected San Francisco physician   a graduate of the prestigious University of Heidelberg, Germany (M.D., 1892), and a professor at Cooper (later Stanford) Medical College. Then he developed some bizarre notions of diagnosis and treatment. The world had become thoroughly "syphilized," Abrams announced, equating "syphilization" with civilization and proposing to cure it by means of electronic vibrations emitted by a magic box called the Oscilloclast. He claimed to be able to determine sex, race, religion, even emotion, as well as illness, from an anonymous drop of blood. He predicted the creation of "love

laboratories" to treat the peculiar vibrations transmitted by people in that emotional state. Abrams lost his job at Cooper Medical School in 1898 when students reported his ideas to the dean. He went on to establish a Clinic of Electronic Medicine in San Francisco, with a clientele of health faddists, spiritualists, and socialists—people who had lost their confidence in elementary physics along with their faith in capitalism and organized religion, as **Kenneth Rexroth** put it. One patient was **Krishnamurti**, the designated world teacher of theosophy, who sent Abrams a blood sample while vacationing in Southern California. By return mail Krishna received a diagnosis

of cancer in the left lung and syphilis of the nose. He dutifully submitted to treatment with the Oscilloclast, but thought it best to keep quiet about the diagnosis as "it would undoubtedly make an awful row." Abrams also claimed to have been consulted during Lenin's last illness. The doctor's credentials were so impressive, and the balance of knowledge and superstition so unstable in the early age of electronics (sound was only just being transmitted by radio) that few felt sure enough to dismiss the fraud outright. *Scientific American* magazine ran a six-part investigation into "ERA" (Electronic Revolution of Abrams), and when the doctor died, the *New York Times* hedged its bets with a full-column obituary.

Ansel Easton Adams

(1902-   ). The dean of American nature photographers was born in San Francisco, grandson of a 49er, and spent a relatively idyllic childhood exploring the dunes beyond the Golden Gate. When the Panama-Pacific Exposition opened in 1915, his father gave him a season pass to enjoy the sights. In 1916 Adams

discovered Yosemite, where he spent several summers as custodian of the Sierra Club lodge and where he took his first pictures with a Brownie box camera. There he also met his future wife; they were married at the foot of Bridalveil Falls. He spent years preparing for a career as a concert pianist but ultimately found a greater sense of personal reward in photography. San Francisco art patron Albert Bender arranged for the folio reproduction of his Yosemite photos in 1928, and also for his collaboration with **Mary Austin** on *Taos Pueblo* (1930). On occasion Adams engaged in social commentary, as with *Born Free and Equal* (1944), a book-length photo essay on Japanese internment during World War II. But he was preeminently a nature photographer, accomplishing on film what **John Muir** achieved in prose: the glorification of the Sierra Nevada. In fact, his highly contrasted black and white studies of the California mountains are so striking that reality pales by comparison and many tourists report disappointment when they stand before the real thing. Adams also enjoys the distinction of having become the richest photographer in history. In 1970 he acquired a business manager and announced his intention to stop reproducing his work, thus creating an instant market for prints at up to $800 apiece. Ten years later, the same prints were changing hands for upwards of $5,000 each. His books also command major prices, like $75 (deluxe edition: $2,500) for *Yosemite and the Range of Light* (New York, 1979).

The Eloquent Light by Nancy Newhall (San Francisco, 1963) is an early biographical study of Adams.

Kurt Herbert Adler

(1905-   ). It is a mark of San Francisco's cultural cosmopolitanism that it acquired its very own brilliant,

temperamental European maestro to rule as dictator of the city opera for 25 years. A cross between Rudolf Bing and Peter Sellers, Adler (not to be confused with the German chemist or the Metropolitan choirmaster of the same names) was born in Vienna and apprenticed under theatrical genius Max Reinhardt. When he took over the San Francisco Opera in 1956, it was a modest provincial company with a wardrobe of musty old costumes and a small but loyal following of society matrons and sentimental paisanos. Adler completely revamped stage and production design, added modern opera to the repertoire, introduced

newcomers like Leontyne Price, and spun off performances in labor halls, public parks, and even a rural vineyard. He bullied, wheedled, coaxed, and flattered his performers to new standards of bravura, and barred hostile critics from the opera house. (Democracy does not work in opera, he explained.) Thanks to Adler's charisma and his obsessive attention to detail, whether musical, theatrical, or financial, he turned the San Francisco Opera into the second company in the U.S. after New York's Metropolitan.

Howard Fieldstead Ahmanson (1906-1968).

Ahmanson was a precocious businessman who started a fire insurance company while still a student at USC (B.A., 1927). The roots of his $1 billion financial empire were established during the Depression in property foreclosure, banking, insurance, and investments. In 1947 he bought a savings and loan company for $162,000, then expanded and merged it into the world's largest, Home Savings & Loan. During the 1950s Ahmanson became active in state politics as a liberal (some said "pink" Republican), managing **Goodwin Knight**'s 1954 campaign for governor and funneling contributions to legislative candidates through Democratic Speaker of the House Jesse Unruh. (This paid off when the legislature gave Ahmanson's fire insurance company exclusive coverage of Cal-Vet homes financed by state aid to veterans.) For all that his

money could buy—a Tudor home in Hancock Park, a 200-acre ranch in the desert, a succession of prize-winning yachts, an art collection—Ahmanson remained a nouveau riche outsider in L.A. society. But as a rich man with an "edifice complex," he was a prime target for fund-raising culture mavens. In 1958 he donated $2 million for an Ahmanson Theater at the L.A. Music Center, plus another $2 million to the L.A. County Museum of Art for an Ahmanson gallery. (He wanted the whole museum named after himself, it was rumored, failing which, he insisted that *his* paintings hang in *his* gallery.) There is also an Ahmanson Center for Biological Research at USC and the Ahmanson Center in L.A., not to mention all those banks designed to look like Masonic temples.

Joe Alioto (Joseph

Lawrence Alioto, 1916-   ). As mayor of San Francisco (1967-1975), Alioto seemingly had it all: power, money, culture, and a clear shot at the political moon. The son of a North Beach fish wholesaler and restaurateur (not a fisherman, he was quick to correct), he graduated from Saint Mary's College and law school at Catholic University in Washington, D.C. Specializing in antitrust law, the dynamic Alioto soon rose to the top of his profession, establishing a family firm in which two of his sons would later join him and acquiring an opulent Renaissance-style palazzo in San Francisco's Presidio Heights. As mayor, he approved downtown redevelopment, pushed minority participation in government, and moved forcefully to put down student antiwar protests at San Francisco State. *Look* magazine hinted at Mafia connections in a 1969 article, but Alioto filed suit for libel and eventually won. Then in 1972, when he announced his candidacy for governor, it all began to come apart. His wife disappeared during the campaign—to punish him for neglect, she told everyone who would listen—and he lost. In 1975, a grand jury criticized the outgoing mayor for conflict of interest in acquiring with his son John a shipping line—which soon went bankrupt. When Alioto divorced and remarried in 1978, all the intimate details made the front page of the local newspapers. "Sicilians don't get divorced," a relative said, while the ex-mayor's ex-wife announced that he looked ghastly from dieting to keep up with his new young wife. And in 1980 a Wyoming rancher won a record malpractice verdict against the Alioto firm in a supermarket price-fixing case, handled by "Little Joe" Alioto with all of his father's arrogance and little of his skill.

Herb Alpert (Herbert Alpert, 1935-   ). The Tijuana Brass, which sold some 30 million records during the 1960s, was born in a Hollywood garage, the creation of a Los Angeles native of Russian-Jewish descent. Alpert, a former U.S. Army trumpeter, hit on the idea of producing slicked up Mexican music while making the proverbial south-of-the-

border pilgrimage to the Tijuana bullfights. He used the profits from "Ameriachi" music to buy the old Chaplin studio in Hollywood, a little medieval principality on La Brea which became headquarters of his A & M (M for partner Jerry Moss), the largest independent in the recording industry. The Tijuana Brass disbanded in 1969, leaving a haze of ethnic confusion. Alpert's brother David told *Los Angeles* magazine he is frequently asked, "How come you're Jewish and your brother's Mexican?"

Juan Bautista Alvarado (1800?-1882). Alvarado was a clerk in the Monterey customs house when he led the 1836 revolution against Mexico to establish home rule. He was considered a liberal with reform ideals—"the ablest man Old California produced," according to **Gertrude Atherton**—but his energies were absorbed during six years as governor (1836-1842) by factional strife and dissipation. In 1838 he asserted his authority by doing battle in the south with the insurgent Carrillo brothers and their friends—a bloodless encounter, **William Heath Davis** reported, "as they took the precaution to keep at a

safe distance from each other." Alvarado earned the undying enmity of many Americans imprisoned in 1840 for plotting against him. Some were sent to Monterey for a day or two, others deported to Mexico. The following year he restricted trade with foreigners, which severely curtailed government revenues then heavily dependent on import duties. But much of the time the governor seemed to let public affairs drift, content, as historian **H.H. Bancroft** said, "to deplore the nonprogressive conduct of the department, and cast the blame on circumstances, on fate, or Mexico." In response to complaints by his uncle and rival **Vallejo**, the Mexican government sent General **Manuel Micheltorena** with an army of irregulars to replace Alvarado. The failure of home rule was humiliating for Alvarado, who pulled support together to help drive out Micheltorena in 1845. However, he took little part in resisting the American conquest which followed within a few years, admiring the creative drive of the Americans even while they proved his ruin. Compelled by

moneylenders to liquidate his assets, he sold his 44,000-acre Rancho Mariposa to **John C. Frémont** and spent the next twenty years fighting for title to a small remnant of his former holdings. Only bill collectors, he sighed, still bothered to address him as "Your Excellency." A small town in the East Bay and a boulevard in Los Angeles were named for him.

Walter Clement Alvarez (1884-1978) and **Luis Alvarez** (1911-   ). Walter Alvarez lived the transition from folk superstition to scientific method in medicine, from family doctor to clinical researcher. Born in San Francisco, he was the son of a Spaniard who came to California in 1880 to make his fortune and remained to study medicine. (The senior Dr. Alvarez went off as a government doctor to Hawaii where his son was raised, later practicing in a Mexican mining town.) Walter graduated from Cooper Medical College (later Stanford) in 1905 and was doing his internship at San Francisco City and County Hospital during the earthquake. A nonconformist, restless and dissatisfied with the primitive state of medical knowledge, he wrote papers against the preoperative custom of purging and against the needless extraction of teeth. He once examined the stomach muscles of a murderer hanged at San **Quentin**, to further his knowledge of the gastrointestinal tract, and he was also interested in heredity and in the psychosomatic dimension of disease. And somehow he found the time to join month-long Sierra Club hikes into the California wilderness. In 1925 Alvarez left his San Francisco practice to join the Mayo Clinic for 25 years. On retiring in 1950 he began a nationally syndicated newspaper column of medical advice for laymen. A scientist who followed his curiosity wherever it led, Alvarez once visited **Ernest Lawrence**'s radiation lab at the University of California, Berkeley. Coincidentally, his daughter Gladys became Lawrence's secretary, and his son **Luis Alvarez** (1911-   ), after earning a Ph.D. in physics from the University of Chicago went to work on Lawrence's cyclotron. Luis worked on radar at MIT during World War II, devising a system of all-weather landing for planes. Later he joined the Manhattan Project at Los Alamos, actually monitoring the 1945 Trinity and Hiroshima explosions from observation planes. Back at Berkeley after the war, he became Lawrence's disciple and protegé, even testifying in Lawrence's stead against **Oppenheimer** as a security risk. Luis Alvarez received a Nobel Prize in 1968 for his research on subatomic particles.

Walter Alvarez wrote Incurable Physician, The Autobiography of America's Family Doctor *(Englewood Cliffs, NJ, 1963) and a slightly updated edition,* Alvarez on Alvarez *(San Francisco, 1977.*

Earle C. Anthony
(1880-1961). Anthony was an automotive and communications pioneer who helped adapt the horseless

carriage and the wireless radio to the California experience. As a teenager in L.A. he built his own primitive automobile, said to have been involved in the city's first traffic accident. After graduation from the University of California at Berkeley (1903) where he founded the campus humor magazine, he opened a Packard dealership in L.A. To fuel his cars, he soon had a string of gas stations; to attract patronage, he imported neon from France for eye-catching signs; and to extend the California driver's range, he suggested an "automobile highway" from Los Angeles to San Francisco. **Bernard Maybeck**, who designed a temple-like showroom for him in San Francisco, described him as a merchant prince, selling autos like so many magic carpets. After World War I, Anthony expanded into radio broadcasting with the purchase of KFI, a powerful L.A. station. After World War II (when his Packard dealerships were converted to Chrysler and Lincoln-Mercury), he moved into the new field of television. KFI-TV began broadcasting in L.A. in 1948, presenting a schedule of Rams games, but somehow TV did not have the same appeal for Anthony as radio. Although he lived in L.A. (in a **Greene and Greene**

bungalow in Los Feliz), he also maintained business and social ties in San Francisco, including a membership in the Bohemian Club, where he was visiting when he died.

Juan Bautista de Anza
(1735-1788). Alta California was thought to be a peninsula like Baja California until Anza set out on his first overland journey from Mexico in 1774. A member of the Spanish military aristocracy whose father was killed by renegade Indians, Anza first crossed the unchartered California desert with only a runaway Indian for a guide, arriving after six weeks of travel at Mission San Gabriel in March 1774. The following year, he led the way from Mexico City to Monterey, California for a party of 240—40 families, 38 soldiers with 29 wives, three padres, four servants for same, three Indian interpreters—the forebearers of the first Latin families in California. Anza's biographer describes the party as a "moving sanitarium"—there were three births and countless medical exigencies en route—presided over by "Dr. Anza." Described by others as brave, cultured and incorruptible, Anza was rewarded for his pathfinding with the post of governor of New Mexico (1777-1787). A national monument in the Southern California desert was named Anza-Borrego in his honor, while other memorials go by the name De Anza, such as De Anza College in Cupertino.

Herbert Eugene Bolton covered the subject exhaustively in his five-volume Anza's California Expeditions *(Berkeley, 1930).*

Fatty Arbuckle (Roscoe Conkling Arbuckle, 1887-1933). Arbuckle's trials for manslaughter, which sold more **Hearst** newspapers than anything since the sinking of the *Lusitania*, marked the end of innocence for Hollywood. He was a comedian from California, a graduate of Santa Clara High School in San Jose who became popular on the vaudeville circuit as a lovable, lightfooted fatman. His life was his work to the extent that his marriage to Minta Durfee in 1908 was performed by the mayor of Long Beach before a full house at the Byde A. Wyle Theatre. Arbuckle went to work for filmmaker Mack Sennett, directing and starring in his own films as the greatest pie-slinger of all time. In 1921, at the peak of his popularity, having completed three films simultaneously for Paramount, he went to San Francisco to unwind over Labor Day. The party in his hotel suite, complete with booze and broads, included Virginia Rappe, a would-be actress with a reputation for taking her clothes off after a few drinks. After a brief spell alone with Arbuckle, she began to complain of abdominal pain and a few days later, the others having returned south, died of a ruptured bladder. Stories immediately began to circulate of rape by Coke or champagne bottle, and Arbuckle's size, once an object of fun, became a source of obscene speculation. He was brought to trial on the basis of sketchy allegations because, the judge explained, "we are trying our present day morals." Finally acquitted after two hung juries, Arbuckle was banned from the screen by the **Hays** Office, at the prompting of Paramount, his own employer. He spent the rest of his life trying to recoup his reputation and his finances as a director under the pseudonyms William Goodrich or Will B. Good.
David Yallop lays to rest two generations of rumor and innuendo in The Day the Laughter Stopped *(New York, 1976).*

Herbert W. Armstrong (1892-   ). One of Pasadena's biggest industries is religion, and one of its liveliest sects Armstrong's Worldwide Church of God. A former advertising man from the Midwest, Armstrong

began preaching in Oregon during the Depression. He had been chosen by God for his sophisticated command of media, he claimed, to prepare the Anglo-Saxon people for nuclear destruction in 1972 and the return of Jesus three years later. Moving to Pasadena in 1947, he communicated with his followers via radio and TV broadcasts in the rapid-fire style of a Paul Harvey. He also published a glossy "news magazine" modeled after *Time*. The WCG faithful (the hard core is estimated at 60,000) were expected to tithe up to 50 percent of their incomes, giving Armstrong larger resources than Oral Roberts and Billy Graham combined. Some of the money was used to establish Ambassador College in Pasadena and some to acquire mansions, limousines, airplanes, and art collections. In the 1960s son Garner Ted Armstrong (1930-   ), who as a youth had been more interested in show business than religion, began to replace his father in the electronic ministry while Herbert assumed the status of elder statesman and world traveler, with his born-again tax consultant in constant attendance. When the date of the predicted holocaust came and went, the Worldwide Church of God began to come apart at the seams. Garner Ted was banished in 1972 for rumored sexual improprieties, and the following year several leading churchmen were excommunicated. Church finances were strained by the opening of the $10 million Ambassador Auditorium in Pasadena in 1974. Arguments about tithing erupted. A group of dissidents published a 1976 lampoon, *Ambassador Report,* with features entitled "Fleecing the Faithful" and "In Bed with Garner Ted." Excommunicated in 1978, Garner Ted traded sensational charges in the press with his father. And in 1979 the Worldwide Church of God was placed in receivership by the attorney general of California at the request of the dissidents. This only served to give Herbert, then in his eighties, a new issue— freedom of religion—and a new lease on life. The state soon backed down, leaving him in absolute control of the remainder of his congregation.
Joseph Hopkins, author of The Armstrong Empire *(Grand Rapids, MI, 1974), describes himself as a concerned layman.*

Gertrude Franklin Atherton (1857-1948). Atherton was California's first liberated woman, a writer who escaped the petty domestic tyranny of country verandah society to go and do as she pleased during a long, eventful life. Raised largely by her grandfather, secretary of **Ralston**'s Bank of California, she ran off at nineteen to marry George Atherton, whose chief qualification

seems to have been that he was her divorced mother's suitor. Soon tiring of her husband, of maternity ("a highly specialized form of martyrdom"), and of life on the Atherton estate south of San Francisco, she borrowed the skeletons from a neighbor's closet to write a shocking first novel. After her husband's unlamented death in 1887, she went off to live in New York, England, and Germany, with research excursions to the West Indies for a biographical novel about Alexander Hamilton, to Alaska to learn about **Rezanov**, a Russian official in nineteenth-century California, and to Greece to study Pericles and Aspasia. Around the turn of the century, Atherton returned to California to reconsider her own heritage. For the 1915 Panama-Pacific Exposition she wrote *California, An Intimate History*, the first of several gossipy appreciations

of local history. (Actually, she appreciated San Francisco but despised L.A., an "upstart pothole," the "Chicago of the coast.") Atherton's facts were not always correct, but her descriptions were superb. Of **Pío Pico**, California's last Mexican governor, for example, she wrote that he was "short and very stout, with a snapping eye and a fat empurpled nose." A close friend of **James Phelan**, she spent the best parts of fifteen years as his guest at the Villa Montalvo. Always controversial, she made scandalous headlines in 1923 with a novel about an aging woman's attempts at rejuvenation. She remained active into her nineties.

Adventures of a Novelist (New York, 1932) is Atherton's autobiography. A prolific writer, she began to repeat herself with Golden Gate Country *(New York, 1945) and* My San Francisco: A Wayward Biography *(New York, 1946).*

Mary Hunter Austin

(1868-1934). Her admirers called her one of the most remarkable women of her generation. Others privately referred to her as "the mother-in-law of God." Austin was born and raised a Methodist in the Midwest, which represented to her everything alien and antithetical to the creative spirit. She came west with her family in 1888 to homestead near the Tejon Ranch, a land which at first seemed as alien as Mars, all dusty sagebrush and perennial drought. But she gradually learned to know the country, its seasons and signs, and found herself deeply attuned to the economy of nature in inland California. Teaching school in

the San Joaquin Valley, Austin was an interested spectator of the great water war against land baron **Henry Miller**, whose "Nordic strength" she admired. After an unsuccessful marriage to an Owens Valley rancher and the institutionalization of their retarded daughter, Austin moved to L.A. in 1899 to break into the circle around **Charles Lummis**. Both supreme egotists, neither could abide the other, so Austin tried her luck in San Francisco. With the publication in 1903 of *Land of Little Rain*, a series of

reflections on the desert ethos, she joined the front ranks of the Northern California literati. Settling in Carmel in 1905, she affected Indian-princess braids and an early model muumuu, claiming clairvoyant powers as the high priestess of local folk art. Austin's novels, which were less successful than her essays, include *A Woman of Genius* (1912) and *The Ford* (1917), the latter about L.A.'s despoiling of the Owens River Valley. After World War I, she settled in Santa Fe, New Mexico, where she remained until her death.

Austin's autobiography, Earth Horizons *(New York, 1932)*, is composed alternatively in the first and third persons, giving credence to the "mother-in-law of God" school of opinion.

Gene Autry (Orvon Eugene Autry, 1907-   ). A former telegrapher from the rural Texas-Oklahoma border, Autry arrived in Hollywood in 1934 to make his movie debut as a singing cowboy. Like **Will Rogers**, he didn't much care for California at first, but western films offered a great way to beat the game. ("In the costume ball of life," he wrote, "you never had to change clothes.") Autry couldn't read music, but he made 300 records, nine of which sold over a million copies. Strictly an amateur actor, he played his engaging self in 93 movies (five basic plots, he estimated) over a twenty-year period. (He took time out to serve as a World War II air transport pilot, the only officer in the Air Corps with permission to wear cowboy boots on duty.) Autry may not have been a great performer, but his arithmetic was good and he knew what to do for an encore. With the demise of the B western in the mid-1950s, he began to manage his diverse interests, which included radio station KMPC in Los Angeles. To maintain the station's sports profile after Dodger director **Walter O'Malley** cancelled Dodger broadcasts, Autry bought his own baseball team, the Los Angeles (later California) Angels. "It looks so simple on the field," remarked the new owner, "and yet within even the smoothest of organizations there are enough

disturbances to make an Italian opera company seem calm." As proprietor of his own sports-media empire, he ranked as one of the richest men in Hollywood.

Autry's autobiography, Back in the Saddle Again *(Garden City, NY, 1978)* is well salted with self-humor.

Joan Baez (1941-   ). As a fifth grader in Redlands, Baez was considered a Mexican because of her dark skin. (Her mother was born in Scotland, her father in Mexico.) But the family moved around a lot, including a year in Iraq where her father taught physics for UNESCO. Her negative self-image gradually evolved into a positive sense of identification with the dispossessed of the world. Singing "Farewell, Angelina" at the 1959 Newport Folk Festival, Baez with her silvery soprano voice and long black hair embarked on a successful career as a performer and activist. Whatever the cause, she seemed to take an anti-Establishment position, turning up in 1964 to lead free speech protestors at Berkeley in "We Shall Overcome," withholding income taxes to protest the Vietnam War, and singing for **Cesar Chavez**'s striking farmworkers. With Ira Sandperls, whom she first met when she was a high school student in Palo Alto, she established an Institute for the Study of Non-Violence in 1965. (Originally in the Carmel Valley, it subsequently moved to Palo Alto, Baez's home base.) She was arrested twice in 1967 for demonstrating at the Oakland military induction center and in 1969 married a former Stanford student-body president who spent most of their short marriage in jail for refusing induction. Always controversial, she aroused hatred on the Right ("Joanie Phoanie," Al Capp called her) and adoration on the Left as Bob Dylan's "sad-eyed lady of

the lowlands." In 1979, speaking out against North Vietnamese violations of human rights, prompting the massive exodus of the "boat people," she momentarily alienated her radical fans as well.

Baez wrote Daybreak *(New York, 1968)*, a short memoir.

Arcadia Bandini Stearns de Baker (1825?-1912). The beautiful daughter of ranchero **Juan Bandini,** she married two of the richest men of her day and at her death left the most valuable estate yet probated in Los Angeles County. Married first at fourteen to **Abel Stearns**, who was older (and richer) than her father, she moved into L.A.'s most sumptuous residence, wore custom-made clothes, and drove around town in a proper Bostonian carriage. She once gave the Empress of China some sheep. The marriage, although childless, was considered a happy one. Three years after Stearns's death in 1874, the still handsome Arcadia married Col. Robert Baker, new owner of the San Vicente Ranch and an associate of Sen. **John P. Jones** in the development of Santa Monica. The beach town's foremost hotel, a great verandahed Victorian structure with a cupola, was named after the regal Mrs. de Baker, who affected a French particle before her second husband's name. Baker tore down Stearns's "Arcadia Block" and replaced it with an impressive office building, in which Arcadia maintained a salon furnished with Aubusson carpets, period furniture, and

Sèvres china. (The "Baker Block" survived until 1942, when it was torn down for a freeway.) Widowed again, Arcadia Bandini Stearns de Baker spent her last years living in Santa Monica, dispensing financial aid to a large circle of impoverished relatives. When she died intestate, 32 lawsuits were filed by 86 hopeful heirs: 35 Bandinis, 41 Stearns, and 10 Bakers. Years later everyone eventually got some small share of the $7 million estate.

Thomas Baker

(1810-1872). Baker was a lawyer and militia colonel from Ohio who helped develop the lower San Joaquin Valley. He was creator in 1855 of Visalia, although Nathaniel Vise usually gets the credit, was elected to the state assembly in 1855, and rose to the state senate in 1861. Thought to be a secessionist, Baker was interned briefly in San Francisco during the Civil War, an experience which made the San Joaquin Valley

seem like a healthy place to retire. In 1862 he set out to reclaim the vast swamplands of the Kern River delta, 400,000 acres that have been compared in fertility to the Nile River delta. Using Indian labor, Baker built a levee and erected a dam at the north end of Buena Vista Lake. The drought of the Civil War years, so devastating to settled rangeland, helped dry out the former swamp. In 1867 the state rewarded him with a grant of 87,000 acres. He built a road to Havilah, then the Kern County seat, and kept open house for travelers along the long road from Los Angeles to Sacramento. In 1869, frustrated in his attempt to return to the state legislature, he decided to lay out a town of his own, Bakersfield. After Baker's death from typhoid, his rich new lands, which would yield oil and gold, were taken over by **Henry Miller** and Charles Lux.

Naomi Bain wrote The Story of Col. Baker and the Founding of Bakersfield, *published by the Kern County Historical Society in 1944.*

Allan Paul Bakke

(1940-   ). The reverse discrimination case that split the U.S. Supreme Court in 1978 and polarized American liberals was filed by an engineer from the Midwest trying to get into medical school in California. Bakke, who graduated from the University of Minnesota (1962) at the top of his class and returned after military service to finish a master's degree there, was working at NASA's Ames Research Center in Mountain View when he applied for admission to UC Davis in 1973. A Davis

interviewer described him as "tall and strong and Teutonic in appearance" but "completely unprepossessing." His grades and other qualifications were good, but at 33 Bakke was considered overage. In 1974, twice rejected by Davis, Bakke filed suit charging that the university's affirmative action program, which reserved sixteen places out of a class of 100 for the "disadvantaged," constituted a violation of the Fourteenth Amendment's equal protection clause. The Bakke case split liberals between groups like the Anti-Defamation League which opposes racial quotas and the NAACP which argues their necessity to overcome past discrimination. The University of California itself seemed ambivalent, concerned to obey the law and to uphold admission standards at the same time. Everyone agreed it was not an ideal case, but it nevertheless went to the state Supreme Court which ruled in 1976 that the program as administered violated the rights of nonminority applicants. The U.S. Supreme Court agreed, although adding that race was a legitimate factor with respect to "voluntary affirmative action." Bakke began his medical education in 1978, age 38, and earned

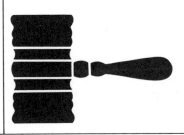

his M.D. from UC Davis in 1982.

Joel Dreyfus and Charles Lawrence, The Bakke Case *(New York, 1979).*

Lucky Baldwin

(Elias Jackson Baldwin, 1828-1909). A fabled character in late nineteenth-century California, Baldwin enjoyed great celebrity for his financial and sexual exploits. Born in Ohio, he started with a hotel and livery business in Northern California during the 1850s and made a killing in the Comstock. There are several versions of how he came to be called "Lucky." According to the story with the widest currency, Baldwin instructed his broker to sell some mining shares but left on a world tour with the shares locked in a safe; while he was gone, the mine came in. Somewhat less felicitous was his investment of large sums in the Baldwin Hotel and Theater in San Francisco, which opened in 1876 and burned to the ground uninsured in 1898. Baldwin was said to have acquired the coveted Santa Anita Ranch in the San Gabriel Valley through luck, but in fact he paid $200,000 for it, a princely sum in 1875. Undeniably, however, he had a talent for being in at the kill. Having loaned $300,000 to L.A.'s Temple and Workman Bank just before it failed, he foreclosed on more valuable property adjacent to the ranch in 1876. The Santa Anita became the great show ranch of Southern California, producing 2,000 pounds of butter a week, 400,000 gallons of wine a year, and a stable of thoroughbreds, including three Kentucky Derby winners. On the other side of the ledger, Baldwin was a notorious skinflint and libertine, constantly involved in lawsuits over nonpayment of debts and seduction of what was then called the fair sex. Chronically short of cash, he kept his ranch laborers in a virtual state of peonage and preferred to pay bills in raw brandy. Married four or five times, he also entertained so many young females that his home became known as "Baldwin's harem." One woman shot him in the arm and later sued him for maintenance of her child. In 1884, a jilted sixteen-year-old inamorata won a $75,000 settlement; and at the age of 60 the financier defended himself against yet another paternity suit on grounds that the 31-year-old mother was old and ugly. Baldwin subdivided Arcadia and sold the townsites of Sierra Madre and Monrovia. One of his last ventures was a race track, opened in 1907. When the state finally legalized wagering in 1933, Baldwin's old track became Santa Anita, the class act of western racing. In a final stroke of luck, oil was discovered in his Montebello pastures and on his La Cienega ranch, now called Baldwin Hills.

C.B. Glasscock's Lucky Baldwin, The Story of an Unconventional Success *(New York, 1933), is very dated.*

Hubert Howe Bancroft

(1832-1918). Bancroft created a controversial San Francisco literary outfit along the lines of an assembly plant, writing history as other entrepreneurs built railroads. An Ohio boy with little formal schooling, he arrived in California in 1852 with a consignment of books to sell for his brother-in-law and soon owned the finest bookstore west of Chicago—a department store, actually, carrying stationery, legal forms, music, and maps, and running its own printing and binding operations. During the 1860s Bancroft began collecting books and other materials on the West Coast; he also employed researchers to take down the memoirs of oldtimers and to copy local archives that could not be bought. An omnivorous reader, he calculated that it would take him 400 years to read his 60,000 volume collection, so he set his researchers to work, organizing, indexing, and digesting the materials. Working from drafts prepared by his assistants, who included a former governor of Baja California and an Italian "general," Bancroft wrote and revised for sixteen years putting in ten-to-twelve hour days to complete a 39-volume history of the Pacific Slope (1874-1890), including eleven volumes on California. The compleat bookman, he printed and published his own books, solicited and arranged reviews, and hired an army of subscription canvassers to sell the $284 set door-to-door throughout the West. Needless to say, the Bancroft method, from research to promotion, was highly

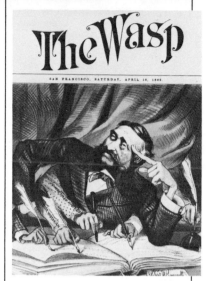

controversial. Bancroft was accused within his lifetime of plagiarizing and exploiting his "researchers," more than one of whom later claimed authorship of entire volumes; of slanting his opinions to favor subscribers; and of extortionary sales techniques. A subsequent publishing enterprise called *Chronicles of the Builders*—a biographical dictionary paid for by the subjects at the rate of about $1,000 a page—brought further disrepute on his history business. Bancroft had become so controversial that it took him a decade to negotiate the sale of his collection to the University of California at the bargain basement price of $150,000. Later and more dispassionate critics would judge his 39-volume history to be ponderous, occasionally amateurish, and insufficiently digested, but a valuable compendium of the materials in Bancroft's larger priceless collection.

Bancroft called his autobiography

Literary Industries (*San Francisco, 1890*), prompting critics to remark that he was more industrious than literary. *John Caughey's* Hubert Howe Bancroft; Historian of Western America (*Berkeley, 1946*) is ponderous but thoroughly professional.

Arcadia Bandini. *See* Arcadia Bandini Stearns de Baker.

Juan Lorenzo Bandini

(1800-1859). One of the most prominent Californios of the last generation of Mexican rule, Bandini arrived in Southern California around 1820 from Peru, an aristocrat claiming descent from Italy's de Medicis. He soon acquired a string of ranchos—Tecate, Guadalupe, Jurupa, Coronado—stretching from Los Angeles to the Baja, and a San Diego townhouse, the Casa de Bandini, furnished with rugs, silver, crystal, and furniture from Europe. Richard Henry Dana, who met him in 1836, described him as an effete gentleman, elegant, proud, and impoverished, a picturesque character out of *Gil Blas*. True, he ordered his shoes from Europe and cut a graceful figure on the dance floor, but Bandini was in fact a leading progressive of the era. He participated in the 1831 *coup d'état* against Governor Manuel Victoria and in the 1837 struggle for power. He even favored American statehood as more efficient than Mexican rule. Three beautiful Bandini daughters sewed the first stars-and-stripes to wave over San Diego and all married Yankees, but statehood did their father little good. He wrote a learned treatise against the U.S. land laws

which dispossessed so many of his compadres whose titles rested on good faith rather than paper. Bandini himself fell deeply in debt during the first decade of statehood and lost much of his land to moneylenders, including his Yankee sons-in-laws. His self-respect went with his land, and he died a broken man.

See "The Bandinis," a three-part series by Merle Clayton in San Diego Magazine (*April-June 1969) and Leonard Pitt,* The Decline of the Californios (*Berkeley, 1970*).

Phineas Banning

(1830-1885). On first arriving in Los Angeles in 1853, diarist Harris Newmark was astonished to find that the picturesque young man wearing short pantaloons, red

galluses, and brogans over tattered socks was the harbormaster. Banning, who came west in 1851, achieved a monopoly of landing facilities and freight handling at San Pedro by sheer energy and drive. Expanding into the hinterlands, he opened stage routes to Fort Tejon, San Bernardino, and Yuma, and negotiated with Brigham Young for a freight and passenger line to Salt Lake City. A large and convivial man, Banning raced teams of wild horses, threw county-wide barbecues and joined vigilante groups, all with great gusto. In 1858 he founded a company town named Wilmington after his hometown in Delaware. (It was described by a contemporary as "an extensive city located at the head of a slough in a pleasant neighborhood of sand banks and marshes.") The Port Admiral, as he was called in respectful jest, built himself a gracious colonial-style home with a cupola from which to sight arriving ships, and acquired the offshore island of Catalina. Some laughed when Banning built a lilliputian 21-mile railroad linking L.A. and San Pedro (1869), for he was a man before his time. He travelled to Washington in search of funds for harbor development, which became a reality fifteen years after his death, and headed a rudimentary oil company that acquired drilling rights to ranchos where oil would be discovered 30 years later. Banning left his name on a windy town in the San Gorgonio Pass along one of his stage routes. His Wilmington home is now part

of the L.A. park system.

Port Admiral (*San Francisco, 1957*) by Maymie Krythe is small town history.

Louise Aline Barnsdall

(1882-1946). She was an heiress with a social conscience, a benevolent eccentric who gave her estate of the city of Los Angeles for a "people's park." Little is known of her personal life. Her father was an Oklahoma oilman whose company drilled off Santa Barbara and near Newhall. She studied art and drama in Europe, bore a daughter whose father remains unknown, and had a spectacular house designed by Frank Lloyd Wright in his pre-Columbian style. (She was a difficult client and had such incorrigible wanderlust that Wright wondered why she wanted a house at all.) More is remembered of her "causes": she deeded her property to the city in 1926 and went off to Geneva to live at the "League for Universal Peace." Barnsdall's bequest contained stipulations: her house was to be used as a club for girls, an obscure type of French dancing was to be taught, and no statue of any political or military figure might be erected on the 13.6 acres. When these stipulations were not observed, she sued for repossession and spent her last decade in acute aggravation with the establishment. She supported Upton Sinclair's campaign to end poverty in California, and contributed generously to the campaign to pardon Tom Mooney, the Bay Area radical convicted of the 1916 Preparedness Day bombing,

erecting "Free Mooney" billboards around her property. After Mooney was pardoned by Governor **Culbert Olson**, whose 1938 electoral campaign she supported, the billboards and even sandwich boards simply changed causes, including independence for India. In 1945 she launched the "Battle of Barnsdall Park," putting up barriers against automobile traffic that she felt endangered neighborhood children. At the end of her life she was a recluse, living alone in her Mayan temple with twelve cocker spaniels running free in violation of city leash laws. Today, Barnsdall Park survives as a welcome oasis in the midst of urban blight.

Washington Bartlett

(1824-1887). California's sixteenth governor, Bartlett was a 49er from Georgia, a printer by trade who started a couple of unsuccessful newspapers in San Francisco during the 1850s. Active in the Second Vigilance Committee, he became San Francisco county clerk (1859-1867) and state senator (1873-1877). In 1883 Bartlett ran for mayor of San Francisco as the **Buckley** machine's concession to respectability. Distinguished in appearance, he also enjoyed what later generations would call name recognition, for the first alcalde of San Francisco, a third lieutenant on **Montgomery's** *Portsmouth*, was a distant relative with the same name. The second Washington Bartlett became mayor by an extremely slim margin. (It was revealed during the campaign that he employed Orientals in his business interests, although his Democratic Party supported Oriental exclusion.) After a second term as mayor, Bartlett ran successfully for governor, but the Buckley machine's finest hour was brief, for Bartlett died of Bright's disease during his first year in office.

L. Frank Baum (Lyman

Frank Baum, 1856-1919). With his first wealth from the popular Oz books, Baum began wintering in Coronado. In 1909 he moved permanently to the land of perpetual summer, acquiring a Pasadena house with an aviary of rare songbirds. Later Baum moved his "Ozcot" to the corner of Franklin and Cherokee in Hollywood, where he tended his prize chrysanthemums wearing a silk shirt, panama hat, and kid gloves. In addition to his fourteen Oz books, he wrote boys' stories under the name Floyd Akers, girls' stories under the name Edith Van Dyne, two serious novels as Schuyler Staunton, and doggerel for a jolly group of fellows started by his neighbor **Harry Haldeman**. The "Uplifters," as Baum named them (motto: "Keep it Up"), with Haldeman as "Grand Muscle" or president, held weekly luncheons, monthly jamborees, and an annual "high jinks" which one year featured Baum's play *Uplift of Lucifer*. Partners in business as well as play, Haldeman, Baum and some of the others started an independent film company to produce Oz features but were defeated by distribution problems. The club turned out en masse to attend Baum's funeral at Forest Lawn.

On the last decade of Baum's life, see Betty Lou Young's Rustic Canyon and the Story of the Uplifters *(Santa Monica, 1975).*

Leone Baxter. *See* Clem Whitaker.

The Beach Boys. The

three Wilson brothers, Brian (1942-   ), Dennis (1944-   ) and Carl (1946-   ), were cleancut boys from Hawthorne who got together with their cousin Mike Love (1941-   ) and friend Al Jardine (1942-   ) to make music about cars, girls, and surfing. They called themselves the Pendletons at first, after the wool shirt-jackets favored by preppie beachbums. "Surfin'," their first single, hit the national charts in 1961, heralding a new national vogue for the carefree sun-fun of California's endless-summer lifestyle. The Beach Boys' "Surfin' USA" album was a big hit in 1963, as were their singles, "Little Honda" (1964), "California Girls" (1965), and "Good Vibrations" (1966). Brian Wilson, the producer, composer, and arranger of the group, moved uptown to Beverly Hills, where he installed his piano in a sandbox—for inspiration, it was said. His was a breezy, mellow style, totally accessible—instant nostalgia. His more serious efforts— "California Suite," included "The Beaks of Eagles," a setting of a poem by **Robinson Jeffers**—did not catch on at all. Individually, members of the group began to experience highly publicized problems with drugs, alcohol, and fame. For a time in 1968, Dennis Wilson's Sunset Boulevard home served as a crash pad for a long-haired hippie named **Charlie Manson** and his tribe of girls. Eventually the Beach Boys went their separate ways—one to Big Sur, one to Colorado, another to Ohio. But thanks to the notoriously short memory of the popular music market, they have managed a comeback every five years: a Carnegie Hall reunion in 1971, a fifteenth-anniversary TV special in 1976, and a twentieth-anniversary concert in Long Beach in the summer of 1981. As captured on documentary film for the twentieth anniversary, the group seems a marvel of tonelessness, rhythmically comatose. If they had sung songs about Connecticut girls and summer at the Cape, would they have lasted twenty minutes?

The Beach Boys by Byron Preiss (New York, 1979) is a photo-album biography.

Edward Fitzgerald Beale

(1822-1893). After the Civil War, prospectors in the Mohave Desert occasionally reported seeing midnight phantoms in the shape of camels. In fact, these were descendants of California's

legendary but short-lived Camel Corps, the brainchild of E.F. Beale. Beale arrived in California in 1846 as a navy lieutenant under **Robert Stockton**, conqueror of California, and remained as Stockton's personal agent after the conquest. He also made several trips overland to the East Coast, bearing on one occasion the first tangible evidence of the discovery of gold. Appointed Commissioner of Indian Affairs in 1852, he gathered 2,500 tribesman on a reservation at El Tejon, midway across the Tehachapis. Having read an account of travels in the Far East, Beale suggested the camel as a means of desert transportation. In 1856 he took delivery on the Gulf Coast of 76 dromedaries from Asia Minor and successfully piloted them overland to California. But Beale's men did not understand the camel temperament nor like the camel smell, so the army decided against keeping them. Beale bought the animals at auction and released them on his 300,000 acre ranch at El Tejon, acquired during a spell as surveyor general of Nevada and California and described by **Nordhoff** as "the most magnificent estate in a single hand in America." (On replacing him, President Lincoln remarked that Beale seemed to become monarch of all he surveyed.) The squire of El Tejon kept a white camel for his personal use, and rode down to L.A. in a camel-drawn sulky. He even claimed to have learned Arabic in order to converse with the beasts. But over the years Beale tired of his

colonial idyll and repaired for long stretches to his Lafayette Square mansion in Washington, D.C., where political assiduity won him a brief tour as U.S. Minister to Austria-Hungary (1876-77). The camels (and/or the miners) died out eventually, and in 1912 Beale's son sold El Tejon to the **Chandler** syndicate.

Stephen Bonsal wrote Edward F. Beale, A Pioneer in the Path of Empire, 1822-1903 *(sic) (New York, 1912). See also* Men of El Tejon *by Earle Crowe (Los Angeles, 1957).*

Bechtel Family

Warren A. Bechtel (1872-1933), founder of one of the world's largest construction companies, started out with a team of mules and a railroad construction job in Oklahoma's Indian Territory in 1898. His sons, Stephen Davison (1900-   ), Warren (1898-1946) and Kenneth (1904-1978) grew up in construction camps all over the West, building roads, more railroads, then dams. The Bechtels claimed to be the first to use a tractor in heavy construction and the first to introduce the diesel-powered shovel. Taking on ever more complex technology, they built a Pacific Gas & Electric pipeline in 1929, collaborated on Hoover Dam and on the San Francisco Bay Bridge. After "Dad" Bechtel's death (on a trip to the Soviet Union to inspect its giant Dnieprostroy Dam) Stephen succeeded him and formed a partnership with John McCone in 1937 to engineer and construct entire

processing plants. During World War II, Bechtel-McCone helped build Fort Ord and other Pacific military installations, as well as record numbers of ships. McCone went his own way after the war (to become head of the Atomic Energy Commission, 1956-1960, and of the CIA, 1961-1965) while Bechtel continued from its California base to tame the jungles, oceans, and deserts of the world. In 1979 Bechtel (now under the leadership of Stephen Jr.) enjoyed an annual income of $6.4 billion. The company's top 56 executives, including at least two past or future U.S. cabinet appointees (George Shultz, Casper Weinberger) were all millionaires, *Newsweek* reported in 1977. Just as compelling as its financial success is the mystique of Bechtel: the Cadillac of the construction industry, it is able as a privately owned enterprise to drive at full speed, writing its own traffic laws. Latter-day Bechtel mega-projects include San Francisco's Bay Area Rapid Transit (BART), something of a lemon, a third of the nation's nuclear-power plants, the Washington, D.C. Metro, the $140 billion Jubail project in Saudi Arabia, and the Trans-Alaska Pipeline.

Robert Ingram's The Bechtel Story *(San Francisco, 1949) is an in-house account.*

Welton David Becket

(1902-1969). A young architect from the University of Washington (1927), Becket designed some of L.A.'s most distinctive buildings in partnership with Walter Wurdeman during the 1940s.

Their Streamline Moderne design for the Pan Pacific Auditorium (completed in 1941) won an international competition, with Wurdeman investing the prize money in a country club membership to cultivate wealthy clients. Other major projects in economical lightweight concrete include the **Bullock**'s Pasadena department store (1944) and the Prudential Insurance building (1947) on Wilshire Boulevard. After Wurdeman's premature death, Becket

bought out his partner's heirs and directed the firm into the concept of "total design," from philosophy and feasibility to space planning and interior decor. The circular Capitol Records Tower (1954) in Hollywood is a case of form imitating function. By the 1950s, Becket was L.A.'s premier architect, the country club membership having paid off in prestigious public and corporate commissions: the Beverly Hilton Hotel (1952), the L.A. Sports Arena (1959), the city's Music Center (1967)

and numerous medium- and high-rise office buildings. He also became supervising architect for UCLA, master planner of Disney World, and designer of Century City. He left his firm to a group of sixteen relatives and associates when he died.

William D. Hunt's Total Design *(New York, 1972) is geared at the architecture profession.*

Alphonzo Edward Bell, Sr.

(1875-1947). Bell was an unlikely entrepreneur, a former seminary student who became the creator of L.A.'s most elegant subdivision. A second generation Californian, he was born near a town named Bell, for his father, and educated at Occidental College, founded by his father and others. Dropping out of the seminary after two years—too timid to face a congregation, his friends thought—he won the Southern California singles tennis championship in 1900, 1901, and 1904. When oil was discovered on his Santa Fe Springs ranch in 1921, Bell invested his new wealth in land and took his family off to Europe where they scouted names for new streets and developments: Castellamar, Amalfi, Posetano. On their return, they moved into Capo di Monte, a 40-room mansion on top of the highest hill in the new community of Bel Air. (There was also a Bar-Bell ranch near Indio and another ranch by the same name in Colorado.) In association with some of his old tennis buddies, Bell formed the Los Angeles Mountain Park Company with a total of 23,760 acres in the Santa Monica mountains and foothills to develop according to his own conservative tastes. A dignified and abstemious man, he refused to sell land to movie stars and as the mortgage holder on the Bel Air Country Club and the Bel Air Bay Club, tried to prevent liquor consumption on the premises. Singularly inept at public relations, he got into a six-year public dispute over his right to quarry limestone in his mountains ("industrializing" the wilderness, critics charged). Bell also offered Occidental College a large tract in Brentwood for a separate men's branch, but the college preferred to remain coeducational. Alphonzo E. Bell, Jr., would later represent the neighborhood—the Forest Lawn of the living, some joked—in Congress.

See John Pohlmann's biography of Bell, Sr., in the September-December 1964 issues of Southern California Quarterly *(Vol. 46).*

Horace Bell (1830-1918). Bell was a lawyer by training, a newspaper editor by avocation, and a soldier of fortune who loved a good fight. Arriving in L.A. in 1852, he joined the Rangers to campaign against the elusive **Joaquin Murieta** and other desperados, went off to Nicaragua with **William Walker**'s army in 1856, served under Mexico's Benito Juarez, and fought as a Union soldier in the Civil War. Back home in L.A., which was openly sympathetic to the Confederacy, the Civil War "continued to rage," Bell wrote, "largely around my person." In his absence, the hospitable Mexicans with their graceful eighteenth-century lifestyle had been largely

dispossessed by Anglo sharpers, leaving the mortgage records of L.A. County "bloodstained and fearful." As editor of the *Porcupine* (motto: "Fearless, Faithful and Free"), Bell lampooned and caricatured the vanities and presumptions of the new usurpers. Two favorite targets were governor **John Downey**, for whom the editor invented a fictitious noble ancestry, later claimed by Downey as fact; and **Griffith J. Griffith**—"the Prince of Wales"—who gave his estate to the city for a park rather than pay taxes on it. Bell also despised self-made historian **H.H. Bancroft** for pandering to the likes of Downey and Griffith, and praised Colonel R. S. Baker for paying *not* to be included in Bancroft's *Chronicles of the Builders*. A familiar local figure on his coal-black

stallion, Bell developed a small estate at Pico and Figueroa into an early L.A. subdivision.

Bell wrote Reminiscences of a Ranger *(1881). After his death,* On the Old West Coast; Further Reminiscences of a Ranger *(New York, 1930) was prepared from his notes and manuscripts.*

Mel Belli (Melvin Mouron Belli, 1907-). Flamboyant is the usual description of Belli, the San Francisco attorney whose celebrity reportedly sticks in the craw of the staid state bar association. Thoroughly Californian, he was born in the mother lode town of Sonora, the son of a banker of Swiss descent. After graduation from UC Berkeley (1929) and Boalt Hall law school (1933), he got a job making anti-**Sinclair** speeches in the 1934 gubernatorial campaign. Belli would later present himself as bringing justice to the poor and downtrodden, but in fact his causes seem to have been chosen for their potential payoff in publicity and/or money. In early years, he represented San **Quentin** clients just to get noticed; later, he developed a lucrative specialty in personal injury cases, breaking new legal ground with the use of "demonstrative evidence" (photos of corpses, and witnesses arriving on stretchers). For comic relief, Belli represented mobster **Mickey Cohen** and the topless waitresses of San Francisco. In 1955, he successfully argued the concept of warranty against Cutter Laboratories, the East Bay pharmaceutical house that produced defective **Salk** polio vaccine. With his

winnings from Cutter, he bought an historic San Francisco building on Montgomery Street—the birthplace of freemasonry in California, according to the plaque—where he worked, surrounded by rococo clutter, in full view of the street. He also planned law offices all over the state, apparently envisaging "Belli's" as the McDonald's of the legal profession. An exhibitionist at heart, he moonlighted in show business with a short-lived talk show, a few bit roles in B movies (*Devil's Dolls*, with Susan Hayward), and a TV pilot for a series about a big-time defense lawyer. But getting down to cases, Belli was responsible for the development of a lot of new law in California.

Belli wrote several litigation texts, and an as-told-to autobiography, My Life on Trial *(New York, 1976).*

Victor Jules Bergeron. *See* Trader Vic.

Busby Berkeley (Busby Berkeley Enos, 1895-1976). He was born in Los Angeles, but only coincidentally, in the proverbial theatrical trunk. Sent to military school while his parents continued touring, he began his own theatrical career designing elaborate military drill patterns during World War I. After a few years' experience on Broadway, Berkeley moved to Hollywood in 1930 to design the most extravagantly elaborate production numbers in the history of film. He delighted in assembling hordes of identically clad extras on revolving platforms, shooting from above to achieve a kaleidoscopic effect. A perfectionist, he planned his long, uninterrupted takes in advance, cutting "in the camera." Some of Berkeley's fabulous films include *42nd Street* (1933), *Babes on Broadway* (1941), *For Me and My Gal* (1941). He also directed an uncharacteristic drama, *They Made Me a Criminal*. Berkeley's career was disrupted by personal problems, including alcoholism and five failed marriages. In 1935 he was indicted for manslaughter after an automobile accident on the Pacific Coast Highway. He was acquitted but spent years paying off $100,000 worth of legal bills. *Take Me Out to the Ballgame* (1949) was Berkeley's last film as a director. He staged elaborate aquatic numbers for **Esther Williams** (*Million Dollar Mermaid,* 1952) before retiring with his sixth wife to the healthier environment of Palm Desert.

Tony Thomas and Jim Terry, The Busby Berkeley Book *(Greenwich, Conn., 1973).*

John Bidwell (1819-1900). When Bidwell set out from Kansas City in 1841 with the first overland emigrant train, it was known only that California was in a general westerly direction. A teacher from New York state, he kept a journal of this odyssey that was later published. Early in 1842 Bidwell joined the staff at **John Sutter**'s Fort, serving for six years as secretary, advisor, bookkeeper, and general manager. Meanwhile, he explored Northern California and the prospect of farming without the heavy rainfall to which easterners were accustomed. Bidwell considered the U.S. war

against Mexico unjust, and took little part in the American conquest of California. Primarily interested in agriculture, he panned just enough gold in the Feather River to buy Rancho Chico which he transformed into a 26,000-acre showplace. Its wheat earned a gold medal as the world's finest at the 1878 International Exposition in Paris. His moral standing and

long California residence made Bidwell an inevitable political candidate. As a delegate to the state Constitutional Convention, he helped define and name the new counties. He was commissioned a general by Governor **Leland Stanford** during the Civil War, served a term in Congress (1865-1867), and was three times a reluctant candidate for

governor. Tall, prim, and principled, he opposed monopoly, persecution of the Chinese, and consumption of alcoholic beverages, for which, in 1892, he was nominated as the Prohibition Party candidate for U.S. president.

Rockwell Hunt's Bidwell, Prince of California Pioneers *(Caldwell, ID, 1942) is highly platitudinous.*

Ambrose Gwinett Bierce (1842-1914?). California has always had its boosters. In Bierce, it found its master of the put-down. Born in Ohio, he rose to the rank of captain in the Civil War, apparently the high point of his personal experience, and came west in 1866 with a surveying expedition. Starting as a "Town Crier" columnist in San Francisco in 1868, he became an editor of *Argonaut* (1876-1879), of the *Wasp* (1881-1887), and in 1887 was approached by the young **W.R. Hearst** himself to write a column of "Prattle" for the *San Francisco Examiner*. He

became known as "Bitter Bierce" for his corrosive cynicism, from which he spared no one. **Gertrude Atherton** could not understand why he was never shot. He called San Francisco a "moral penal colony," a place where nobody thought, and denigrated its leading literary organ, the western answer to the *Atlantic Monthly*, as a "warmed-*Overland Monthly*." Also a misogynist, Bierce toasted woman: "Would that we could fall into her arms without falling into her hands." In his own life, he more or less banished his wife and children to suburban cottages while he did as he pleased on the San Francisco cocktail circuit. An asthmatic and practicing hypochondriac, for a while he also maintained his own small cabin in the rarefied air of Mount Saint Helena. But when one of his sons died in a lurid lover's triangle, the fastidious Bierce was highly sensitive to the scandal. Many considered him a poseur. **Mary Austin** thought he had immense provocative capacity but was embittered by "failure to achieve direct creative power." Bierce insisted on loyalty from his protégés, who included **George Sterling**, but was loyal to no one himself. In 1896 Hearst sent him to Washington, D.C., to fight the railroad funding bill, using the columnist's cynicism as a weapon against the Southern Pacific. In 1914, during an expedition into Mexico to find Pancho Villa, Bierce disappeared and was presumed killed. He had written, "to be a Gringo in Mexico—ah, that is

Euthanasia."

Bierce's Devil's Dictionary *was first compiled in 1906 from his columns. Carey McWilliams,* Ambrose Bierce, A Biography *(New York, 1929,); Richard O'Connor,* Bierce, A Biography *(Boston, 1967).*

John Bigler (1806-1871). In 1850, Bigler, a lawyer of Pennsylvania German descent, arrived in California friendless and penniless. Only two years later he was elected the state's third governor, a miracle of upward mobility accomplished in alliance with **David Broderick**'s Democratic machine. Bigler's two terms of office (1852-1856), both marked by electoral irregularities, have been described as a "reign of ruffianism." "A dull companion [but] an astute politician," in the words of a contemporary, he permitted the sale of San Francisco water lots to enrich the Broderick machine, granted questionable prison contracts, pardoned a notorious cutthroat, favored squatters against landowners, and exploited anti-Chinese prejudice but was unable to achieve passage of any exclusionary legislation. He also favored the removal elsewhere of California's Indians. Defeated for a third term as governor, Bigler used his national connections to win appointment as U.S. Minister to Chile (1857-1861). There he befriended Harry Meiggs, a fugitive from California justice. When Meiggs made a fortune in South American railroads, he rewarded Bigler with the price of a home in Sacramento, where the ex-governor spent

his last years. Just before his death, the state legislature named for Bigler the beautiful lake on the California-Nevada border, which later reverted to its honorable Indian name of Tahoe.

Warren Knox Billings (1893-1972). He was just a kid looking for adventure when he left home at nineteen to join Pancho Villa in Mexico. Instead, he wound up in Folsom Prison with a life sentence for his role in the San Francisco labor wars. Billings was convicted in 1913 of transporting dynamite (unknowingly, he claimed) for use against strike-bound Pacific Gas & Electric. Released in 1914, an incorrigible radical, he briefly considered storming Utah State Prison to free Joe Hill. Arrested along with his friend **Tom Mooney** after the 1916 Preparedness Day bombing that left ten dead and scores injured in San Francisco, Billings was tried first and sentenced to life at Folsom. Mooney, whose death sentence was commuted to life in 1918, served for the

next twenty years as the central focus of an international campaign to expose the convictions as a frame. While Mooney did his time in the celebrity spotlight at San Quentin, Billings passed the years in prison quietly and almost cheerfully. He got along with everybody at Folsom, particularly with the Wobblies, on whose prison baseball team he played first base. He studied law and Latin, played winning chess by correspondence, and became the prison watchmaker. Mooney was pardoned in January 1939, but Billings remained in prison until October. His sentence was then commuted to time served, because of his prior record. He ran a watch shop on Market Street and was quietly active in union affairs for the rest of his life. In 1961 Governor **Pat Brown** pardoned him.

Billings was interviewed in 1957 by the UC Berkeley Oral History Project. See Frame-Up *by Curt Gentry (New York, 1967) and* The Mooney Case *by Richard Frost (Stanford, 1968).*

Willie Bioff (William Bioff, 1899?-1955). It was one of the bolder extortion schemes of recent history. Bioff, whose name suggests onomatopoetically his object in life ("buy off"), was a racketeer from Chicago who managed to hold Hollywood ransom for $100,000 annually and eventually hoped to acquire half ownership of all the studios. His vehicle was *IATSE*, the movie technicians' union, for which he recruited members with a combination of intimidation and benefits. In order to "protect" the industry against strikes, Bioff exacted an annual tribute on a sliding scale based on studio size. "I had Hollywood dancing to my tune," he boasted. The moguls, whom he considered "nothing but two-bit whores with clean shirts and a shine," had to deliver their payoffs to him in person at his fortress home in the San Fernando Valley. The Screen Actors Guild finally joined with *Daily Variety* to expose Bioff's racket in 1940. In the ensuing investigation, **Joe Schenck**, head of Twentieth Century-Fox, testified that he "loaned" Bioff $100,000 and was himself convicted of tax evasion. Bioff was convicted of extortion but got off after three years in return for informing on other mobsters. Living under an assumed name in Phoenix where he was reduced to fencing stolen goods, he was killed by a bomb wired to the ignition of his pickup truck.

Rose Elizabeth Bird (1936-   ). The push for feminist equality played itself out in the California Supreme

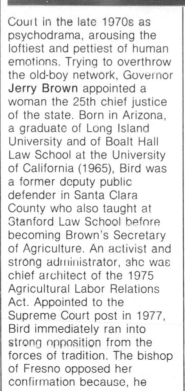

Court in the late 1970s as psychodrama, arousing the loftiest and pettiest of human emotions. Trying to overthrow the old-boy network, Governor **Jerry Brown** appointed a woman the 25th chief justice of the state. Born in Arizona, a graduate of Long Island University and of Boalt Hall Law School at the University of California (1965), Bird was a former deputy public defender in Santa Clara County who also taught at Stanford Law School before becoming Brown's Secretary of Agriculture. An activist and strong administrator, she was chief architect of the 1975 Agricultural Labor Relations Act. Appointed to the Supreme Court post in 1977, Bird immediately ran into strong opposition from the forces of tradition. The bishop of Fresno opposed her confirmation because, he

testified, she was vindictive and unstable. The right wing, infuriated by her civil libertarian rulings favoring the underdog, vigorously opposed her confirmation in 1978 (She won approval by 51.7%) and maintained the threat of a recall campaign. The 1978 election was complicated by charges that a controversial ruling had been postponed for political reasons, the subject of an inconclusive 1979 investigation. Within the male-dominated legal profession, Bird's background was not considered good enough. An otherwise reputable UC law professor wrote a virulent anti-Bird book, putting down her record as "undistinguished but not otherwise remarkable." Even the chief justice's hairdo aroused controversy, for when she changed it there were rumors of recurrence of

an earlier cancer. As evidence of the seriousness with which even sophisticated Californians took Bird, columnist **Herb Caen** described the tall, fair chief justice, towering over a court of short, elderly men, as Snow White and the six dwarfs.

Russell Juarez Birdwell (1903-1977). A former crack reporter for **Hearst**'s *L.A. Examiner*, Birdwell became Hollywood's most outrageously original publicity agent. During an era when rivals were perpetrating outright hoaxes to attract attention, Birdwell achieved a certain bemused credibility with his merely "manufactured" incidents. Hired by producer **David O. Selznick** in 1935, he painted the world's longest sign in Culver City to ballyhoo a film, hired a famous G-man to guard the studio's ideas, and orchestrated the nationwide search for Scarlett O'Hara. Employed by **Howard Hughes** for seven years at $1,500 a week to arouse mounting anticipation for *The Outlaw*, Birdwell made Jane Russell a star before she ever appeared on the screen. ("What two things are responsible for Jane Russell's success?") Other duties included midnight assignations with the reclusive millionaire and the defense of Russell's décolleté before **Hays** Office censors. Other Birdwell clients, including ex-King Carol of Rumania, used to call him for approval on wardrobes, social engagements, even prospective spouses. Possessed with the courage of his crazy ideas and given to musing in front of a map, he once asked the town of Fairbanks, Alaska, to add a "Jr." after its name in honor of a Birdwell client, and invited the entire population of Zenda, Canada, to fly to the premiere of *Prisoner of Zenda*. Birdwell remained active into the early 1960s, but the fun seemed to have gone out of it. He wrote the longest press release in memory (184 pages) for **John Wayne**'s *The Alamo* (1960), part of a high-pressure campaign to corner some Oscars for the year's most patriotic film.

Birdwell wrote a fictional memoir, I Ring Doorbells (New York, 1939), which he personally launched with a PR campaign. Also see Alva Johnston's four-part profile of the publicist in The New Yorker, August-September 1944.

Eugene Warren Biscailuz (1883-1969). As sheriff of Los Angeles county from 1932 to 1958, Biscailuz occupied a ceremonial position equivalent to dean of the diplomatic corps in a burgeoning banana republic. The county has always been a crazy quilt of cities, special districts, and unincorporated areas with their own special interests, and the sheriff, an elected official, frequently had to negotiate his authority in any given situation. Biscailuz was born in L.A. of Basque, Spanish, and Anglo ancestry. His Yankee grandfather was killed in the line of duty as a city marshal in 1870. A graduate of Loyola, he started out as a foreclosure clerk in the sheriff's office, studying law in his spare time, and won promotion to undersheriff in 1920. In 1923 he made front-page news on a trip to Central America to extradite an escaped murderess. He became a familiar figure at weddings, funerals, and parades as "the first caballero of Los Angeles," riding a palomino with silver-studded trappings. After eighteen months in Sacramento organizing the state Highway Patrol, Biscailuz returned home in 1932 to be appointed sheriff and reelected to six terms. His was a relatively easy-going attitude to law enforcement, cautious and courteous. He refused to participate in the Depression-era roadblocks designed to turn away Okies and Arkies and was reluctant to move against the offshore gambling ships of the same period. (A grand jury in 1951 would accuse him of laxity in prosecuting vice.) Biscailuz

pioneered in the establishment of honor ranchos, where county prisoners could do their time in fresh air, funded by the sheriff's annual barbecue. The barbecue evolved over the years into a full-scale rodeo and pageant at the L.A. Coliseum, with 100,000 in attendance in 1949.

Biscailuz, Sheriff of the New West (New York, 1950) by Lindley Bynum is quaintly provincial.

Shirley Temple Black. *See* **Shirley Temple**.

Thomas Blythe (Thomas Williams, 1823?-1883). In 1877 a Welsh-born San Franciscan filed a claim under the Swamp and Overflow Act to 40,000 acres of land periodically inundated by the Colorado River. Blythe planned to divert the mighty river, envisioning a fertile new Nile Valley in the Southern California desert, but he suffered a stroke and died before the realization of his dream. His estate, which also included a million acres in Mexico, and the San Francisco block bounded by Geary, Grant, and Market streets, was tied up in litigation by putative heirs until 1905. The desert land was eventually sold to a syndicate which laid out the town of Blythe in 1910. Until the completion of Hoover Dam in the 1930s, the town waged an annual battle with the Colorado. As for the new Nile Valley, Blythe had the right idea but the wrong location. Extensive irrigation created a garden hothouse farther south in the Imperial Valley, leaving Blythe a sleepy little town on the interstate highway to Los Angeles.

E(lias) Manchester Boddy (1891-1967). Boddy was an itinerant publishing gadfly—associated at one time or another with the *Encyclopaedia Britannica,* the "War Volume Department" of the *New York Times*, and the Mexican Year Book Co.—who in 1926 took over California's major Democratic newspaper. The *Los Angeles Daily News* had been established in 1923 by Cornelius Vanderbilt, Jr., a black-sheep liberal who was soon forced out of business, it was said, by the *L.A. Times*. Boddy used the *Daily News* as a personal vehicle for his philosophical ideas ("Living is merely an endeavor to tune in," he wrote in a series of newspapers essays), which

included a flirtation with "technocracy" during the Depression. But he was important by virtue of his singularity in a Republican-dominated profession. (The *Daily News* was the only newspaper in California to support **Culbert Olson** for governor in 1942.) On the side, the crusty and increasingly conservative publisher developed the 150-acre Descanso Gardens, later purchased by the county, and in 1950 ran against **Helen Gahagan Douglas** for the Democratic nomination to the U.S. Senate. Retiring after the electoral defeat, he sold his newspaper a few years later to the **Chandlers**.

Bill Bonelli (William George Bonelli, 1895-1970). For sixteen years Bonelli represented Southern California on the Board of Equalization (1938-1954), the powerful state agency charged with tax assessments and liquor licenses. A Phi Beta Kappa graduate of USC (1916) with an M.A. from Occidental (1923), he taught political science before going into politics. Bonelli survived two major attempts to link him with corruption and racketeering: in 1940 he was indicted for bribery but acquitted, and late in the 1940s he was questioned by the Kefauver Committee. Then in 1953 the *Los Angeles Mirror*, the second-string Chandler newspaper, ran an exposé of California's "saloon emperor," master salesman of liquor licenses. Bonelli knew where a few Chandler bodies were buried, too, and retaliated with a ghostwritten book about the publishing family, including some undoubtedly authentic material on gross underassessment of Chandler property. The upshot was that Bonelli was defeated for reelection, indicted for election code violations and income tax evasion, and fled as a fugitive, first to Arizona, and then to Mexico, where he died after years in exile. In 1955, authority over liquor licenses was transferred to a new state Alcoholic Beverage Control Department. It is not known what action if any was taken to reappraise the Chandler properties.

Bonelli's Billion-Dollar Blackjack (Beverly Hills, 1954; actually written by Leo Katcher), for years the only book published about the Chandlers, now ranks as an underground classic.

Winifred Black Bonfils.
See Annie Laurie.

Newton Booth
(1825-1892). The modest and scholarly Booth was considered the greatest orator of all California governors. A 49er, he once compared the American settlement of the state to "first love, the memory of which is sweeter than present possession." Born in Indiana of Quaker parentage, Booth graduated from Asbury College (later De Paux) in 1846 and was admitted to the bar before joining the westward movement. Finding the frontier flooded with lawyers, he went into the grocery business in Sacramento. He ran for governor in 1871 as a Republican on an anti-railroad platform, speaking eloquently against "soulless corporations" and the centralization of wealth. (His repertoire also included a lecture on Charles James Fox, the British advocate of U.S. independence, and another on mystic Emmanuel Swedenborg.) Booth's administration (1871-1875) has been described as lacking in incident. The governor himself became an issue by lobbying for a vacant U.S. Senate seat midway through his term, which was considered somewhat improper. Trying again in 1875, Booth was elected to the U.S. Senate where he made impassioned speeches against U.S. imperialism in Hawaii. He died, ironically, of cancer of the tongue. A nephew and namesake back home in Indiana was (Newton) Booth Tarkington.

Christopher John Booth
Boyce (1953-   ) and **Andrew Daulton Lee** (1952-   ). The biggest American spy scandal of the 1970s was nurtured in Palos Verdes, the former **Sepulveda** ranch north of Long Beach which became in the aerospace age an enclave of mindless affluence and moral amnesia. Boyce and Lee both grew up in privileged circumstances there, classmates at Saint John Fisher parochial school. (From the roof of the school they could look down and see Watts burning during the 1965 riots.) After graduation from Palos Verdes High School, Lee, the adopted son of a wealthy doctor, found himself unprepared to earn a living as anything but a dope dealer. He was busted seven times during the 1970s, and served a few months at the Wayside Honor Rancho, resuming his high life of crime after each interruption. Boyce, the son of a former FBI agent, enrolled at and dropped out of a series of local colleges. His main interest in life was falconry, which led him to enroll at Cal Poly in San Luis Obispo for its proximity to a federal sanctuary for peregrine falcons. In 1974 through his father's contacts he got a $140-a-week job as a clerk at TRW, which soon cleared him to work on a clandestine CIA project involving satellite surveillance. One night while doing drugs together Boyce and Lee came up with the idea of selling CIA secrets to the Soviets. Like everything else in their lives, treason was too easy. TRW security was ridiculously lax, enabling Boyce to take home with him as many secret documents as he could carry. Lee, who had drug contacts in Mexico, simply presented himself to the Soviet Embassy there and offered to deal, selling secrets as if they were so much hash. The two were too incompetent or perhaps simply too stoned to properly focus the mini camera the Russians bought them. Lee, who seems to have been motivated primarily by desire to play a big-spending hot-shot, even bragged to friends about the deals going down in Mexico. Incredibly, this amateur espionage went on for two years, thoroughly compromising major U.S. spy networks, until Lee was apprehended in Mexico entirely by accident in 1977. Tried separately and swiftly to confine the national embarrassment, Lee was sentenced to life in prison and Boyce to 40 years. Boyce escaped from Lompoc prison in 1980, living dangerously as a bank robber in the Pacific Northwest until his recapture in 1981. His sentence was extended 25 years on robbery charges.

Robert Lindsay, The Falcon and the Snowman *(New York, 1979) will undoubtedly give rise to a Hollywood update of* Rebel Without a Cause.

Louise Arner Boyd

(1887-1972). The granddaughter of a 49er, Boyd was a debutante and heiress who became one of the world's great arctic explorers. She graduated from Miss Murison's School in San Francisco as an accomplished horsewoman and hunter, properly Episcopalian and Republican. On her father's death in 1920 she became president of Boyd Investment Company, but soon found better use for her freedom and fortune: a polar expedition which she organized, financed, and led in 1926. Two years later, she participated in the search for missing explorers Roald Amundsen and Umberto Nobile. Altogether, she led eight expeditions, exploring Greenland and eastern arctic Canada in the 1930s, and becoming the first woman to fly over the North Pole in 1955. Always properly ladylike and impeccably groomed

(even on her expeditions), Boyd repaired between voyages and honors (including France's Chevalier of the Legion of Honor) to the family home in San Rafael, Maple Lawn. Never married, she sold the mansion in 1962 to the Elks Club. On her death ten years later, it was found there was nothing left of the family fortune. Assuredly, she had enjoyed every penny of it.

Ray Douglas Bradbury

(1920-   ). The most popular of contemporary science fiction writers, Bradbury arrived in twentieth-century Los Angeles from nineteenth-century Waukegan, Illinois, at the age of fourteen. Somehow he managed to preserve the ethos of a bicycle-powered, homemade-ice-cream, front-porch world while leading a fantasy life out of Buck Rogers and Flash Gordon. As a senior at L.A. High School Bradbury founded a magazine called *Future Fantasia*, his first literary effort. He practiced writing for the pulps while earning a living as a streetcorner newspaper vender. His first book, *The Martian Chronicles* (1950), a collection of stories about the colonization of space, became a popular favorite. *Farenheit 451* (1953), an allegorical protest against McCarthyism, described a future world without books or fantasies, while *Dandelion Wine* (1957), explored the metaphor of the circus in midwestern childhood. For Bradbury, who never learned to drive and refused to fly, the Cheviot Hills area of L.A. became the base for extraterrestrial or merely whimsical "trips," the source

of a continuous stream of short stories, poetry, screenplays, and an opera scheduled for production shortly.

Thomas Bradley

(1917-   ). In the period between the two world wars, the University of California at Los Angeles enrolled an extraordinary group of young blacks. **Ralph Bunche** blazed a unique trail through international politics, while Kenny Washington (1918-1971) and Jackie Robinson (1919-1972) helped open the gates of professional sports to black athletes. Bradley, who moved to L.A. from Texas as a child and earned an athletic scholarship to UCLA, made his mark in California politics. In 1940 he joined the Los Angeles Police Department, one of the first in the country to employ blacks. Working his way up through the system, playing carefully by the rules, he became the city's first black police lieutenant. Bradley earned a law degree at night school and after retiring from the force in 1961 went into politics, serving two terms on the city council. In 1973, on his second try for mayor, he defeated incumbent Sam Yorty and moved up from his small frame house in Leimert Park to Getty House, L.A.'s new mayoral mansion. Tall and handsome, low-key and deliberate, Bradley as mayor behaved more like a civil servant than a political personality, emphasizing administration rather than achievement. Rapid transit, his top campaign promise and the city's major headache, advanced nowhere during his

two terms as mayor. His chief accomplishment seemed symbolic rather then substantive: he made the white establishment feel comfortable with black leadership. Running as the Democratic candidate for governor in 1982, he lost.

Leslie Carlton Brand

(1859-1925). "One of the empire builders of the Southland," according to his obituary in the *Los Angeles Times*, Brand carved out his own little fiefdom in Glendale at the turn of the century. He was born in Saint Louis, where he learned the real estate title business before migrating west in 1886. As president of the Title Guarantee and Trust Company, he acquired 20,000 acres in the northern San Fernando Valley including 1,000 acres in Glendale, where he established a water and light company, a telephone company, a bank, and an electric railway along what is now Brand Boulevard. Brand literally put Glendale on the map with his Strawberry Line connecting the city to downtown L.A. and with his twice weekly ads in the L.A. press: "Have You Ever Been to Glendale?" His most enduring creation was Miradero, a "country home" at the foot of the Verdugos modeled after the East Indian Pavilion at the Chicago World's Fair. An early aviation buff, he used to fly his guests in for weekend house parties. As the largest landowner at the eastern end of the valley, Brand was invited to join **Harry Chandler**'s "Los Angeles Suburban Home" syndicate which profited handsomely from the Owens River Aqueduct. Stricken at his summer place at Mono Lake, he was buried at Miradero, which he left to the city of Glendale.

Samuel Brannan

(1819-1889). Setting out around the Horn to San Francisco in 1846 at the head of a party of Mormon colonists, Sam Brannan had visions of driving the Mexicans into the sea. Finding on arrival that **Frémont** and the Bear Flag bunch had in effect done so, he turned his considerable energies to becoming San

Francisco's first millionaire. Only a token Mormon, he was excommunicated after a dispute over tithes collected from the new colonists. Elected city councilman, he arranged for the sale of public lands to himself among others; charged with misappropriation of public funds, he survived the city's first jury trial. Brannan also had a hand in the subdivision of **John Sutter**'s land in Sacramento. His own holdings eventually included a biscuit factory and a bookstore, 200 acres in the Western Addition and an 1,800-acre Feather River ranch. Tiring of the city, Brannan discovered and developed the hot springs resort of Calistoga in the Napa Valley. A major consumer of champagne, he is supposed to have predicted in his cups that the resort would become the "Calistoga of Sarifonia,"—the Saratoga of California. Brannan was cheerful, bombastic, generous, restless, careless. He entertained the peripatetic **Lola Montez** regally, and built rococo houses for

mistresses and relatives. His wife, after thirteen years abroad, returned to divorce him for "notorious intemperance." Always eager for action, he considered filibustering in Hawaii, instead, he bought $1.5 million of Juarez bonds and raised volunteers for the Mexican Revolution. His fortunes declined through carelessness and extravagance, and he spent his last years trying to recoup this Mexican investment. Brannan died poor but ever hopeful in an Escondido boarding house. The Brannan Island State Recreation Area, 300 acres reclaimed from the Sacramento delta, was later named for him.

Louis J. Stellman's Sam Brannan of San Francisco *(New York, 1953) is a perfunctory biography.*

Richard Brautigan

(1935-   ). The J. D. Salinger of the hippie generation, Brautigan arrived in San Francisco in 1954 from the Pacific Northwest. In his first novel, *A Confederate General from Big Sur* (1964), he described hippie nirvana, the Northern California coastline where stoned dropouts imagine faint echoes of ancestral drums. Most of Brautigan's early work is inlaid with images of San Francisco and of himself, a tall, blond character with long hair and moustaches, got up to look like a backwoods California colonel. *Trout Fishing in America* (1967), an ode to water pollution in the age of Aquarius, opens with a picture of Brautigan at **Cogswell**'s statue of Benjamin Franklin in San Francisco, an obsolete

monument to temperance. *The Abortion, An Historical Romance 1966* (1970) is a gentle sexual fantasy of pneumatic bliss, set in a S. F. library devoted to the unpublished works of monomaniacs. With bestsellerdom, Brautigan left San Francisco in 1971, settling on a Montana ranch to write hip-sophisticated versions of *Field and Stream*.

Harry Bridges

(Alfred Renton Bridges, 1900?-   ). The most radical U. S. labor leader of his generation was an Australian sailor who came ashore to work on the San Francisco dock in the 1920s. Bridges rose to leadership during the longshoremen's 1934 strike for recognition, a strike that ranks in local history as a virtual civil war. After 83 days of skirmishing, one major confrontation at Rincon Hill, and a three-day general strike that shut down the city, the longshoremen won most of their demands. Bridges then moved inland to organize warehousemen. In 1937 he took his union into the CIO as the Independent Longshoremen's and Warehousemen's Union (ILWU). Personally, he was frugal, honest, a hardnosed pragmatist, ever distrustful of the upper classes, and apt to be seen around town with a real "looker" on his arm. Proudly independent, he tolerated Communists and other nonconformists in his union, for which the U.S. government spent fifteen years trying to deport him as an undesirable alien. A ten-week immigration hearing on Angel Island in 1939, covered by the local press as if it

were a war, exonerated Bridges of Communist Party affiliation. But in 1940 Congress voted 330-42 to deport him as ''a symbol of the Fifth Column'' and a second immigration hearing went against him in 1941. The Supreme Court reversed the 1941 ruling in 1945, by which time Bridges had become a naturalized U.S. citizen. The government then moved to convict him of perjury for having denied any Communist affiliation on his citizenship application. Convicted in 1949, Bridges was again reprieved by the U.S. Supreme Court, and again tried, before the charges were finally dropped. Meanwhile, his union launched a socio-economic revolution in Hawaii by organizing field workers and kept peace on the San Francisco waterfront for a generation. By virtue of sheer integrity and longevity, Bridges finally won acceptance from the San Francisco establishment. Mayor **Joe Alioto** appointed

him to the port authority in 1970, and in 1975, smiling sardonically, the 74-year-old labor leader was feted as a ''distinguished citizen.''

The only available work on this key figure in American labor is Charles Larrowe's Harry Bridges, The Rise and Fall of Radical Labor in the U.S. *(New York, 1972).*

David Colbreth Broderick (1820-1859).
The first man of "humble" origin to reach the U.S. Senate, Broderick was a controversial political genius whose career ended prematurely in the most famous duel in California history. Born in Washington, D.C., the son of an Irish immigrant stonemason employed on the Capitol building, he grew up in Tammany, New York. Finding his advancement as a Democratic ward politician blocked by class prejudice, he set out in 1849 for classless California, land of political opportunity—"where labor is honorable," Broderick said in a Senate speech, and "no

station is so high and no position so great that its occupant is not proud to boast that he has labored with his own hands.'' Broderick established a Tammany-style organization in San Francisco and in alliance with Governor **John Bigler** soon controlled local and state politics. He ran into stiff opposition from the ''Chivalry,'' pro-slavery Southern Democrats whom he fought tooth and nail for free soil and free labor (as well as patronage), and was a chief target of the Second Vigilance Committee. (Newspaper editor **James King of William** called him David *Catiline* [after the demagogic Roman politician] Broderick, ''the Pandora's box from whence spring all these evils.'') But Broderick fought back to win election to the U.S. Senate in 1856, having extorted from fellow California Senator **William Gwin** promise of control of all California patronage. In Washington, however, the self-educated Broderick found himself ranked as a crude outsider. Back home on the eve of the Civil War, Broderick, having spoken out eloquently against slavery, was challenged to a duel by fighting judge **David Terry**, an ardent exponent of the ''Chivalry.'' It is said that the senator went almost fatalistically to his death.

A century later, Broderick still arouses strong partisanship. Compare Broderick, A Political Portrait *by David Williams (San Marino, 1969) with Lately Thomas's biography of Gwin,* Between Two Empires *(Boston, 1969).*

Jerry Brown (Edmund Gerald Brown, Jr. 1938-).
The son of a folksy, backslapping politician,

Governor **Pat Brown**, Jerry Brown was cold and devoid of social graces. He was often rude, scornful, contentious, with a "whim of iron." An advocate of less-is-more and of ''conspicuous austerity,'' he proved masterful at stating the obvious in esoteric terms. He was liberal on issues, conservative in action, and often opposed to action altogether, but whatever your opinion, Jerry Brown was not boring. He seemed to have been cloned rather than born in San Francisco, graduating from parochial school to enter a Jesuit seminary in Los Gatos. Changing direction, he enrolled at Yale Law School, joined an L.A. law firm after his 1964 graduation, and ran for the local school board as a warm-up for statewide office. Elected secretary of state in 1970, Brown won points for enforcing campaign disclosure laws. After his successful 1974 gubernatorial campaign designed right out of McLuhan's *Understanding Media*, he gave the shortest inaugural address on record (seven minutes) in his opening round against political pomp and circumstance. His appointments were a study in

new-age consciousness—lots of women and minorities to shake up the old-boy network. A bachelor, Brown scorned the governor's mansion for an ordinary apartment and the customary limousine for a Plymouth. "Governor Moonbeam," as he became known, talked about space as if it were California's private new frontier, preferring to ignore more earthly problems. Everything about him was unorthodox for a politician except his ambition. An erstwhile presidential candidate, he lost his 1982 bid for the U.S. Senate.

J. D. Lorenz, Jerry Brown, The Man on the White Horse (Boston, 1978); Robert Pack, Jerry Brown, The Philosopher Prince (New York, 1978); Orville Schell, Brown (New York, 1978).

Pat Brown (Edmund Gerald Brown, 1905-   ). "In Washington they call it the Great Society. We just call it California," quipped Pat Brown, the ebullient, gregarious 32nd governor of the state (1959-67). Born Irish Catholic in San Francisco where his father ran a theater and cigar store, Brown acquired the nickname "Pat" at Lowell High School for imitating Patrick Henry. After graduation from San Francisco College of Law (1927) he went into private practice, ran as a Democrat for district attorney of San Francisco (1944-1950), state attorney general (1951-1959), then governor, defeating **William Knowland** over the right-to-work issue. He won re-election in 1962 by defeating **Richard Nixon**. Brown's proudest achievements as governor are considered to be the statewide water plan and the

master plan for higher education, involving construction of three new branches of the University of California. On the other side of the ledger, he first reprieved convicted criminal **Caryl Chessman**. then let him die; punished UC student protestors but could not control them; and resorted to budgetary gimmickry to postpone a necessary tax increase. After his 1966 defeat for reelection, he appointed 80 friends to judgeships, wrote a book full of sour grapes (*Reagan and the Two Californias*, 1970), and resumed private law practice in Beverly Hills.

J[ohn] Ross Browne
(1821-1875). Browne was a "primordial T-man," a confidential government agent in gold-rush California. He was also a satirical writer who reveled in the very human foibles that as a government agent he worked zealously to expose. Based in the Bay Area, he traveled throughout the West for a decade, but it was San Francisco, then a hotbed of corruption and profiteering, that absorbed most of his attention. Browne recommended pay cuts for some civil servants and tried to eliminate others altogether—to wit, the "Measurer of Tonnage" and the "Spirit Entry Clerk." His most famous case involved a gold shortfall at the San Francisco Mint. He had already recommended firing **Agoston Haraszthy**, assayer of the mint, for being too absorbed in private affairs; now he collected evidence for a fraud indictment, despite his

inclination to accept Haraszthy's explanation that the missing gold went up the flue in smoke. Browne's zeal was possibly motivated by envy: his greatest ambition was to be a man of leisurely letters. During the 1860s he managed to support his family in Europe by his writing. (Haraszthy exonerated himself and apparently bore Browne no ill will, for he later asked· after the former government agent when both were in Germany.) As a writer, however, his best-seller was the *Report of the Debates* (1849) which he recorded as secretary to California's Constitutional Convention. Browne served briefly as U.S. Minister to China in 1868 but was so lacking in diplomacy

that he soon retired to his Oakland home, Pagoda Hill. Satirizing himself in the third person, he once wrote: "He was a fellow of infinite jest. There was something so exquisitely comic in the idea of taking official instructions literally. . . ."

Richard Dillon, Confidential Agent in Old California (Norman, OK, 1965).

Avery Brundage
(1887-1975). A college discus champion from Chicago, Brundage became a wealthy construction engineer, a major collector of Asian art, a social leader of Santa Barbara, and the dictator of Olympic sports. "He was not so much a born athlete as he was a great fighter," a competitor said of Brundage, who scored fifth in the

decathlon at the 1912 Olympic Games. (That was the year Jim Thorpe won, but had to return his medals because he had played a season of semi-pro baseball.) As chairman of the U.S. Olympic Committee and later of the International Olympic Committee (1952-1972), Brundage would always insist that the games go on—in Hitler's Germany in 1936 and in Munich after the massacre of Israeli athletes in 1972. He also fought indefatigably to keep the Olympics ''pure'' and free of commercialism and professionalization. He once disqualified an American swimmer for sipping champagne and warned a Canadian athlete against accepting a gift from admirers. Cyril **Magnin**, San Francisco merchant prince, described him as a "curmudgeon of the first order." During his world travels, Brundage put together an impressive collection of

Asian art. Some pieces were lost when his Santa Barbara house burned in a 1964 brush fire, but the bulk of the collection went to San Francisco's **De Young** Museum, which opened a new wing to house it in 1966. At one time the owner of the Montecito Country Club, the El Presidio, and the Montecito Hotel, Brundage remained to rebuild his home after the 1964 fire. After his death, ironically, it was revealed that the moral arbiter of Olympic sports was the father of two illegitimate sons.

Heinz Schobel's, The Four Dimensions of Avery Brundage *(Leipzig, 1968), a European production, lacks any California dimension.*

Christopher Augustine Buckley

(1845-1922). The ''Blind Boss of San Francisco'' or ''blind white devil,'' as the Chinese called him, Buckley started his career as a streetcar conductor. He became a bartender and went into partnership with impresario **Tom Maguire**. During the 1870s Buckley lost his sight, due to dissipation, some said, but developed a distinct ability for leadership. (According to legend, he recognized men by their hand grasp.) It was a period of industrialization and urbanization with ethnic and occupational groups groping for strength in numbers. Taking advantage of the chaos created in the local Democratic party by Kearneyism, Buckley chose a majority of city supervisors even as **Denis Kearney**'s candidate won the 1879 mayoral election. Not content with patronage alone, the Blind Boss is said to have

controlled the political economy of San Francisco, expediting contracts, awarding franchises, and granting favors impartially— for a price. In 1880 Buckley moved up from the crowded fifth ward to the suburban Western Addition, also acquiring a 75-acre estate in the Livermore Valley where he weekended as a country squire. The first rumbles of revolt were felt in the mid-1880s over patronage in the schools, where half of city jobs happened to be located. In 1887-88 a smallpox epidemic aroused charges of malfeasance by the city health department, and **W. R. Hearst**'s *S.F. Examiner* came out against the Blind Boss, even though Buckley had helped elect Hearst's father U.S. Senator. Indicted for bribery in 1891, Buckley wisely absented himself on a trip to Europe. He was never tried, but never recovered his political hegemony either. He had enough of a nest egg left over, however, to purchase the **Mackay** mansion on O'Farrell Street in 1896. After the '06 earthquake he retired to his country estate, living out his sunset years as the ''Lord of Livermore.''

Buckley inspired R. L. Stevenson's 1892 novel, The Wrecker. *William Bullough's* Blind Boss and His City *(Berkeley, 1979) is good social history but suffers from verbosity.*

James Herbert Budd

(1851-1908). The nineteenth governor of California (1895-1899), Budd has been described as ''forceful, pugnacious, epigrammatic.'' He was born in Wisconsin, came to California as a child, and graduated in the first class to complete four years

at the University of California, Berkeley (1873). As a student he was also a precocious member of the Democratic state central committee. Budd read law under his father (later a San Joaquin county judge) and won election to Congress in 1882 but preferred after a single term to resume his law practice in Stockton. (The stature of a lawyer on the valley good-old-boy network was probably greater than that of a junior congressman in Washington and certainly more remunerative. Budd is said to have earned $100,000 as counsel for Charles Fair.) Nominated for governor in 1894, he attracted attention by a campaign described as ''pyrotechnic,'' commuting by buckboard as often as possible to dramatize his opposition to the Southern Pacific monopoly. ''Breezy'' and ''truly western'' in the conduct of the state's highest office, he hung a sign on his door, ''Jim's In.'' Despite his personal popularity, he chose not to run for reelection, claiming ill health. He had recovered sufficiently in 1902 to help his friend **William Randolph Hearst** campaign in New York for Congress but declined an invitation to join the Hearsts on their honeymoon trip to Europe soon afterwards.

Don Budge (John Donald Budge, 1915-   ). Considered by some the greatest tennis player of all time, Budge began playing at public parks in middle-class Oakland where he grew up. After winning his first big title, the state Juniors, he was approached by tennis czar Perry Jones, who forbid him ever to play again in dirty tennis shoes. Going to the opposite extreme, Budge became the last player of his generation to wear proper long white flannels in competition. He dropped out of UC Berkeley his freshman year (1934) to join the U.S. Davis Cup team and three years later won the singles titles at Forest Hills and Wimbledon. In 1938 Budge won the first grand slam of French, British, Australian, and American singles titles, a feat not repeated for 24 years. Turning pro on the eve of World War II, he spent his best years playing exhibitions for troops in the Pacific. He lost his first postwar tour to **Bobby Riggs**, but proved consistently strong enough with his formidable backhand and perfect mechanics to remain on the pro circuit for years. After an unsuccessful Hollywood marriage he moved back east with his second wife, running a summer tennis camp in the Poconos and wintering at racquet clubs in the Caribbean.

He wrote the obligatory memoir, Don Budge: A Tennis Memoir *(New York, 1969).*

Benny Bufano
(Beniamino Benvenuto Bufano, 1898-1970). A sculptor with the short stature and quixotic fancy of a child, capable of works of great beauty and of monumental kitsch, Bufano was San Francisco's cultural mascot for nearly 50 years. He arrived from Italy via Brooklyn to work on the 1915 Panama-Pacific Exposition, returning to stay after extensive travel through China and India. On the WPA payroll during the Depression Bufano evolved his own distinctive style and media: smoothly rounded animal forms in granite and tall icons sheathed in stainless steel. He was considered a radical, and much of his work ended up in storage, whether through inadvertence or suppression. There were also reports of vandalism, and the suggestion that Bufano himself may have been responsible. Benny, according to his friends, played games with words, with art and with life. Appointed a city art commissioner in 1944, he denounced museums as graveyards and advocated free public art. Most of his surviving work now belongs to the streets and the people of San Francisco. A colossal statue of Saint Francis, after years in storage and temporary display at Si's Charbroiler in Oakland, now stands in front of the Longshoremen's Union at Fisherman's Wharf. Bufano's *Peace*, a bosomy witch with a four-eyed child—commonly regarded as a colossal piece

of kitsch—is now installed on a little used access road at San Francisco Airport. Among his masterpieces are the steel-sheathed **Sun Yat-sen** in Saint Mary's Square, and his animal sculptures at Alcoa Center and the Hillsdale Shopping Center. Chronically improvident, Bufano lived most of his life off the generosity of others. He had a room at the S.F. Press Club, where his black cat sculpture occupied pride of

place, and a studio on Minna Street, courtesy of **Trader Vic Bergeron**. He earned a lifetime pass to eat at Moar's Cafeteria by executing three huge mosaic panels there. After his death, the cafeteria went bankrupt and the murals were dispersed to the boondocks.

Howard Wilkening, who with Sonia Brown wrote Bufano, An Intimate Biography *(Berkeley, 1972), is a psychologist.*

John Gillespie Bullock
(1871-1933). L.A.'s merchant prince was Canadian by birth and a frugal Scot by descent. Seeking his fortune in

Southern California he got a job as a salesman in Arthur Letts's Broadway chain store. As a reward for the young man's diligence and virtue,

Letts built a new store at Seventh and Broadway, "put my name on it," Bullock remembered, "and gave me $250,000 to outfit it as I liked." The store opened with a band concert and pony show just in time for the panic of 1907 but Bullock persevered, prospered, and expanded. In 1921, when he proposed to link two buildings by a bridge over Saint Vincent's Place, **Hearst**'s *Examiner* fiercely opposed the plan but it was approved by voters in a city referendum. In 1927 Bullock's, Inc. was formed to purchase the store from Letts's estate. Two years later, a fabulous new branch in high Gothic style was opened on Wilshire Boulevard, followed by a Westwood store in 1932. Rising to civic leadership, Bullock worked for the Colorado River Aqueduct and was a backer of Western Air Express, predecessor of Western Air Lines. On his death, he was widely eulogized as a "practical idealist," the sainted founder of a great institution. Bullock's stores, which would survive and prosper by refining the art of local consumption, merged with I. **Magnin** in 1941 and later became part of the Federated Department chain.

Ralph Johnson Bunche

(1904-1971). Life was relatively good for blacks in Southeast L.A. during World War I when Bunche was growing up, because they were few in number and because some racial antagonism was drawn off by Mexicans. Born in Detroit, Bunche had moved with his

family in 1916 to Albuquerque where his mother died of tuberculosis and his father abandoned the family in discouragement. He came with his grandmother to Los Angeles—"a Southern climate without being a Southern state"—and graduated as class valedictorian from Jefferson High School in 1922. At UCLA he became president of the debating society, went out for sports, and graduated summa cum laude in 1927, again the commencement speaker. Offered a tuition fellowship to Harvard graduate school, Bunche left home with financial assistance from local black women's clubs. He never looked back. He earned a Harvard Ph.D. (1934), the first in political science ever awarded to an American black; taught at Howard University and assisted Gunnar Myrdal with his major study of U.S. race relations (*An American Dilemma*, 1944); worked for the State Department during World War II, and went to the U.N. as the highest ranking American diplomat, winning the Nobel Peace Prize in 1950 for the

1948 Arab-Israeli peace negotiations. UCLA named a highrise building on campus in honor of its most illustrious graduate, an orphan from East L.A.

Peggy Mann, Ralph Bunche, UN Peacemaker *(New York, 1975) has the inspirational quality of young adult literature.*

May Sutton Bundy

(1887-1975). In her day she was considered the greatest woman tennis player the world had ever seen. Born in

England, the daughter of a British navy captain who sailed with his family to the new world, May Sutton was raised with her three sisters on a ten-acre ranch in Pasadena. Playing with the aggressive style of a man, she won the Southern California Women's Championship at thirteen and the U.S. women's singles title at seventeen. In 1905 she became the first "colonial" to take the British title at

Wimbledon, a feat she repeated in 1907. Returning home in triumph, she was chosen queen of the Pasadena Tournament of Roses, an honor then conferred for achievement rather than pulchritude. ("Magnificently muscular," the British remarked, "she appears to care nothing for the social graces. . . There is no tripping after the ball with her, no showing off of her figure at the net.") May Sutton retired from competitive tennis after her marriage to Tom Bundy, also a tennis star, and with his four brothers a West L.A. real estate developer. She continued to teach, made occasional comebacks, and could be seen well into her eighties, the grande dame of American tennis, playing with her sisters at the Uplifters Club in Santa Monica Canyon.

Luther Burbank

(1849-1926). Santa Rosa seemed to Burbank like a botanist's Garden of Eden, "the chosen spot of all the earth as far as nature is concerned." A Yankee from Massachusetts, he grew up among elderberries and woodchucks in Walden Pond country, a loner and a self-educated scientist. At 26 he moved west to join three older brothers, delighting in the Sonoma Valley's pure sweet air, soft sunshine, and varied vegetation, from majestic oaks to orange blossoms and tropical plants. He began to experiment, painstakingly selecting and cross-fertilizing to achieve new and better plants. Within five years of his arrival Burbank published his first

catalog, offering for sale 100 species from all over the world. Within ten years he was well established, with a widespread clientele. A practical rather than a theoretical genius, concerned with improving stock rather than increasing knowledge, Burbank is credited with between 800 and 1000 "introductions" of new vegetables, plants and flowers during his lifetime. Best known of these are the Burbank potato, the Santa Rosa and other plums imported from Japan which he developed into a huge local industry, and the Shasta daisy. The Russet Burbank accounts for 40 percent of U.S. potato sales today. Burbank's 1893 catalog, *New Creations in Fruits and Flowers*, became a collector's item. ("What Shakespeare was to poetry and drama," according to the back cover, "Luther Burbank is to the vegetable world.") The local post office had to expand to handle his mailings, and tourists including Henry Ford and Thomas Alva Edison

made pilgrimages to his experimental gardens. In his later years Burbank became known nationwide as an eccentric and possible charlatan. A believer in eugenics, he wrote an article for *Century Magazine* on "Training of the Human Plant." (More tolerant than most eugenicists, he considered mass immigration a golden opportunity to improve the race.) He also believed in clairvoyance, "suggestive thought" even "love vibrations" between man and plant. He told his friend and admirer **Yogananda** that he had developed a spineless cactus by mental persuasion: "You don't need your protective thorns. I will protect you." Described by an acquaintance as "a strange combination of childlike simplicity and Yankee shrewdness," he was easy prey for sharpers trying to make money off his name. A twelve-volume encyclopedia of his work was a critical and financial fiasco, while the Luther Burbank Company, which took over his catalog and marketing in 1912, soon went bankrupt. When he died, he was buried under a deodar tree near his Santa Rosa greenhouse.

Burbank's autobiography, The Harvest of the Years *(Boston, 1927), was ghostwritten. See* A Gardener Touched with Genius; The Life of Luther Burbank *(New York, 1975) by Peter Dryer.*

Gelett Frank Burgess

(1866-1951). One of the most infectious lines in all poetry, "I never saw a purple cow" was written during the Gay Nineties by an expatriate Bostonian in Bohemian San

Francisco. Burgess came west after graduation from MIT (1887), took a studio on Russian Hill, and joined a group of aesthetes called "Les Jeunes" (The Young Ones), who proclaimed luxury a necessity and whimsy a virtue. He taught topographical drawing at the University of California, Berkeley, until asked to resign because of a prankish attack on the downtown S.F. fountain-statue of the eminent teetotaler **Henry Daniel Cogswell**. Burgess found work on a local society paper, *The Wave* ("a journal for those in the swim"), and was a founder in 1895 of *The Lark*, which carried his purple cow quatrain in its first issue. *The Lark*, tastefully printed on rice paper, was succeeded after 23 issues by the even more precious *Petit Journal des Refusées*, with pages made of trapezoidal pieces of wallpaper, and finally by *Phyllida*, which committed suicide after two numbers. ("The renaissance of the light essay has not yet come in California," Burgess explained.) At the end of the Gay Nineties he moved to London and later to New York, achieving popular success as the author of books on manners for children. (He introduced creatures called goops or slobs as negative examples.) Eventually, he retired to California, home of the young at heart.

The Book Club of California published two handsome limited editions of Burgess's local writings, Bayside Bohemia *(San Francisco, 1954) and* Behind the Scenes *(San Francisco, 1968).*

Ah, yes, I wrote the "Purple Cow"—
I'm Sorry, now, I wrote it;

But I can tell you Anyhow
I'll Kill you if you Quote it!

Peter Hardeman Burnett

(1807-1895). In 1849, when California was no longer a Mexican colony but not yet a state, Burnett led the movement to establish a de facto government. Drawing inspiration from the American Revolution, he argued that to remain without any government at all was worse than taxation without representation. As a reward for his eloquence (it is also suggested that his attractive daughters increased his popularity in the bachelor legislature), he was elected first governor of the not-quite-state. Born in Tennessee, Burnett had practiced law in Missouri before migrating in 1843 to Oregon where he became a judge and converted to Catholicism. Joining the Gold Rush in 1848, he made his fortune in fees on the sale of **John Sutter**'s town lots in Sacramento. As governor (1849-1851), Burnett proposed capital punishment for cattle rustling, a major problem of the day, opposed the immigration of free Negroes and Chinese, and proclaimed Thanksgiving a Saturday. At the beginning of the 1851 legislative session—the "legislature of a thousand drinks," whose members had responded churlishly to his annual message—he resigned suddenly citing personal reasons. Burnett later served a year as a state Supreme Court justice (1857-1858), wrote a book about his religious conversion, and in 1863 joined with **Sam Brannan** to found the People's Bank, the state's first chartered commercial bank.

Burnett's memoirs, An Old California Pioneer *(New York, 1880), were reprinted in Oakland in 1946.*

William John Burns

(1861-1932). Burns was the Sherlock Holmes of his day, a flamboyant private detective with a flair for dramatic discovery. A veteran of the U.S. Secret Service, he played a key role in the two most important trials in early twentieth-century California. Hired by millionaire **Rudolph Spreckels** to backstop the San Francisco graft investigations, Burns proceeded to entrap and outmaneuver Boss **Abe Ruef** into pleading guilty in 1908. The ensuing trials of Ruef's confederates eventually bogged down in legal technicalities. Using his San

Francisco team as a nucleus, the short, stocky, red-haired sleuth (he was caricatured by the **Hearst** press as Colonel Mutt, later of Mutt and Jeff) went on to establish a national detective organization. A specialist on the management side of labor disputes, Burns was already working on a similar case when the *Los Angeles Times* was dynamited in 1910; coincidentally, the detective knew the source of the explosive. He tracked down the purchasers, continuing at his own expense after the city of Los Angeles withdrew its support, and illegally held his suspects captive for several days until extradition papers arrived from California; meanwhile, he also "convinced" one of them to turn state's evidence. Faced with an ironclad case in an era unconcerned with due process, the **McNamara** brothers pleaded guilty. Burns was himself indicted by a grand jury for kidnapping, his license was eventually revoked by several states, and a U.S. attorney general once accused him of bribing jurors. He was appointed head of the U.S. Justice Department's Bureau of Investigation in 1921, but his fast-and-loose techniques and his uncharacteristic passivity during the Harding-era scandals combined to tarnish his reputation. Burns resigned in 1924 and was succeeded by a young assistant named J. Edgar Hoover.

The Masked War (New York, 1913), Burn's autobiography, is flagrantly self-serving. Incredible Detective by Gene Caesar (Englewood Cliffs, NJ, 1968) is only slightly less adulatory.

Edgar Rice Burroughs
(1875-1950). Among the legions of midwesterners who emigrated to California after World War I was Burroughs,

already well known as the author of tropical and science fiction adventures. A rugged outdoorsman on the model of Theodore Roosevelt, Burroughs failed in several business adventures before beginning to write at age 35. Out of his love of nature, his belief in the survival of the fittest, and his surprisingly fertile imagination, he created Tarzan, son of a British nobleman who grows up to become lord of the jungle. Combining business with literature, Burroughs pioneered in the syndication and marketing of his fictional creations, spinning off Tarzan bathing suits, archery sets, and movies. The first Tarzan film, featuring 60 men in ape suits tailored to Darwinian

specifications, was released in 1918. His daughter Joan married one of the movie Tarzans, Jim Pierce. He purchased the 540-acre **Otis** estate at the western end of the San Fernando Valley, where for a few years the Burroughs family enjoyed the good life California-style, with their own swimming pool, movie theater, and a little gentleman-farming on the side. But the farming venture failed, the swimming pool lacked modern filtration and turned into a murky hole, the family was divided by divorce in the 1930s, and Burroughs seemed increasingly to get the short end of the deal in protracted negotiations with Hollywood producers. The land-poor writer tried

subdividing Tarzana, offering 50 acres for sale at a jungle barbecue and launching an unsuccessful country-club venture. He lived in Malibu for awhile, serving as mayor of the beach outpost, and later tried to recoup his fortunes in Hawaii. He was buried in Tarzana where, according to the law of the jungle, more rapacious realtors eventually reaped the profits. But his literary properties have continued to pay dividends to the third generation of California Burroughses.

An inveterate traveller like so many California writers, Burroughs wrote an early Auto-Biography, now virtually unobtainable, based on his "auto-gypsying." Edgar Rice Burroughs (Provo, UT, 1975) by Irwin Porges is an entertaining photobiography.

Juan Rodriguez Cabrillo (?-1543).
The world was half a thousand years younger and man's sense of wonder and fear more acute, when Cabrillo set sail in 1542, from the west coast of Mexico in search of a northwest passage to the Atlantic. Europe was in the throes of the Reformation; in England Henry VIII was intriguing for a new wife. In

the half century since Columbus, Spain had explored Central America, the Caribbean, and Mexico in search of El Dorado, the fabled seven cities of gold, and the legendary land of "California," imagined by a contemporary as an island paradise inhabited by a race of black Amazons. Sailing north along the coast they decided to call California, Cabrillo's crew felt tense expectation. The historian of the voyage wrote of coastal mountains "which reach the sky," so formidable "it seems as if the mountains will fall upon the ships." The expedition stopped at two harbors which Cabrillo named San Diego and Monterey, and at the coastal islands. They encountered Indians but no females resembling Amazons. Returning south for the winter, Cabrillo fell and broke his arm near the shoulder, a mishap from which he died. He was buried on one of the islands off Santa Barbara. Point Loma, where the expedition first came ashore 28 September, 1542, is now

Cabrillo National Monument. The site of the explorer's landing in Santa Barbara, now a private estate, recently changed hands for $2.25 million.

Little is known of Cabrillo's life. Richard Pourade wrote a moving account, "In Search of Cabrillo" (Southern California Quarterly, June 1962) of visiting Guatemala, where Cabrillo lived for twenty years and built the ships that carried him to his death in California.

Herb Caen (Herbert Eugene Caen, 1916-   ).
Color is what makes a city great, according to Caen, whose personal mission it was for decades to brighten up San Francisco's day with his column of gossip, inside political dope, and sheer whimsy. A confirmed cosmopolite—he once defined the "boondocks" as where they put the Velveeta cheese in the gourmet department— he was born and raised in boonie capital Sacramento but claims to have been conceived while his parents were visiting the Panama-Pacific Exposition in San Francisco. Caen dropped out of school at sixteen to become a local sportswriter, moving up four years later to the staff of the *San Francisco Chronicle*. During the 1950s he went over to the rival *Examiner* for eight years, then returned to the *Chronicle* with his three-dot Walter Winchell-style of sophisticated civic boosterism. Caen also developed a lucrative sideline in books such as *Baghdad-by-the-Bay* (1949) and *One Man's San Francisco* (1976). A fellow traveler of the city's intelligentsia and a confirmed "namephreak," he coined the cognomen *beatnik*, from beat

+ nik as in Sputnik, meaning "far out." He also "discovered" a Chinese dish called sum dum goy, one of thousands of Caen contributions toward keeping San Francisco mellow.

James Mallahan Cain
(1892-1977). A former teacher and journalist from Maryland, Cain came to California during the 30s to write film scripts but found that the movie industry inspired him mostly with contempt. His first assignment, a remake of *The Ten Commandments*, he dismissed as a "masterpiece of hokum." Instead, he began weaving the local suburban landscape into tightly constructed little novels about wishes that come true with a vengeance. All three of Cain's major works—*The Postman Always Rings Twice* (1934), *Double Indemnity* (1936), and *Mildred Pierce* (1941)—use Glendale as a geographic synonym for the banality of the American dream. *Mildred Pierce* is a novel about pride, respectability, a woman's overweening love for her daughter, and the relative status of Glendale and Pasadena. A Depression-era divorcée, Mildred is faced with the necessity of going to work. Too proud to accept employment as a maid and too respectable to wait on tables, she promotes a gift for baking into a good little restaurant business. For her daughter Veda, however, a musical wunderkind and calculating snob, the "pie-wagon" is beneath contempt and Glendale rates as Ellis Island overlooking the promised land of Pasadena. Veda's wishes come true,

thanks to her mother, but with disastrous results. Ironically, considering Cain's opinion of the movies, all three of his Glendale novels were made into excellent films, none better than *Mildred Pierce* (1945) featuring Joan Crawford as the hard-boiled survivor of divorce, adultery, and murder. Mildred endured as a female archetype into the 1970s, when a hip San Francisco restaurant was named in her memory. By this time, Cain, after nearly two decades in Hollywood, three divorces of his own, and an abortive attempt to organize an author's union, had returned home to Maryland.

David Madden's James M. Cain (New York, 1970) is a literary biography— more literary than biographical. Ray Hoope's biography of Cain was scheduled for publication in 1982.

Patrick Calhoun
(1854-1943). The longest and most violent streetcar strike in U.S. history took place in San Francisco in 1907. The strike and the striking union were both eventually broken by Calhoun, a grandson of John C. and "an aristocrat of the buccaneer breed."
Gertrude Atherton claimed that Calhoun provoked the strike in the first place to distract attention from the municipal graft trials in which he was charged with making a $200,000 payoff for a 25-year streetcar franchise. Certainly Calhoun, who fought the last *code duel* in the South, was not lacking in bravado. During the strike he drove around town in an open limousine, blatantly defying "anarchic labor scum" to touch him. And during his trial for bribery he maintained an air of outraged innocence—

despite his refusal to testify on grounds of self-incrimination. His United Railroad Company was also clearly implicated in violent attempts to silence prosecution witnesses. The jury deadlocked and the indictments were eventually dismissed, but Calhoun was financially crippled by the ordeal. He was also unable to float a bond issue without producing the books that would convict him of bribery. He lost control of United Railroads in 1913 and declared bankruptcy three years later. Even in (relative) poverty, Calhoun remained vigilant of his honor: in 1931 the first edition of **Lincoln Steffens**'s autobiography had to be withdrawn because

Calhoun objected to remarks about the San Francisco graft trials. In the 1930s he amassed a new fortune in San Joaquin Valley oil operations. He died in Pasadena after being struck by a hotrodder.

Donaldina Mackenzie Cameron (1869-1968).
California's foremost crusader against "yellow slavery" was a gentle-born Scots lady raised on ranches in the San Joaquin and San Gabriel valleys. At the age of 25, Cameron joined the Presbyterian Foreign Mission Home near San Francisco's Chinatown, the only "foreign" mission in the U.S. She spent the next 42 years there, marching forth with upright

and soldierly bearing to rescue — or kidnap if necessary — young Chinese women from domestic or sexual slavery. Cameron made a total of 3,000 such rescues, sending some of the girls back to China and raising or rehabilitating others at the mission home on Sacramento Street where the best Chinese traditions were observed along with Anglo-Saxon propierties. Cameron was devout enough to believe that the key to world salvation lay in converting the Chinese but hardheaded enough to forswear romantic sentimentalization of her work. Nor was she a prim-lipped old spinster, though some called her the Carrie Nation of Chinatown. Reminiscing in later years about the old Chinatown that had largely ceased to exist, she called it admirable and appealing for all its evil. Cameron, who kept her British citizenship and her Scots burr all her life, retired to a cottage in Palo Alto in the 1930s. In 1939 the Presbyterian Mission on Sacramento Street became a

school, and Portola Alley, the scene of many rescue sorties in the old days, was renamed by San Francisco in honor of Cameron.

Both Mildred Martin's Chinatown's Angry Angel, The Story of Donaldina Cameron *(Palo Alto, 1977) and Carol G. Wilson's* Chinatown Quest; The Life and Adventures of Donaldina Cameron *(Stanford, 1931) tend to the sanctimonious.*

Frank Capra (1897-   ).
Instead of having a revolution during the Great Depression, America went to the movies to see films like Capra's. He grew up poor in L.A.'s Little Sicily, sold newspapers after class at Manual Arts High School, and worked his way through Cal Tech to win an engineering degree in 1918 only to find there were no jobs. A charter member of the "huddled masses yearning to breathe free," he wandered the West for awhile, discovering in himself the social message he would later translate into film: that the common man has God-given resources of energy and moxie with which to triumph over adversity. First a gagman for Mack Sennett, Capra became a writer-director for Columbia Pictures early in the reign of "His Crudeness" **Harry Cohn**. He figured out how to work the studio system to make some of the film classics of the Depression era, from the screwball comedy *It Happened One Night* (1934) to the utopian vision of *Lost Horizon* (1937). Most typical of Capra's sentimental populism ("*Saturday Evening Post* socialism," somebody called it) in which idealism and optimism triumph over corruption and cynicism were

Mr. Deeds Goes to Town (1936) and *Mr. Smith Goes to Washington* (1939). After World War II, which he spent making the *Why We Fight* series for the U.S. Army Morale Department, something seemed to go out of filmmaking for Capra. Power had shifted from the studios to the conglomerates, the stars, and their agents. Rather than hassle with the new system, Capra preferred to make educational films or no films at all, gradually withdrawing from his occupational addiction to movies.

Capra's autobiography, The Name Above the Title *(New York, 1972), is dedicated to "weavers of the Magic Carpet" including Aristotle, Edison, and Gary Cooper.*

Horace Walpole Carpentier (1824-1918).

The town of Oakland started out as the personal fiefdom of Carpentier, an audacious New York-educated 49er. Having cleverly divested the Peralta family of its 19,000-acre Rancho San Antonio, he laid out the town, named it Oakland and in 1852 became its first mayor. In addition to techniques that reportedly included co-opting and selling unoccupied local land, Carpentier further enriched himself by offering to build Oakland's first school in exchange for control of the city waterfront in fee simple forever. Such a cavalier attitude toward land ownership led to decades of litigation. Some measure of local stability was achieved by the adjudication of compromise titles in 1869, but the city of Oakland did not recover its waterfront until 1910, and the Peraltas fought nearly as long, but unsuccessfully, to reclaim their lands. Carpentier spent the last two decades of his life in New York. Unmarried, he figured peripherally as "uncle" and "guardian" to beautiful young girls, most notably San Francisco-born Maud Burke (1872-1948) who grew up to become Lady Cunard. Carpentier left his California riches to endow chairs of Chinese and medicine at Columbia University, of which he was the oldest living alumnus at the time of his death.

Leo Carrillo (Leopoldo Antonio Carrillo, 1880?-1961).

A true son of Los Angeles, Carrillo was born in an old downtown adobe of proud but impoverished ancestry. A prized family possession was volume two of *Bancroft's History of California*, which listed four pages of Carrillos, including his great-great-grandfather who accompanied explorer-priest **Junípero Serra** and his great-

grandfather, the first native-born governor. Leo was a street-smart kid who learned to mimic Chinese, Italian, and other ethnic groups in the city's melting pot. Later the family moved to the more halcyon environs of Santa Monica, where Leo's aunt **Arcadia Bandini**, a major landowner, had his father elected mayor. Carrillo became a vaudeville dialect comedian, moving up to Broadway as the Italian modiste in *Lombardi* and the cowardly southern heir in Booth Tarkington's *Magnolia*. He invested his first earnings in a ten-acre ranch in Santa Monica Canyon so steep that **Will Rogers** called it a ranch you could lean against. Later, he acquired 3,000 acres with a view of the Camino Real near Carlsbad. At the age of 70, Carrillo began a second career as the quixotic sidekick Pancho on television's *Cisco Kid*. Through the years he was also a familiar fixture on his palamino with silver-studded trappings at Pasadena's annual Rose Parade and other ceremonial occasions, a mock personification of the Spanish heritage. (When not on horseback, he could frequently be found behind the wheel of a 1948 Chrysler convertible wagon with the horned head of a bull mounted on the grill.) Active in conservative politics, he was a leading spokesman against the "Red Peril," urging the House Un-

American Activities Committee to clean the ''Communist rattlesnakes'' out of Hollywood. He served for several years on the state Parks Commission, which named a rustic beach campground in his honor.

Carrillo's The California I Love *(Englewood Cliffs, NJ, 1961) is an idealization of ''the twilight of the pastoral era.''*

Kit Carson (Christopher Houston Carson, 1809-1868). At sixteen Carson ran away from home in Missouri to join a wagon train to Santa Fe. For the next seventeen years he wandered the West as a hunter and trapper, learning Indian languages and ''memorizing'' the land itself. One beaver-hunting expedition took him through the Mojave to San Gabriel and north to the Sacramento Valley, then Mexican California. Underemployed when beaver hats went out of style, Carson joined **John C. Frémont**'s first three Western expeditions as a guide. Theirs was a relationship based on mutual admiration. Carson, three years older and

infinitely more experienced in trail lore, would have followed the courageous, dashing Frémont anywhere he said. Frémont, for his part, made Carson a national hero, the West's most famous guide, with his best-selling reports. On the first expedition (1842-1843), Carson led Frémont to the South Pass of the Rockies. The second expedition forced a midwinter crossing through the Sierra to **Sutter**'s Fort. On the third (1845-1846), they traversed impassible stretches of desert to reach California in time for the Bear Flag revolt. Carson distinguished himself at the Battle of San Pasqual by escaping through enemy lines to get help. He was also involved in the most discreditable episode of the American conquest, the killing of three Californios, shot because Frémont wanted no prisoners. Carson made two cross-country trips as a courier to Washington, D.C., where he had a personal audience with President James K. Polk and was nominated for a second lieutenant's commission. But the Senate refused to ratify the commission, perhaps hoping to strike back at the ambitious Frémont, and Carson returned home to New Mexico a plain citizen, unspoiled by either celebrity or disappointment. He spent his later years as an Indian agent, and was promoted to brigadier general for his pacification of rebellious tribes during the Civil War.

Dear Old Kit; The Historical Kit Carson (Norman, OK, 1968) by Harvey Lewis Carter contains a bibliographical essay and an annotated version of Carson's own memoirs. For a traditional

biography, see Bernice Blackwelder's Great Westerner, The Story of Kit Carson *(Caldwell, ID, 1962).*

Neal Cassady (1926-1968). Cassady was a seminal figure in the Beat generation, a character out of 1950s underground mythology who resurfaced in the 1960s as one of **Ken Kesey**'s Merry Pranksters. A reform school alumnus from Colorado, he sought out **Allen Ginsberg** and **Jack Kerouac** in New York, hoping some of their urban intellectual sophistication would rub off on him. Actually, he taught them the manic energy of the open road, the freedom of the outlaw, and the wild pull of the West. Ginsberg fell in love with Cassady, Kerouac became his alter ego, and both of them followed him to the Bay Area. Kerouac cast the jailkid from Denver as Dean Moriarty, the central character in *On the Road* (1957) and used him again in *Visions of Cody* (1959). Cassady's juvenile delinquencies all involved what he called ''autoeroticism,'' joyriding in stolen cars. Later he became obsessed with horse racing. A compulsive personality, addicted to danger, he literally asked for the marijuana conviction that sent him to San Quentin for two years. When he got out in 1960 the Beat generation was finished, submerged in alcohol and middle age. Attracted by the combination of drugs and literature, he turned up at Ken Kesey's place in Stanford to become a charter member of the psychedelic generation. Cassady was the driver, the

''mad Ahab'' at the wheel of the Pranksters' bus on its trip across the country. But that scene faded too, and one day he turned up dead in Mexico of too many pills and too much alcohol.

Lawrence Ferlinghetti published Cassady's First Third *(San Francisco, 1971) a Kerouac-style memoir of his early years.*

Carlos Aranha Castaneda (1925?-   ). In the early middle ages of the psychedelic era, a California anthropologist made the cover of *Time* as the mystery author of best-selling underground classics. A Latin American whose precise name, birthdate, and other vital statistics remain elusive, Castaneda surfaced in Los Angeles in 1955, enrolled at UCLA a few years later, and finally won his doctorate in anthropology in 1973. By that time his dissertation, usually a tedious, mechanical exercise, had already been published as his third best-seller: *Journey to Ixtlan* (1972), following *The Teachings of Don Juan* (1968) and *A Separate Reality* (1971). All feature Don Juan, a Yaqui sorcerer, adept at manipulating power and perception, whom Castaneda claimed to have met in an Arizona bus depot. Best-sellerdom aroused curiosity and animosity in academia. Were Castaneda's purported field reports science, fiction, or a mixture of the two? Richard DeMille, self-described ''Master of Castanedics,'' made a career out of writing witty, incisive explanations and interpretations of the whole phenomenon. Castaneda was a shaman of academe, he

CARLOS
CASTANEDA:

MAGIC AND REALITY

Florence May Chadwick

(1918-   ). For most children growing up in coastal California, the Pacific Ocean is an awesome primal force, arousing respect if not outright fear. Chadwick conquered that force and that fear. The daughter of a San Diego policeman, she got a precocious start in marathon swimming, making it across the San Diego Bay channel when she was ten. Later she won the 2-1/2 mile La Jolla race ten times. She appeared in a 1945 **Esther Williams** film, but the teamwork and seemingly effortless beauty of water ballet were not her thing. Chadwick went in for the long, hard haul, solitary and punishing. In 1948 she worked her way to Europe as a secretary for the Arabian American Oil Company, practicing in the Persian Gulf

for a shot at the English Channel. In 1950 she set a new record for swimming from England to France in thirteen hours, twenty minutes. One of the alltime great channel swimmers, she swam the Straits of Gibraltar, the Bosphorus, the Dardanelles, the English Channel (three times), and California's Catalina Channel, establishing seventeen world records in her day. At last report Chadwick was a San Diego stockbroker, still swimming weekends in Mission Bay.

Harry Chandler

(1864-1944). Chandler built a fortune on real estate, croneyism, Yankee shrewdness, and the power of the press. He arrived in Los Angeles in 1883 with little money and poor health but soon recouped strength and solvency by farm work in the San Fernando Valley. Newspaper circulation routes were bought and sold in those days, and Chandler bought up enough of them to acquire bargaining power with *Los Angeles Times* publisher **Harrison Gray Otis** who made the young go-getter his business manager in 1894. After the death of his first wife, Chandler married Otis's daughter Marion and minded the store while Otis went off to war in 1898. In the early years of the century, armed with inside knowledge about the Owens River Aqueduct, Chandler put together his first syndicate of cronies to buy up San Fernando Valley lands which would appreciate fabulously with the provision of water and other public utilities at taxpayer expense.

wrote, "the Neil Simon of metaphysics," a plagiarizer and popularizer of Big True Ideas. (In the same vein, Marcello Truzzi described Don Juan as "the biggest hoax in anthropology since the Piltdown Man.") DeMille does, however, give Castaneda credit for imaginative effrontery. Castaneda himself, seemingly impervious to the flap, continued to produce best-

sellers (*The Eagle's Gift* in 1981) that, cumulatively, support DeMille's concept of the author as inspired fabulizer.

Richard DeMille wrote Castaneda's Journey *(Santa Barbara, 1976) and* The Don Juan Papers *(Santa Barbara, 1981).*

The profits from this venture financed another Chandler syndicate operation, the 300,000-acre Tejon Ranch, called the "right-of-way" ranch because the state highway commission selected it over a more economical and populous route for Interstate 5. By the 1930s Chandler was a land baron with two million acres including a large piece of Baja California and the Santa Anita Ranch, **Lucky Baldwin**'s showplace. He also acquired diverse manufacturing, transportation, tourist, and other interests, usually through syndicates or dummy corporations, and served on some 50 boards of directors. Like Otis, whom he succeeded in 1917 as publisher of the *Times*, Chandler was aggressively Republican and antilabor. Citing the threat of international Bolshevism, he supported corrupt municipal governments during the interwar period in exchange for a police "Red Squad" to put down strikes and investigate subversives. The Depression was only psychological, according to Chandler, who thought economist Maynard Keynes was a pinko. **Upton Sinclair**, who hoped to end poverty as a candidate for governor in 1934, he considered the devil incarnate, calling down on California a hoarde of penniless vagrants. ("Come on, Harry!" Sinclair joked, alluding to Chandler's own arrival penniless, "Give the *other* bums a chance.") In 1942 the *Times* won a Pulitzer Prize and respectability for defending freedom of the press; the particular freedom

in question was that to urge stiff sentences in labor disputes. After Chandler's death, family holdings were so extensive that *Times* editors and reporters reportedly sometimes had difficulty keeping track of which issues to softpedal. In the third generation of publishing, Norman Chandler (1899-1973) is said to have begun his newspaper career as a paperboy in a Model T. His wife, Dorothy Buffum Chandler (1901-   ), first used family power for public philanthropy, singlehandedly spearheading the drive for the Los Angeles Music Center, with a philharmonic hall there named for her in 1964. (As president of the Symphony Association, she also claimed the prerogative of hiring and firing conductors.) Their son Otis Chandler (1927-   ) is credited with bringing the *Times* into the twentieth century and abandoning boosterism for professionalism. Under a board of directors representing the Southern California establishment, the *Times* also became a publishing conglomerate, putting out everything from art books to telephone books, James Bond paperbacks, Bibles, and election ballots. However, Otis Chandler, who maintained his hobby of surfing into middle age, seemed to lack his grandfather's business sense. Or perhaps the quality of cronies was just starting to slip. In 1972 Chandler was revealed as an unwitting partner with a former Stanford classmate in the $30 million GeoTek scandal, an oil exploration scam for which

the classmate went to prison. *See* Thinking Big; The Story of the Los Angeles Times *by Bob Gottlieb and Irene Wolt (New York, 1977).*

Raymond Thornton Chandler (1888-1959). His Southern California was a soulless metropolis bounded by Long Beach, Malibu, and San Bernardino, a nightmare of seedy streets, dark canyons, and offshore gambling ships, a world dominated by corruption and greed. American born and British educated in the

classics, Chandler was always an odd man out. He became a successful oil company executive at the Signal Hill fields in Long Beach but was laid off during the Depression, reportedly for reasons of inebriation rather than economy. Making a methodical study of pulp fiction at the age of 44, he created a new genre of literate detective fiction featuring a hardbitten idealist named Marlowe, later played by Humphrey Bogart with cynical class. After the

success of *The Big Sleep* (1939), *Farewell, My Lovely* (1940) and *The Lady in the Lake* (1943), Chandler turned to filmwriting, collaborating with Billy Wilder on *Double Indemnity* and adapting some of his own novels for the screen. Too shy and reclusive to enjoy film society, he went into self-imposed exile in La Jolla with his wife Cissy Pascal, eighteen years his senior. There he wrote *The Long Goodbye* (1954), his most cynical work. Repeated editions, translations and films of Chandler's novels have given the world and successive generations an ineradicable image of Depression-era L.A. Taking a clue from San Francisco's **Hammett** cult, one enterprising group of trench-coated guides recently offered tours of Chandler's L.A., or what is left of it. Marlowe's office building at Sunset and Cahuenga is no longer there, and Los Feliz, where he lived in seedy apartments, has come up in the world since his day.

Frank MacShane, The Life of Raymond Chandler *(New York, 1976).*

Cesar Chavez (Cesario Estrada Chavez, 1927-   ). A quiet, unassuming former farm laborer, Chavez drew on the models of Saint Francis and Gandhi to organize the wretched of the California earth, bringing farm-labor relations from the feudal age into the twentieth century. He was born in Arizona where his family had a ranch in the Gila Valley. The ranch was lost to taxes during the Depression, and the whole family joined the migrant stream of laborers to California,

harvesting everything from peas to watermelons from the Imperial to the Sacramento valleys. (Topping sugar beets is the most back-breaking work, Chavez once recalled, followed by thinning lettuce. Cotton and broccoli are also difficult to pick.) In 1952 he went to work as an organizer for Saul Alinsky's Community Service Organization, conducting voter registration and citizenship drives and listening to people's problems for ten years. In 1962 Chavez resigned from CSO to found his own farm workers' union, and in 1965, when Filipino laborers went out on strike against the grape growers, Chavez took his workers out, too. Eventually, the United Farm Workers lined up against the big names in California agriculture: **Di Giorgio**, Perelli-Minetti, Giumarra, Roberts, Bagdasarian, Zaninovich. At first the growers refused to recognize their workers, got injunctions and restraining orders, and hired scab labor.

Chavez responded with prayer vigils, mass marches, and boycotts. When violence threatened to break out, he began to fast, turning the strike into a moral pilgrimage—a mission to restore the dignity of labor. In 1970, as the last new contracts were being signed in the grape industry, the UFW began a three-cornered struggle in the lettuce industry, the Teamsters having already signed sweetheart contracts with conglomerates like United Fruit. And when the grape contracts began to come up for renewal in 1973, the UFW again found itself up against the Teamsters.

Peter Matthiessen's Sal Si Puedes: Cesar Chavez and the New American Revolution *(New York, 1969) and Jacques Levy's* Cesar Chavez, Autobiography of La Causa *(New York, 1975) are both sympathetic to the labor organizer.*

Caryl Whittier Chessman (1921-1960). Chessman's life story reads like a black tale in which the bad fairies call all the turns of fate. As a child in Pasadena and Glendale, he suffered from pneumonia, asthma, encephalitis and diphtheria. An automobile accident left his mother paralyzed, and his father went on relief during the Depression. Chessman first began stealing to put food on the table, he claimed. Then he needed money for an operation for his mother, or to trace her parentage (she was abandoned in infancy). There was also, unquestionably, a thrill in lawlessness. Joyriding in a stolen auto, he reported, made him feel free, creative, triumphant. Caught near a burglary scene with a car

belonging to the postmaster of Pasadena, he was sent to reform school in Northern California. There was a second stretch in Road Camp Number Seven in the mountains near Malibu. L.A.'s ''Boy Bandit'' spent his twentieth birthday in San Quentin, sentenced to sixteen-to-life as a repeat offender. Obviously of above-average intelligence, he joined the prison debating team, wrote radio scripts, and was transferred to a minimum security facility in Chino from which he escaped with an improbable tale of infiltrating a local fascist group to put the ''snatch'' on Hitler. Prisons have personalities, wrote Chessman, who made a comparative study: maximum-security Folsom, where he was next remanded, was ''tough, contemptuous, challenging,'' but so was he. Released on parole in 1947, he returned to prey on L.A. bookmakers. Having educated

himself during the long years of incarceration, he thought of himself as a criminal Alexander the Great. He also identified with Franc[92ois Villon, the medieval French poet and murderer. In 1948 Chessman was accused of committing the ''red light'' (so-called because the perpetrator drove a car with a red light) robbery-rapes on the lovers' lanes of L.A. He denied the charges and conducted his own defense, rather poorly. Despite the fact that no murder was involved, Chessman, the mean, dangerous, arrogant habitual criminal, loomed in the popular imagination as a combination Jack the Ripper and Boston Strangler. Condemned to death, he spent twelve years on death row writing appeals and literate accounts of criminal sociopathy before his execution. A distinguished group including Albert Schweitzer, **Aldous Huxley** and the queen of Belgium protested his death in the gas chamber.

Cell 2455 Death Row (New York, 1954), Chessman's criminal autobiography, sold over a half a million copies. For a more impartial account of his life and trials, see Frank Parker's Chessman, The Red Light Bandit *(Chicago, 1975). Legal standards in 1948 were somewhat looser than they are today, prompting William Kunstler to write* Beyond a Reasonable Doubt; The Original Trial of Caryl Chessman *(Westport, CT, 1961).*

Haakon Maurice Chevalier (1901-   ). Outside of war and other such extremities, few men ever have occasion to test the ultimate loyalty and integrity of their friends. Chevalier, a leftwing French instructor at the University of California at Berkeley (1927-1946), found that he had been betrayed almost gratuitously by his best friend, a man he idolized and would have defended to the death, **J. Robert Oppenheimer**. The notorious ''Professor X'' of Oppenheimer's 1954 security hearings, Chevalier was born in the United States of French-Norwegian parentage and graduated from Berkeley (Ph.D., 1929). An authority on Anatole France and the translator of André Malraux's *Man's Fate* and numerous other works, he became friends with Oppenheimer through common radical sympathies in the late 1930s.

One day in 1943, just as the physicist was leaving for Los Alamos, Chevalier mentioned a mutual friend who had means of passing information to the Russians. Some months later Oppenheimer mentioned this to security officers, but declined to name Chevalier, who went into the files as ''X.'' Chevalier left Berkeley in 1946 and experienced difficulties finding another job. He was subpoenaed by the **Jack Tenney** committee and branded ''one of the most ubiquitous figures in the Communist set at Berkeley,'' for reasons which did not become fully apparent until 1954. Security hearings then revealed that Oppenheimer had reported what Chevalier

considered an innocent conversation. Feeling betrayed and rejected, Chevalier found relief in writing. His novel *The Man Who Would Be God* (1959) was a Faustian tale of a scientist destroyed by his own invention. Later, in *The Story of a Friendship* (1965), he searched Oppenheimer's past for character defects, concluding that the brilliant physicist shared with classic figures of literature the tragic flaw of pride.

Christo (Christo Javacheff, 1935-   ). In 1976 a Bulgarian-born neo-dadaist arrived in Northern California proposing to construct a perfectly useless 24-mile fence from Petaluma to the

sea. Christo, who started by "wrapping" cans, cars, buildings, and then whole landscapes in white canvas, was the veteran of a similar fence project (*Valley Curtain*) in Colorado. His *Running Fence* would cost two million dollars, to be provided by the artist; it would take six months to erect; and after two weeks of display it would vanish completely, all materials going to the 59 ranchers whose land would be traversed. After seventeen hearings in Sonoma and Marin counties, three appeals to the state Supreme Court, application to the U.S. Army Corps of Engineers, and completion of a 265-page Environmental Impact Report, Christo won permission to launch his experiment in the aesthetics of transience. The result proved a rare community experience for the people of Sonoma and Marin counties, who moved from hostility and skepticism to support of the offbeat artist. So what if it was a totally useless fence? It became "our" fence, a shimmering vapor trail stretching over rolling hills into the Pacific sunset, redefining relations between people and space, art and society, dream and reality.

The Running Fence Project (New York, 1977) is a photographic documentary of the experience. A television documentary was also made and runs occasionally on public television.

William Andrews Clark, Jr. (1877-1934). The
son of a copper baron and U.S. Senator from Montana— one of the hundred men who "owned" America, it was said—young Clark enjoyed all the advantages of education,

travel, and culture. Trained as a lawyer at the University of Virginia (1899), he was also a gifted violinist and a brilliant conversationalist who was knowledgeable about astronomy, oenology or the study of wine, and sumo wrestling. In 1908 he acquired a winter home on then-elegant Adams Boulevard in Los Angeles where he housed his growing private collection of books. Unable to compete with the "rare-book imperialism" of **Huntington** in San Marino, he specialized and cornered the market on Dryden. In 1919 Clark personally founded the Los Angeles Philharmonic, putting up $1 million to hire musicians "removed from any participation in cabaret shows, parades, or fatiguing employment." Happily free from any such personal necessity himself, he used to rehearse with the orchestra's second violins. To give the new orchestra cachet, he tried unsuccessfully to hire Rachmaninoff as conductor. Other benefactions included the Mary Andrews Clark Residence in L.A., a French-

style chateau run by the YWCA as a home for impoverished gentlewomen. He also bequeathed his home and library to UCLA. At the time of his death, he had spent a total of about $4 million to bring culture to Southern California.

Eldridge Cleaver (Leroy
Eldridge Cleaver, 1935-   ). After the proverbial athletes and entertainers, the best-known blacks in California are outlaws. Cleaver, who first went to Folsom Prison at eighteen for getting caught with a shopping bag full of marijuana, later served nine years for assault. During his prison years he educated himself in the radical classics, became the leader of inmate Black Muslims, and wrote a memoir, *Soul on Ice*, in which he discussed the revolutionary significance of raping white women. When he got out on parole in late 1966, the Muslims with their bean pies and small-business mentality were taking a back seat to the new macho of the Black Panthers, whom he joined in 1967 as Minister of Information. Cleaver soon clashed with the Panthers for consorting with hippies and the white radical-chic fringe. (A racial relativist rather than a black nationalist, he had grown up in an L.A. Chicano neighborhood where he had learned to admire the pachuco style of defiance.) In 1968, after a shootout with Oakland police, he went underground and surfaced in Cuba, which he later described as "San Quentin with palm trees." He moved on to Algeria, supporting himself by means learned in

East L.A.—car boosting and forging passports—and to France, where he is rumored to have been kept by the prime minister's mistress. It was in the south of France that the former Panther became, improbably, a born-again Christian. In 1975, after seven years' exile, Cleaver came home to face charges, getting off with probation thanks largely to his new-found piety. (The Panthers, who had long since written him off as a defector, suspected him of finking to the FBI as well.) Joining the Christian celebrity circuit, Cleaver flirted alternately with the Moonies and the Mormons, affected cod-piece trousers and blue-denim robes, and defended the doctrine of wife-beating. In 1981 he was talking about running for mayor of Oakland, scene of his former martial glory.

Cleaver has almost enough facility as a writer —Soul on Ice (New York, 1968) followed by Soul on Fire (Waco, TX, 1978)— to obscure the moral and legal dimensions of his actions.

Samuel Langhorne Clemens. See Mark Twain.

Henry Daniel Cogswell
(1819-1900). "If fame is to be judged by gross tonnage of statuary," Idwal Jones once joked, "Dr. Cogswell was as conspicuous a man in his age as Pompey or Queen Elizabeth were in theirs." An orphan from Connecticut who survived trials worthy of Horatio Alger to become a dentist, Cogswell joined the Gold Rush to San Francisco, filling miners' teeth with gold straight from the placers. Investing in sandlots, he became rich enough to retire at 35 and devote the rest of

his life to the cause of temperance. Hoping to replace alcohol with water, "nature's own beverage," he financed a series of ornamental drinking fountains all over the U.S. Most of these featured a life-size statue, usually of himself, although Ben Franklin is the subject of a surviving San Francisco monument. Unfortunately, Cogswell's fountains fairly invited vandalism. Of six erected in San Francisco, **Gelett Burgess** and friends brought one to its knees during the Gay Nineties and four others have disappeared. A Cogswell fountain in Washington, D.C., became such an eyesore that Senator Sheridan Downey of California introduced a resolution in Congress for its merciful removal. The do-gooding dentist's most lasting monument is the massive

Cogswell College on Nob Hill, started in 1877 as a free vocational high school for boys. (A home for fallen women seems to have gone the way of the fountains.) Clearly suffering from an edifice complex, Cogswell designed his own mausoleum at Oakland's Mountain View Cemetery, adding to the trio of faith, hope, and charity, a statue of temperance. "A veritable work of art," he described his final resting place, "and scarcely suggestive of a sepulchre."

Mickey Cohen

(Meyer Harris Cohen, 1913-1976). Racketeer Mickey Cohen grew up in Boyle Heights, an East L.A. ghetto where his widowed Russian-Jewish mother ran a small store. A graduate of the school of the streets, he was hustling newspapers downtown at six, was busted for bootlegging at nine, and in adolescence became a prize fighter, a well-traveled route into the racket world of money, prestige, and power. Cohen rose to the top of what he called L.A.'s "main events"—cards, shylocking, betting, and fixing—during the 1940s. He also ran nightclubs and a Hollywood haberdashery. (He didn't like to sell his merchandise, which would only have to be replaced, but was generous in giving away ties to admirers.) A snappy dresser, high liver, and big tipper, he loved to be seen with celebrities. At the height of his power he held a fundraiser for Israel's Irgun (pocketing the money, it was rumored) and contributed to **Richard Nixon**'s campaign against **Helen Douglas**. But

his house was bombed during the underworld "Battle of Sunset Strip," he was wounded in a 1949 shootout at Sherry's Restaurant, and he ultimately became a victim of his own compulsion for publicity. Convicted in 1952 of income tax evasion, he spent three years in charge of a prison clothing commissary, trading new uniforms for influence. On his release he opened an ice cream parlor in Brentwood with a bookie operation in the back room and was seen around town

with stripper Candy Barr. During a second long stretch for tax evasion (1961-1972), he was attacked by another inmate with a pipe and permanently crippled. But he never lost his moxie, his good humor, or his faith in the big fix. The problem was to figure out whom to fix. "There's no politics in Southern California you can deal with," he explained. "It's anarchy."

See his autobiography, Mickey Cohen: In My Own Words (*Englewood Cliffs, NJ, 1975*).

Harry Cohn (1891-1958). He was the autocrat of Columbia Pictures, a tough wheeler-dealer from New York's East Side who built a backstreet Hollywood operation into a major studio by the sheer force of his vulgarian personality. His criterion of film quality was simple: "If my fanny doesn't squirm, it's good." His brother Jack held the financial pursestrings, exercising

constant nagging supervision from New York, but within the boundaries of the studio on Gower Street, Cohn exercised absolute power. A short, natty man with a fetish for cleanliness, he reigned from a desk raised above the floor like Mussolini's, connected by two-way intercom to the whole lot. "That was lousy," his disembodied voice might interrupt shooting on a remote set. "Do it again."

(When a startled visiting actor asked who was speaking, the voice replied, ''God.'') He liked to rename his stars and, as the author of their celebrity, rule over their lives, public and private. (''When you're at this studio, you keep your pants buttoned,'' he told young **John Wayne**, and he reportedly pulled some underworld strings to break up a romance between one of his actresses and a black entertainer. Writers and directors had a high turnover rate at Columbia. Writer Ben Hecht privately called his boss White Fang, and director Charles Vidor sued him for abusive treatment. (The judge ruled that Cohn's abuse was habitual, not punitive, in an extraordinary profession.) Fascinated by power, Cohn brought the world Willie Stark, the demagogue of *All the King's Men* (1949) and Harry Brock, the loud-mouthed junk dealer of *Born Yesterday* (1950), in his own image. Personally, however, he chose to maintain a low public profile. (When a young reporter, catching him off guard in a barber chair, asked how he liked his job, Cohn replied, ''It's better than being a pimp.'') When he died, a studio sound stage was converted into a funeral chapel, and he was buried in Hollywood Cemetery, within shouting distance of Columbia Studios.
Bob Thomas's King Cohn *(New York, 1967) is a Hollywood classic.*

Lillie Hitchcock Coit

(Eliza Wychie Hitchcock Coit, 1843-1929). Fires were so frequent and so devastating in early San Francisco that firefighting became something

of a civic duty and firewatching a municipal pastime. According to her biography, which reads like a Harlequin romance, Lillie Coit had a traumatic early experience of fire. Not only did she personally experience some of the early San Francisco conflagrations, she also accompanied her mother, an unreconstructed Southern belle, to put the torch to the old family plantation rather than have it fall to squatters. Fire-engine chasing was also a form of publicity indulged in primarily by actresses in early San Francisco, but also by exhibitionistic society women. The daughter of an army physician posted to San Francisco in 1851, Lillie made

up in daring what she lacked in looks to become the reigning debutante of her day. Typically she would leave cotillions or even weddings to arrive by barouche, with coachmen and dancing partner in attendance, at the latest fire. Sent to Paris during the Civil War to keep her out of trouble (she was of course a rebel), she turned up at a Parisian masked ball in a fireman's uniform. After a string of broken engagements, she married Howard Coit, a handsome San Francisco stockbroker with a reputation as a lady-killer. In 1872 the young society matron's photo was placed in the cornerstone of the new city hall as the outstanding woman of the day. But hers was a style that

did not age gracefully or well. The Coits separated, and Lillie began spending more time at her ranch in the Napa Valley, where she was known for driving her coach at breakneck speed over country roads. In 1904, when an acquaintance was shot and killed in her Palace Hotel suite, that was too much even for Lillie Coit. She spent 25 years in European exile, returning only to die in San Francisco. She left part of her fortune to the city, which erected in her memory the Coit Tower on Telegraph Hill (over the objections of **Gertrude Atherton**, who said it looked like an incinerator) and a Washington Square monument to fire volunteers, inscribed: ''In those stern pioneering days, a man was a man—and a fireman.''
Helen Holdredge's Firebelle Lillie, The Life and Times of Lillie Coit *(New York, 1967) is prime soap opera.*

William Tell Coleman

(1824-1893). Vigilantism had its origin in California, made respectable by men like Coleman. **Robert Louis Stevenson** called him the ''lion of the vigilantes,'' the ''intermittent despot'' of San Francisco. ''As haughty as a prince of Persia,'' historian **H. H. Bancroft** remarked. **Josiah Royce** credited him with sound judgement and firm balance, **William Tecumseh Sherman** with character and assurance. Kentucky-born William Tell Coleman (son of Napoleon Bonaparte Coleman) came overland to San Francisco in 1849. Self-educated and, a successful merchant by the age of 27, he was appointed prosecutor of the first

Vigilance Committee's "people's court" (which incidentally convicted, then reprieved, an innocent man). In 1856, after the shooting of **James King of William**, Coleman became head of the second Vigilance Committee which seized military control of the city, standing off the governor with daring coolness until satisfied that order was restored—"This is no mob, no distempered faction, but San Francisco herself that speaks," in the deathless words of Chairman Coleman. Although the second committee was active for only three months, the influence of the businessmen's revolution, as Royce called it, lasted for

24 years. Coleman spent most of that time in New York, where he married well and extended his business interests, including a prosperous clipper line. In 1870 he returned with his wife to San Francisco, whose streets he had been so instrumental in making safe for women, children, and democracy. The Colemans acquired a Nob Hill mansion and a large summer estate in San Rafael, both furnished lavishly by the formidable Mrs. Coleman. During the anti-Chinese labor unrest of 1877 Coleman was again called on to restore order, this time through a Committee of Public Safety. He was also

active in the Chamber of Commerce, the Society of California Pioneers, the state Democratic party, and the California Immigrant Union which recruited "desirable" new citizens abroad. Having invested heavily in Death Valley borax, a form of which was named "colemanite," he was ruined in 1888 when Congress removed the U.S. tariff on borax.

James Scherer's Lion of the Vigilantes *(Indianapolis, 1939) is an oldie but goodie.*

David Douty Colton

(1832-1878). An early Southern Pacific crossroads east of Los Angeles is named after Colton, the man, ironically, who precipitated California's first major railroad scandal. Born in Maine, he was a gold rusher who served a term as county sheriff of Siskiyou. He became associated with the **David Broderick** machine in San Francisco, and somehow inherited most of the California senator's real estate. The aggressive and ambitious General Colton, as he liked to be called, became cronies with his neighbor on Nob Hill, **Charles Crocker**, who brought him into the Southern Pacific machine. Given an option on $1 million worth of SP stock, Colton merely had to come up with the money—how he didn't know. In anticipation of his initiation into an expanded "Big Five," he developed an exaggerated sense of his own importance. After Colton's premature and somewhat mysterious death, his widow was told of certain "irregularities" in his accounts and obliged to settle

up with the SP. She got a certain amount of satisfaction, however, out of producing Colton's correspondence with **Collis Huntington**, evidence of the railroad's practice of buying and selling state and federal legislators. The Colton trial provided the first impetus for the long campaign to get the SP out of politics.

Colton functions as the coda in Oscar Lewis's symphonic The Big Four *(New York, 1938, 1969).*

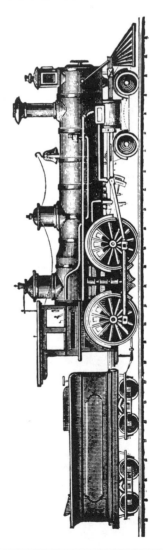

Walter Colton

(1797-1851). "I had dreamed in the course of my life, as most people have, of the thousand things I might have become, but it never entered my visions that I should succeed to the dignity of a Spanish alcade." So wrote Colton when, having arrived in 1845 as chaplain on the U.S.S. *Congress*, he was pressed into extraordinary service as mayor of Monterey, California. For three years he discharged his unaccustomed duties with compassion and wit, as recounted in a diary full of homilies and perceptions. Colton was constantly struck by the contrast between shrewd Yankee acquisitiveness and Mexican generosity. "There is hardly a shanty among them which does not contain more true contentment, more genuine gladness of heart, than you will meet with in the most princely palace," he said of the Californios, although conceding that "Yankees are good when mountains are to be levelled, lakes drained, and lightning converted into vegetable manure." Colton was also a witness and participant in the Gold Rush, which he considered a great democratic leveller: "The master has become his own servant and the servant his own lord," he wrote, portending the revolution in class distinctions.

Colton's Three Years in California (Stanford, 1949) is a minor classic.

Jack Kent Cooke

(1912?). A dapper Canadian media millionaire who retired to Pebble Beach in 1961, Cooke embarked on a whirlwind second career as the sports wizard of Southern California. First he bought the Los Angeles Lakers basketball team for $5 million. Then he was awarded the local hockey franchise in 1966 for his Los Angeles Kings. Barred by competitors from the L.A. Sports Arena, he proceeded to build his own stadium in Inglewood, an 80-columned "forum" modeled after a Montreal stadium. The Forum opened in 1967 to become the Madison Square Garden of the West, a goldmine of a convention center and concert hall as well as sports arena. Cooke's other interests included advertising and cable TV, all complementary. In 1979, however, in the wake of a painful divorce, he walked away from it all. The Lakers, Kings, and the Forum, along with a 13,000-acre Sierra ranch, were sold for $67.5 million.

Ina Coolbrith

(Josephine Donna Smith Carsley, 1841-1928). Although she was married at the age of seventeen and was widely believed to be the sweetheart of the California literary giants of her day, Coolbrith was called "the virgin poetess." The title reflects the role of ritual martyrdom she assumed, rather than actual sexual status. She was born in Nauvoo, Missouri, the city founded by Mormon prophet Joseph Smith, her uncle, who was murdered there. At ten she crossed the plains in a covered wagon, becoming the first white child to enter California through Beckwourth Pass. After the failure of her early marriage to Carsley and the death of her sister,

Coolbrith assumed the burden of supporting her sister's orphaned children as well as the illegitimate half-Indian daughter of her friend **Joaquin Miller**. After her divorce she assumed her mother's maiden name, reasoning that her own maiden name, Smith, was not distinguished enough for her new aspirations as a potess. In 1874 she became the first public librarian of Oakland, where she imparted her reverence for the printed word to such youngsters as **Jack London** and **Isadora Duncan**. They recalled her sitting at her library desk as if it were a throne. She, however, considered it a prison and longed for the freedom to write poetry. In 1898 Coolbrith moved to the Mercantile Library in San Francisco and in 1899 to the Bohemian Club, whose members treated her with courtly reverence and chipped in to help her over hard times. Unfortunately for Coolbrith, life seemed to be one long hard time. What poetry she wrote is remarkable chiefly for its lugubrious quality and its preoccupation with duty and death, frustration and sorrow. In 1915 she was crowned poet laureate of California at the Panama-Pacific Exposition. **Luther Burbank** named a poppy for her, and after her death at an august old age a mountain in Sierra County was named in her honor.

Ina Coolbrith, Librarian and Laureate of California by Josephine Rhodehamel and Raymund Wood (Provo, UT, 1973) is printed, appropriately, in lavender ink.

Copley Family

. It reads like an Edna Ferber epic: childless for two generations, a family perpetuates itself by adopting children who turn against one another for control of the patrimony. Colonel Ira Clifton Copley (1864-1947) was an Illinois utilities magnate, a Yale graduate who led troops against striking workers in the 1894 "Pullman War" and served six terms in Congress as a Republican from Illinois. He bought his first newspaper in 1905 to promote his political career and expanded into California in 1928 with the purchase of the *San Diego Union* and *Evening Tribune* along with a mansion in Coronado, from sugar baron **John Spreckels**. The colonel, who once declined to buy the *Chicago Tribune*, preferring to remain a bigger frog in a smaller puddle, as he put it, eventually acquired a ring of newspapers around Los Angeles. These included the *Hollywood News*, the *Pasadena Post*, the *Glendale Press*, the *Santa Monica Outlook*, and the *Long Beach Sun*, as well as an L.A. TV station renamed KCOP (sold in 1957). On the colonel's death, James Strohn Copley

(1916-1973), a sickly orphan raised in his foster father's manly image and educated like him at Andover and Yale, prevailed over his younger adopted brother, an expatriate artist. The colonel had run his newspapers like a personal fiefdom, collecting all the cash and doling it out for expenses, but Jim, who looked like a smaller version of Nelson Rockefeller, put everything on a sound financial basis. Politically, however, the Copley Press remained staunchly conservative, devoted to the Constitution, free enterprise, and national defense. Jim also adopted two children and reigned as the squire of La Jolla. But the stage was set for another house divided when he replaced his first wife with a Cinderella of a secretary. The second Mrs. Copley personally took over the company on her husband's death, thus forestalling the confrontation between her son, legally adopted by Copley, and the adopted son of his first marriage.

The Thin Gold Watch by Walter Swanson (New York, 1964) is a loyal account of Copley family history.

James John Corbett

(1866-1933). The San Francisco boy who defeated world heavyweight champion John L. Sullivan, Corbett came from a large, demonstrative Irish family in Hayes Valley where his father kept a livery stable. Twice expelled from parochial school for fighting, he joined **John Mackay**'s Bank of Nevada as a teenage messenger and advanced to assistant teller. Working out at the Olympic Club, Corbett

was soon able to take on his older brothers ("chesty," they complained), and won his first major fight in 1889 against another local boy, Joe Choynski, on a barge in San Francisco Bay. Corbett had already met John L. Sullivan at a sparring exhibition in full evening dress at San Francisco's Grand Opera House; in 1892, billed as "the California Wonder," he defeated Sullivan for the heavyweight title in New Orleans. Five years later, he lost the title to Robert Fitzsimmons, and failed in two later attempts to regain it from **James Jeffries.** Called "Gentleman Jim" because of his dapper dress and cafe-

society lifestyle, Corbett was a scientific boxer rather than a slugger, fast and smart enough to compensate for his slender build and relatively weak hands. A loving and loyal family man as well, he used his first big winnings to pay off the mortgage on his father's livery stable and to set up his brother Harry in Corbett's Cafe. (Another brother played professional baseball.) During and after his years as a champion, Corbett went on stage as a curiosity act, work he accepted with good humor and grace. *Gentleman Jack*, a melodrama specially tailored for him, had a third act consisting entirely of a prize

fight. The play was later made into a film, starring Errol Flynn in one of his better roles.

Corbett wrote The Roar of the Crowd (New York, 1925).

Errett Lobban Cord

(1894-1974). The "next-to-last tycoon," someone once called Cord, creator of the most glamorous automobile ever manufactured. Born in the Midwest where his Scots father was a grocer, he grew up in Los Angeles tinkering with the newly contrived automobile, rebuilding engines and remodeling chassis in his garage. In 1925 he was approached by Chicago banking interests to take over the failing Auburn Automobile Company in Indiana. He completely retooled Auburn in five years to bring out the car with "It"—the longer, lower, faster Cord, with front-wheel drive, unit body construction, bucket seats, tuckaway headlights, and aristocratic perfection. Cord personally road-tested his creation on a crosscountry drive, as a result of which he called for more liberal speed laws; he also wrote his own ad copy and had the car photographed in front of his own and other impressive Beverly Hills mansions. The Cord became *the* car for movie premieres. John Barrymore bought one, as did **Edgar Rice Burroughs** and Jean Harlow; **Frank Lloyd Wright** kept his for 30 years. But during the Depression, few were interested in a car that at $2,695 cost nearly $1,000 more than a Cadillac. Besides, Cord was becoming bored. He dabbled with airplanes for awhile and tried to take over American Airlines. In the mid-thirties he moved to England, prompted by kidnap threats, it was said, but later returned to Beverly Hills to build Cordhaven, a mansion with 22 bathrooms, a shooting gallery, soda fountain, and live organ music piped throughout. Cord's L.A. real estate interests at one time included the Pan Pacific Auditorium and eight blocks of prime Wilshire Boulevard frontage. In 1953, however, he moved again, this time to Nevada where, except for an appointment as state senator, he led a reclusive life.

Dan Post's Cord, Without Tribute to Tradition *(Arcadia, CA, 1974) is a celebration of the automobile. Griffith Borgeson is preparing a biography.*

Tony Cornero (Antonio Stralla Cornero, ?-1955).

He was a leading character in the Depression-era saga of the offshore "gaming vessels," pleasure palaces floating just beyond the law in the waters off Los Angeles. A colorful villain with a ten-gallon hat and a rolling gait,

Cornero had worked the shores between Mexico and Malibu during Prohibition as a rumrunner, for which he served two years in federal prison. Later he ran a distillery in Downey. He lost his first gambling ship in a game of cards but returned in 1938 with the *Rex*, promoting it with full-page newspaper ads and skywriting stunts. Anchored in Santa Monica Bay and connected by water taxi to the pier, the *Rex* was raking in $100,000 a month for the Capone mob until **Earl Warren**, crime-busting attorney general of California, put it out of business. While Warren watched through binoculars from a beach club, the *Rex* held off an invasion force of Fish and Game Commission boats with fire hoses but was eventually subdued and had its expensive gaming equipment dumped into the sea. When booked, Cornero gave his profession as "mariner." He spent World War II as a casino manager in Las Vegas,

returning to the coast in 1946 with another ship, the *Lux*, anchored six miles off Long Beach. This time it took an act of Congress prohibiting gambling in U.S. territorial waters to put him out of business. Cornero returned to Vegas, where he dropped dead at a crap table in 1955. Detective novelist **Raymond Chandler** used a Cornero-type ship for the de[91nouement of his *Farewell My Lovely* (1940). It was made into a 1975 film starring Robert Mitchum, who—coincidentally—grew up in Long Beach, home base of Cornero's ships.

Juan Vallejo Corona

(1934-   ). In the annals of crime, it was a grisly record: 25 bodies buried in shallow graves along the Feather River near Yuba City, the largest mass murder in history. Corona, a labor contractor to local growers and orchardists, had first come north from Mexico as a wetback, worked briefly as a laborer on the Folsom Dam, later got a green card (labor permit) and learned the business of contracting from his older brother Natividad. In 1971 when the bodies of fruit tramps, winos, and drifters began to be uncovered, most of them with fractured skulls, knife wounds, and exposed genitals, Corona came under suspicion because he had been seen in the area and because some receipts bearing his name were found in a grave. He had also spent three months in a state mental hospital in 1956, haunted by visions of bodies after a killer flood, and had recently been involved in a

homosexual altercation in Natividad's bar. A search warrant turned up a ledger with some of the victim's names and assorted bloodstains on Corona's vehicles. The case against the labor contractor, developed during a five-month trial in 1972-1973, was circumstantial and so ineptly prepared with such confusion over the location and identification of victims that defense attorney Richard Hawks rested after cross-examination. Hawks, a city slicker in a cow town, also overestimated ethnic support for the labor contractor, a job analogous to slavedriver in the Old South. Nor did Corona, a courteous and respectful businessman with heart trouble, identify with the Chicano movement. The jury returned a verdict of guilty which was overturned on appeal, on grounds that Corona received inadequate representation. A second trial began in 1982. This time Corona's new lawyer tried to prove that the murders were actually committed by Natividad Corona, described by the lawyer and other members of the family as an "aggressive homosexual." The older brother was not around to answer the charges as he had died from third stage syphilis some time before. Juan's only defense was, "*No recuerdo*", "I don't remember". That wasn't enough for the jury, who found him guilty, nor for an angry public which would not soon forget the price tag for the second trial—over $5 million.

Several recent books on Corona include Burden of Proof *by Ed Cray (New York, 1973) and* Jury; The

People vs. Juan Corona (*Boston, 1977, New York, 1978*). Details of the 1982 trial were lurid enough that a new biography will no doubt appear momentarily.

Douglas Corrigan

(1907-   ). Corrigan was not the first man to fly a plane nor did he set any records for speed or distance, but for sheer boyish enthusiasm he reigned supreme in the new era of aviation. As a boy in L.A. where his mother kept a roominghouse across from Westlake Park, he explored the town while making deliveries for a bottling company. Later, working on a construction gang, he saw a cloud of dust near Exposition Boulevard. It turned out to be an airplane, and his life was never the same again. In 1938, after a nonstop flight from the West Coast to the East Coast Corrigan took off for the return trip in a fog, with no radio or safety device in his dilapidated plane. He landed in Ireland—mistakenly, he claimed. He had been refused the necessary permits for a trans-Atlantic flight. "Wrong Way Corrigan" returned to the U.S. a hero. He rode in parades, was initiated into Indian tribes, and wrote an autobiography, *That's My Story* (1938), distinguished chiefly for his simple pleasure in joyriding in the sky. (The author presented to the Los Angeles Public Library a copy which is autographed no less than three times, inscribed twice, and has its illustrations supplemented by a personal photo.) Corrigan starred in a film of his life, *The Flying Irishman* (1939). After World War II duty as a bomber pilot he ran unsuccessfully for the

U.S. Senate in 1946 on the Prohibition party ticket.

Henry Dixon Cowell

(1897-1965). A path-breaking figure in American musical history, Cowell grew up largely without schooling in a Menlo Park cottage. His father, scion of an illustrious British family, was a wanderer and dilettante whose only known accomplishment seems to have been that he gave **Helen Wills** tennis lessons. Ellen Rolfe **Veblen**, estranged wife of the Stanford professor, gave Cowell his first music lessons and encouraged him to see Professor Charles Seeger at the University of California, Berkeley, who took the literally unwashed fifteen-year-old as a special student for three years. A born musician, completely unhampered by formal instruction or prohibition, Cowell became an innovative and eclectic composer. He pioneered in the use of tone clusters (groups of notes struck

simultaneously) and "elastic form," leaving freedom for choice and improvisation. He invented the rhythmicon, a keyboard percussion instrument, and incorporated Eastern instruments and forms into his compositions. A radical in politics as well as music, he joined a composers' collective and

helped record and promote contemporary music. Cowell spent most of his adult years teaching at the New School in New York City, except for one devastating interlude in California. Arrested on a morals charge in 1937, he spent three and one half years in San Quentin before a good lawyer got him out.

Lotta Crabtree

(1847-1924). Crabtree was the **Mary Pickford** of her day, a child actress from the Mother Lode who played youthful parts until she was middle-aged. **Lola Montez** is said to have taken an interest in her young Grass Valley neighbor, giving Lotta dancing lessons and offering her a tour of Australia. Mary Ann Crabtree, the proverbial stage mother, declined—just as well, because the tour was a flop. Lotta made a local debut at seven, arousing the affection of miners starved for home and family. She conquered San Francisco at twelve, made her New York debut at sixteen, and was soon a national favorite as Little Nell in an adaptation of Dickens's *Old Curiosity Shop*. (Throughout her career she usually played gamins or waifs in Cinderella stories of separation from and reunion with her "true" family.) In 1869 the Crabtrees returned by the new transcontinental railroad to San Francisco, which welcomed Lotta as a civic celebrity. Wealthy thanks to her mother's real estate investments and frugality, she commissioned a fountain for the city, modeled after a prop in one of her popular plays. The fountain, located at the intersection of Geary, Kearny

and Market, was dedicated as a local landmark in 1875. Lotta Crabtree made a final sentimental journey west for the 1915 Panama-Pacific Exposition, invited by the city for a command appearance at her fountain. It was a moving spectacle, with an honor guard dressed as miners, a chorus bursting into the "Hallelujah Chorus," and Lotta's largest and last audience.

David Dempsey wrote a so-so biography, The Triumphs and Trials of Lotta Crabtree *(New York, 1968).*

Charles Crocker

(1822-1888). Crocker is a prime example of frontier opportunism, an amateur engineer who could claim to have built the mighty Southern Pacific Railroad. Born in New York, he came overland to Sacramento in 1850, went into business, and became a "Know-Nothing" city councilman. Joining with his fellow merchants

Hopkins, Huntington and Stanford in the new railroad venture, Crocker was appointed to carry out the construction contracts they awarded themselves. (One of Crocker's brothers handled railroad legal affairs, and another was a labor contractor.) He assembled one of the largest single forces of workmen ever, mostly Chinese ("They built the Great Wall of China, didn't they?"). A massive man with a bird's nest of a beard, "Cholly Clocker" got the job done, sacrificing safety and economy to speed and mileage, in competition for every government-subsidized mile with the Union Pacific building east from Chicago. It was Stanford who drove the golden spike joining the two lines in Utah in 1869, but Crocker got his opportunity a few years later, presiding over a similar ceremony linking Los Angeles with San Francisco. Basically an

outdoorsman with little ability or inclination for administration, Crocker sold out his railroad holdings in 1871 but found himself bored and bought back in two years later. While Huntington and Stanford ran the SP, Crocker occupied himself with real estate and banking. He also kept his hand in at construction, personally supervising the erection of his ornate Nob Hill mansion, described by Willis Polk as "a delirium of the wood carver." (The "spite fence" between this mansion and a Chinaman's shanty next door would be the site of Denis Kearney's finest hour.) Crocker's last effort was construction of the SP's Del Monte Hotel, where he lived during his last years. A venerable old resort hotel, improbably equipped with a lagoon and gondolas, the Del Monte was an important watering hole for the robber barons of the day. Although

they were the most "humbly born" of the Big Four, the Crockers went on to become the most social of the railroad heirs. Charles Crocker's sons built the Saint Francis Hotel in San Francisco and ran it like a country club. They also built up the family banking interests which merged in 1926 with James Phelan's 1st National into the Crocker Bank, one of the state's largest. Son William H. Crocker (1861-1937), the king of Snob Hill, became head of the state Republican party and a chief backer of San Francisco's 1915 Panama-Pacific Exposition. In the third generation the family produced an extravagant flapper, the five-times married Aimee Crocker, who wrote a memoir entitled *I'd Do It Again* (1936).

Oscar Lewis's The Big Four *(New York, 1938, 1969) is excellent.*

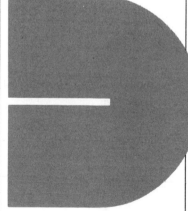

Richard Henry Dana

(1815-1882). California was a foreign country in 1835, a "half-civilized coast at the end of the world," when Dana first sighted its shores after a six month journey around the Horn. Having taken a leave of

absence from his Harvard studies to ship out as a seaman, Dana proceeded to study the exotic natives, their character, dress, and institutions, like an anthropologist observing a primitive tribe. A proper Bostonian with an uncompromising Puritan ethic, he pronounced the people free of all disease except "California fever," or laziness—they are "an idle, thriftless people, and can make nothing for themselves." Politically, he classified the country as an "arbitrary democracy," suffering frequent revolutions. Economically, there were no banks nor even a proper currency, hides serving as "California banknotes" (worth about $2 apiece) in exchange for the silks, spices and other luxuries brought by ships like Dana's *Pilgrim*. As for ecology, the young seaman found the coast desolate, its trees chopped down for fuel, no lighthouses or even buoys. San Diego seemed a snug little harbor compared to San Pedro, a miserable hole, while

Monterey presented the most civilized appearance of all. (The landing offshore from Mission San Juan Capistrano, where there was no harbor at all and hides had to be thrown from the palisades for loading aboard ship, would later to be named Dana Point.) Dana described his "two years before the mast" in an 1840 book that soon became a popular classic; during the Gold Rush, when people were hungry to read about the new land, it was virtually the only recent work available. The author returned to California in 1859, 24 years later, to find the land greatly changed. San Francisco with a population of 100,000 had become the "emporium of the Pacific," and Los Angeles had grown to 20,000 inhabitants, although San Diego was still a sleepy Mexican town. Everyone had read his book, Dana found, and even the natives he had characterized as lazy and thriftless welcomed him graciously. (The Spanish women were still beautiful, he noted, attributing the preservation of their looks to the climate.) Among recent arrivals, he encountered three Harvard classmates and newly elected Governor **Latham**, whom he mistakenly thought a native of Massachusetts. Back home in Boston Dana practiced law and dabbled in politics and diplomacy, without notable success, everything else in his life paling by comparison to the drama and immediacy of his two trips to California.

Kevin Starr, Americans and the California Dream *(New York, 1973) has an excellent short sketch of Dana's California idyll.*

Clarence Seward Darrow

(1857-1938). A labor lawyer of national stature and celebrated eloquence, Darrow reached his Gethsemane, the nadir of his career, in Los Angeles. He arrived in 1910 to represent the **McNamara** brothers, charged with bombing the *Los Angeles Times*, and remained two years, broken in health, wealth, and spirit, to defend himself. The bombing had polarized the community, which reacted against the anti-union excesses of the *Times*-dominated establishment by threatening to elect a Socialist mayor in 1911. The McNamara brothers were widely considered victims of a *Times* frame-up, so it came as a great shock when Darrow changed their plea to guilty, convinced that the prosecution had an ironclad case. The timing of the announcement, dictated by the *Times* in exchange for saving the McNamaras from the death penalty, resulted in a Socialist defeat at the polls. Darrow was accused by labor of betrayal, but that was the least of his troubles. His brother-in-law and a jury investigator for the defense had both been caught trying to suborn jurors—the brother-in-law motivated by an excess of zeal, the jury investigator possibly an agent provocateur for the prosecution. Darrow moved into a downtown apartment, read Tolstoy to steel himself for the ordeal, and hired celebrated defense attorney **Earl Rogers** to represent him. (Rogers apparently despised his client as a "lugubrious wretch," according to the account by

his daughter **Adela Rogers St. Johns** in *Final Verdict*. When his first trial ended in a verdict of not guilty, he was tried on a second count of bribery, this time culminating in a hung jury. His reputation impugned, he gave up his law practice and joined the national lecture circuit (refusing any bookings in Southern California). Darrow eventually returned to the law, wiser and sadder, declining labor cases to specialize in criminal defense. His reputation for brilliance restored, he squared off against fundamentalist William Jennings Bryan in the epic 1925 Scopes trial.

Darrow's Story of My Life *(New York, 1932) says very little about the Los Angeles period—"no reader will blame me if I do not unduly dwell on this part of my story." See Irving Stone,* Clarence Darrow for the Defense *(New York, 1941).*

George Davidson

(1825-1911). When the first argonauts sailed west to join the Gold Rush, many of them were equipped with little more than school atlases as navigational aids to the unfamiliar Pacific. Davidson, a graduate of Philadelphia's Central High School (1845) who became the ranking scientist of nineteenth century California, arrived in 1850 to chart headlands, capes, and other marine landmarks for the U.S. Coast Survey. Going beyond the call of duty, he also noted shipwrecks, tides, harbor facilities, and local history for his 1858 *Directory for the Pacific Coast*, called "The Coast Pilot" in its later editions, or simply Davidson's Bible. Pitching in wherever needed, Davidson became an expert on document authentication, providing key testimony at the trial of **José Limantour.** An avid astronomer, he built his own observatory in San Francisco's Lafayette Park, and suggested to **James Lick** the idea of building a mountain observatory for better vantage. In 1872 Davidson fixed the precise California-Nevada boundary from the Oregon line to Lake Tahoe, following the 120th meridian; he later surveyed and marked the 405-mile diagonal south to the Colorado River. He visited Alaska to report on its possible American acquisition, and headed an astronomy expedition to Japan. He taught at UC Berkeley for over 30 years (first geography then geodesy and astronomy), was an authority on irrigation and reclamation, and conducted research on the early explorers. An amateur seismologist, he rated the 1906 quake as "A 1," or nine on a scale of ten. Although he personally favored the retention of original Indian and Spanish place names,

Davidson left his name all over the Western landscape: on an Alaskan glacier, a peak in Nevada's Comstock, and an ocean "river," the Davidson Inshore Eddy Current. Mount Davidson in San Francisco is the site of annual Easter sunrise services.

George Davidson, Pioneer West Coast Scientist (Berkeley, 1954), by Oscar Lewis, is a minor effort by a ranking California historian.

Marion Davies (Marion Douras Brown, 1897-1961). She was a good-time girl from Brooklyn, a Broadway chorine who became the richest star in Hollywood thanks to her relationship with publishing tycoon **William R. Hearst.** He was 52 when they met and she was only eighteen, but the broad-with-a-heart-of-gold actually fell in love with the lumbering old giant and remained faithful in spirit if not always in fact until his death 35 years later. Hearst compensated for his age and his inability or unwillingness to divorce his wife and marry Davies (her stage name) by creating a lifestyle so

extravagant that no other man could compete. He founded a film production company to showcase Davies, installed her at MGM in a fourteen-room bungalow fit for Marie Antoinette, and paid her on the inflated scale of $10,000 a week plus $100,000 annually as company president. (When told there was money in making movies, Hearst replied, "Yes, mine.") Unfortunately, his money and his insistence on casting Davies as a saccharine-sweet heroine (*When Knighthood was in Flower*, 1922) created the aura of purchased fame that Orson Welles parodied in *Citizen Kane*. Actually, Davies had a real flair for comedy, as evidenced in *Show People* (1928), a satire on the Hollywood scene. She was also an accomplished hostess at Hearst's ranch in San Simeon and at her beach house in Santa Monica, a Georgian-style mansion with 37 fireplaces. Her annual masquerade ball was *the*

social event of the Hollywood season. And she had a shrewd eye for real estate, some of which she liquidated to aid Hearst when he got into financial trouble in the late 1930s. When Hearst died in 1951, his body was reclaimed by family and corporation. His mistress consoled herself by marrying a former stuntman ten weeks later.

Fred Guiles wrote Marion Davies *(New York, 1972). The Times We Had (New York, 1975) is a posthumously published memoir.*

Angela Yvonne Davis (1944-   ). When she first arrived in San Diego in 1967 to earn a graduate philosophy degree under **Herbert Marcuse,** she used to drive around searching for causes. Born in Alabama, educated in Eastern establishment schools, and fresh from two years study in Germany, she was eager to put her radical activist theory into practice. She scoured the dorms for black students to protest against radical discrimination at the local Navy base, but San Diego was thoroughly conservative; the real action was farther north, in L.A. Davis tried out various organizations including the Black Panthers before joining the Che-Lumumba Club, the black cell of the Communist Party in L.A. (1968). She soon became her own *cause célèbre*, when Governor **Reagan** and the Regents of the University of California tried to prevent her as a Communist from teaching at UCLA, citing a McCarthy-era clause (later declared unconstitutional by the courts). Then in February 1970 she saw, on the front page of the *Los Angeles Times*, a photograph of Soledad Brother **George Jackson**, chained and shackled. She went to visit him in the prison at Soledad (which reminded her of the South), and lectured in his behalf. In August 1970, implicated in a shootout at the Marin County Courthouse which left four dead, she went underground—a fugitive slave of the black power movement. Captured a few months later, she spent a year in jail awaiting trial before she was allowed free on bail pledged by a white farmer in Fresno County. Acquitted of murder, kidnapping, and conspiracy charges in June 1972, she was launched onto the international radical circuit.

At the age of 30, while a guest in Castro's Cuba, Davis wrote the thoroughly uppity An Autobiography *(New York, 1974).*

James Edgar Davis

(1889?-1949). Davis was the Depression-era police chief of L.A. who invented the "bum

blockade" and ran a "Red Squad" to investigate subversives. First appointed chief in 1926, he was demoted to the traffic division in 1929 on charges of incompetency and neglect of duty. Davis claimed that the underworld was out to get him because of his effectiveness in keeping mobsters out of L.A. He also warned that white Communist females were cohabitating with Negroes and that the Communists would overthrow the U.S. government within six years. Returned to power after the election of Mayor **Frank Shaw** in 1933, he allowed the special investigative unit called the Red Squad to hire out as strikebreakers on the side. In 1936, with "sheer, calm audacity," Davis installed a blockade near California's desert border to discourage indigents. The *L.A. Times* called the bum blockade "the kind of outrage that ought to have been perpetrated in California several years ago," but the state attorney general simply called it unconstitutional. In addition to his rather cavalier violations

of the Constitution and Bill of Rights, Davis was also charged with letting hoodlums (presumably the elected mayor and his friends) run the city. In 1938, the chief of the Red Squad was implicated in the attempted murder of an individual investigating political corruption. Mayor Shaw was recalled that year, and Davis followed him into retirement, moving over to Douglas Aircraft as head of security.

William Heath Davis

(1822-1909). Davis had a ringside seat for the unfolding drama of nineteenth-century California history. The son of a Yankee sea captain, he was born in Hawaii, his maternal grandmother a Polynesian princess. Moving to California at sixteen to join his uncle Nathan Spear in Yerba Buena (later San Francisco), he became known as "Kanaka" ("Hawaiian") Davis and fit easily into the pastoral society of the prestatehood era. After a proper two-year courtship he married Maria Estudillo of one of the great landowning families. Traveling up and down the coast as sailor and trader, he seemed to be present wherever the action was: he first escorted **John Sutter** up the river to claim his Sacramento settlement; he sailed on the ship carrying Governor **Manual Micheltorena** into exile in 1845; and he provided supplies to **John C. Frémont** (who never paid for them) during the Bear Flag revolt. However, fortune seemed to elude Davis. He liquidated his San Francisco holdings before the Gold Rush made them

fabulously valuable, and he moved south to develop San Diego a decade before its time. Davis anticipated the development of Oakland—as San Francisco's "Brooklyn"—but again, others reaped the profits. Settling on his father-in-law's Rancho San Leandro, he struggled with squatters and the long effort to establish title under U.S. law. His greatest success was as a writer, recording with appreciation and rich detail the character of old California and the worry-free lifestyle that made gray hair a rarity among Californios. (He also described frankly the widespread custom of smuggling in Mexican California.) The last survivor of his generation, he finished his life in San Francisco working on a memoir describing first sixty and ultimately seventy-five years of local history.

Davis's Seventy-Five Years in California *was published posthumously in San Francisco in 1929.*

William Deane-Tanner.

See William Desmond Taylor.

Charles E. Dederich

(1913-   ). Dederich's Synanon started out as a drug rehabilitation program, gathered momentum as a civil libertarian *cause célèbre,* and fell into disrepute as an authoritarian cult. A recovered alcoholic from Ohio, Dederich split off from AA in the late 1950s to concentrate on drug rehabilitation in an Ocean Park (Los Angeles) store-front. Primarily by means of a no-holds-barred variant of group therapy called "The Game," he claimed to be keeping his junkies clean and gainfully employed at the Synanon gas station in West L.A. and at other group enterprises. When Synanon moved upshore to the cavernous old Del Mar Beach Club, the neighbors objected and the city of Santa Monica jailed Dederich for zoning violations. Liberals rallied to Synanon's support, lionizing Dederich as a counterculture guru. (Chuck Norris played him in a 1965 Hollywood movie.) An independent network of "game clubs" arose to recruit "straight" support for Synanon, which also developed a successful advertising novelty business, selling personalized pens to corporations. In 1964 Synanon shifted its main base of operations to a 65-acre ranch in remote Marin County. By 1978, when the trouble began, the facility there included three boats, six airplanes, a sophisticated computer and communications center, and a population of 900. These included some former addicts, a "punk squad" of juvenile incorrigibles, and a loyal cadre of true believers, all of whom wore overalls and had their heads shaved. Reports began to leak out of sexual experiments, of large salaries and perks enjoyed by Synanon leaders, and of violence and coercion. Dederich was disarmingly frank about some of the charges. Synanon is modeled after General Motors, not the Salvation Army, he explained of his $75,000 annual salary and $500,000 retirement bonus. He also freely admitted his fascination with manipulating behavior

tolerances, whether sexual or sartorial. Synanon's large new weapons acquisitions, however, were not so easily dismissed. In 1978 members of the group were charged with a rattlesnake attack against an L.A. attorney who had won a child custody suit against the cult. Arrested, reportedly inebriated in Arizona, he was extradited to L.A. and pleaded no contest. In 1979, a Marin County weekly won a Pulitzer Prize for revealing how Synanon managed to evade all local, state, and federal authority and regulation. At last report, Synanon was regrouping across the Arizona state line in Lake Havasu.

See The Light on Synanon *(New York, 1980) by Dave and Cathy Mitchell and Richard Ofshe. Guy Endore's* Synanon *(New York, 1968) is an early, sympathetic account of the Santa Monica days.*

Alonzo Delano

(1806?-1874). For Delano, who arrived overland from Illinois in 1849, the Gold Rush turned out to be a wild goose chase. Instead of big strikes and fabulous wealth, he found only weariness and disappointment, fire and flood. His wife died young, his son became an invalid, and his daughter went insane. Turning to produce marketing, Delano lost everything in a wharf fire. Everything seemed to fail him except his cheerful realism and the wry humor with which he wrote of the loneliness and pathos of the miner's life. "The only alternative was to dig or starve," he wrote of prospecting. "I did both. I dug first, and I starved afterwards." Just a plain American except for a nose as proverbial as Cyrano's, he

called himself "Old Block" and prepared with illustrator Charles Nahl a series of *Pen-Knife Sketches* which sold— astonishingly—15,000 copies in California. (Many were sent back East to give the folks at home a first taste of California life and humor.) Moving up in the world, Delano became the Wells Fargo agent in Grass Valley and is said to have enjoyed **Lola Montez**'s salon. Ironically, after his death one

of his mining claims paid off handsomely.

Delano published two additional books, Across the Plains and Among the Diggings *(Auburn, NY, 1854; reprinted Ann Arbor, MI, 1966) and* Old Block's Sketch Book *(Sacramento, 1856; reprinted Santa Ana, 1947).*

Stanton Delaplane

(1907-). A journalist who started out as editor of *Apéritif* magazine (1933-1936), Delaplane became a gourmand of local color for the *San Francisco Chronicle*, winning a Pulitzer Prize in 1942 for his bemused account of a Northern California succession movement. Ever since it got together the state had been threatening to break up, most notably in 1859 when Southern California tried to secede as a territory called Colorado. But this was a little different. Residents of Siskiyou, Modoc, Del Norte, and Lassen counties, the site of a prospective new state called Jefferson, really only wanted better roads. The secessionists drew up a state seal (a double cross on a mining pan) and threatened to withhold strategic ores mined locally "until Governor **Culbert Olson** drives over these roads and digs us out." Every Thursday, the citizens of Jefferson celebrated a patriotic rebellion, setting up a border patrol and roadblocks to man their perimeter; in the evening, they adjourned to a local tavern. A few days after Delaplane's reports from Jefferson ran in the *Chronicle*, the Japanese bombed Pearl Harbor and nothing was ever quite the same again. Delaplane went on to become something of a tourist among journalists, sampling local culture all over the world for his *Chronicle* column.

Cecil Blount DeMille

(1881-1959). The archetypal Hollywood director with his jodhpurs, puttees, and delusions of historical grandeur, DeMille came from a New York theatrical family. On arriving in California in 1913 to film his first "feature play," he fell so much in love with the country that he

insisted on two conditions in every contract he signed: absolute authority as director, and refusal to work elsewhere without prior agreement. During the early Hollywood years DeMille made a series of sophisticated film comedies of sexual morals (*Why Change Your Wife?* 1920). When the **Hays** Office put sexual sophistication out of style, he turned to biblical epic, with the emphasis on great mass spectacle. He made *The Ten Commandments* twice (1923 and 1956), along with *Cleopatra* (1932) and *Samson and Delilah* (1949). In life as in art, DeMille cultivated the grand effect. His office,

decorated with props from some forgotten film, looked like a Shinto shrine. Home was a Florentine palazzo in Los Feliz, with a weekend hideaway in Little Tujunga Canyon, its entryway dominated by gates from *Kings of Kings*. To get into the spirit of Tujunga, male dinner guests were provided with loose silk tunics and colorful cummerbunds. During World War I, DeMille commanded a home guard unit that drilled on Vine Street with a brass band. A flying buff, he used a vacant lot at Wilshire and La Cienega as "DeMille Field." He was also active in conservative Republican circles. Radio

buffs will remember him signing on and off from Hollywood for the original soap opera, Lux Radio Theater—a job he gave up in 1944 rather than pay union dues. He then established the DeMille Foundation for Political Freedom, a leader in the anti-union right-to-work movement.

See The Autobiography of Cecil B. DeMille *(New Jersey, 1959) and his brother William DeMille's* Hollywood Saga *(New York, 1939). (A writer and director, Bill DeMille married* Henry George's *daughter and fathered* Agnes DeMille, *the dancer.)*

Ruth Dennis. *See* Ruth St. Denis.

Charles de Young

(1845-1880) and **Michael Henry de Young** (1849-1925). Journalism was a dangerous profession in nineteenth century San Francisco. Besides **James King of William**, a second editor to fall in the line of business was Charles de Young, founder at age twenty of San Francisco's *Dramatic Chronicle*. The de Youngs, of Dutch Jewish descent, arrived on the coast with their widowed mother in 1854. A third brother, Gustavus, became a map publisher. From little more than a theater handbill, the *Chronicle* evolved into a leading daily newspaper, thanks in part to its scoop on the Lincoln assassination. In the early years, the de Youngs carried on a longstanding feud and public fisticuffs with impresario **Tom Maguire**, were hit with a dozen suits for criminal libel, and were widely suspected of blackmail. **Isaac Kalloch**, Baptist minister and successful 1879 mayoral

candidate, replied to *Chronicle* revelations in kind—Mother de Young ran a whorehouse, he claimed, while Gustavus was in an asylum—for which Charles de Young shot and nearly killed him. Six months later, Kalloch's son shot the editor and killed him. After his brother's death, Michael de Young had a similar contretemps. In 1884, **Adolph Spreckels** shot him following *Chronicle* allegations that he had been involved in stock fraud . But Michael de Young survived to become a respectable pillar of the conservative Republican establishment and a patron of local arts. He built the city's first "skyscraper" in 1890, the ten-story *Chronicle* building on Market Street, and rebuilt it after the earthquake. He promoted an International Exposition in 1894, the profits of which he suggested go into a permanent art museum, for which he personally travelled the world collecting art.

(Later, he donated a new building to the De Young Museum.) His children were educated in Europe, presented at the Court of Saint James, and returned to take their places at the head of local society. When Michael de Young died, flags were lowered to half-mast in San Francisco, courts were adjourned, the archbishop presided over his funeral, and the *Chronicle* devoted a whole section to a thoroughly expurgated version of his life story, never once referring to the wild west beginnings of the de Young boys.

Michael Henry de Young. See Charles de Young.

Edward Augustus Dickson (1879-1956). Dickson chose the old Wolfskill ranch in West Los Angeles as the site for a new university, UCLA, because the setting near the Santa Monica Mountains reminded him of the University of California nestled against the hills of Berkeley. As a student at Berkeley he had been editor of the *Daily Californian*; after graduation (1901), he became political editor of the *Los Angeles Express* and a leading figure in the successful statewide campaign (1906-1910) to drive the Southern Pacific out of politics. In 1913 Governor **Hiram Johnson** appointed him the youngest regent in the history of the University of California and the only one, at that time, from the south. Dickson became editor and publisher of the *Express* in 1919, taking time on the side to scout the land and push the bond issues for UC Berkeley's "southern campus." (UCLA opened its doors in 1929.) Increasingly conservative with age, he sold his newspaper in 1931 (it was absorbed into **Hearst**'s *Herald*) and entered the savings and loan business. But throughout 43 years as a regent, the "father of UCLA" continued to watch and worry over the fortunes of his offspring. He kept a scrapbook of local society births, marriages and obituaries, even a stray embezzlement, each item a clue to potential benefactors to his school. He was so partisan, it was said, that he hated to see civic appointments going to USC grads.

See Dickson's UCLA, Its Origin and Formative Years (L.A., 1955) and the UCLA master's thesis by F. M. Medeiros, "Dickson: A study in Progressivism" (1968). Dickson left most of his papers to UCLA, except for his scrapbook of potential benefactors which is in the Los Angeles Public Library.

Joan Didion (1934-   ). (*Visualize* Maria Wyeth, surrendering to "freeway rapture," following the flow of highway energy to her rendezvous with abortion, divorce, and despair, driving as carefully as if "reconnoitering an atmosphere without gravity.") Like the central character of her novel *Play It as It Lays* (1970), Didion is small, the possessor of a Corvette Stingray, and given to paralyzing anxieties. Born and raised in California's heartland capital, she graduated from **C.K. McClatchy** High School (a year behind "Honey Bear" Warren, the governor's daughter), and went on to the University of California, Berkeley. She won an editing job in New York City, remained eight years and published a first novel with a Sacramento setting. In fiction as well as nonfiction she became skilled at expressing the "unspeakable peril of the everyday," the extraneous detail seen with the startling clarity of hallucination. (*Visualize* **Huey Newton**, as Didion described him for a magazine assignment: bleeding from a bullet wound in the stomach after a Black Panther-police confrontation, arguing with the nurse about hospital admission procedures.) In the 1960s Didion moved with her husband, writer **John Gregory Dunne**, back to California, continuing to explore the ironies, absurdities, and compulsive rituals of the West Coast experience. She wrote an essay enshrining Bishop **Pike** as a literary character, found escape in Hawaii and Las Vegas, become knowledgeable about shopping center theory and water politics. (*Visualize* water moving through aqueducts and siphons, weirs and surge tanks, the veins and arteries of California life.) She also learned the Hollywood art of the big film deal, became rich and famous—and returned to her childhood home in Sacramento to finish each of her books.

In addition to her novels, Didion has published two excellent collections of essays, Slouching Towards Bethlehem *(New York, 1968) and* The White Album *(New York, 1979), most of them about California.*

Joseph Di Giorgio

(1874?-1951). "Fruit is nothing but water and labor and more labor and freight," according to Di Giorgio, a Sicilian by birth who became the world's largest shipper of fresh fruit, the model for Gregorio in **John Steinbeck**'s *Grapes of Wrath.* During the interwar period Di Giorgio acquired 10,000 acres in California, including a 5,000-acre vineyard near Delano. He also bought a lumber company to produce his own boxes, and a packing company and a winery, which together with Di Giorgio's Baltimore Fruit Exchange and his labels (S&W,

TreeSweet) gave him control of his product from the fields to the marketplace. As an employeer Di Giorgio was considered notoriously anti-union. His workers, who numbered 3,000 in 1940 and 10,000 a decade later, went on strike in 1939, 1947, and 1960 before finally gaining recognition in 1966. The 1947 strike, lasting 31 months, was particularly hard fought. (The defeated AF of L made a film, "Poverty in the Valley of Plenty," the subject of a protracted libel suit that outlasted the strike.) By the time **Cesar Chavez** finally won the right to organize Di Giorgio (now run by nephews of the "fruit king," who died childless), the conglomerate was rapidly exiting from agriculture altogether, prompted by changes in the supply of two of the three vital ingredients, labor and water. The family was too mired in feudal traditions to make the transition to unionized agriculture, and the water table under family land was sinking, foreboding dependence on government irrigation projects with their 160-acre limitation. By the late 1970s Di Giorgio income derived almost exclusively from processing and marketing operations.

Ernesto Galarzo's Spiders in the House, Workers in the Field *(Notre Dame, 1970) describes the 1947 strike from the worker's point of view.*

Joe DiMaggio (Joseph Paul

DiMaggio, 1914-   ). Back in the early middle ages of baseball, when teams traveled by train and players carried their own bats, the Galahad of the game was a tall, quiet Italian boy from San Francisco. DiMaggio was the

eighth of an immigrant fisherman's nine children. His pop played *bocci*, or Italian lawn bowls, but he and his brothers preferred baseball, and they were good. After dropping out of Galileo High School, Joe followed his brother Vince to the S.F. Seals of the old Pacific Coast League, where he was such a

batting sensation that the New York Yankees bought up his contract in 1936. In the outfield he made it look easy, always anticipating the breaking play; and at the plate he stood tall, his bat high in the air, confident of hitting any pitch, in any inning. DiMaggio compiled a hitting streak of 56 consecutive games in 1941, and helped the Yankees win six straight World Series pennants (1936-1939, 1941, and 1947). Off the field and on, he had dignity and old-world authority. A family man, he went home during the winters to San Francisco, where he and his brothers ran a restaurant. He married two glamorous actresses and mistakenly assumed they would stay home while he was out with the boys. **Marilyn Monroe**, his second wife, refused. She even took time out from their honeymoon to entertain the troops in Korea. ("Oh, Joe, you've never heard such cheering," she said on returning. "Yes, I have," he replied.) Ever practical (base hits are to a ball team what sales are to a broker, he wrote in a perfunctory autobiography), the former all-star traded on baseball nostalgia in his later years to make awkward TV commercials for savings banks and coffee pots.

DiMaggio wrote Lucky to be a Yankee *(New York, 1951). See Maury Allen's* Where Have You Gone, Joe DiMaggio? The Story of America's Last Hero *(New York, 1975).*

Walt Disney (Walter Elias

Disney, 1901-1966). The three geniuses in the development of the film art are considered to be **David W. Griffith**,

Irving Thalberg, and Walt Disney. A high school dropout from the Midwest, veteran of World War I ambulance corp and ex-president of a bankrupt cartoon company, Disney arrived in Los Angeles in 1923 with $40 in his pocket. With his brother Roy, who had been recuperating from tuberculosis at the local veterans hospital, he developed animation from the simple cartoon strip into narrative film. The first Disney superstar was Mickey Mouse, "a little fellow trying to do the best he could"—in that respect, resembling his creator. Training teams of animators, Walt established a patriarchal production-line system to put out the *Three Little Pigs* (1933) and *Snow White and the Seven Dwarfs* (1937), the first cartoon feature. Roy Disney handled finance and administration, the animators did the actual work, and Walt provided the creative spark, acting out his original conceptions and prodding his people to greater production. Disney Studios in Burbank has been compared to Santa's workshop, full of men struggling to endow dwarfs with distinctive personalities or to make an everyday insect into an endearing Jiminy Cricket. It was an extremely costly process and by World War II, the Disneys were $4 million in debt. After the war, the studio moved into more profitable live-action films as well as the televised *Mouseketeers* program. The fascination of movie-making had worn off for Walt Disney, who wanted something experimental to tinker with. For years he nurtured the concept of a

Mickey Mouse Park, constantly adjusting the continuity, flow, scale, and mood of the fantasyland arising in Anaheim. Disneyland opened in 1955 to become the most successful amusement park in history. A few years later, it was followed by Disney World in Florida, planned on an even larger and more futuristic scale. In his last years, Disney experimented with the latest challenge in animation, audio animatronics—the endowing of robots with personality and expression. He is also said to have been interested in cryonics, or freezing the dead for future reanimation. **Ray Bradbury** once suggested him for mayor of Los Angeles, considering him the only person with the technological imagination to run the megalopolis. Disney declined—"I'm already king." He was also the fairy godfather of California Institute of the Arts in Valencia, a utopian approach to art education.

Former Life *Magazine movie critic Richard Schickel is highly critical of what he calls* The Disney Version *(New York, 1968), Bob Thomas, who wrote* Walt Disney *(New York, 1976), is not.*

Maynard Dixon

(Lafayette Maynard Dixon, 1875-1946). For an artist born in the San Joaquin Valley, Dixon once said, it is necessary to go east to see the West. Self-educated in emulation of Frederick Remington, Dixon became a newspaper and magazine illustrator, using his studio in San Francisco's Montgomery Block as a base from which to explore the mountains and deserts of California. He worked for the *Morning Call* for two years, illustrated some of **Jack London**'s early books, and designed sets and costumes for Bohemian Club

plays. When his early work was destroyed and his life thoroughly disoriented by the 1906 earthquake, Dixon decided to give New York a try but lasted there only five years. In 1913 Anita **Baldwin** gave him his first major commission, a mural for her Santa Anita ranch. Subsequently, Dixon executed murals for the Mark Hopkins Hotel, the California State Library in Sacramento, and the Bureau of Indian Affairs in Washington. In the 1920s he gave up commercial art completely to concentrate on large, pastel-suffused landscapes of the Southwest in its aboriginal beauty. During the Depression Dixon did a series for the WPA on Hoover Dam, or "man vs. rock"; he also made sketches of "the forgotten man" and other variants on poverty, dispossession, and labor strife. Suffering from chronic ill-health, the artist who was as lean and worn-looking as one of the dustbowl refugees photographed by his second wife, Dorothea Lange, gave up his San Francisco studio

for good in 1937. Merging life with art, he spent his last years absorbed in the desert Southwest of his epic canvases.

Wesley M. Burnside, Maynard Dixon, Artist of the West *(Provo, UT, 1974).*

Doheny Family. Teapot Dome is in Wyoming, but the same Harding-era scandal also involved navy oil reserves in California and a local tycoon named Edward Laurence Doheny (1856-1935). The son of a poor Irish immigrant, he was a former roughneck and prospector in the Southwest who arrived in Los Angeles in 1892 and discovered crude oil bubbling in Hancock Park. Within five years he controlled the state's oil production, then moved south to make a killing in the Tampico oilfields of Mexico. By the 1920s Doheny was one of the richest men in the U.S., a big spender who affected aristocratic manners along with his lavish lifestyle. In addition to the family

estate on Chester Place in L.A. ("their own little kingdom," a servant called it), the Dohenys owned a yacht and a 400-acre ranch in Beverly Hills, later Trousdale. They also built their own neighborhood Catholic Church, the imposing Saint Vincent de Paul. Doheny's second wife, Carrie Estelle, would become a papal countess for her benefactions, which included the USC library and an eye hospital. It was therefore purely out of patriotism and not for any base financial motive, Doheny explained, that he had his son E. L., II (1893-1929) hand-deliver $100,000 in cash to his friend Albert Fall, U.S. Secretary of the Interior, for rights to the Elk Hills naval oil reserves in California. Thanks to the eloquence of a silver-tongued attorney, also of Irish ancestry, Doheny was twice acquitted of offering the bribe that Fall was convicted of accepting. But the "oil trials" marked the beginning of a time of family troubles. His patriotism impugned ("the last refuge of scoundrels," the prosecutor orated), Doheny tried unsuccessfully to interest **Cecil B. DeMille** in making a film to exonerate him. E.L. II, the "bag man," was murdered by his male secretary at Greystone, the 40-room Doheny palace in Beverly Hills, built at a cost of $4 million in 1925. As a monument to E.L. II, a replica of the Temple of Santa Sabina in Rome was constructed at Forest Lawn. Much of the family fortune was swallowed up in the Depression, and a later heir, E. L. IV (1943-73) would be found dead of a

drug overdose at 30, reportedly despondent over money.

Stephen Birmingham's Real Lace: America's Irish Rich *(New York, 1973) is the best current source on the Dohenys.*

Robert Dollar
(1844-1932). Dollar was a Northern California lumberman of Scots descent who went into the shipping business at age 60, expanding from the China trade to create the first regular round-the-world passenger service. In 1921, the Dollar Steamship Company consisted of 23 vessels, named after the founder's four children and fifteen grandchildren. Dollar then acquired a dozen war-surplus vessels and financial backing from the U.S. Shipping Board to start his worldwide American President Lines, each ship carrying a signature dollar sign on its funnel and the name of an American president on its bow. An abstemious and self-righteous patriarch, Dollar served no liquor on his ships and bitterly fought the efforts of his employees to organize and better their lot. He was a leading opponent of the 1915 Seamen's Act, moving his headquarters to Vancouver, sailing under the British flag, and using Oriental crews to escape regulation. At one point, he even suggested the U.S. government subsidize the difference between Oriental and U.S. seamen's wages. Despite his own lucrative subsidies and combinations in restraint of trade—government loans and mail contracts, plus a 1930 agreement with **William Matson** to split the Pacific rather than compete—Dollar's

shipping business fell on hard times during the Depression. After his death, a U.S. Maritime Commission investigation revealed heavy cash withdrawls through "a milking system of holding companies" designed to "insulate the personal resources of the principal owners." The U.S. government took over the American President Lines in 1938.

Dollar wrote a three-volume autobiography, privately published in San Francisco in 1917-1925.

Donner Party. It was summer 1846 when the Donner party left the Oregon Trail at the Continental Divide, cutting south in hopes of saving 300 to 400 miles on the overland journey to California. This was the first of a sequence of events and misjudgments culminating in the greatest tragedy of the westward movement. The party of 87 included a cross-section of humanity, and the road ahead would put all to the ultimate test, arousing generosity and greed, heroism and cowardice. Titular head of the party was George Donner, a 62-year-old farmer from Illinois, patriarch of an extended family including his brother and brother's wife and children. Donner's primary qualification for leadership, as historian George Stewart points out, was wealth. As long as certain democratic amenities were observed, the pioneers respected men of property. Delayed by erroneous information, poor cooperation, and worse luck, the party found itself stranded at Truckee Lake by an early snowfall on 28 October with

provisions nearly exhausted. Setting out on improvised snowshoes, seven of a group of fifteen struggled into the San Joaquin Valley on 17 January after 33 harrowing days en route. In February a relief party arrived to be greeted with the question, "Are you men from California or do you come from heaven?" and got back over the pass to California with 23 people, of whom nineteen survived. Left behind were the four Donner elders who in the extremity of starvation sacrificed the most deeply held conventions of civilization, eating the flesh of the dead to insure the survival of their children. It was late April 1847 before the last survivor of "starved camp" was rescued. None of the senior Donners was among the 47 to come through the winter alive, but seven of the offspring of the two brothers survived. That summer, the **Kearny** party on its way east burned the abandoned huts and buried the last traces of the camp. Reports of the disaster undoubtedly encouraged many 49ers to endure the hazards of crossing the Isthmus of Panama rather than attempt the overland journey. Donner Pass and

later Donner Memorial State Park were named in grim testimonial to the imponderables of the human spirit.

George Stewart's Ordeal by Hunger *(Boston, 1936, 1977) is a classic.*

Donald Wills Douglas

(1892-1981). One of the legendary figures in the history of aviation, Douglas was a Naval Academy dropout who enrolled at MIT in 1912 to learn more about the new field of aeronautics. He came west in 1915 as chief engineer for **Glenn Martin**, returning alone after World War I to build his own airplanes when Martin set up shop in Cleveland. Flying conditions were better in L.A., Douglas reasoned, the climate was better for his family; a canny Scot, he also figured he would save money by not having to heat his hangars. Starting out in the back of a barbershop on Pico Boulevard in 1917, Douglas Aircraft moved up to an abandoned movie studio in Santa Monica three years later, gradually building up from one contract to another. The early years were difficult, but Douglas and his crew (which included such early aviation geniuses as **John Northrop**) were young and fired by enthusiasm for their work. Wearing knickers to work, they spent their lunch hours playing volleyball and their weekends unravelling the mysteries of

aerodynamics. The big breakthrough came in 1932 with the TWA contract for the DC (Douglas Commercial) 1. This was "stretched" into the DC-3, one of the most durable planes of all time, when American Airlines asked for a wide-bodied pullman plane a few years later. Eventually, it grew into the DC-7, followed by the jetliners. During World War II Douglas turned out some 30,000 aircraft ("one of the great feats of industrial history," according to *Fortune* magazine), making Los Angeles the Detroit of aeronautics. By now the firm, based at Santa Monica's Clover Field, had expanded to include its own police, telecommunications, health, and welfare systems—a total patriarchy ruled by loyalty and respect to the Douglases. Retiring in 1957, Donald Douglas was succeeded by his son. In 1966, weakened by the staggering sums

involved in the transition to the jet age, Douglas Aircraft was taken over by McDonnell of Saint Louis.

Skymaster *by Frank Cunningham (Philadelphia, 1932) is an early biography of Donald Douglas.*

Helen Gahagan Douglas (1900-1980).

The first actor in California politics was an actress, considered by critic Heywood Broun to be singlehandedly, "the ten most beautiful women in the world." Born in Brooklyn, raised in privilege and educated at Barnard, she was a stage actress and dramatic singer who married Melvyn Douglas, her leading man in *Tonight or Never*, in 1931. In Hollywood, Melvyn Douglas was active in Screen Actors Guild politics while Helen worked to improve the conditions of migrant labor. Both Douglases were delegates to the 1940 Democratic convention, and they were invited to the White House. ("The First Lady collected people," Helen Douglas wrote in *The Eleanor Roosevelt We Remember*, 1963. "Melvyn and I were among those collected.") Elected to Congress from L.A.'s fourteenth district in 1944, Helen Douglas was billed as "the Democrats' answer to Clare Boothe Luce." She served on the House Foreign Relations Committee where she supported the U.N., opposed Cold War aid to Greece and Turkey, and recommended coexistence with Red China. In domestic politics, she staunchly opposed the House Un-American Activities Committee and loyalty oaths. In 1949 **Jack Tenney**'s California Un-American

committee listed her as a "fellow traveler." Her rival for the Democratic nomination to the Senate called her "red-hot." And **Richard Nixon**, the Republican nominee, pilloried her as the "pink lady, . . . pink all the way down to her underwear," with a voting record favorable to Communism. (In turn, Douglas dubbed Nixon "Tricky Dick.") After her defeat by Nixon Douglas made a brief return to the stage, moved back East, and stumped for Stevenson and McGovern. At the time of Watergate, a bumpersticker began to be seen around Southern California: "Don't blame me. I voted for Helen Gahagan Douglas."

Douglas's autobiography, A Full Life *(New York, 1982), was published posthumously.*

John Gately Downey (1827-1894).

Downey, who became California's seventh governor (1860-1862), was a champion of lost causes. Arriving during the Gold Rush, the Irish-born apprentice pharmacist opened L.A.'s first drugstore, although L.A. seemed "the healthiest place

in the world." He married a young Spanish Californian and moved easily between the two cultures, acquiring one of the old ranchos, the Santa Gertrudes, for an absurdly small sum at a sheriff's auction in 1859. Downey was elected lieutenant governor in 1880 and that year, at the age of 32, became governor when **Milton Latham** appointed himself to the U.S. Senate. His sympathy for the South in the Civil War (although officially he maintained a posture of Union loyalty) and for the apprenticeship of California's surviving Indians proved politically catastrophic, and Downey was not even nominated for reelection. Returning home to his mansion opposite Saint Vibiana's Cathedral in L.A., he was active in the movement to create a separate state in Southern California. He also backed Senator **John Jones**'s unsuccessful attempt to create an ocean-going harbor at Santa Monica. Downey's most lasting accomplishment was the subdivision and sale of the Santa Gertrudes, for settlement by small farmers whom he idealized as "yeomen." The area was later named for the ex-governor and eventually absorbed into the sprawling metropolis of Los Angeles. In 1880 Downey gave $1 million worth of land for the establishment of the University of Southern California by the Methodist Church. His wife was killed in an 1883 train crash in the Tehachapis, from which he never recovered. He took off on a three-year trip around the world accompanied by

medical attendants, arousing newspaper speculation that the wealthy former governor had been kidnapped by his nephew, J. Downey Harvey. It was never clear what the motive would have been, since Harvey, later a pillar of San Francisco society, had already been designated his uncle's heir.

Charles Russell Quinn's History of Downey *(Downey, 1973) touches briefly on the founding father.*

Francis Drake (1540?-1596).

In 1579, seeking the Northwest Passage during his second circumnavigation of the globe, Drake put ashore in his schooner, the *Golden Hind*, somewhere on the coast of Northern California. The white cliffs and the "faire and good Baye" reminded him of Dover, though the land was otherwise exceedingly strange. Drake noted a large population of "Conies" (squirrels), whose skins the Indians used for the "kings holidaies coate." Before leaving Drake nailed up a brass plate claiming this New Albion for England. The bay named for him near Point Reyes was long considered to be where he landed, but 400 years later scholars were still arguing about it, the other leading candidates being Bolinas, Bodego Bay, and San Francisco itself. In 1936 a picnicker found a crudely engraved brass plate which was authenticated by leading contemporary scholars and apparently confirmed Drake's Bay as the site of the landing. In 1977, however, the plate was revealed as a hoax. The debate on the location of Drake's landing resumed at

a certain amount of hometown sentimentality prevailed in the prison community. When a condemned killer asked for hamburgers and a coke, "Mother Duffy" herself went to the local all-night grocery for the ingredients. Articles about the reform warden appeared in *Reader's Digest* and *Life*, and his memoirs were serialized in the *Saturday Evening Post*. Two movies were made on San Quentin, which became popularly known as Duffy's Tavern. Such celebrity was anathema to the correctional establishment, and Duffy compounded the problem by lining up on the wrong side of Governor **Earl Warren**'s proposed prison reforms. In 1951, after eleven years as head of San Quentin, Duffy was transferred to the state parole board.

See The San Quentin Story *(New York, 1968) by Duffy as told to Dean Jennings. Gladys Carpenter Duffy also wrote a book,* Warden's Wife *(New York, 1959) as told to Blaise Lane. For a longer perspective, see Kenneth Lamott's* Chronicles of San Quentin *(New York, 1961).*

an international conference of scholars convened for the 400th anniversary of the event, and San Francisco judge Harry Low's "Court of Historical Review" also argued the case. A replica of the *Golden Hind*, fitted out in England, sailed over Drake's

original route and came to anchor in San Francisco Bay which, although the least likely of the possibilities, commanded the superior attraction of tourist dollars.

Warren L. Hanna, Lost Harbor; the Controversy over Drake's Anchorage *(Berkeley, 1979).*

Clinton Truman Duffy
(1898-1982). The best-known prison warden of his day, Duffy was born and raised in San **Quentin,** the son of a guard. State prison employees typically had large families and formed their own hometown community, "prison town," which many of the wives considered decent and safe compared to Sodom and Gomorrah (San Francisco) across the bay. Duffy married into the prison family—his wife's father was captain of the yard—and worked for several years as

assistant to the warden. Appointed acting warden after a prison scandal in 1938, he closed down the dungeon, replaced brutal guards, and abolished the tradition of head shaving. An enlightened reformer, he promoted basketball and chess tournaments, hobbies, movies, and other forms of recreation. San Quentin even developed its own radio program which was broadcast over the Mutual Network during World War II and opened with inspirational remarks by the warden. During the Duffy era,

Isadora Duncan (Dora
Angela Duncan Essenin, 1878-1927). A plaque near the corner of Geary and Taylor streets in San Francisco marks the house where Duncan, world-famous modern dancer, was born. She lived there only briefly, however. Her father, a former clerk at **William Ralston**'s Bank of California, abandoned his family to a succession of rooming houses, mostly in the East Bay. To help make ends meet, Duncan began teaching dance at an early age. One of her pupils was **Gertrude**

Stein's brother Leo. She left San Francisco for good at the age of seventeen, appearing first in Chicago as the "California Faun" and later in Europe. The uninhibited Duncan danced Salome-style, barefoot and draped in clinging veils, liberating dance from the formal rigidity of contemporary ballet and ballroom. Later, she would write that her first rhythmic influence was the sea, by which she had danced as a child. She returned to San Francisco only once, in 1922, hiring a car after a performance at the Columbia Theater to revisit scenes of her childhood.

See Duncan's My Life *(New York, 1927); Allan Ross Macdougall,* Isadora: A Revolutionary in Art and Love *(New York, 1960); and Victor Seroff,* The Real Isadora *(New York, 1971).*

John Gregory Dunne
(1932-   ). Educated easterners have long come west to observe and sneer, invariably confirming their own prejudices and sense of superiority. Dunne, an Irish

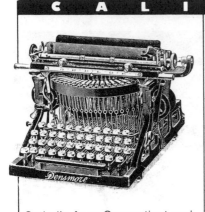

Catholic from Connecticut and a Princeton graduate (1954), was instead receptive. He found a virgin field of subjects and issues to explore and developed in the process into a fine writer. First, he observed the social fabric of agrarian California in *Delano* (1967), where **Cesar Chavez**'s striking farmworkers and the fiercely clannish vineyard owners were locked into battle with "the deadening tenacity of the Hundred Years' War." Next, he explored the "subtropical abstraction" of Hollywood in *Studio* (1968), hanging around Twentieth Century-Fox for a year to record with devastating impartiality the dialogue, mind-set, and tricks of the trade. (Dunne and his wife **Joan Didion** also moonlighted very successfully as screenwriters.) Suffering from an attack of nonspecific angst, he took refuge in *Vegas* (1974), recounting in a "memoir of a dark season" random encounters with private investigators, Kelvinator salesmen, and hookers. Trying his hand at fiction, Dunne transposed to L.A. two eastern archetypes, the tough mick cop and his brother the priest, whose *True Confessions* (1977) are a

chronicle of favors, fixes, and prejudices. Perhaps the novelty of California was wearing off, the writer becoming desensitized to his environment. With *Quintana and Friends* (1978), a collection of essays written over a fifteen-year period, Dunne revealed an increasing drift away from the role models, rituals, and unspoken assumptions of California life to a new subject—himself. Then again, that may be the ultimate California subject.

Will Durant (William James Durant, 1885-1981). The most comprehensive historical survey ever attempted by one man was composed for the most part in a Spanish-style house in the hills of Hollywood. Durant, a night-school philosopher and author of the best-selling *History of Philosophy* (1926), was a former Roman Catholic of French-Canadian descent who passed through atheism, socialism, and pacifism to a sort of benevolent humanism. Visiting early Hollywood as a peripatetic lecturer, he was wined and dined by **Will Rogers**, Doug Fairbanks, Jr., and Charlie Chaplin. He taught summer school at UCLA during the 1930s, living in nearby sorority houses. Describing his busy schedule, he wrote in 1938: "I introduced 'The Ten Greatest Thinkers' to the young ladies of the junior college at Pasadena; I solved 'The World Crisis' at the Ebell Club, the First Congregational Church, and the Polytechnic High School in Long Beach." During World War II Durant decided to make L.A. his home between "hunting

expeditions" around the world for material for the *Story of Civilization*, begun in 1935 and completed 22 years later with the collaboration of his wife Ariel (Ida Kaufman Durant, 1898-1981). Durant joined in the intellectual life of the movie colony, participating in a debate with Irene Dunne and Eddie Cantor on "Is War Impairing our Moral Standards?" He wrote a Declaration of Inter-Dependence that **Shirley Temple** read at a 1947 banquet at the Ambassador Hotel. For many locals, he provided a rare exposure to the world of ideas, however second-hand. **Sam Yorty** remembered attending a "Parliament of Man" featuring the philosopher. The Durants also made front-page news after being burglarized of $300,000 worth of stocks and bonds (soon recovered). "They can have material things as long as they leave me ten more years of life," the philosopher told the press. A lifelong advocate of vegetarianism and high colonics, he lived to the venerable old age of 96.

Will and Ariel Durant wrote A Dual Autobiography *(New York, 1977).*

Charles Eames (1907-1978). A Renaissance man among contemporary designers, with interests ranging from furniture and architecture to set design and film production itself, Eames made an art form out of the chair. He studied briefly at Washington University in Saint Louis, then at Saarinen's Cranbrook Academy of Design in Michigan, before settling in Los Angeles in 1941 with his wife and professional collaborator Ray, a Sacramento-born sculptress. L.A. then represented "a quiet place to work where we didn't know anybody and we could concentrate." For years most of their clients were in the East. They designed their own home in the Pacific Palisades (1949), a monument of modern architecture with multicolored panels of glass and concrete resembling a Mondrian painting. In their Venice garage-shop, they experimented with techniques for molding plywood to produce modernistic chairs, which were exhibited at New York's Museum of Modern Art in 1946. Later Eames chairs included a lounge with ottoman, prompted by director Billy Wilder's desire for something he could relax on in his office without connotations of the casting couch; and the molded plastic shell, eventually copied and manufactured for mass production. Charles Eames also designed museum exhibits, MGM sets, and an entire pavilion at the 1964 New York World's Fair. Absorbed by the challenge of visually presenting information, he wrote and produced twelve films for the U.S. Information Service as well as an Emmy award-winning TV special on "The Fabulous Fifties."

Connections: The Work of Charles and Ray Eames *is the catalogue of an 1976-1977 UCLA exhibit of their work.*

Hubert Eaton

(1881-1966). A former mining engineer from Missouri, Eaton took over a struggling Glendale cemetery in 1913 and transformed it into the world's most parodied burial ground, Forest Lawn. He started out with a marketing gimmick, the "Before Need Plan," gradually upgraded the physical premises, then plundered the history of art for suitable objects of adornment. A cemetery should be an uplifting locale, Eaton believed, not the dismal, depressing place of popular lore. He banned deciduous trees with their falling leaves, replaced tombstones with flat tablets to create vistas of sweeping lawns, and planted speakers in the shrubbery to intone soothing refrains ("Indian Love Call" or bird songs). The grounds of Forest Lawn were staked off into "theme" areas such as Lullabyland and the Vale of Memory, with chapels kept small to avoid the mournful feeling of empty pews. Funerals requiring pomp and circumstance, could schedule the larger Church of the Recessional, inspired by the poetry of Rudyard Kipling. Combing Europe like a Booth Tarkington businessman, Eaton put together the largest collection of marble statuary in the U.S., using art as a "silent salesman" to "fire the imagination." What he

couldn't buy he had copied, including a Michelangelo *David* specially outfitted with a fig leaf to meet Glendale standards of propriety, and a stained-glass version of Leonardo da Vinci's *Last Supper.* Eaton's largest acquisition was a 195 x 45 foot painting of the *Crucifixion,* for which a special hall had to be built. Dissatisfied with the traditional stern depiction of the Lord, he launched a search for paintings of a smiling Christ. In matters of more purely professional interest, Eaton was also an innovator. He campaigned during the 1930s to eliminate California's legislative separation of mortuaries from cemeteries, adding to Forest Lawn a Tudor-style mortuary complete with Slumberrooms resembling boudoirs where the departed reposed in cosmetic tranquility. As a final resting place, Forest Lawn appealed to flamboyant tastes. **Aimee Semple McPherson** is buried there, as are Florenz Ziegfeld and Jean Harlow. It also captured

the sardonic imagination of British writer Evelyn Waugh who wrote a caustic description of Forest Lawn for *Life* magazine (29 September l947) followed by a short burlesque, *The Loved One* (1948), featuring Eaton as "The Dreamer."

Adela Rogers St. Johns, who got religion late in life, wrote a properly reverential biography, First Step Toward Heaven: Hubert Eaton and Forest Lawn *(Englewood Cliffs, NJ, 1959). See also Ralph Hancock's* The Forest Lawn Story *(Los Angeles, 1955).*

Werner Erhard (Jack Rosenberg, 1935-   ).

During the late nineteenth and early twentieth centuries, California attracted a number of experimental communities. More recently, it has become the world capital of experimental individualism. A former car salesman from Philadelphia, Erhard started experimenting on himself. He dropped out and turned up on the West Coast in the early 1960s with a new name out of a magazine article on Germany. Working as a salesman of educational materials, he began to explore the fields of behavior modification and psychocybernetics. Aggressive and enterprising, a "rogue genius" with strong personal charisma, he put together a package called "est," a mixture of Dale Carnegie, transactional analysis, and public library metaphysics. Erhard's main innovation was the marathon group therapy session, first held at San Francisco's Jack Tar Hotel in October 1971. For a total of 60 hours over two weekends, trainees were taught to expand their "human potential" ("humpo,"

Will Schutz called it). During the 1970s, est seminars enrolled 200,000 people nationwide. Erhard, described by his biographer as an "imposter by choice," bought a Victorian townhouse in San Francisco and a Mercedes with personalized plates, SO WUT? Searching for a new angle for the 1980s, he first launched a campaign to end world hunger. Scaling down his ambitions, he then created Project "Breakthrough Racing," a high-performance team starting from scratch to master the complex skill of auto racing, with the guru himself in a flame-proof suit at the wheel.

William Bartley wrote Werner Erhard; The Transformation of a Man: The Founding of est *(New York, 1978), a sympathetic biography by an aspiring philosopher.*

Christopher Evans

(1847-1917) and **John Sontag** (John Contant, 1862-1893). As railroad bandits they were not notably successful, but they became popular heroes for evading the hated Southern Pacific's

efforts to capture them. Evans, born in Canada, was a U.S. Army scout under Custer for ten years before marrying and settling in to farm the Sierra Nevada foothills in the late 1880s. When the railroad raised its rates, he had to ship his crops at a heavy personal loss. Sontag, a former SP brakeman, was discharged after being seriously injured in a railyard accident. In 1892 he and Evans were said to be holding up trains in the San Joaquin Valley, although this was never conclusively proved. In late summer 1892, when the authorities came to apprehend them, a man was killed in the shootout and Evans and Sontag went into hiding, now wanted for murder. During the following winter, while the railroad spent thousands of dollars trying to catch them in the Sierra, **Hearst's** anti-Southern Pacific *Examiner* drummed up sympathy with admiring poems and interviews by **Ambrose Bierce** and **Joaquin Miller**. The outcome, however, was grim and bloody. Trapped by a posse, Sontag died an excruciating death from gunshot wounds, and Evans who lost an eye and an arm in the final shootout, went off to Folsom Prison for life. The rest of the story is pure California: Evans's wife and children went on the stage in a play about the late events (a rank melodrama, but daughter Eva got good notices), while their father was writing a book in jail about a mythical country with a perfect government. After seventeen years in Folsom he was released, but not

pardoned, by anti-railroad governor **Hiram Johnson**. Novelist **Frank Norris** modeled Dyke in *The Octopus* after Evans.

Just as Evans and Sontag were amateur criminals, Prodigal Sons; The Adventures of Evans and Sontag *(Boston, 1951) by Wallace Smith is amateur biography.*

Max Factor (1877-1938). Hollywood's first makeup artist, Factor was an immigrant from Russian Poland who pioneered in the art of cosmetic illusion. Setting up shop in downtown Los Angeles in 1909, he devised special makeup blends as well as wigs for clients such as **Mary Pickford** and Rudolph Valentino. With each advance in film technology, from black and white to Technicolor and

eventually television, Factor and later his sons created makeup appropriate to the properties of the film. In 1928 Factor was awarded a special Academy Award for his work on makeup for Panchromatic film. He launched an elaborate marble cosmetics place near Hollywood and Highland boulevards with an opening party attended by 10,000 people in 1935. The building also contained research labs and a menagerie of guinea pigs on which to test new products for the Hollywood and mass drugstore market. As of 1980 the old Hollywood shop was falling into decrepitude, but family fortunes were sufficiently healthy to endow Factor pavilions at UCLA Medical Center and at Cedars-Sinai Hospital in L.A.

James Graham Fair (1831-1894). Of the Big Four Comstock tycoons, Fair is remembered as the most unfair—"Slippery Jim," a money-grubbing egotist. Born in Ireland, he came to Chicago at twelve and at eighteen joined the Gold Rush. Eventually he became superintendent of the Ophir and Hale & Norcross mines in the Comstock, then struck it rich during the 1870s in partnership with **John Mackay**, **James Flood** and William O'Brien. Fair invested most of his wealth in San Francisco real estate, including the Lick House where he was to spend his last years alone. (He was planning to build a mansion on Nob Hill; after his death, his daughters built a hotel there instead, the Fairmont.) He bought himself a term as

U.S. Senator from Nevada (1881-1887), during which a newspaper remarked that "he has had the good sense to sit silent while matters of which he knows nothing are under debate." Fair's most objectionable trait was to plant purposely misleading market tips, driving up the value of his holdings at the expense of everyone else, including on occasion that of his wife. She divorced him for habitual adultery, then a sensational charge against a U.S. Senator, and his eldest son committed suicide at 27. In his own death as in his life, Fair generated greed and duplicity. His first will disappeared mysteriously and a second appeared in the hands of a widow who also proved to have property deeds and a marriage contract. A succession of claimants won nothing but notoriety, for the Fair children, it was revealed years later, gave a state Supreme Court justice a $400,000 bribe to settle the $50 million estate to their satisfaction. It didn't do them a lot of good. Fair's remaining son died soon afterwards in an auto accident, and one of his two daughters went insane.

See Oscar Lewis, Silver Kings (New York, 1947, 1967).

Lawrence Ferlinghetti

(1919-   ). The publisher of the post-World War II San Francisco literary renaissance, Ferlinghetti was an orphan in search of a spiritual home. Raised by foster parents in New York, he followed the trail of writer Thomas Wolfe to study at the University of North Carolina (B.A., 1941), earned a Ph.D. in Paris on the GI Bill, then chose San Francisco as the closest American equivalent to the French capital. His autobiographical verse (Coney Island of the Mind, 1958) enjoyed a certain vogue, but Ferlinghetti made his real mark publishing the poetry of others. In 1953 he bought into San Francisco's City Lights Bookstore, named after the Chaplin film. The first exclusively paperback bookstore in the country, something of a coffeehouse without coffee, City Lights became a landmark on the North Beach literary scene and its house imprints made national literary waves. Ferlinghetti put out Ginsberg's Howl (1956) in an inexpensive pocket edition, then defended it in an obscenity trial which brought City Lights national recognition. He continued to publish Ginsberg, but was less comfortable with the other Beats. He turned down On the Road, for example, but was generally sympathetic and encouraging to writers. He loaned Kerouac his Bixby Canyon cabin where Kerouac had a nervous breakdown, then wrote a novel about it, casting Ferlinghetti as a genial businessman named Monsanto. With the waning of the Beat generation, Ferlinghetti moved with the flow, exchanging his coat and tie for hippie garb and conventional marriage for less restrictive relationships. He traveled extensively on the international counterculture circuit, a self-described anarchist-populist poet crusading for peace and literary brotherhood. City Lights published the first translations of dissident Soviet poets Yevgeny Yevtushenko and Andrei Voznesensky, also sponsoring their appearances in San Francisco. A book by Ginsberg won a National Book Award in 1972, but that year City Lights also got stuck with thousands of copies of Thoughts by Jerry Brown when the California governor's presidential campaign fizzled out.

Neeli Cherkovski's Ferlinghetti; A Biography (Garden City, NY, 1979) is practically reverential.

Stephen Johnson Field

(1816-1899). Like the colonies of empire which provided haven and fortune for the younger sons of the British aristocracy, Gold Rush California attracted a certain number of junior Yankee patricians. Field, who became the longest-sitting Supreme Court justice in U.S. history (until William O. Douglas), was the younger brother of powerful New York lawyer David Dudley Field. Another brother was cable pioneer Cyrus Field. After graduating from Williams College and apprenticing in his brother's law office, he set out for California in 1849. Possessed of a keen sense of his natural superiority and a vocabulary of "high vituperative excellence," he soon got into

trouble: he became the first person ever held in contempt of court in California and the first attorney ever disbarred, thanks to feuds with not one but two judges. Reinstated, Field was elected to the California Supreme Court in 1857 and became its chief justice in 1859 when **David Terry** resigned. When the U.S. Supreme Court was reorganized and expanded to ten members in 1863, Field was chosen, thanks to his family connections, to represent the new tenth circuit, the Pacific coast. In those days, Supreme Court justices rode circuit in their home or assigned regions, so Field's ties and conflicts with California remained strong during 34 years on the federal bench. His decisions regarding the Chinese and railroad matters made him extremely unpopular locally, to say the least, arousing what his biographer called "envenomed bitterness." A supporter of the inalienable rights of individuals and of corporations, Field invalidated several of the petty humiliations imposed on California's Chinese and supported the Southern Pacific's efforts to remain free of taxation and regulation. As a result, the Chinese paid homage to the Supreme Court justice whenever he arrived at the Palace Hotel, railroad baron **Leland Stanford** made him a trustee of his new university, and he was frequently charged with corruption, if not conflict of interest. Field's decisions were not always wrong, one scholar wrote, but his reasons for them usually were.

Field's memoirs were published as California Alcalde *(Oakland, 1950). See also Carl Swisher's* Field, Draftsman of the Law *(Washington, D.C., 1930).*

F. Scott Fitzgerald

(Francis Scott Key Fitzgerald, 1896-1940). Fitzgerald's death in Hollywood is a cautionary tale of literature shipwrecked on the hostile shores of commerce. Unlike many of his colleagues, the celebrated novelist of the Roaring Twenties considered film an art form appropriate to his talents. Film writing also promised easy riches to restore his badly sagging fortunes. When Fitzgerald first arrived in 1927 with his wife Zelda Sayre, playing out their final round of Russian roulette with marriage, the town seemed new and fresh and hopeful. Then Zelda was institutionalized and Fitzgerald returned alone in 1931, hired by **Irving Thalberg** at $1200 a week to make Jean Harlow a star. This time he was fired after puncturing the upperclass presumption of a Thalberg soirée with a bawdy song. By 1937 when

Fitzgerald made his final assault on Hollywood, he was a forlorn figure, a pale, apologetic man in crumpled tweeds and bow tie, struggling against alcoholism and rejection. He accepted the basic premise of the film industry, "Action is Character," compiled a card file of plot lines, but couldn't seem to find the right tone. He worked on *Madame Curie* for two months but lasted only two weeks on *Gone with the Wind*. ("They think Margaret Mitchell is Shakespeare," he reported.) Sent to Dartmouth to soak up atmosphere for a college weekend script, he went on an epic bender with junior writer **Budd Schulberg**, who later wrote a novel about the trip. A Fitzgerald screenplay titled *Infidelity* was shelved by the **Hays** Office, and an original script of *Babylon Revisited* to star **Shirley Temple** aroused something less than enthusiasm. Fitzgerald's only screen credit, in fact, is *Three Comrades* (1938), actually

heavily rewritten by Joe Mankiewicz. During these years he sold stories to *Esquire* magazine about a class-D Hollywood writer called Pat Hobby and started a Hollywood novel, *The Last Tycoon* (posthumously published in 1941) using Thalberg as a model. There was also an affair with gossip columnist **Sheilah Graham**, who has described the domestic side of Fitzgerald's last years in sad detail. Graham rescued him from the Bohemian disorder of the Garden of Allah, where Robert Benchley and other East Coast writers held court, and installed him in a beach house, but he avoided sunlight like the plague and never went near the ocean. Later, living in the San Fernando Valley, Fitzgerald seemed lost in a giant bowl of silence. His few pleasures included chocolate malts at Schwab's drugstore and football games at the L.A. Coliseum. Some other curiosities of the local landscape, described in the

half-finished *Last Tycoon*, were the 1933 earthquake, a midnight grunion run ("very punctual fish"), and the studio system in which the writer is merely a factory worker while the producer reigns as philosopher-king.

Aaron Latham's Crazy Sundays; F. Scott Fitzgerald in Hollywood *(New York, 1970) is basically a rehash of Sheilah Graham's* Beloved Infidel *(New York, 1955) and Andrew Turnbull's biography,* Scott Fitzgerald *(New York, 1962).*

Jose Figueroa

(1792-1835). Appointed governor of California in 1833, Figueroa, a former comandante-general of Sonora and Sinaloa, won popular affection and respect during two tranquil years in office. The major event of his administration was the 1834 secularization proclamation under which the property of the missions was divided between the Indians and the public. (Possessed of Aztec blood, he was said to be sympathetic to California's Indians.) Figueroa's "public morals" were considered above average although privately he was given to gambling and to dallying with his mistress, according to local historian Myrtle McKittrick. Suffering from ill health, he died at San Juan Bautista en route to convalesce in the warmer south. Many years later, two legitimate sons turned up from Mexico to claim their father's property. **Abel Stearns**, for one, found it expedient to pay them $10,000 to clear title to the Rancho los Alamitos, formerly owned by Figueroa and acquired by Stearns after the governor's death. A street named for Figueroa in downtown Los Angeles is now a major thoroughfare.

Herbert Fleishhacker

(1872-1957). The son of a San Francisco paper manufacturer, Fleishhacker married into the banking business, moving up in 1909 to the presidency of the London Paris-American Bank (later Anglo-London-Paris). He and his older brother Mortimer (1868-1953) proved daring, even reckless financial titans, with powerful political connections. After San Francisco mayor **James Rolph** went broke, he became "heavily and perennially" indebted to Fleishhacker, a relationship that increased in value when Rolph was elected governor. Another recipient of Fleishhacker financial support was **Robert Dollar**, whose shipping line ran aground and was taken over by the government in 1938. Competitor **A.P. Giannini** suspected the Fleishhackers of leading a bear movement against his Bank of America, and derived some satisfaction when Herbert resigned in 1938, accused by bank stockholders of mismanagement and nonpayment of personal loans. He was legally exonerated, but lost control of his bank (later merged into the Crocker-Anglo National Bank) and had to liquidate such assets as diamond cufflinks to satisfy his creditors. He did however maintain his status as president of San Francisco's Park Commission, which he ran as if it were his own private club. On a trip to India, or so it was said, Fleishhacker was inspired by the smell of animals to endow his native city with a zoo. He was also instrumental in the construction of the War Memorial Opera House and in 1925 gave San Francisco the world's largest salt-water swimming pool, an enormous white elephant that finally shut down in 1952.

James Clair Flood

(1826-1889). As the proprietor of San Francisco's Auction Lunch, Flood served a fine fish stew and mixed some of the best drinks on the West Coast. Then he backed a Comstock longshot which in 1872 catapulted him and his partners to fabulous wealth. The most financially astute and the most highly conspicuous consumer of the "Irish Big Four," the popular former barkeeper soon aroused public outrage over Comstock stock manipulations. (His partner at the Auction Lunch, William O'Brien, the most obscure of the Four, was content to retire in reasonable affluence.) To dramatize his wealth, Flood built a massive brownstone on Nob Hill, so solid that it survived the 1906 earthquake to become the exclusive Pacific Union Club. He also built a turreted, gabled Victorian palace in suburban Atherton called Flood's Weddingcake, an object of curiosity until it was razed in 1938. A master manipulator, Flood joined with **John Mackay** in founding San Francisco's Nevada Bank in 1876. (**James G. Fair**, excluded by his former partners, pronounced it a "Floodiavellian" rather than a

"Mackayavellian" trick.) Like Fair, Flood left a dubious moral legacy. A suit by a supposed illegitimate daughter was settled out of court in 1926. His son James L. Flood, who lost a paternity suit of his own, was best known for throwing a lavish costume ball during the depths of the Depression.

See Oscar Lewis, Silver Kings *(New York, 1947, 1967).*

Joseph Libbey Folsom

(1817-1855). The state's tough Folsom Prison takes its name from a New Hampshire-born West Point graduate (1840) who made a killing in early California real estate. Arriving in 1847 as quartermaster with the New York volunteers, Captain Folsom included among his extensive local purchases a string of barren sandhills in downtown Yerba Buena. After the discovery of gold and the metamorphosis of Yerba Buena into San Francisco, these became enormously valuable. Folsom also moved swiftly to acquire **William Leidesdorff**'s estate, chiefly a 35,000-acre rancho on the American River. He even traveled to the West Indies to buy off Leidesdorff's probable heirs for $75,000, a mere fraction of the land's eventual worth. Folsom spent a decade fighting squatters and lawsuits for title to his land, which included the town later named for him and a nearby granite quarry, later site of Folsom Prison. He served as collector of the port of San Francisco and as a member of the 1851 Vigilance Committee. Historian H. H. Bancroft described him as "an honorable gentleman of superior education and refinement, somewhat formal and haughty in manner." He was also one of the wealthiest men in California. When he died at age 38, the executioners of his estate gave him a princely funeral. After years of litigation, the estate brought an eventual total of $1.5 million.

John Anson Ford

(188?-   ). It took four weeks to drive from Chicago to Los Angeles in 1920, recalled Ford, an advertising and PR man from the Midwest, son of a Presbyterian minister. He had followed the old Santa Fe Trail for want of an interstate highway. Elected to the Los Angeles Board of Supervisors as a virtual unknown in 1934, the year of Upton Sinclair's EPIC (End Poverty in California) campaign, Ford remained on the board for 24 years, from the Depression to the age of Sputnik, consistently putting conscience over expedience. Then as now, L.A. County was responsible for welfare, taxes, elections, and justice, while the city took care of police, sewage, and other "housekeeping" functions. Concerned with the proper administration of County General Hospital, Ford launched an investigation that eventually led to the recall of Mayor Frank Shaw and the

retirement of Police Chief James Davis, whose joint reign was the closest L.A. ever came to machine-style politics. (Normally, Ford pointed out, L.A. is run by "clean" establishment interests.) Ford opposed the Depression-era "bum blockade," the World War II internment of California's Japanese, and McCarthy-era witchhunts. He was state chairman of Adlai Stevenson's campaigns for president. And he was particularly active in developing county parks, recreational, and cultural facilities, one of which, the former Pilgrimage Theater, site of the local passion play, was renamed in his honor in 1977. As Will Durant put it, Commissioner Ford embodied the hope that "the Ten Commandments are not incompatible with political success."

Ford wrote Thirty Explosive Years in Los Angeles County *(San Marino, 1961) and* Honest Politics My Theme *(Hollywood, 1978), both memoirs. The earlier is the better book.*

William Fox

(1879-1952). Fox was the mogul who would be king of Hollywood. He entered the film business in 1904, buying, leasing and building a string of "motion picture palaces." Then he began making films to exhibit in his theaters, first using a rented barn across from Mack Sennett's studio, later a large lot at Sunset and Western in Los Angeles. Fox is credited with discovering Tom Mix and creating Theda Bara, but his real forte was finance. In 1930 he laid the cornerstone of a new Fox "Movietone City" equipped for sound production. There were also plans to convert his

1,000-strong theater chain to an enormous new wide screen called "Grandeur." But Fox lost his legal battles over the talking-picture patents, after years in court. More important, he lost a bid to take over MGM and merge it with Fox into a superstudio. The producer found an unlikely champion in muckraker Upton Sinclair, who wrote a melodramatic account of him as lone wolf locked in combat with Wall Street for industrial freedom. Fox emerged from his apparent stock manipulation scheme with $5 million, but it was all downhill from there. He declared bankruptcy in 1936 and later went to federal prison for fraud in connection with the bankruptcy. One of Hollywood's forgotten men, his name nevertheless remained on the studio taken over by the Skouras brothers and merged in 1935 with Twentieth Century. A generation later, when the film industry as a whole fell on hard times, the Fox back lots were sold off for the high-rise condos and high-price shops of Century City, giving the studio a new lease on life.

Upton Sinclair Presents William Fox (Los Angeles, 1933) is a period piece. See Glendon Allvine, The Greatest Fox of Them All *(New York, 1969).*

John Charles Frémont

(1813-1890). Frémont is a problematic figure in American history—either a gallant and picturesque hero, or a vain, bullying opportunist. From the national point of view, he was the Pathfinder, a brave explorer whose army expeditions and literate accounts of them helped open the continent; he also got into some trouble in

California, for which he was courtmartialed—there is a hint of injustice here—and ran unsuccessfully as the first Republican candidate for U.S. President in 1856. From a purely California viewpoint, the Pathfinder's warts are exaggerated and his character flaws loom larger than his accomplishments. The problems began on his third expedition across the country, reaching the West Coast in December 1845. It is disputed to this day whether Frémont actually possessed secret instructions, as he claimed, about the acquisition of California. In any case, he seized on the Bear Flag insurrection as a vehicle to conquer the Mexican colony. Claiming grievous insult to the U.S., he challenged the Mexican authorities to fight. If that were not enough provocation, he took Mariano Vallejo prisoner and held him under humiliating conditions. Sutter reported that Frémont bullied the Bear Flag rebels into submission, that he took "perverse pleasure" in magnifying differences, and that he demonstrated his military valor by murdering unarmed Californios in cold blood. Sutter's colleague Bidwell, who considered the Pathfinder "tactless, humorless, and strangely lacking in any expression of gratitude," blamed him for launching a war without any notice to defenseless Americans scattered over the countryside. And from the Mexican point of view; Frémont rated as "the first gringo," a marauder who took what he wanted, an exploiter, an imperialist. Whatever his motivation—and personal

aggrandizement played an undoubted role—Frémont succeeded in unleashing the forces of manifest destiny. Where he got into trouble was with regular army discipline and authority. Frémont claimed the military governorship of California, as did General Stephen Kearny. Relieved of his command, the Pathfinder was remanded to Washington, D.C. and courtmartialed for mutiny and insubordination. He later returned to California as a civilian, acquired a ranch in the Mother Lode and a home on San Francisco Bay, was elected the state's first U.S. Senator, and saw a rich vein of gold discovered on his Mariposa ranch. But it all seemed to turn to ashes in his hand. He lost his fortune to sharpers and to railroad speculation. His term in the Senate was only six months long, and he lost his San Francisco house, the city's first political and literary salon, during the Civil War. After the defeat of his national ambitions, Frémont returned to live briefly in Los Angeles, under relatively straitened circumstances,

passed by in the sweep of history.

Frémont's Memories of My Life *(1887) is a rare book. Allan Nevins wrote a standard two-volume biography* Frémont, Pathmarker of the West *(New York, 1939, 1955). For a fictionalized account from the viewpoint of Jessie Frémont, see Irving Stone's* Immortal Wife *(New York, 1944).*

Elda Furry. *See* Hedda Hopper.

Andrew Furuseth

(1854-1938). The expression *shanghaied* is said to have originated in late nineteenth-century San Francisco, home of some particularly rapacious boardinghouse owners who specialized in separating sailors from their wages, then delivering them to shipboard servitude. To eliminate this practice (also called crimping), Furuseth helped organize the Coast Seamen's Union (later Sailor's Union of the Pacific) in 1885, serving as secretary of the union for 45 years. A dour and crusty Norwegian (when he arrived in California in 1880, 90 percent of coastal seamen were fellow Scandinavians), Furuseth was renowned for his integrity and for his

eloquence during the long struggle to establish justice on the seas. He spent a good part of every year lobbying in Washington, D.C., although he seems to have been present in San Francisco for key events of labor history. He served as manager of the 1901 general strike. For decades he personally crusaded for reform legislation, warning that the lowly yellow races would soon rule the seas if working conditions were not improved for white sailors. A Seamen's Act was finally signed into law in 1915. Many of Furuseth's tenaciously held ideas have not stood the test of time. He opposed any form of unemployment insurance or pension for workers and was particularly hostile to the longshoremen (in his day, a real sailor loaded his own cargo) whose union eventually superseded his own in national power.

Hyman Weintraub's Andrew Furuseth; Emancipator of the Seamen *(Berkeley, 1959) is thoroughly ponderous.*

Henry Tifft Gage

(1852-1924). California's twentieth governor was a lawyer from Michigan who established a lucrative private practice in Los Angeles in

1875. Married to a descendant of the Lugo family, he lived on his extensive landholdings like the last of the dons. Diarist **Harris Newmark** described him as "a handsome man, of splendid physique. . . and powerful and persuasive in oratory." Nominated for governor in 1898 by the Southern Pacific-dominated Republican machine, he won and was inaugurated in a ceremony replete with bespangled colonels and captains, it being the era of the Spanish-American War. When the **Hearst** press ran a cartoon of railroad tycoon **C.P. Huntington** leading the governor around on a leash, Gage signed legislation restricting journalistic license with respect to politics. His administration was also troubled by an outbreak of bubonic plague in San Francisco, which he officially denied, and by labor unrest in the same city. He was not nominated for reelection, and returned to his L.A. law practice. He squared off against celebrated defense attorney **Earl Rogers** in two flamboyant criminal cases during the early years of the century, supported American adventurism abroad, and served as U.S. Minister to Portugal (1909-11), the state's fifth former governor to receive a similar diplomatic assignment.

Ernest Gallo (1910-   ) and Julio Gallo

(1911-   ). The Gallo brothers founded their company in Modesto in 1933, driven by the Depression-era suicide of their parents to create the fastest-growing

and most innovative winery in the world. Beginning with red table wines only, they introduced their own label (featuring a rooster or *gallo*) in 1940 and soon expanded their distribution nationwide. By automating and integrating from the grape in the fields to the bottle on the shelf and by catering to American tastes with popular confections like "Thunderbird" and "Ripple," Gallo was producing half of all California wine by 1970. Then the company shifted its emphasis from quantity to quality, gradually upgrading product and price. Ernest Gallo, the stern elder brother and marketing genius (as different from smiling production manager Julio Gallo as "whisky from wine") is considered chiefly responsible for the firm's success. (A third brother runs his own small vineyard nearby.) The Gallo Winery with its huge stainless steel tanks looks like a petroleum refinery, dominates the skyline and the economy of Modesto, and commands respect if not always love. As the leading edge of the California wine industry, Gallo sets wages as well as prices, which has brought the company under attack from **Cesar Chavez**'s United Farm Workers and under investigation by the FTC for aggressive marketing practices.

Erle Stanley Gardner

(1889-1970). Oxnard was a brawling, wide-open town when Gardner first hung out his shingle as an attorney in 1911. Born in Massachusetts of pilgrim stock, Gardner came west with his family in 1899 and grew up as a sort of maverick, full of restless energy that often got him into trouble. Even as a lawyer he was a "wrong-way Corrigan," biographer Alva Johnston noted, challenging authority with his unorthodox tactics. Once he pulled a legal coup by playing musical chairs with his clients, a group of Chinese gamblers; when the wrong men were arrested, thanks to Anglo inability to tell one Oriental from another, he got the cases dismissed. (For such prowess the local Chinese called him Tai Chong Tzee—the great counselor.) An outdoorsman who liked to hunt with a bow and arrow, Gardner first tried writing as a means of gaining financial independence from his law office. He began with westerns, then drew on his legal knowledge to create pulp-magazine detective fiction. After a decade of dictating stories after hours, Gardner was in a position to "take off," literally, as a nomadic writer with a caravan of camper-trailers for secretaries and guests. For 30 years his base of operations was a 3,000-acre ranch near Temecula. An incurable gypsy, he also kept a beach house at Oceanside, cottages at Palm Springs and Idyllwild, plus assorted plots of land for caravan campouts. Gardner's restless wandering satisfied some inner need and also enabled him to recharge after writing himself out. Beginning with his first book (published in 1933), he wrote a total of 82 Perry Mason mysteries, another series of 29 under the pseudonym A.A. Fair, and a number of travel books, for a grand total of 141. With such titles as *The Case of the Haunted Husband*, or *The Case of the Negligent Nymph*, the books sold rapidly in inexpensive paperback editions, spinning off the radio and television series that made Gardner a wealthy man. He needed the money, a friend remarked, for no one "ever lived the essentially simple life so expensively."

Alva Johnston's The Case of Erle Stanley Gardner *(New York, 1946, 1947) is an appreciative character sketch.* The Case of the Real Perry Mason *by Dorothy Hughes focuses on Gardner's relations with his publisher. (NY, 1978).*

Charles Mills Gayley

(1858-1932). The son of a China missionary, Gayley joined the faculty of the University of California at Berkeley in 1889 and remained for 35 years as an all-time favorite English professor. Possessed of a musical baritone and a contagious fund of enthusiasm, he inspired generations of students with his love for the classics. His Great Books course became so popular that it was moved in 1909 to the Greek Theater, where classes of over a thousand listened in rapt attention. Gayley somehow found time to coach the debating society that defeated Stanford ("brain vs. brawn"), to found a society of comparative literature, and to teach the university's first extension courses in San Francisco. He also wrote the university hymn and the "Golden Bear" song which inspired the choice of the university mascot. Gayley was a man of great causes and prejudices. He excluded women from his literary debates, limited the enrollment of "giggling girls" in his courses, and extolled the muscular patriotism of Rudyard Kipling. For 24 years he was head of the California branch of the Mayflower Descendants of America. During World War I, he became known as the "dean of California patriots," delivering frequent renditions of his "Smash the Kaiser" speech, wearing the same shabby suit for four years in order to buy war bonds, and keynoting university armistice celebrations with a discourse on "How art thou fallen, O Lucifer."

Ben Kurtz's biography, Charles Mills Gayley *(Berkeley, 1943), is just adequate.*

John White Geary

(1819-1873). Geary arrived in San Francisco as U.S. postmaster in 1849 with ten sacks of mail and carried them all ashore himself, rather than pay Gold Rush porter fees. A native of

Pennsylvania and veteran of the Mexican War, he possessed great natural assets for establishing authority on the unruly frontier: he stood six feet, five inches and weighed 260 pounds. Elected alcalde of San Francisco in August 1849, then mayor (1850-1852), he found the town "without a single requisite for the promotion of prosperity, the protection of property, or the maintenance of order." Geary doubled as judge, sheriff, coroner, and fire chief when necessary. Once during a waterless moment, he demolished a burning building to stop a fire. When the irate owner shot at him, Geary knocked the man down and proceeded with his task. He may have been overworked, but his salary was reputedly greater than that of the U.S. president and he multiplied it by investing in local real estate. Disappointed in his hope of winning **Frémont**'s U.S. Senate seat in 1852, Geary returned east a wealthy man—age 33. A few years later he was appointed governor of "bleeding" Kansas Territory, and rose to the rank of Union general in the Civil War. He served two terms as governor of Pennsylvania.

Harry M. Tinkcom, John White Geary, Soldier Statesman *(Philadelphia, 1940).*

Arnold Genthe

(1869-1942). The son of a German scholar, Genthe came to San Francisco in 1895 for his *wanderjahr* after earning his dueling scar and a Ph.D. in classics. To illustrate his letters home, he began taking photographs of the city in a soft focus that conveyed

the misty effect of the ocean fogs. Genthe soon became a fixture around Chinatown, unobtrusively recording the spectacle of street life on film. His ethereal unposed portraits of such local beauties as Alma de Bretteville (later **Spreckels**) won the attention of the rich and powerful, and he was soon San Francisco's leading society photographer. Most of Genthe's early work was lost in the 1906 earthquake and fire except for photos which Will Irwin, his collaborator on *Pictures of Old Chinatown*

(1908), had insisted be stored in a vault. But he managed to save a camera and captured the most enduring images of the disaster on film. During the hectic period of reconstruction, Genthe spent long periods at his bungalow in Carmel, where as a supremely eligible bachelor he went carousing with his friends **Jack London** and **George Sterling**. He opened a new studio in San Francisco, but his bonds to the city had been loosened. In 1911 Genthe moved on to New York and a new set of

photographic challenges, including commissions to photograph two presidents of the U.S. during office.

Genthe's As I Remember *(New York, 1939, 1979) is handsomely illustrated with the photographer's own pictures.*

Gorgeous George

(George Raymond Wagner, 1915?-1963). Wagner was a high school dropout from Texas, a mediocre professional wrestler who gave new life to an ancient ritual with his elaborate affectations. The scene of his finest hours was L.A.'s Olympic Auditorium, a 10,000-seat arena stinking of piss and liniment. Preceding the wrestler down the aisle would be his morning-coated valet bearing on a silver tray a silken towel and perfume with which to disinfect the

ring. After the referee and the opponent, the star would arrive mincing and primping to the strains of "Pomp and Circumstance," his hair bleached and curled, his embroidered or fur-trimmed robe swishing over orchid-colored trunks. The wrestler's air of dignified aloofness would soon give way to injured innocence, encouraging the jeers, whistles, and catcalls of the crowd. Gorgeous George (he changed his name legally in 1950) usually lost his fights, but he sold out 27 of 32 appearances at the Olympic and catapulted wrestling into televised melodrama. Soon other fighters were affecting outrageous names and styles, but none ever rivalled George's fame. In private life, he drove an orchid-colored Cadillac and acquired a turkey farm near Beaumont, promoting his "Gorgeous Broad-Breasted" birds with typical flair. In his prime the wrestler went through $250,000 a year. Twice-divorced, he died broke and alone in his Hollywood apartment after a heart attack on Christmas Day. Fans took up a collection to bury him in an orchid-covered coffin at Valhalla Memorial Park in North Hollywood. The Olympic Auditorium survives, the last weekly fight club left in the United States.

Henry George

(1839-1897). Economics was an armchair science in the second half of the nineteenth century when a San Francisco editor rose to challenge its conventional wisdoms. To Henry George, a self-educated former sailor

and printer from Philadelphia, it was almost as if he could see the origins of poverty in the new frontier society, as if California were a laboratory in which the flow of wealth was visibly congealing. In 1871 George became editor of the *San Francisco Evening Post*, a one-cent paper. (The Bank of California had to lay in a local supply of pennies so newsboys could make change.) While riding his old plug from the Mission District to work, he often pondered the great riddle of modern economics, why the enormous increase in productivity brought by the industrial revolution did not alleviate poverty. All of the great fortunes were in land and land value increased with population growth. Along with such causes as sailors' rights, prison reform, anti-monopoly, and aid to the oppressed, he began to argue that land alone should be taxed (a "single tax") and that private property, the source of inequality of wealth, should be abolished. After his newspaper was taken over by mining millionaire **John P.**

Jones, George was appointed state inspector of gas meters, a sinecure which enabled him to extend his travel and observations. During **Denis Kearney's** rist to power when the very foundations of society appeared to be breaking up, he worked on his magnum opus at his Bay-view home near First and Howard in San Francisco. *Progress and Poverty* was first published in 1880 in San Francisco, a feat in which half the printers of the state would eventually claim participation. The book became an international best-seller, and George was hailed as "the prophet of San Francisco," America's answer to Marx. California, having nurtured his intellectual development, now seemed to him mired in materialism. After 22 years of residence, he left with his family to make New York the world capital of the single-tax movement.

See Charles A. Barker, Henry George *(New York, 1955) and Anna George de Mille,* Henry George *(Chapel Hill, NC, 1950).*

Rudi Gernreich

(1922-   ). Until the 1950s, Southern California had several swimwear manufacturers but no "fashion" industry per se, relying instead on inspiration from New York's Seventh Avenue. Gernreich, who arrived in L.A. at sixteen, a refugee from the Nazi takeover of Austria, changed all that. After ten years as a dancer and costume designer for the Lester Horton Dance

Troup, he went into fashion design, starting by removing cumbersome inner bracings to create a boneless bathing suit for women. Taking inspiration from the theater of the streets and from the future rather than the past, he suggested machine-gun belts, body decals, and unisex jump suits. His topless bathing suit in 1964 was an idea before its time and his see-through blouse did not have a great vogue, but the "no-bra look"

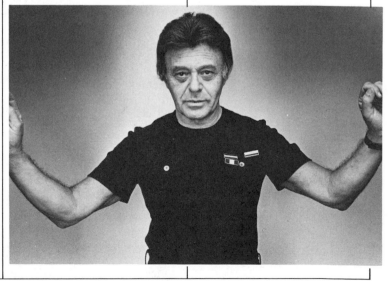

started a definite trend. Gernreich won two coveted Coty awards in the 1960s, causing distinct rumblings of disaffection in the snobbish eastern fashion establishment. In the late 1960s, with the revival of the peasant and preppie looks ("editing rather than designing"), he declared fashion irrelevant and left California on a world trip. Later, he diversified into homewear (towels, pillows), returning to the futuristic swing in the 1980s with more of his way-out jumpsuits, body paint, and jackets made from bicycle parts.

J. Paul Getty (Jean Paul Getty, 1892-1976). The two principal industries in Los Angeles during the interwar period, oil and film-making, involved similar measures of high risk, hard work, and rough play, Getty once observed. The son and heir of an attorney with profitable oil investments, he made his own first million before he was 24, having dropped out of both USC and the University of California (too "juvenile"). As a working playboy Getty found himself very much at home in the world of Hollywood. He entertained show business celebrities at his Santa Monica beach house and at his oil rigs in Long Beach, where they arrived by limousine with picnic hampers to see how oil was drilled. Getty counted Jean Harlow, Gloria Swanson, and Joan Crawford among his friends. Five times married and divorced, he admitted to rivalry with Charlie Chaplin over girls (including Joan Barry, who dated Getty and sued Chaplin for paternity).

Getty had all the makings of an international jet-setter (his friends also included the Duke of Windsor, Aristotle Onassis, and Hugh Hefner) except that he hated to fly. In 1951 he left his 60-acre villa on the coast north of Santa Monica and moved to Europe, his oil interests in the Middle East and the North Sea having eclipsed his California holdings. As home and corporate headquarters he acquired Sutton Place, the princely former estate of the Duke of Sutherland 30 miles from London. In his memoirs Getty compares Sutton Place with **Hearst**'s San Simeon, admitting to a shared admiration for splendor but claiming better business sense than the publishing magnate. Like Hearst, he collected art, shipping the overflow back to his California villa which was opened to the public in 1954. Through the years in Europe, Getty continued to pay his taxes in California, to vote by absentee ballot there (for friend **Richard Nixon** every time), and to maintain his home as a museum, expanded in 1974 to include an entire Pompeiian villa. He himself never set foot in his California home during the last 25 years of his life.

Getty wrote a few how-to books of the inspirational genre, including an autobiography, As I See It *(Englewood Cliffs, NJ, 1976).*

Amadeo Peter Giannini (1870-1949). The history of California is full of people and businesses that prospered thanks to loans from Giannini, the greatest innovator in modern banking history. Born in San Jose, he became a successful

"You can't fall California back!"

commission produce dealer while still in his teens. In 1904 he opened his Bank of Italy in San Francisco, prospering after the earthquake destroyed all records because he personally knew his clients and knew their net worth by heart. From a first branch established in San Jose in 1909, a statewide chain of branch banks eventually rose, over the opposition of conservative state and federal banking authorities. Giannini ran his Bank of America, as it was renamed in 1930, by "ear" and by force of personality rather than outright ownership. The entire family including brother Attilio Henry Giannini (1874-1944), called "Doc" because he graduated from UC Medical School, owned less than nineteen percent of the banking operation. In a 1931 proxy fight against a Wall Street combine, A.P. Giannini won by stumping the state for stockholder votes. A rare liberal in a conservative

business, he voted for FDR and supported the New Deal. He also dispensed neighborliness and homely wisdom along with loans. (One client, clearly a paisano, came into the local branch requesting a divorce and remarriage.) A major source of financing for Hollywood films, Giannini expressed personal concern about the moral quality of the collateral and appointed conservative producer **Cecil B. DeMille** a loan officer in his Hollywood branch. His son Lawrence Mario Giannini (1894-1952) succeeded to the presidency of the bank in 1936, but there was little question who was in charge while A.P. lived. L.M. also succeeded his father as a UC regent, but resigned in conservative pique when the university voted down a McCarthy-era loyalty oath. L.M., a hemophiliac, survived his father by only a few years.

Marquis and Bessie James wrote Biography of a Bank, The Story of the Bank of America *(New York, 1944), an authorized account and a better source of information than* A.P. Giannini; Giant in the West *by Julian Dana (New York, 1947).*

Jerry Giesler (Harold Lee Giesler, 1886-1962). Giesler liked to think of himself as just a "country lawyer," but the country was Hollywood and his cases inclined to the sensational. Born in Iowa, he moved to L.A. in the early years of the century, working his way through USC as an office boy for prominent defense attorney **Earl Rogers**. He was asked to help defend **Clarence Darrow**, but didn't make a name for himself until the

Alexander Pantages case in 1929. Defending the middle-aged Greek theater owner on charges of raping a teenage girl, he established a point of law on the admissibility of evidence of resistance or cooperation. Giesler went on to defend other Hollywood lotharios (notably, Errol Flynn and Charlie Chaplin) in seduction cases. He defended **Busby Berkeley** on manslaughter charges involving alleged drunk driving, and Edward G. Robinson, Jr.; on grand theft. Few of his clients were ever convicted, with the exception of Robert Mitchum, who spent two months in jail on a marijuana rap. Taking a cue from Hollywood, Giesler had

his office decorated like a stage, with a pinpoint spotlight illuminating only his face, flanked by portraits of Darrow and Rogers. But he was the least glamorous of men, a sedate, balding figure, always conservatively dressed and unfailingly polite, managing to make even the most salacious details tedious on cross-examination. "How was he dressed then?" he asked one of Flynn's alleged rape victims. "What color were his pajamas? Striped? Did the pajamas have a sash around them? Were they buttoned in the shirt? Were they stuffed inside the pajama pants? Was he wearing slippers?"
Giesler wrote a memoir, The Jerry Giesler Story *(New York, 1960).*

Eliza Gilbert. See Lola Montez.

Irving John Gill
(1870-1936). Gill moved west for his health at the age of 22, choosing San Diego because the newly completed Santa Fe Railroad ended there. Having apprenticed as an architect under Louis Sullivan in Chicago, he found Southern California a "blank page" awaiting the sophisticated imprint of a master builder. The predominant style of the day, from the 1890s to World War I was Mission Revival, a version of the original Spanish "improved" with frills and flourishes. Gill removed the excrescences to give the Spanish line a pristine modernity, somehow reflecting such disparate influences as **Frank Lloyd Wright**'s Prairie Style and the International Style then evolving in Europe. He built

residences for the upper classes in San Diego's Hillcrest and Coronado areas as well as public buildings and churches, including two for local Christian Scientists. Gill was also interested in "social architecture," experimenting with low-cost, labor-saving, chastely simple housing. Workers in the model town of Torrance rejected his "minimum houses" (1913-1916) in favor of more traditional styles, but his Lewis Courts in Sierra Madre (1910), also designed for the working class, proved so popular that rents were raised for more discerning residents. Gill lost out as architect of San Diego's 1915 Panama-California Exposition, because the organizers preferred the Spanish Colonial style to modern. Commissions were few and far between during his last years, and he died broke. His much-admired Dodge house in West Hollywood (1916) has been torn down, leaving his best work in La Jolla: the Women's Club (1913), Bishop's School (1909-1916), and the Scripps House (1915), now La Jolla's Museum of Contemporary Art.
See Esther McCoy's Five California Architects *(New York, 1960).*

James Norris Gillett
(1860-1937). Gillett's term as California's 22nd (1907-1911) governor has been described, perhaps unfairly, as the "rottenest" administration in state history. Born in Wisconsin where he was admitted to the bar in 1881, he moved to Eureka, California, in 1884 to practice law. He was elected to the state senate as a Republican in 1896 and in 1902 to the

Photograph of Dinner Party given to
JAMES N. GILLETT

Republican Nominee for Governor, and his friends on the day that he was nominated, to celebrate his nomination.

Justice F. W. HENSHAW, Republican Candidate for Supreme Court — RUDOLPH HEROLD — GEO. HATTON, S. P. Politician — JAMES N. GILLETT — WALTER F. PARKER, S. P. L. A. Politician — WARREN PORTER, Rep. Candidate for Lieut. Governor — Congressman JOS. KNOWLAND

Judge J. W. McKINLEY, S. P. Attorney and Politician — ABE RUEF, S. F. Political Boss — FRANK McLAUGHLIN, S. P. Attorney — Judge F. R. KERRIGAN, Rep. Nominee for Supreme Court

U.S. House of Representatives where he became known as a staunch supporter of Southern Pacific interests. At the 1906 Republican convention in Santa Cruz Gillett was nominated for governor in a maneuver by Boss **Ruef** to increase his own power. A photo taken on the occasion, showing Gillett with Ruef and others (including *Oakland Tribune* publisher **Joseph Knowland**),was widely circulated as "the Shame of California." Once elected, however, Gillett does not seem to have been guilty of any gross favoritism. He did not seek reelection in 1910, retiring to practice law and to lobby for the oil industry, the last governor selected by the old machine-dominated convention system that his successor **Hiram Johnson** put out of business.

Allen Ginsberg

(1926-   ). The first reading of Ginsberg's poem *Howl* at San Francisco's Six Gallery on 13 October 1955 has been called the birth trauma of the Beat generation. A friend of **Jack Kerouac** from Columbia University, Ginsberg came west in 1953 to see **Neal Cassady**. He worked as a market consultant in San Francisco for a while, then dropped out to write poetry in an expansive, whitmanesque style, the content ranging from the mystical to the scatalogical. Published by **Ferlinghetti**'s City Lights Books in 1956, *Howl* resulted in Ferlinghetti's arrest and trial on obscenity charges. (The 1957 ruling on the case paved the way for publication in the U.S. of *Lady Chatterley's Lover* and *Tropic of Cancer*.) Ginsberg sat out the trial in Algiers visiting fellow outlaw-writer William Burroughs. Later he traveled to India to explore yoga and meditation, returning as the Om-chanting guru of "flower power," or passive activism. Basically a New York person, Ginsberg had a tendency to gravitate back to San Francisco for major events in the evolution of the counterculture. He gave the first reading of another of his major poems, *Kaddish for Naomi Ginsberg*, at Garibaldi Auditorium in 1959 and was one of the organizers of the first "Be-In" in Golden Gate Park in January 1967. He also continued to publish his work in San Francisco, including his 1972 National Book Award-winning *Fall of America*.

Jane Kramer, who wrote Allen Ginsberg in America, *(New York, 1967), accompanied the poet on one of his trips to the Bay Area.*

Elinor Sutherland Glyn

(1864-1943). Glyn was a pedigreed Englishwoman driven by financial necessity to write mildly titillating novels about beautiful women, handsome men and perfect love. Her *Three Weeks*, the *Peyton Place* of 1907, featured a seduction scene on a leopard-skin rug. Invited to Hollywood in 1920 as an international authority on romantic sex, she created a

sensation with her flaming red hair, crimson lipstick, and long purple veils. Glyn took over the penthouse at the Ambassador Hotel and mixed only with the elite of local society: **Mary Pickford**, whose "natural refinement" she approved, Gloria Swanson, who had married into European royalty, and **Marion Davies**, who gave "gay and intelligent parties" with her "friend" **William Hearst**. (Glyn herself was the "friend" of the eminent Lord Curzon for eight years.) She was invited to parties on the Hearst yacht and to weekends at San Simeon, where the jumbled art and antiques disturbed her. Not least because they formerly belonged to people like herself. At the studios, she insisted on correct details, removing nicknacks and spittoons from the sets of supposed English drawing rooms. She also spent a lot of time intriguing against others. **Jesse Lasky** complained bitterly about paying her $50,000 for one word, even though the word was "It," the title of both a *Cosmopolitan* novelette and of the Clara Bow film which became synonymous with sex appeal. Glyn was almost universally seen as a terrible snob who accused others of her own worst trait, an exaggerated sense of self-importance ("the California curse," she called it). But she had pluck. When Curzon got married without even telling her, she never said a word. Stranded in the wilds of Mexico en route to a Hearst house party, she spent the night laughing with Charlie Chaplin and emerged impeccably groomed the next morning. And when all else failed financially, she made a vaudeville tour lecturing on romantic love. All but forgotten today, her name turns up occasionally in crossword puzzles.

See her autobiography, Romantic Adventure *(London, 1936). Her nephew Anthony Glyn wrote* Elinor Glyn; A Biography *(London, 1955).*

Rube Goldberg (Reuben Lucius Goldberg, 1883-1970). One of New York's alltime great cartoonists was a San Franciscan, born and raised in Boss **Ruef**'s urbane city by the Bay. His German-Jewish father dabbled in real estate and politics, serving as ward boss, fire chief, police commissioner, and general wheeler-dealer. A graduate of Lowell High School, Rube commuted three and a half hours daily from the family home in San Francisco to Berkeley to attend the University of California School of Mining. There he encountered the proto-original Rube Goldberg device, a complicated contraption called the "Barodik," invented by one of his professors to measure the weight of the earth. Inspired with a lifelong appreciation of human eccentricity in the Machine Age, he graduated (1904) to a job mapping sewer pipes and water mains, then abandoned engineering to become a sports cartoonist for the *San Francisco Chronicle*. At 24 Goldberg left home for New York—"ringside" he called it, the main event in U.S. journalism—where he remained for the rest of his life. In early years his father used to come east for the annual ritual of contract negotiations, which eventually

yielded an income of $50,000 a year. One of the few college-educated humorists, Goldberg was intrigued by the impact of technology on everyday life, and particularly by complex new inventions to perform the simplest of tasks. He invented a few of these himself—garage door openers, self-washing windows—always meticulously laid out in chain-reaction absurdity. The most coveted award in cartoonery, the Reuben, was named in his honor. By the time Goldberg won his own biggest prize, a 1948 Pulitzer for a cartoon about the atomic bomb, most of the humor had gone out of the contraption business.

See Peter Marzio's Rube Goldberg; His Life and Work *(New York, 1973).*

Sam Goldwyn (Samuel Goldfisch, 1882-1974). Legend has it that Goldwyn was such an independent child that he left his home in Poland's ghettoes at eleven or twelve and emigrated to the U.S. to become the greatest teenage glove salesman of all time. In any case, he became Hollywood's only successful independent producer, so independent—or so impossible—that his partnerships with **Jesse Lasky**, the Selwyn brothers, MGM, and United Artists were soon dissolved. Certainly he was always persuasive. As a biographer put it, "He would not acknowledge, let alone accept, rejection. He had an answer for every argument, a ploy for every occasion. He could not be insulted. He could not be deterred. He could not be withstood." Goldwyn has been romanticized by press agentry

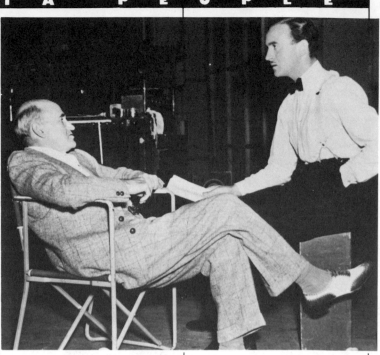

as the lovable author of such endearing malapropisms as "include me out," but he could in fact be crude and boorish. He was also very good at playing people off against one another and at humiliating them. In that department he was a little folksier than **Harry Cohn**—Khrushchev, say, rather than Stalin. He did have good taste and money. The best-dressed producer in Hollywood, he produced very well-dressed films and financed them himself. But to produce such film classics as *Wuthering Heights* (1939) and *The Best Years of Our Lives* (1946) he hounded and schemed and put his staff through the mill. One studio PR man got his revenge by arranging a photo session of Goldwyn seated at a desk on which is prominently displayed a multi-volume *History of the Jews.*

Goldwyn's Behind the Scenes *(New York, 1923) is an early, ghostwritten memoir. See Alva Johnston,* The Great Goldwyn *(New York, 1937) and Carol Easton,* The Search for Sam Goldwyn *(New York, 1976). Goldwyn figures largely in Garson Kanin's* Hollywood *(New York, 1964, 1974).*

Pancho Gonzales (Richard Alonzo Gonzales, 1928-   ). Only in California, where there is no country club class barrier in tennis, could a self-taught player from the *barrio* have risen to world championship status. The eldest of seven children of a Chicano housepainter, Gonzales taught himself to play at the Exposition Park courts in the shadow of the Los Angeles Coliseum. Perry Jones, the autocratic head of the Southern California Tennis Association, tried to exclude him from competition on the grounds that he was a chronic truant. But by the

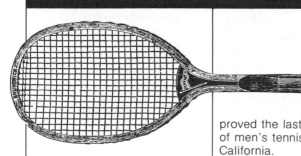

time he was nineteen and beyond the authority of school, nothing could stop the tall, thin, fiercely determined Gonzales. That year he won the Southern California championship, going on to take the U.S. singles titles at Forest Hills in 1948 and 1949. Turning pro at twenty, he was defeated on the 1949-1950 tour by **Jack Kramer**, who with his blond crewcut seemed the very antithesis of the darkly scowling Chicano. Gonzales retreated to the tennis shop at Exposition Park for a few years, then returned to the pro circuit and dominated it until the early 1960s. He had great appeal on the courts, simultaneously hero and villain, exciting, controversial, a master of the "big game." He seemed to be mad all the time, Kramer remarked, but he played better mad. If open tennis had come after World War II, Kramer thought, Gonzales would have swept the world titles—both pro and amateur—until 1963. When the new regime finally arrived in 1968, he played some remarkable matches against kids half his age. Personally somewhat reclusive, he still enjoyed a Hollywood celebrity lifestyle with a Malibu ranch and multiple marriages, two of them to the same former Miss Rheingold. Curiously, he

proved the last of a long line of men's tennis stars from California.

Gonzales, Man With a Racket as told to Cy Rice (New York, 1959).

Bertram Grosvenor Goodhue (1869-1924). Goodhue was a distinguished New Englander, as his name implies, and a renowned architect. Nurtured by his mother on Saint Augustine and Saint Francis of Assisi, he specialized in the design of ornate churches, usually Gothic, including the chapel at West Point, Christ Church in New Haven, Saint Bartholomew's in New York, and even a cathedral in Havana. He also designed grandiose homes for the wealthy with dining rooms resembling refectories. Goodhue's first Southern California commission seems to have been the Gillespie house (1903-1905) in Montecito, where he later designed the Country Club (1916-1917) and a home for himself (1918). Thanks to his connections and his study of Spanish colonial architecture he was appointed directing architect of San Diego's 1915 Panama-California Exposition. Goodhue's Churrigueresque-style State Building (1913-1915) for the Exposition, as imposing as a cathedral, is the epitome of the Iberian influence in California. He also helped plan Cal Tech in Pasadena. His last local commission and his greatest

was the Los Angeles Public Library (1922-1926), conceived as a temple of learning with Egyptian, Byzantine, and Islamic motifs.

Goodhue—Architect and Master of Many Arts, Charles H. Whitaker, ed. (New York, 1925) is a handsome illustrated production but difficult to find.

Bill Graham (Wolfgang Grajonca, 1931-   ). In the late 1960s, Graham transformed first an ice-skating rink, then a drafty old Irish dancehall in San Francisco into the Fillmore Auditorium, world capital of acid rock. Featuring such switched-on local groups as the Grateful Dead and the Jefferson Airplane, with multi-media light shows and psychedelic decor, he expanded to New York City in 1968, opening a Fillmore East to match his Fillmore West. Then in 1971 Graham pulled the plug on both Fillmores, complaining about the greed and ingratitude of rock stars, who in turn called him the dictatorial "robber baron of rock." Born in Berlin and orphaned during World War II, Graham had made his way to New York, then earned a bronze star during the Korean War and a business degree from City College of New York (1955) on the GI Bill. "You guys are hippies and I'm a square," he told one of **Kesey**'s Merry Pranksters, but that wasn't quite it. Graham was really sort of a late-model hip beatnik with a head for the hard sell. After closing the Fillmores, he went on to organize the 1973 Watkins Glen (New York) concert, Bob Dylan's 1974 tour, and other class rock acts. At last report he was

living in a $1 million house in Marin County and putting together a team from Stanford, Princeton, and Wharton business schools to create an entertainment conglomerate, bringing together everything from merchandising and equipment rental to advertising and concert booking. Down the road, he forecast total-recreation centers, combining the features of singles bars, rock concerts, and sports clubs—meeting places for a brave new world of pleasurable business.

Sheilah Graham (Lily Sheil, 1908?-   ). "Hollywood to me was sham and glitter," she wrote on becoming the North American News Alliance's movie columnist, "and I thought myself qualified to understand sham and glitter." After a Dickensian childhood in a London orphanage, she traded up from chorus girl to society matron, counting a marquess among her suitors. But in 1935 she gave up society to become a gossip columnist, and the marquess for **F. Scott Fitzgerald**, premier novelist of the Roaring Twenties who during the 1930s was fading into alcoholism and oblivion. During the last four years of his life, Fitzgerald played Pygmalion to Graham's Galatea, while Graham in return kept a watchful eye on his drinking and his housekeeping arrangements. A seemingly incongruous couple, the literary prince and the journalistic showgirl shared one glittering illusion. Fitzgerald thought "the rich were a special race,"

Hemingway once wrote. So did Graham. She saw herself as a beautiful Fitzgerald heroine—the life of the party, a woman who like Jay Gatsby had invented herself—and she became one, the elusive Kathleen in *The Last Tycoon*, Fitzgerald's unfinished novel about Hollywood. When Fitzgerald died, Graham went on to more mundane relationships. (One of her husbands was W.S. ''Bow Wow'' Wojchiechowicz, a movie PR man.) After a long career of exposing the intimate details of others' lives, she began to cannibalize her own. Altogether she wrote four books about her relationship with Fitzgerald, comparing him for good looks with Robert Redford. The royalties made her rich at last.

Graham's books, all of which tend toward sexual autobiography, include Beloved Infidel *(New York, 1955) and* Confessions of a Hollywood Columnist *(New York, 1969).*

Sidney Patrick Grauman (1874-1950). The son of a San Francisco vaudeville impresario, Grauman built palatial showcases in Los Angeles for the new art of film. His grand entryways, plush carpeting, ornate furnishings and motifs from ancient history—all widely imitated by the theater chains of the day—were calculated to transport the humble moviegoer into never-never land even before the film began. In 1918 Grauman held a gala opening for his Million Dollar Theater and in 1923 remodeled the Rialto, both on Broadway in downtown L.A., trying to rival New York's Great White Way. But L.A. was just too spread

out, and fans and producers alike preferred to attend their gala premieres (a Grauman invention) at his Egyptian (1922) and Chinese (1927) theaters in Hollywood. Grauman looked like the Mad Hatter, **Anita Loos** remembered—''small and wiry with an enormous nose and a halo of fuzzy red hair''—and was a legendary prankster as well as consummate showman. He once turned up in a blonde wig as a blind date for **Sam Goldwyn**. His publicity stunts included bombs bursting overhead, Assyrian armed guards on 24-hour patrol, and hand-and-feet imprints by stars in the concrete courtyard of the Chinese Theater, one of the area's top tourist attractions. Grauman also took impressions of **William S. Hart**'s six-shooters, Harold Lloyd's glasses, Betty Grable's whole leg, and Joe E. Brown's mouth. But nothing is forever.

Grauman's theater is now Mann's Chinese.

Jackson Alpheus Graves (1852-1933). Graves came to California as a boy with the Civil War-era stream of refugees from the South. Writing his memoirs 60 years later, he described his new home as a paradise where deer and antelope still roamed. After graduation from Saint Mary's College in San Mateo (B.A., 1872; M.A., 1873), he passed an oral exam before the state Supreme Court (some of the justices were personal acquaintances) and moved to Los Angeles to practice law. A congenial fellow, he claimed to have met everyone in town within six months. Specializing in real estate law, he represented some of Southern California's largest landowners, including the **Irvine** ranch and **Van Nuys**' L.A. Farming and Milling Company. Graves went into

partnership with **Henry O'Melveny** in 1885, when it was just becoming fashionable for businesses to incorporate. They drew up the papers and represented L.A.'s new corporations, including nearly every bank in the city. A pillar of the city's turn-of-the-century establishment, Graves agreed with his friend General **Otis** about ''the curse of trade unionism.'' A pretty astute businessman himself, he once managed a client's bank, and turned an $800 investment in an oil well into a $100,000 bonanza before retiring to his Alhambra ranch.

Graves wrote My Seventy Years in California, 1857-1927 *(L.A., 1928) and, as an afterthought,* California Memories *(L.A., 1930).*

Charles Sumner Greene (1868-1957) and **Henry Mather Greene** (1870-1954). The bungalow, originally conceived by the British as a comfortable, unpretentious home-away-from-home, achieved its apotheosis in Pasadena, California, as a winter home for wealthy eastern imperialists. This was accomplished by two brothers with a proper Bostonian pedigree and MIT training in architecture. Arriving in Pasadena to visit their parents in 1893, Charles and Henry Greene remained to develop their art and the highest standards of craftsmanship. After exploring a variety of styles from Queen Anne to Spanish Mission, they evolved around the turn of the century their own distinctive synthesis of the log cabin, the Swiss chalet, and the Oriental teahouse. They also believed in total design, from

landscaping down to leaded glass and custom cabinetry. Greene and Greene houses were relatively expensive, but the brothers were fortunate enough to attract clients who could afford the luxury of handmade screws and dowels. Two outstanding examples of their bungalow mansions are the Blacker (1907) and Gamble (1908) houses in Pasadena, the latter now run as a museum by the University of Southern California. Just around the corner from the Gamble house is an enclave called "Little Switzerland" where the brothers built their own more modest chalets. Henry was the businessman of the firm, handling finances and working drawings, while Charles saw to the refinements of design and execution. When styles changed and commissions began to drop off around World War I, the brothers went their separate ways. Charles moved to Carmel

where he built a stone mansion on a promontory overlooking the sea and pursued a lifelong interest in Oriental philosophy. (Locals called him the "Buddhist architect.") Both brothers survived into their venerable eighties, when they were honored by new generations of architecture buffs.

Randall Makinson, curator of the Gamble house in Pasadena, wrote Greene and Greene: Architecture as Fine Art *(Salt Lake City, 1977) and* Greene and Greene: Furniture and Related Designs *(Salt Lake City, 1979).*

Zane Grey (Pearl Zane Gray, 1872?-1939). A former New York dentist with a degree from the University of Pennsylvania (1896), Grey became a top western writer and one of the world's greatest sportsfishermen. He first visited Catalina Island on his honeymoon in 1906 and returned frequently in pursuit of the most prized of all catches, the Pacific swordfish. He also had

business to attend to in Hollywood, which made over 100 films of his novels, including four versions of *Riders of the Purple Sage*, published in 1912. An astute bargainer, Grey leased the rights to his books for seven years only, thus reaping the windfall on remakes. He insisted on authenticity, often requiring that his films be made on location. In 1918 Grey moved his family into a three-story Spanish mansion in Altadena, also acquiring an Indian-style home for summers on Catalina. (It is now a hotel.) His great novels were written back East, but during the California years he turned out *Wanderer of the Wasteland* (1923) about Death Valley, and *Hoover Dam* (1923), based on personal research during construction of the giant dam. Financial pressure led to overproduction, with the result that books denied publication

during his lifetime were issued by his sons after his death. A loner in Hollywood, he was a conservative and an old-fashioned moralist, a handsome, taciturn figure with some resemblance to Randolph Scott, who starred in many of his remakes. According to his obituary in the *Los Angeles Times*, Grey's "red-blooded, clean stories" were responsible for elevating the cowboy from "the paperbacked dime novel into the $2 deluxe edition."

Frank Gruber, Zane Grey *(New York, 1970).*

Merv Griffin (Mervyn Edward Griffin, 1925-   ). In melting-pot California, an L.A.-born Harvard professor once suggested, personality is a more vital identity factor than ethnic background. Case in point is Griffin, a third-generation Irish Catholic Californian, born and raised in the country club suburbs south of San Francisco. His father and uncles were all tennis stars who used sports as their entré to society. (Uncle Elmer made **Ripley**'s *Believe It or Not* for winning a tennis match without a racket.) Even as a boy, Merv Griffin was always "on," producing backporch productions to entertain the children of Eldorado Street in San Mateo. He became a touring crooner with Freddy Martin's band, and tried to break into the movies without success. His most marketable commodity was neither his voice nor his dramatic ability but his personality. Rising through the jungle of TV game shows, he became a talk show host, purveying personality into the new mass-cult of celebrity. Griffin's style was wide-eyed and low-key, Mr. Nice Guy. When all else failed, he would croon one of his sentimental standards (''Tonight We Love,'' ''Lost in the Stars'') or stage a pro-am tennis tournament. Griffin formed his own production company and syndicated his own show, with a sideline in game shows and real estate. The latter included a Tudor mansion with a view of Pebble Beach, room at the top echelon of mainstream California.

Merv; An Autobiography (New York, 1980) is pure plastic.

D.W. Griffith (David Wark Lawrence Griffith, 1875-1948). The first great master of film started out as an itinerant actor, traveling to Hollywood for such bit parts as an Indian in the silent film version of **Helen Hunt Jackson**'s *Ramona*. His nom du cinéma: Granville Warwick.) He returned in 1913 at the head of his own repertory company of actors to make film history. *Birth of a Nation* (1915), Griffith's epic Civil War drama, was filmed during nine weeks on location in Southern California, with white actors in blackface as the slaves and the desert in cottonface as Southern fields. Premiered in L.A.'s Clune (later the Philharmonic) Auditorium as *The Clansman,* the film went on to earn a reputed $100 million on an investment of $100,000. Griffith, the descendant of impoverished Southern gentry who looked like one of the characters in his own films, proceeded to sink his share of the profits in

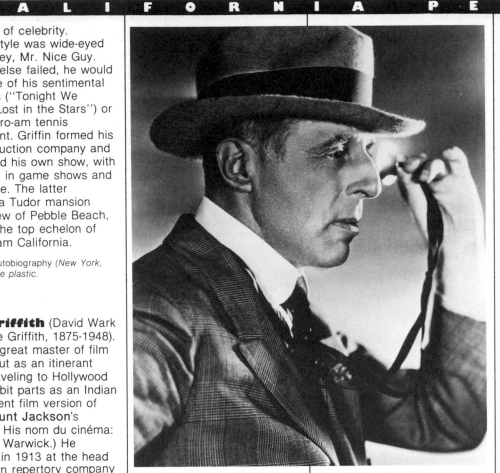

Intolerance (1916), for which he constructed a Babylonian city—the largest set ever built—on Sunset Boulevard. There were a few more epics, most of them filmed elsewhere, and Griffith went into the history books for writing the new idiom of film: the longshot, close-up, fade-in, and fade-out. But even before the advent of sound his exaggerated silent film style was already considered passé. For years he tried to promote a film on *Christ and Napoleon* as a sequel to *Intolerance*. Unemployed the last seventeen years of his life, he died alone and all but

forgotten, a resident of Hollywood's Knickerbocker Hotel.

See R.M. Henderson, D.W. Griffith, His Life and Work *(New York, 1972);* The Man Who Invented Hollywood; the Autobiography of D.W. Griffith *(Louisville, 1972);* Lillian Gish, The Movies, Mr. Griffith and Me *(Englewood Cliffs, NJ, 1969).*

Griffith Jenkins Griffith (1850-1919). Griffith, who gave most of his 4,000-acre Los Feliz ranch to the city of L.A. as a Christmas gift in 1896, was the son of a Welsh coal miner. He became wealthy through mining investments in the western states and moved

to Los Angeles in 1881, intending to farm his extensive new holdings. He also raised ostriches and established an ''Ostrich Farm Railway'' to bring sightseers from downtown. In addition to donating the land, he financed construction of an observatory and Greek theater at Griffith Park, the second largest municipal park in the U.S. Somewhat less well known is the fact the Griffith, described as short, vain, and overbearing (''a midget egomaniac''), served one year in San Quentin for the attempted murder of his wife at Santa Monica's Arcadia Hotel. (His lawyer **Earl Rogers** argued the first ''alcoholic insanity'' defense.) The reformed philanthropist emerged from prison (an objectionable personality still, **Adela Rogers St. Johns** remarked, but chastened, apparently sane, and still very rich) to write a study on rehabilitation and a short treatise on *Public Parks and Playgrounds* (1910).

Ferde Grofé

(Ferdinand Grofé, 1892-1972). A former violist with the Los Angeles Symphony, of which his uncle and grandfather were also members, Grofé composed orchestral suites evocative of the western landscape. Most popular of these was his *Grand Canyon Suite* the first piece of American music ever recorded by Toscanini. Late, Grofé's "clip-clop" theme (donkeys on the trail) gained commercial immortality by incorporation into a famous Philip Morris cigarette ad. He also wrote a *Death Valley Suite* and a *Hollywood Suite,* trying to explain America by music, he said. In addition to composing, he worked as an arranger for Paul Whiteman's band and as an occasional conductor at the Hollywood Bowl.

Abraham Livingston Gump

(1869-1947). Solomon Gump, the son of a cultured German merchant, arrived in San Francisco in 1863 to sell decor for the palatial homes of the nouveau riche silver and railroad barons. His son A.L. grew up in the business, surrounded by ornate bric-a-brac, marble mantels and cornices, and above all paintings, enormous canvases of Arab chieftains and Normandy landscapes. As a boy A.L. made deliveries and supervised installations in the **Stanford, Spreckles, C.P. Huntington,** and **Coleman** mansions. He learned to compensate for near-blindness by careful study, an uncanny sense of touch, and courtly manners. Taking over the family business and

rebuilding on Post Street after the 1906 earthquake, A.L. steered civic wealth and taste from garish gilt to the refinements of silver and jade. Combing ancient trade routes, his buyers brought back fabulous museum-quality orientalia, including the world's premier collection of jade. Gump's also established a custom design studio which revolutionized interior corporate decor. A trip to Gump's became *de rigueur* for visiting celebrities (the store advertised in the *New Yorker,* "leave New York at noon. . . shop here at 3 p.m.") and A. L. corresponded with customers like Franklin Roosevelt who were too busy to stop by. In the third generation, A.L. was succeeded by his son Richard, composer of a *Polynesian Symphony* and author of *Good Taste Costs No More* (1951), who ran the store for awhile by remote control from the South Seas. (Richard's brother Robert was married briefly to **Sally**

Stanford, who referred to the family business as a museum with cash registers.) In 1969, the Gump family sold out to Macmillan, Inc., the publishers.

Gump's Treasure Trade (New York, 1949) by Carol Wilson is the next thing to an authorized biography.

William McKendree Gwin

(1805-1885). Gwin set out for California in 1849 with the express intention of becoming the new state's first U.S. Senator. A Tennessean by birth and a Jacksonian Democrat by inheritance, educated as a doctor and a lawyer, he was elected to Congress in 1840 from Mississippi where he had a plantation. He arrived via Panama with a copy of Iowa's constitution which, along with his experience in Washington, gave him a leg up on other delegates to the state's Constitutional Convention. Just as he hoped, Gwin was elected by the legislature to the U.S. Senate and took his seat in 1850 as soon as California was admitted to the union. In his first term he introduced a battery of bills to provide a U.S. mint and customhouse, a federal judiciary, a coastal survey, lighthouses, Indian agents, and other necessities of statehood. One of his most significant efforts was the land act favoring new settlers over land grantees. Gwin was judged harshly by nineteenth-century historians. Bancroft described him as "avaricious, heartless, and devoted to his own aggrandizement." Royce considered him "intellectually the most admirable of all the unprincipled political

intriguers in the history of California." The main source of contention is his rivalry with **David Broderick,** also a carpetbagger and a Democrat but a member of what was jokingly called the "shovelry" while Gwin represented Southern "chivalry." When Gwin came up for reelection in 1855, the legislature deadlocked between him and Broderick. His U.S. Senate seat remained vacant for two years until he came to an arrangement with his rival. As set down in what **Gertrude Atherton** called "the scarlet letter," Broderick was to receive control of federal patronage in return for Gwin's reelection. (Thanks to his patronage monopoly, Gwin had appointed so many impoverished southerners to the San Francisco Customs Office that it became known as the Virginia Poor House.) With the outbreak of the Civil War, Gwin, sympathetic to secession but unwilling to actively support it, became a "wandering Jew." He spent some time in Paris and considered a mining and colonization scheme in Sonora, Mexico. (When rumor filtered back to San Francisco of Gwin's appointment as "Duke of Sonora," **Joshua "Emperor" Norton** warned his fellow citizens against accepting any such spurious titles of nobility.) In 1868, Gwin returned to San Francisco and invested his remaining assets in a neglected gold mine in Calaveras County which paid off handsomely. "California has all the elements that contribute to human happiness and prosperity," he wrote to a friend, although he considered Californians, just as Bancroft considered him, selfish and rapacious—"always striving for more."

Lately Thomas rehabilitates Gwin's reputation in Betwen Two Empires, The Life Story of California's First Senator *(Boston, 1969).*

Henry Huntley Haight

(1825-1878). The son of a New York judge, Haight graduated from Yale at nineteen and studied law before joining the Gold Rush to California in 1850. His extended family also came west, including his father (later a federal district court judge in Southern California), a banker uncle (after whom the San Francisco hippie street was later named), and seven siblings. A former free-soil Democrat, Haight switched his support to the Republicans on the eve of the Civil War but changed his mind with the abolition of slavery, which in his opinion exceeded the president's constitutional authority. Elected governor in 1866 as a Democrat on a platform appealing to anti-Negro and anti-Oriental prejudice, he was nonetheless considered a man of moral stature, "ardently devoted to the great principles." Haight opposed Southern Pacific landgrabbing and subsidization, but considered the railroad itself, completed during his administration, as "the crowning work of Anglo-Saxon civilization." Nonetheless, pondering the moral character of the future, he warned that "corruption and vice can travel on railways with as much ease as in stage coaches." Under Haight's leadership, the state legislature refused to ratify the Fourteenth and Fifteenth Amendments to the U.S. Constitution, rejecting the principles and practice of Reconstruction. The governor's stature was such that he was mentioned as a presidential candidate in 1868 although he was defeated for reelection as governor that year. Oddly, he died in what the papers described as a "Russian bath establishment." His grandson Raymond Haight was a progressive candidate for governor in 1934.

Harry Marston Haldeman

(1871-1930). Haldeman was a large, convivial pipe company executive from Chicago who founded a sort of Elks Club for the Los Angeles establishment. Formerly the "big bug" of a lively faction in the Chicago Athletic Club, he became "grand muscle" or leader of the Uplifters who split off from the L.A. Athletic Club in 1909. (The titles and humorous ditties were created by L. Frank Baum of

Oz fame.) The Uplifters met weekly, held annual outings, and concocted elaborate practical jokes and tableaux featuring men dressed as women. In 1920 they established their own country club in Santa Monica's Rustic Canyon, where Haldeman and other members also built private cabins. When the club began drifting away from mere good fellowship into polo and tennis, Haldeman resigned as president in 1925. By now he had more serious things on his mind: C.C. Julian's oil pools which promised fabulous wealth but instead ended in fraud and his indictment as an investor; and the Better America Foundation, founded by Haldeman to oppose Bolshevism, Socialism, the union shop, and the eight-hour work day. ("A masterpiece of flood, fear, and alarm," in the words of Morrow Mayo, the BAF saw "a Bolshevik lurking behind every palm tree.") He was also head of the local Red Cross, active in Republican politics, and a crony and business associate of Harry Chandler. Haldeman died dramatically on the witness stand while testifying in a civil suit. His grandson H.R. (Bob) Haldeman (1926-   ) inherited the Republican self-righteousness but none of his grandfather's congeniality. A former advertising executive, he joined the Nixon vice-presidential team as an advance man in 1956 and worked his way up to White House Chief of Staff in 1968. He was sentenced to two-and-a-half-to-eight years in prison for his involvement in the Watergate affair.

Betty Lou Young's Rustic Canyon and the Story of the Uplifters *(Santa Monica, 1975) covers the light side of family history.*

George Ellery Hale

(1868-1938). As an astrophysicist Hale was one of the first of the "high-pressure, heavy hardware, big-spending, team-organized scientific entrepreneurs," in the words of writer Hunter Dupree. He was also a lifelong neurasthenic who in later years found a new outlet for his energies in the politics of Pasadena culture. Born in Chicago, the son of an elevator tycoon, he enjoyed his own backyard observatory as a boy and at 21 invented the spectroheliograph, a major contribution to the astrophysical revolution he would lead. After graduating from MIT (1890), he promoted, built, and presided over the University of Chicago's Yerkes Observatory. Just after the turn of the century Hale came west for his health and settled in Pasadena where he built his second major observatory atop Mount Wilson. Colleagues recall the astrophysicist singing Schubert and Beethoven symphonies as he made frequent hikes up the 5,700-foot peak, dressed for his explorations in a three-piece suit. Thanks to support from wealthy benefactors whom he adroitly involved in his projects, Hale completed the Mount Wilson Observatory in 1904, first installing a 60-inch reflector donated by his father and later replacing it with a 100-inch reflector. (Plans for a 200-inch reflector were finally realized in 1948 at Mount Palomar, the advent of smog having diminished the prospects from Mount Wilson.) In 1908 Hale made an important professional breakthrough with the discovery of magnetic fields in sunspots. But in middle age he suffered two nervous breakdowns which severely curtailed his scientific activities. For the sake of his chronically agitated nerves, doctors confined him for a time to the backyard observatory at his South Pasadena home, from which he could monitor the activity on Mount Wilson only through

a telescope. Seeking new diversions, Hale became a member of the group that planned the Pasadena Civic Center with its handsome auditorium and library; he was founder and first president of the local music and art association; and he was instrumental in the transformation of Throop Polytechnic into Cal Tech in 1920. He also spent years coaching his neighbor **Henry Huntington**, a streetcar magnate like Yerkes of Chicago, on the final disposition of his art and book collections. Huntington rejected Hale's suggestion for a library on the model of the Parthenon, but he did appoint the astrophysicist a trustee of the library-museum endowed on his San Marino "ranch."

Helen Wright, Explorer of the Universe, A Biography of George Ellery Hale *(New York, 1966). Hale's own works include* Depths of the Universe *(New York, 1924) and* Beyond the Milky Way *(New York, 1926).*

Henry Wager Halleck

(1815-1872). Halleck is the type of personage who figures prominently in historical society journals. A graduate of West Point known as "Old Brains" for his scholarly stuffiness, he arrived in California in 1847 as an army lieutenant of engineers and was soon appointed secretary of state in the military government pending California's admission to statehood. Halleck played an important role in drafting the state constitution, although his proposal to extend the state's boundaries to the Rockies, to close forever the question of slavery in the West, did not find favor.

Having become knowledgeable on Mexican law, he became the leading land-claim lawyer of the day. The Californios who hired him had little evidence of title, made terrible witnesses in court, and neglected to pay even when they won their cases. But Halleck earned enough to acquire a 30,000-acre ranch in Marin County, to buy into the New Almadén quicksilver mine near Santa Clara, and to erect a four-story office complex in downtown San Francisco. The Montgomery block, or "Monkey Block" as it was affectionately known, became a landmark on the turn-of-the-century literary scene. It survived the 1906 earthquake, only to be razed for a parking lot in 1959 and

eventually replaced by **Pereira**'s Transamerica Pyramid. Halleck, meanwhile, returned to the army during the Civil War. Despite his priggish personality and a reputation for military ineptitude, he was promoted to general and then chief of staff by Abraham Lincoln. Idwal Jones, author of *Ark of Empire* (1951), a history of the Montgomery Block, describes him as a prolific writer on such subjects as refractory ores, pontoon-building, and the habits of pelicans.

Vincent Hallinan

(1896-   ). San Francisco's top radical lawyer was the son of a cable car conductor of Irish rebel descent. Physically as well as intellectually pugnacious, Hallinan won his parochial school boxing championship before going on to law school (USF, 1921). He started out in personal injury and criminal law, defending San Francisco public defender Frank Egan against murder charges in 1932, and madam **Sally Stanford** against harrassment in the line of her profession. He also worked to reform a jury system corrupted by powerful local interests. Although constantly described by the local press as "the millionaire mouthpiece," Hallinan remained first and last a maverick. He once challenged the Catholic Church to produce the precise geographical coordinates of heaven and hell. In 1949 he successfully defended labor leader **Harry Bridges** against renewed government deportation efforts, exposing a succession of perjured prosecution witnesses and winning a six-month contempt sentence for himself. Bridges was convicted, but his conviction was later overturned by the U.S. Supreme Court. Nominated as the U.S. presidential candidate of the Progressive Party in 1952 ("Win with Vin"), Hallinan sat out most of the campaign at McNeil Island Federal Prison serving his contempt sentence. As a prominent dissenter during the McCarthy era, he was a prime target for government harrasment, culminating in another prison term for income tax evasion. Unbowed, Hallinan and his sons, four of whom in succession won the middleweight intramural boxing championship at UC Berkeley, continued to fight the system. Terence ("Kayo") and Patrick ("Butch") Hallinan both became lawyers, defending antiwar activists during the Vietnam years. Their mother Vivian Moore Hallinan, a shrewd businesswoman who made some of the family millions in real estate, served as national coordinator of the Women's International League for Peace. Vincent Hallinan was appointed to referee the free food program demanded by the Symbionese Liberation Army after the kidnapping of heiress **Patty Hearst**, and his sons were briefly involved in her defense, until Hearst corporate interests dictated the retainer of legal big-shot F. Lee Bailey.

Hallinan wrote A Lion in Court *(New York, 1963). Vivian Hallinan wrote* My Wild Irish Rogues *(New York, 1952), chiefly an account of radical child-rearing.*

Armand Hammer

(1898-   ). His is another life story out of *Believe It or Not*. Born in New York, he managed to get through Columbia College and medical school while making a fortune as head of his father's pharmaceutical company. Sailing to the Soviet Union at the helm of his own "hospital ship" in 1921, he got Lenin's personal approval to establish a pencil factory, to run an asbestos concession, and to represent western trading concerns. He also amassed a treasure trove of art and antiques. Back in the U.S. during the 1930s Hammer arranged for the sale of this collection through such unorthodox outlets as department stores, including **Bullock**'s in Los Angeles; a few years later, he would use the same outlets to liquidate **W.R. Hearst**'s huge collection. Having become known as a man who could buy or sell anything, he made one fortune in the whiskey business and another in cattle-breeding. Retiring to California with his third wife in 1956, Hammer looked around for a tax shelter for his wěalth and came up with a decrepit oil company. With Hammer's backing, Occidental Oil would make some valuable finds in California, obtain two key Libyan concessions, and make another strike in the North Sea to become a multi-billion dollar conglomerate. Only in the Pacific Palisades was he frustrated—by environmentalists—from exploring a beachside site obtained in a controversial swap with Mayor **Sam Yorty** for some mountain acreage. There were other minor

aggravations—being investigated for illegal campaign contributions to **Nixon**, for violations of SEC regulations, plus IRS prosecution for inflated tax deductions on art contributions—but Hammer remained unbowed. Using art as his ticket into the establishment, he generously loaned out his new acquisitions, including a

Leonardo da Vinci notebook modestly renamed the "Codex Hammer." He donated $4 million to the Salk Institute, and on his death, the Los Angeles County Museum of Art will inherit his collection.

Bob Considine, biographer of "Believe It or Not" Ripley, wrote The Remarkable Life of Dr. Armand Hammer *(New York, 1975).*

Dashiell Hammett

(Samuel Dashiell Hammett, 1894-1961). On a dead-end

alley off Bush Street in San Francisco, a plaque marks the historic spot where the fictional Miles Archer was done wrong by Brigid O'Shaughnessy, archetype of the beautiful dangerous woman. The plaque is as much a tribute to hip civic boosterism as it is to Hammett who lived in San Francisco during the 1920s and made it the scene of his *Maltese Falcon* (1930), starring the original cynical detective Sam Spade. A lean former Pinkerton detective from Maryland, Hammett was disabled by tuberculosis in San Francisco and began to write detective fiction for the pulps, his only source of income for several years. He abandoned his wife and two daughters in San Francisco and left a trail of unpaid bills there when his novels first began to sell. In the 1930s he moved to Hollywood to collect munificent sums for film rights and screen treatments. But after *The Thin Man* (1932), which became a film and radio series, "the hard-boiled novelist grew soft," as biographer Richard Layman put it. He never wrote again except for a history of World War II in Alaska, where he had served in the army. Hammett's last years were plagued by alcoholism, by political persecution for the radical beliefs he shared with Lillian Hellman, his companion of 30 years, and by tax troubles, for he was as careless about paying his taxes as his debts. But in the world of detective fiction he was a brief shining light, the creator of Sam Spade and Nick Charles and of such criminalese as *shamus* and *gunsel*.

Richard Layman's Shadow Man *(New York, 1981) is little more than a paraphrase of Hammett's writings with footnotes from legal and medical records on the writer's troubles with VD and debt collectors. The first biography authorized by Lillian Hellman is being prepared for publication.*

Henry Hancock
(182?-1883) and **George Allen Hancock**
(1875-1965). A Harvard-educated lawyer who came around the Horn in 1849, Henry Hancock drew on his legal training and his exploring instincts as a U.S. deputy surveyor in Los Angeles. Completing the city's second survey in 1854, he predicted L.A. would one day become the Italy of America. On Hancock's 3,000-acre Rancho La Brea were found some tar pits containing extensive Pleistocene-era fossils, the first of which he donated to the Boston Society of Natural History. During a term in the state legislature (1851-1852) he met **Agoston Haraszthy**, whose daughter Ida he later married. A formidable woman who survived her husband by 30 years, Ida Hancock leased the Rancho La Brea out for oil exploration and built herself a Florentine villa at the corner of Wilshire and Vermont. Their son Allen grew up to be something of a Renaissance man California-style with interests in oil, banking, business, farming, music, and science and the purse to pursue them all. He played the cello well enough to join the Los Angeles Symphony Orchestra on occasion, and he acquired a series of yachts, *Velero I, II, III,* and *IV*, on which he hosted scientific expeditions to the Galapagos Islands and elsewhere. An explorer with a purpose, like his father, he could not take a simple pleasure cruise to Mexico without calling it a fact-finding trip. With oil nearing depletion, Allen Hancock gave the tar pits and remaining fossil specimens to the county in 1915, removed the oil derricks, and subdivided the ranch, parts of which would later be transformed into L.A.'s "Miracle Mile" plus Hancock Park, the elite residential area. Following the death of his son in the 1925 Santa Barbara earthquake and extortion threats against his daughter in 1926, he settled in Santa Maria, where his activities included scientific farming, a railroad, an ice company, an airfield, and a flying school which later became Hancock College. One of his primary beneficiaries was USC, which received a lucrative parcel of the ranch land (developed as Park La Brea), several ornate rooms from Ida Hancock's villa when it was demolished in 1939, the *Velero IV* "marine lab", and other tokens of an active and affluent life.

A Hancock family album of pictures and momentos was edited by Dewitt Meredith (San Jose, 1964). For a narrative, see Sam Clover's A Pioneer Heritage *(Los Angeles, 1932).*

Agoston Haraszthy
(1812-1869). A titled and affluent refugee from imperial Hungary, Haraszthy became a sheriff, politician, vineyardist, gold assayer, and *cause célèbre* in Gold-Rush California. He settled first in Wisconsin on coming to the U.S. in 1840 but, afflicted with asthma and wanderlust, brought his family overland to San Diego in 1849. Chosen sheriff of the county, he engaged in a little enterprise on the side, winning a contract to construct a new jail. When the walls proved too fragile, he got another contract to fortify them. Haraszthy was elected as a Jeffersonian Democrat to the state legislature in 1852 and moved to Northern California, serving for a time as Assayer at the U.S. Mint in San Francisco. (For a while, a group of Hungarians had a local monopoly on refining gold.) Confronted with a shortfall of $130,000, he successfully argued that the missing gold went up the flue "in smoke". He became a pioneer vineyardist in Sonoma County, where he built a Pompeian-style villa, Buena Vista, with a view equal to any in Europe. Using Chinese labor and redwood casks, he proved that wine could be successfully produced without irrigation. On the move again, he secured a commission from the state legislature to study European wine-making and a New York contract for the publication of his report. Setting out with his family, he toured the Continent as an economic diplomat from the fabled land of gold and desperadoes. California refused to reimburse the expenses of the trip, and many of Haraszthy's valuable cuttings were scattered and lost, but the diary survives. Possessed of great impulsive energy, Haraszthy literally lacked staying power. Having lost control of his Sonoma vineyards, he set off for the new frontier of Nicaragua to establish a sugar plantation. He disappeared into the

jungle one day and was never seen again. His sons Attila and Arpad, named after princes of Hungarian mythology, married the twin daughters of General **Mariano Vallejo** and remained to cultivate their patrimony in Sonoma.

Father of California Wine: Agoston Haraszthy (Santa Barbara, 1979), edited by Theodore Schoenman, is a reprint of the 1862 travel diary.

Asbury Harpending

(1839-1923). The central figure of the Great Diamond Hoax of 1872, Harpending was so crazy for adventure that he left home in Kentucky at age sixteen to join **William Walker**'s 1855 invasion of Nicaragua. Moving on to California, he claimed $60,000 in gold his first year, then went off to the mines of Mexico where he made a million dollars before reaching his majority. Back in San Francisco, he bought **William Ralston**'s Rincon Hill mansion and joined a Civil War plot to secede from the Union—a plot which failed, Harpending implies, only because the rebels could not take Nevada's Comstock out with them. Then the young millionaire became involved in some real estate roguery—a plan to push Montgomery Street south to the Bay which was foiled by the stubbornness of former Governor **Milton Latham**, whose house stood in the way, and by the "inexperienced, ignorant, venal and scandalously cheap" state assembly. Then came the Great Diamond Hoax. Ralston, who first heard about a fabulous find in the Rockies from some old miners, sent Harpending and

a mining expert to check it out. After arousing a speculative frenzy exceeding even that over the Comstock, the mine proved to be a phony, salted with cheap scraps from South Africa. Harpending claims that he, Ralston, and other principals absorbed all losses, but there is little substantiation for his account, which was serialized in the *San Francisco Bulletin* in 1913. (Some of the details are even contradicted by Harpending's own papers in the possession of the California Historical Society, according to scholar Glen Dawson.) During his last years in California, Harpending kept the stars and stripes flying over his home, which neighbors thought odd for a former Confederate rebel.

Harpending's The Great Diamond Hoax *(1913) was republished by the University of Oklahoma in Norman, 1958.*

Job Harriman

(1861-1925). Harriman was a Marxist lawyer, described by **Aldous Huxley** as resembling a revivalist or Shakespearean actor, who nearly became mayor of Los Angeles. It was 1911, and the one-time Socialist candidate for state governor (1898) and for U.S. vice president (1900) started out on an "anti-aqueduct" platform, condemning the theft of water from the Owens Valley for the benefit of L.A. real estate speculators. As a member of the **McNamara** brothers defense team, he found his prospects tied to public opinion about the accused dynamiters of the *Los Angeles Times*. "McNamaras Not Guilty! Vote for Harriman!" his campaign

literature urged. Harriman won the mayoral primary handily to the great alarm of the *Times*, which warned that eastern financiers would withdraw their investments and hordes of aliens would descend upon a "red" L.A. But when the McNamaras changed their plea to guilty on the eve of the election, Harriman was defeated. In 1914 he went into the desert wilderness to create a more perfect community, the cooperative colony of Llano del Rio in the Antelope Valley, which broke up after three years of factionalism and mismanagement. Harriman tried another unsuccessful utopian experiment, New Llano in Louisiana, before returning to Los Angeles, where he died.

For an account of the Llano del Rio experiment, see California's Utopian Colonies *(San Marino, 1953; New Haven, CT, 1966) by Robert Hine.*

Thomas Lake Harris

(1823-1906). In 1875, guided by an inner vision of great trees and vast oceans, Harris moved his Brotherhood of New Life from upstate New

York to a new Eden in the West. Located two miles north of Santa Rosa, Fountain Grove was variously considered to be propitious for gold-mining, wine-making, and for the brotherhood's theo-socialistic sexual mysticism. The English-born Harris was a "theological vagabond," a former Swedenborgian who broke away to found his own total community based on a spartan lifestyle, communication with the dead, and a form of sexual hocus-pocus featuring bridal play with angels. Eventually encompassing 700 acres, Fountain Grove showed early promise as a vineyard. (The sect considered wine "a vehicle of the quickening influence.") But the colony was soon rocked by internal schism and public scandal. Harris's most eminent devotees, a member of the British Parliament and his titled mother, broke away and filed suit for the return of funds donated to the

community. And in 1891 a defector named Alzire Chevaillier began to give lectures on "Harricism: Secrets of the Sonoma Eden Unveiled," charging the "pivotal man" with autocracy and sexual license. Harris and most of his followers decamped in 1892, leaving Fountain Grove to remaining members of the sect. The vineyards and Harris's house, described by writer Idwal Jones as originally resembling "a mansion Louisa May Alcott might have lived in," eventually fell into disuse, another of God's ghost towns.

See A Prophet and a Pilgrim *(New York, 1942) by Herbert Schneider and George Lawton, and* California's Utopian Colonies *(San Marino, 1953, New Haven, 1966) by Robert Hine.*

William S[urrey] Hart

(1874-1946) He was an itinerant stage actor who at age 40 became Hollywood's first cowboy film star. As a child in the Midwest he had learned to speak conversational Sioux or so he claimed, a handy bit of business when it came to convincing producer **Tom Ince** to give him his first Western film role—never mind that this was the *silent* film era. Concerned with authenticity, Hart set out to correct the prevailing conception of the cowboy as a cross between a Wisconsin woodchopper and a Gloucester fisherman. His Rio Jim was a good badman, a knight of woeful countenance and solemn chivalry, with a scene-stealing horse named Fritz. Writer and director as well as star, he did his own stunts and scouted locations to boot: Topanga passed for the Grand Canyon, Playa del

Rey for desert sands, and Victorville for Dodge City. Hart's national popularity was so great that he was chosen along with Chaplin, **Pickford**, and Fairbanks to tour the U.S. promoting Liberty Bonds during World War I. In Hollywood, however, he was known for the tenacity of his grip on a nickel and for his sanctimoniousness, parodied by Buster Keaton in *The Frozen North* (1922). Hart retired to his 200-acre ranch near Newhall to write nostalgic books about the old West and an autobiography, *My Life, East and West* (1929). When the nearby Saint Francis Dam collapsed in

1927, Sheriff **Gene Biscailuz** was startled to be offered hospitality by a rancher whose face seemed awfully familiar. A lone wolf to the end, Hart left his ranch to L.A. County. His relatives contested the will and lost, but litigation shrank the bequest in half and delayed opening of the ranch to the public for a decade.

Bret Harte (Francis Brett

Hart, 1836-1902). The first California writer to achieve national recognition, Harte created the stereotype of the westerner as sentimental swaggerer. He was born and raised in genteel poverty in

New York, coming west in 1854 when his widowed mother remarried. After several years of wandering as a teacher, printer, and casual laborer, he became a protégé of Jessie Benton **Frémont** who got him a sinecure at the U.S. Mint in San Francisco. This supported him for seven years while he was writing his first Dickensian stories of frontier life featuring such deathless characters as the rugged miner, the "heathen Chinee," and the harlot with a heart of gold. In 1868 Harte became editor of the new *Overland Monthly*, which published his first and best stories: "The Luck of Roaring Camp," "The Outcasts of Poker Flat," etc. These proved so popular that he was offered an appointment as Professor of Recent Literature at the University of California at Berkeley. Harte declined, believing he had better cash in on his new

celebrity status. Returning east in 1871 as California's first man of letters, he was lionized by literary society in Boston and New York. Although he thought of himself basically as an easterner, those who witnessed him delivering a lecture at Harvard wearing green gloves had no doubt that this was a creature from the outer spaces of the West. Harte's literary style, too, was strictly regional and did not lend itself to a change in venue. He spent his last quarter century in Europe, mining an increasingly tired vein of Californiana to support his expensive lifestyle. Contemporary **Josiah Royce** accused him of romanticizing predatory violence, while **Mark Twain** considered him a literary hypocrite, coldly "pumping up the tear of sensibility," but they remain a distinct minority.

Richard O'Connor, Bret Harte: A Biography *(Boston, 1966).*

Burnette Haskell

(1857-1907). In 1885 a group of radicals filed land claims to establish a utopian community on the fringes of what is now Sequoia National Park. They were a motley crew, as historian Robert Hine points out—dress-reformers, phonetic spelling advocates, devote's of uncooked food— under the leadership of Haskell, himself a problematic figure. Born of a pioneer family, he attended the University of California but did not graduate, was admitted to the bar but did not practice law. Given a labor organ to publish, he became an anarcho-socialist and founded the International

Workingmen's Association, a secretive group advocating the use of dynamite. (One recommended target: the Hall of Records, in order to confuse land titles.) It always seemed possible that Haskell was an agent provocateur, for he would egg others on, then drop out. He was argumentative and unreliable, erratic and unstable—a genius, his friends claimed. The utopian Kaweah Colony (named for a nearby river) was itself founded on a characteristic misapprehension. Although the law prohibited commercial timber operations, the idealistic colonists figured they could still harvest timber cooperatively. Up to 300 of them at a time found refuge at Kaweah from the "cold, competitive world." Pictures from the colony show tiny people against a background of giant trees, which they named after radical heroes. The end of Kaweah came in 1890 when Congress decreed the establishment of the national park, refusing to compensate the colony even for such improvements as their road, long the only access to the area. Kaweah's Karl Marx Tree was renamed for General Sherman, and Haskell spent his last years poor and friendless.

See Robert Hine, California's Utopian Colonies *(San Narino, 1953; New Haven, CT 1966).*

Charles Mallory Hatfield (1876-1958).

Charles and his brother Paul, midwestern Quakers transplanted to Southern California in boyhood, became pioneers in the pseudo-science of pluviculture— rainmaking. They studied

weather charts and employed evaporating tanks filled with secret chemicals to assist nature in releasing moisture. Known throughout the West as the Rainmaker, Charles Hatfield actually and repeatedly produced record rainfalls as contracted. In Los Angeles in 1903 he called forth one inch of rain in five days; in 1905 he took credit for eighteen inches in four months. He had a standing contract in the San Joaquin Valley for several years and filled a reservoir in Hemet in 1912. In 1916, however, Hatfield called down a host of troubles on San Diego—two dams overflowed and a third went out altogether—by producing too much rain. (His magic was too powerful to control, some thought.) This incident plus the development of statewide aqueducts and irrigation systems put Hatfield's career into eclipse, but his legend survived to inspire the play *The Rainmaker,* with a 1956 film version starring Burt Lancaster as Hatfield. (A later

musical, *110 in the Shade,* was based on the play). The real rainmaker, who lived to the age of 82, carried his secrets to the grave, although he said of modern experiments with dry ice, "They'll make it."

Samuel Ichiyě Hayakawa (1906-   ).

Nothing is quite as it seems, Hayakawa proved in state education and politics. He moved to California in 1955, a Canadian-born professor of Japanese descent, and author of *Language in Thought and Action*, an improbable book-of-the-month-club bestseller. During thirteen years of teaching at San Francisco State College, students and colleagues came to question his scholarly credentials, writing him off as more of a promoter or exhibitionist than an original thinker. Off-campus, he was a leader of the Anti-Digit Dialing League, which opposed the replacement of prefixes with numbers. In 1968, in the

midst of a strike led by militant black students, Governor **Ronald Reagan** appointed Hayakawa president of the school, a position which he discharged with great relish and some originality. A day of student-police confrontation was his most exciting experience since his first roller-coaster ride, he told the press, for whom he turned literal somersaults during interviews in his office. The strike dragged on for over six months, and the black students won many of their demands, but Hayakawa emerged as the big winner. A comical little figure in his plaid tam-o-shanter, he made national headlines for standing up to the students, on one occasion personally pulling the plug on their amplifying system. Now a public figure, he wrote a syndicated weekly column and used his fan mail as the basis for a political fund-raising operation. In 1976 Hayakawa ran as a Republican to defeat an incumbent and enter the U.S. Senate as a seventy-year-old freshman with an idiosyncratic opinion on every issue. Appointed to the Senate Foreign Relations Committee, he announced that we "stole the Panama Canal fair and square," also suggesting that bribery might be good for international trade. In domestic affairs, he caused a flap with his statement that the poor don't need gas. Falling asleep in the Senate and tap-dancing in the corridors, Hayakawa ranked in Washington as a political fluke from beyond the fringe.

Dikran Karagueuzian, Blow it Up! The Black Student Revolt at San Francisco State and the Emergence of Dr. Hayakawa *(Boston, 1971), reads like a student effort.*

Tom Hayden (Thomas Emmett Hayden, 1940-   ). Hayden and his actress wife Jane Fonda (1937-   ) represent the ultimate in radical chic in latter-day California. A former student activist from Detroit, Hayden was an early SDS leader and community organizer before his indictment as one of the Chicago 7, charged with conspiracy for demonstrating against the Vietnam war at the 1968 Democratic convention. He moved west in 1970 to join the Red Family, a Berkeley commune, but was drummed out as a publicity-mongering political opportunist. He met Fonda in 1971 and they collaborated on a mixed-media antiwar presentation, a fusion of leftist ideology and psychodrama. Their alliance and marriage in 1973 gave new life to both their careers. Fonda, who was considered practically untouchable by the film industry for her politics during the Vietnam years, found new acceptance in *Julia* (1977) and *The China Syndrome* (1979). Hayden put on a pinstriped suit and joined the political mainstream as a candidate in the 1976 Democratic U.S. senatorial primary. He lost but emerged from the campaign with an organization called Campaign for Economic Democracy (CED), which claimed a membership of 8,000 by 1980. CED focused on lifestyle rather than social issues, stressed ecology rather than morality, and appealed to an upwardly mobile, celebrity-conscious constituency in the affluent beachside community of Santa Monica where the Haydens maintained a house. There was also a solar-powered summer camp near Santa Barbara, where they had a 120-acre ranch. Although Governor **Jerry Brown** gave CED token political recognition, Hayden and Fonda remained political outsiders, their ambitions a source of malicious amusement to the California establishment. In 1982 Hayden scaled down his ambitions and won a state assembly seat.

Will Hays (William Harrison Hays, 1879-1954). He was hired in 1922 after the **Fatty Arbuckle** scandal to help the movie industry improve its image, just as baseball acquired a judge as commissioner after the 1919 World Series fix. A consummate politician, his primary qualification for the job was that he had gotten Harding elected president in 1920, and that as U.S. Postmaster General (1921-1922) he had been responsible for fighting "smut" in the mails. (He had also "borrowed" $260,000 from the oil industry but managed to ride out the Teapot Dome scandals.) As head of the Motion Picture Producers and Distributors of America, Inc. (MPPDA) at a princely salary of $100,000, Hays proceeded to clean up the movie industry, by blacklisting and voluntary censorship. (Constitutionally, film was then considered a business, not a communications medium

entitled to First Amendment protection.) Rulings by the Hays Office represent the triumph of philistinism. **Disney** was required to remove the udders from animated cows and to drape garlands around the necks of female centaurs. **Selznick** reportedly argued for four hours for approval to retain one of the most famous lines in film history: "Frankly, my dear, I don't give a damn." Gloria Swanson reported in her memoirs that they used to film two versions of every screen kiss, one ten seconds maximum to meet Hays Office rules, and a longer version for European distribution. From his base in New York, Hays made regular visits to the front lines, beginning with an all-industry rally at the unfinished Hollywood Bowl in 1922. Eventually he built a ranch in Hidden Valley, where **C.B. DeMille**, whose religious films he heartily approved, was a neighbor. But Hays's territory was really the world. He negotiated international trade agreements, cultivated the approval of the Vatican League of Decency, and handled a Mexican government protest over the movie image of Mexicans as *banditos*. Closer to home, he placated the Yellow Cab Company when it complained that too many bad guys were escaping by taxi, and Huey Long, who established state censorship in Louisiana in reprisal against an unflattering newsreel. The Hays Office was superceded in 1940 by the Breen Office.

Hay's Memoirs *(Garden City, NY, 1955) were published posthumously.*

Edith Head (1898?-1981). Head grew up in western mining camps and earned an M.A. in French from Stanford. Hired to teach at the Hollywood School for Girls, she bluffed her way into a job as a junior designer at Paramount, then a Barnum and Bailey world where elephants were costumed in tasseled headdresses and an actress's wardrobe included everything down to handmade lingerie. The challenge of costume designing is to convey character via costume without crossing the fine line into clumsy disguise, Head learned. In Hollywood, this complicated by the needs and demands of image-conscious supernovas. Mae West wore her dresses so tight that she couldn't sit down, Head recalled in her memoirs, and had to rest against a reclining board between takes; Sophia Loren absolutely refused to wear blue jeans; Shirley Booth always scrambled the pieces of her studio wardrobe to create her own frumpiness; and Anna Magnani was anxious to find an appropriately earthy underslip for *The Rose Tattoo*. In 1945 Head became a regular on Art Linkletter's radio advice program, which later moved over to TV, sharing her expertise on how to dress in character and on clothing as therapy. For herself, she maintained the same distinctive persona through three generations in Hollywood—that of a petite, conservatively tailored woman in bangs and prescription sunglasses. Head won eight Oscars for costume design.

Head wrote The Dress Doctor *(Boston, 1959) with J.K. Ardmore.*

George Hearst

(1820?-1891) and **Phoebe Apperson Hearst** (1842-1919). A legend in American mining, Hearst found, by a combination of instinct and luck, three of the country's most fabled mines: the Ontario in Utah (1872), the Homestake in South Dakota (1875), and the Anaconda in Montana (1881). Born in Missouri, he joined the Gold Rush to California and got in at the beginning of the Comstock strike. After his marriage in 1862 to a girl back home, the petite and refined Miss Apperson, he made San Francisco the base of his extensive operations ranging throughout the West and Mexico. A crude but kindly character, almost illiterate and completely lacking in affectation, George Hearst nonetheless nourished political ambitions. In 1886 he was appointed to fill a vacancy in the U.S. Senate, and the following year spent a small fortune through Boss **Buckley**'s Democratic machine to win election to the seat which he held until his death, "the silent man of the Senate." Despite his great wealth, Hearst enjoyed a reputation as a man of the people. "Taking his wealth from the hills," says the engraved legend on the Hearst Mining Building at UC Berkeley, "he filched from no man's store and lessened no man's opportunity." His estate, valued at $18 million and rapidly appreciating, included two items vital to the future of his only child, **William Randolph Hearst**: the *San Francisco Examiner*, and a 48,000-acre ranch at San Simeon. Immediate control of the estate passed to Phoebe Hearst, who shared her husband's reluctance to trust their supremely overindulged son and only heir. Returning home to California after the years in Washington, she made her base at the family ranch in Pleasanton but also kept a house near the university in Berkeley, over which she hovered as fairy godmother. In addition to the mining building bequeathed in her husband's memory, she underwrote the university's architectural master plan and donated Hearst Hall, a baronial gymnasium and social center for women students designed by Bernard

Maybeck. She also endowed scholarships, built the university museum to house artifacts from her extensive travels, and hosted an annual picnic in Pleasanton for the graduating class. It was estimated after her death that she gave away $21 million to educational and other causes. Her greatest single charity was probably her son, to whom she "loaned" $10 million during her lifetime and left an additional $11 million.

W.R. Hearst had Cora and Fremont Older write the official biography of his father, George Hearst, California Pioneer (San Francisco 1933; Los Angeles, 1966) and commissioned sob sister Annie Laurie to do the same for his mother, The Life and Personality of Phoebe Apperson Hearst (San Francisco, 1928). Both books leave much to be desired, as does The Hearsts, Family and Empire (New York, 1981) by Lindsay Chaney and Michael Cieply.

Patricia Campbell Hearst (1954-   ).

She grew up as a veritable California princess, enjoying the benefits and privileges of a granddaughter of **W.R. Hearst**. Home was a spacious gracious mansion in Hillsborough, with summers and weekends riding Arabian horses around her grandfather's enchanted castle at San Simeon. She was willful enough to claim exemption from certain rites of class, refusing to play the role of debutante, and aggressive enough to pursue an affair with a young teacher at her exclusive Hillsborough finishing school housed in a former **Crocker** mansion. Hearst was living in Berkeley with her fiancé in February 1974 when she was kidnapped by an erratic group of leftists called the Symbionese Liberation Army, whose first act had been the murder of a popular black school superintendent in Oakland. For two months the SLA kept Hearst in a closet, calling her Marie Antoinette for her blithe ignorance of political reality. By a gradual process of "brainwashing," the spoiled young princess was transformed into an urban guerrilla queen. Hearst preferred to think of herself as a prisoner of war, a slave, as she went along with the SLA, helped them rob a bank owned by her best friend's father, and made no effort to escape or even to contact family or friends. Yet she retained some sense of her former identity. In her memoir, written after the resumption of her old lifestyle, she described herself as mortified at the photo of herself as Tanya the bankrobber and humiliated at hearing her tape recordings broadcast to the world. She did what she had to in order to survive, she claimed, including bank robbery—but stubbornly refused to go with SLA members to see *Citizen Kane*, the fictionalized film about her grandfather. Captured after nearly two years underground, Patty Hearst raised her fist in defiance, then was brought to trial for robbery. One damning detail was the Olmec figurine of a monkey which she kept, the prosecution argued, to recall her love for fallen guerrilla colleague Cujo. She couldn't stand Cujo, Hearst claimed, and only kept the piece because "all my life I have been surrounded by art." (Shana Alexander had the wit to compare this to one of the most famous arias in grand opera, Tosca's "Vissi d'arte"—I lived for art.) The Olmec relic was a phony, it turned out, and the jury decided Hearst was, too. (She didn't have a brain to wash, cynics said.) Convicted of bank robbery, she was sentenced to seven years, of which she served two at a Pleasanton correctional institution near her grandmother's old estate. Collaborating now with the feds to convict her fellow guerrillas, she signaled her contempt for them by arriving in court dressed to the hilt, including bright red fingernail polish. Would the princess live happily ever after her release in 1979? She married her bodyguard, resumed a life of suburban affluence, and made the cover of *People* magazine when her first child was born.

Shana Alexander, Anyone's Daughter, The Times and Trials of Patty Hearst (New York, 1979); Patty Hearst, Every Secret Thing (Garden City, NY, 1982).

Phoebe Apperson Hearst. *See* George Hearst.

William Randolph Hearst (1863-1951).

The largest American publishing empire of the first half of the twentieth century was founded by a second-generation Californian, the extraordinary Hearst. He grew up in San Francisco undisciplined and totally indulged, going off on art-buying sprees to Europe with his mother while his father was absorbed in mining interests. Young Willie spent a miserable three semesters at a New England prep school, hating the "weak, pretty scenery" and the whole prep ethos, and was expelled from Harvard during

his junior year for a prank. Back home, he persuaded his father to give him the moribund *S.F. Examiner* in 1887. A maverick to custom and class, Hearst proceeded to transform the *Examiner* into the leading western vehicle of "yellow journalism" with screaming headlines and outrageous stories calculated to entertain rather than to inform. For all his wealth, he was also a champion of the underdog and foe of the Southern Pacific. Having conquered San Francisco journalism, he set out to do the same in New York with the purchase of the *Journal* in 1895. For the next 25 years Hearst made New York the base of his campaign to become president of the U.S., manipulating his growing publishing empire (thirteen newspapers and six magazines by World War I) in whatever ruthless, truthless manner might promote circulation and ambition. He was elected to Congress as a Democrat from New York in 1902 but narrowly lost his anti-Tammany campaign for mayor of New York City in 1905 and failed to win election as state governor in 1906. During the next generation he would haunt the corridors of every Democratic presidential nominating convention, powerful enough to deny the nomination to others but never strong enough to grasp it for himself. Accustomed to the immediate gratification of his every wish (his father once said, "When he wants cake, he wants cake, and he wants it now"), Hearst turned from the frustration of his political ambitions to

conspicuous consumption on a gargantuan scale. Leaving his wife and five sons in New York, he returned home to California after World War I with his mistress, former showgirl **Marion Davies**, for whom he established a movie production company and built a Santa Monica beach castle (actually, five connecting colonial mansions) with 110 rooms and 37 fireplaces. Hearst's most grandiose creation was of course the castle at San Simeon, an architectural orgy showcasing his $50 million art collection. The San Simeon "ranch," which also possessed the largest private animal collection in the U.S., was the scene of baronial house parties during the interwar period. Guests included world leaders and ranking Hollywood stars, but the most interesting person there was always the host. A tall, shy man, given to screaming ties and green suits which looked as if they had been sent out for rumpling, Hearst moved "with the stately grace of a circus elephant," writer **Anita Loos** remarked, exercising a gently persuasive tyranny over all about him. During summers when it got too hot at San Simeon, the house party might adjourn to Wyntoon, the family castle in Northern California which Hearst had rebuilt as a Bavarian village with wall murals of Miss Davies as Cinderella, Goldilocks, and Snow White. With age, the publisher became more conservative. The former champion of the underdog adamantly opposed **Upton Sinclair**'s EPIC (End Poverty in California) campaign for

governor in 1934, and complained loudly of confiscatory state taxes, although his compulsive spending continued unabated during the Depression. But by 1937 the Hearst publishing empire (22 dailies and nine magazines at its peak) was in such dire straits that the chief had to be removed from financial control, put on a strict allowance, and required to sell off some of his vast art collection. Hearst nonetheless continued to exert his influence editorially; an indelible image has come down of him in the massive library at San Simeon, totally absorbed, turning the pages of his newspapers with his feet. Wherever he happened to be, his nearest editor would be under the gun, sure to receive late night calls from the chief. In his startling soprano voice ("like the fragrance of violets made audible," **Ambrose Bierce** said), Hearst would criticize a story or perhaps mobilize the staff to gratify his latest whim, which might be for rhubarb and soda or for some elusive object like trivets for his Halloween party witches' cauldron.

Hearst inspired a classic film, Citizen Kane, *(1941) and an amusing novel by Aldous Huxley,* After Many a Summer Dies the Swan *(1939). His real life, however, was infinitely more complex and fascinating than any fictional recreation. W. A. Swanberg, whose* Citizen Hearst *(New York, 1961) is one of the great biographies, describes his subject as a Jekyll and Hyde figure, great and contemptible, puritan and libertine, true and false, democrat and king.*

Francis Joseph Heney

(1859-1937). Despite a prim, bespectacled appearance, Heney, the muckraking prosecutor of the San

Francisco graft trials, was a lawyer in the tradition of the Wild West. He grew up in the tough working-class neighborhood "south of the slot" in San Francisco, compensating for his small size by sheer pugnacity. After working and saving to enter the University of California, he was expelled for fighting, although he managed to finish his law studies at Hastings and won admission to the bar in 1883. Heney practiced law in Arizona, where he shot and killed a man in self-defense. In 1903 the U.S. Justice Department appointed him to a land fraud investigation in Oregon, where in collaboration with sleuth **William Burns** he succeeded in convicting a U.S. Senator. Recruited by crusading newspaper editor **Fremont Older** to clean up municipal graft in San Francisco, Heney and Burns spent five years trying to nail down the culprits, from Boss **Abe Ruef** and Mayor **Eugene Schmitz** to local leaders of society and finance. Public feeling ran high during the trials. Heney was caricatured in the **Hearst** press as the cross-eyed, slobbering, cap-wearing "Beany" in the Mutt and Jeff cartoon. (To express solidarity, Berkeley students began wearing "beany" caps.) Shot through the head in 1908 by a disgruntled former juror, Heney miraculously survived and even returned to the courtroom. But he was unable to get the convictions he sought, and the graft indictments were finally allowed to lapse. Heney ran for D.A. of San Francisco in 1909, for U.S. Senator in 1914, and for governor in 1918, all without success. Unable to sustain a private practice in San Francisco where feeling still ran high against him, and too much of a loner to join a law firm, he moved to L.A. where he became a Superior Court judge in 1931.

Eugene Woldemar Hilgard

(1833-1916). To many early settlers, the alkali-encrusted valley and desert lands of California looked as if some wrathful god had sowed the earth with salt so that nothing would grow. The first to understand and unlock its great fertility was a German-born agricultural scientist who joined the University of California, Berkeley faculty in 1875. After earning his Ph.D. at Heidelberg, Hilgard had taught for twenty years in the American South. Middle-aged in 1875, an embittered southern secessionist with tendencies to Catholic spiritualism, he found himself rejuvenated by the challenge of the California environment. He first established an agricultural station on the UCB campus, plowing plots at various levels to test moisture conservation; later he created a chain of such stations throughout the state. He had to overcome the opposition of California's farmers, who opposed the expansion of the old agricultural school; they sent their sons to a university, if at all, to become lawyers. Hilgard's soil analysis of the state for the 1880 U.S. census proved a bonanza for agriculture in the entire Southwest. Historically, the professor pointed out, early civilizations arose in arid regions rather than rain forests because it is easier to irrigate than to deforest. To reclaim alkali lands, he suggested applying gypsum as an antidote, cropping with salt-absorbing plants, and underdraining, a combination of methods successfully used to reclaim a large portion of the earth's surface. Hilgard was also a prophet before his time with respect to California viticulture. His own 30-acre vineyard near San Jose eventually fell victim to phylloxera, but once that scourge was surmounted the way was clear to a major state agribusiness.

Hans Jenny, E.W. Hilgard and the Birth of Modern Soil Science *(Pisa, Italy, 1961).*

David Hockney

(1937-   ). An expatriate English artist with an ironic appreciation of the exotic, Hockney enshrined Los Angeles as swimming-pool suburbia in the annals of modern art. He first came to California in 1963, a bleached blond with owlish glasses, drawn by the climate of homosexual hedonism. In his first paintings he explored the juxtaposition of palm trees against glaring facades highlighted by mesmeric street signs ("Wilshire," "Melrose") written in tropical esperanto. Introduced into the homes of art collectors, Hockney found a sameness of plush carpets, striped paintings, and primitive sculpture. The showers and swimming pools of Los Angeles, however, fascinated him, suggesting variations on the bather as a traditional subject of art. Absorbed by the quality of moving water itself, Hockney sometimes left out the bather altogether, creating in *The Splash* (1966) and *A Bigger Splash* (1967) a strong statement about the elemental starkness of L.A. life. Between trips to New York and Europe, he made his home in Southern California. "All the painters of joy," he once said, "move to the south. Matisse didn't live in Paris; he lived in Nice."

David Hockney by David Hockney *(New York, 1977);* David Hockney *by Marco Livingstone (New York, 1981).*

Eric Hoffer

(1902-   ). He would have been an original, a loner, wherever he lived, but he chose California because he heard it was a good place for the poor. The only child of a German couple who emigrated to New York City, he went blind at age seven and remained so, completely unschooled, for ten years. When he was twenty he bought a bus ticket for Los Angeles and rented a cheap room near the public library, supporting himself by odd jobs while he read voraciously to make up for lost time. During the 1930s he worked as a migrant farm laborer, collecting cards from smalltown libraries all over the state. (Later in life, whenever he got restless, Hoffer would get on a bus with $5, descend at some new town, and survive.) Rejected by the U.S. Army in 1941, he took the hardest job he could find—dockwork on the San Francisco waterfront. It was like "being on the bum in one place," he recalled; he could earn enough in a weekend to read for the rest of the week. For seventeen years he lived in a rented room on McAllister Street, reading and distilling the essence of his reading into aphorisms. With the publication in 1951 of *The True Believer*, a treatise on the psychology of mass movements, Hoffer became a working-class celebrity. He was invited to join the UC

Berkeley faculty as a "senior research political scientist" but found himself out of sympathy with student protestors who wanted to make history rather than learn it. Retiring gradually, he spent several hours a day walking the streets of San Francisco, a self-appointed "building inspector" and observer of the human condition. There are those who consider Hoffer about as profound a philosopher as **McKuen** is a poet, but he is, nonetheless, unique.

Eric Hoffer, An American Odyssey *by Calvin Tomkins (New York, 1968).*

Rodney Hooper. *See* Rod McKuen.

Herbert Clark Hoover (1874-1964). The formative experience of Hoover's life, from which all else followed, was his education at Stanford University. When he arrived in 1891 to enroll in the "pioneer" freshman class, the new tuition-free school was just emerging from the wheatfields of the Santa Clara Valley. Working his way through school, the Iowa-born

orphan of Quaker ancestry established a laundry and a newspaper delivery service which he subcontracted to others. He was also chosen junior class treasurer and financial manager of the athletic association, personally taking in $30,000 for the first Big Game between Stanford and Cal. Opposed to the smug snobbery of fraternities, Hoover and his friends became known as "Barbs," short for barbarians, confident of their ability to succeed by virtue of rugged individualism

and personal enterprise. Graduating in 1895 as a mining engineer, Hoover became an international consultant, widely sought after for his business and organizational skills. Even during the years abroad he and his wife—Lou Henry, a Stanford geology student whom he married at the Carmel Mission—maintained a house near their alma mater and close contact with schoolmates and professors. Hoover became a trustee of the university (his brother Theodore served as dean of

the Engineering School), and nominated friend and fellow Barb **Ray Lyman Wilbur** for president of Stanford (1917-1943). Whatever the problem, the solution involved Stanford. During World War I Hoover drafted several professors and alumni, including journalist Will Irwin, to man the Belgian Relief Commission. Having assembled a huge collection of wartime documents, "fugitive literature" usually lost to history, he turned it over to Stanford for a Hoover Library on War, Revolution, and Peace. On election day in 1928 and again in 1932, he returned "home" to Stanford to vote. As U.S. president (1929-1933) Hoover surrounded himself with school cronies, fellow believers in individual enterprise, including Ray Wilbur who took a four-year leave of absence as university president to serve as Secretary of the Interior. The Hoover administration's collective failure to come to terms with the Depression may be attributed in part to the Stanford ethos of Social Darwinism and laissez faire economics.

The Memoirs of Herbert Hoover; Years of Adventure (1874-1920) *(New York, 1951).*

Mark Hopkins (1813-1878). His name would be associated by future generations with an art institute and a world-famous hotel, but Mark Hopkins was anything but a cosmopolite. He was 35 when he joined the Gold Rush—old by California standards and by outlook as well. Tall, thin, and schoolmasterish, he was thrifty and prudent, a vegetarian who grew his own turnips and cabbage. By an accident of economic life he went into business in Sacramento in 1856 with **Collis Huntington**, mastermind of the Southern Pacific Raiload. The least active of the Big Four, Hopkins was little more than a glorified accountant. When the completion of the railroad made him a millionaire many times over, his wife persuaded him to abandon his lifetime frugality and build a Nob Hill mansion that looked like a medieval castle. After Hopkins died, his widow moved her construction activities back east, where she married an interior decorator over twenty years her junior, Edwin Searles. It was he who gave the Nob Hill castle to the San Francisco Art Association in 1893 for a school. In 1923 the school moved to Russian Hill and the property was sold for construction of the present hotel, opened in 1926, incorporating on its south side the wall of the original mansion—a railroad culvert.

Oscar Lewis, The Big Four *(New York, 1938, 1969) is a classic.*

Hedda Hopper (Elda Furry, 1890-1966). A Pennsylvania Quaker by birth, she was pretty enough to make a minor sensation as a Broadway actress and proper enough to seek marriage to an older character actor named DeWitt Hopper. (Her first name was devised by a numerologist to distinguish her from Hopper's previous wives, Ella, Ida, Edna, and Nella). She went to Hollywood and played bit parts (**Marion Davies**'s mother in *Zander*

the Great) but it wasn't until she was 50 and financially pinched that she found her ultimate role as a gossip columnist. Beginning in 1937, she was syndicated to thirteen newspapers— including the local paper, the *L.A. Times*, which put her a leg up on competitor **Louella Parsons**. Hopper became known by her hats, symbols of propriety and conservatism, which she acquired at the rate of 150 a year and deducted from her income tax. Fiercely protective of feminine virtue, she personally abetted Joan Barry's paternity suit against Charlie Chaplin and conducted regular crusades in her column against sexual libertinism. Other phobias included Communism ("Metro-Goldwyn-Moscow" was a favorite target) and pointed-toe shoes. "Who are we fighting today?" she would announce on arriving at her Hollywood Boulevard office, crowded with aspiring actors and informers, where she

dictated her column out loud as if she were trying out new lines. The *L.A. Times* got **Cecil B. DeMille** to review Hedda's first book, but her second volume led to an out-of-court libel settlement with actor Michael Wilding. A tenacious woman with a keen eye on the Hollywood caste system, she lived and died alone in a Beverly Hills mansion she called "the house that fear built."

Hopper wrote From Under My Hat *(Garden City, NY, 1952) and* The Whole Truth and Nothing But *(Garden City, NY, 1962). The gossip columnist left a priceless collection of publicity photos, all featuring herself prominently, to the Academy of Motion Picture Arts and Sciences.*

Alonzo Erastus Horton (1813-1909). After **Juan Cabrillo** and **Junípero Serra**, Horton ranks as the founding father of San Diego. Born in Connecticut, he had already established one town, Hortonville, Wisconsin, before joining the Gold Rush to California. He made his first fortune selling ice in the Mother Lode during the hot summer, then set himself up in San Francisco as a furniture dealer. On a trip to San Diego in 1867 he picked up 960 acres at auction for only $265, land which became Horton's Addition or New Town, the nucleus of present-day San Diego. Horton used his proceeds from land sales to build a hotel, several business blocks, a wharf, and a succession of homes for himself, culminating in a mansion on First Street with a bay view. The city's principle employer during the early years of construction, he paid his workers in land and

required them to vote Republican. He offered free lots to churches and traded San Francisco publisher **H. H. Bancroft** a city block in exchange for books to serve as the nucleus of a public library. During its first 50 years the San Diego economy proved particularly susceptible to boom-and-bust cycles, each downswing thinning out the population to Horton and a hard core of "geranium growers" (retirees). Eventually succeeded by younger tycoons like **John Spreckles**, Horton lived on in San Diego to a venerable old age, for which he gave some credit to the "fountain of youth" at nearby Warner's Hot Springs. He left his imprint all over San Diego, down to the spot where he was once thrown from a burro into a patch of poison ivy, thenceforth known as "Horton's Slide."

Elizabeth MacPhail's The Story of New San Diego and of its Founder, Alonzo E. Horton *(San Diego, 1969, 1979) is local history at its best.*

Howard Robard Hughes (1905-1976). Snapshots from Los Angeles in the 1920s reveal a tall, engaging young man, shyly holding hands with Jean Harlow or standing slightly apart at a celebrity beach party in Santa Monica. Orphaned at eighteen, he had turned his back on Texas and his father's tool company to join his Uncle Rupert in Hollywood. (Rupert Hughes, 1872-1956, author of a debunking biography of George Washington, became a screenwriter and leader of the film industry's right wing.) At twenty Howard Hughes was a film producer and

playboy, undeterred in his search for the perfect woman by a brief marriage to a Texas debutante; at thirty he was a world-record-breaking pilot with a genius for adapting planes to fly across the continent and around the globe; at forty he was a billionaire defense contractor, increasingly strange and reclusive. During forty years in Southern California Hughes left the mark of his eccentric genius all over the landscape. There is Hughes Aircraft, a top electronics firm with eleven branches and 1,200 acres of prime real estate in Culver City; Hughes managed to get the state to route Highway 1 around the property but was finally unable to prevent the county from taking 100 acres of beachfront to develop Marina Del Rey. There is the one and only home he ever owned at 311 Muirfield, which he auctioned off with all its contents including the family

silver during World War II; henceforth he would live in hotels (including a bungalow at the Beverly Hills Hotel) and in rented mansions such as the French chateau in Bel Air where he installed actress Jean Peters as his bride in 1957. There is the unmarked office at 7000 Romaine Street, formerly the home of Multicolor, a premature Hughes venture into color film, which served for decades as the 24-hour message center of the Hughes Empire. Not far away is RKO, which he bought in 1948 ("between blondes," it was joked), ran by remote control, and eventually sold at a large profit. Before he became a full-time recluse, Hughes, who had the imagination of a fortune-teller, **Jack Warner** thought, personally directed *Hell's Angels* (1930) and *The Outlaw* (1946).There are scenes of aviation triumphs and disasters: Martin Field in

Santa Ana where he set a new world speed record of 352 mph in 1935, and the Beverly Hills house which he demolished in a 1946 crash-landing of a reconaissance plane, barely escaping with his life. (Another time, he made an emergency landing on the golf course of the Bel Air Country Club.) Then there is the Spruce Goose, the huge wooden cargo ship **Henry Kaiser** urged him to build, which occupied a Long Beach hangar for 38 years. And finally there are numerous planes which he left to rust at local air fields and a fleet of anonymous Chevrolets in which the Huck Finn of U.S. industry liked to conduct midnight business conferences, buying and selling airlines, hotels, and politicians. Ironically, when Hughes left California for good, it was by train, the closed "mystery" train that in 1966 made an unscheduled stop in Pomona to pick up an unknown passenger bound for exile in hermetically sealed penthouse suites all over the western hemisphere.

Best of the Hughes biographies are Bashful Billionaire by Albert B. Gerber (New York, 1967) and Howard, The Amazing Mr. Hughes by Noah Dietrich (revised 1972).

Bernhard Hühne

(1547-1611). When the first volumes of Appleton's *Cyclopaedia of American Biography* were published in the late 1880s, they contained sketches of such unsung heroes as Hühne, a hitherto unknown German navigator who had piloted a Spanish expedition to California in 1661 and left a valuable chart of the waters between Mexico and Alta California. As it

turned out, however, Hühne and at least 47 others in Appleton's *Cyclopaedia* were created out of whole cloth by some whimsical impecunious writer whose remuneration increased acording to the number of words contributed, true or false. Moral: beware the Jubjub bird, the frumious Bandersnatch, and the conventional biographical dictionary, written for money, not love. (All *California People*, however bizarre, are real.)

Collis Potter Huntington

(1821-1900). The mastermind behind the Southern Pacific Railroad was a former Yankee peddler from New York state. Setting out for Gold Rush California, he arrived richer for some astute trading en route in Panama. In Sacramento he went into business with **Mark Hopkins**, second of the shopkeepers who would become the Big Four. (**Leland Stanford** and **Charles Crocker** were the others.) Until 1862, historian Oscar Lewis remarked, Huntington was involved in "nothing more spectacular than attempts to gain temporary control of the local supply of potatoes and shovels or gunpowder." Then he moved back East to pull the political and financial strings that turned the Southern Pacific into the West's greatest money-making machine and most thoroughgoing monopoly. Huntington once remarked cynically that the railroad was nothing but "two streaks of rust and a right-of-way," with, of course, a government construction subsidy and a land grant of 12,800 acres for every mile. He proved adept at manipulating bonds, loans, and congressmen, whom he never hesitated to bribe, he told **Bancroft**'s scribes, if he thought it right. On trips west he stayed at the Palace Hotel until acquiring **David Colton**'s Nob Hill Mansion in 1891. Huntington did not like California, considering its climate good only for weaklings. He does not seem to have liked his partners much either. "Ruthless as a crocodile," as a local obituary called him, he humiliated Stanford in 1890 by forcing him out of the titular presidency of the SP. Back home in New York, where he lived on the corner now occupied by Tiffany's, Huntington presided over larger interests including shipbuilding and coal mining, a ranking American symbol of predatory wealth.

David Lavender wrote The Great Persuader *(New York, 1970).*

Henry Edwards Huntington (1850-1927).

Nephew and heir of **Collis Huntington**, he first came west at age 40 to help run the Southern Pacific Railroad. An enthusiastic convert to "Californianism," he preferred the south to the north, predicting that Los Angeles would one day be the most important city in the U.S. After his uncle's death, he sold the SP to E.H. Harriman for $50 million, bought a 600-acre ranch in San Marino, and put together an interurban railroad linking the entire Los Angeles basin. (Huntington Beach at the southern end of the line was named after H.E., who

became the largest landowner in Southern California, but Huntington Palisades to the west was one of his uncle's railroad acquisitions.) The newspapers called H. E. "the Trolley Man." A 1906 banquet for him in Pasadena featured a four-foot-long floral streetcar, trolley-shaped ice creams, and mini-trolleys filled with nuts for guest favors. His other interests included Pacific Light and Power Company, and a share in the **Harry Chandler** syndicate which made a killing in the San Fernando Valley. In 1910 he sold his interurban lines (again to Harriman) and became increasingly absorbed in his library, which grew into the greatest private collection of books in the world. H.E.'s

second wife Arabella, who as his Uncle Collis's widow inherited another third of the SP fortune, preferred to spend her money on art. Their collections, along with the San Marino "ranchhouse" and botanical gardens, were endowed as a prestigious museum and research institution.

Henry Huntington and the Pacific Electric by Spencer Crump (L.A., 1970) is a picture album. The Founding of the Henry E. Huntington Library and Art Gallery: Four Essays edited by James Thorpe (San Marino, 1969) contains some biographical details. Arabella Huntington figures prominently in Stephen Birmingham's Grandes Dames *(New York, 1982).*

Aldous Leonard Huxley (1894-1963).

A ranking member of the British intellectual aristocracy, Huxley travelled the world in search of a salubrious climate. "I value sunshine more than people, culture, arts, conversation," he once said. In 1938 he settled in Southern California but continued to travel, spiritually if not physically. A chronic medical case (he suffered from poor eyesight, allergies, bronchial infections, lumbago, and a long string of other complaints), he had always gone in for fad diets and quack cures. In California during the 1940s and 1950s he experimented with hypnosis, astrology, entelechy or E therapy, and animal magnetism, all of which he considered emotional substitutes for religion and medicine. Long before they became fashionable, he tried acupuncture, dianetics, and LSD, describing some of his efforts at self-transcendance in *The Doors of Perception* (1954). (In fact, he requested an intramuscular injection of LSD when he lay dying at a friend's house on Mulholland Drive). Other works of Huxley's California period include *After Many a Summer Dies the Swan* (1939), a gentle satire on **Hearst** and the quest for eternal, lubricious youth; and *Ape and Essence* (1948), a post-atomic vision of Los Angeles in the year 2013, when library books are burned for fuel in Pershing Square. He also earned some "filthy lucre" writing for the movies, including the film adaptation of *Pride and Prejudice* (1940), possibly Hollywood's most literate screenplay. Huxley described his Hollywood experience as alchemy in reverse, turning gold into lead. But he loved the city's sleazy glamor and is one of the few expatriate intellectuals to thrive there. He explored the deserts and mountains of Southern California, was a regular patron of the Farmer's Market at Third and Fairfax, and liked to take houseguests to Forest Lawn to admire the pink marble statuary. And he was remarkably philosophical about that archetypal Southern California *rite de passage*, the brush fire. "It was quite an experience," Huxley reported after losing his house in the Hollywood Hills, and all his possessions in 1961. "It does make one feel extraordinarily clean." clean."

Sybille Bedford's Aldous Huxley; A Biography *(New York, 1974) is comprehensive.*

Thomas Harper Ince

(1880-1924). In the fall of 1924, producer Tom Ince had just completed a lavish 25-room "hacienda" in Benedict Canyon, Días Doradas, which was featured in *House Beautiful* and *Architectural Digest*. In November, after attending the premiere of his latest film, he joined a **Hearst** yachting party to celebrate his 44th birthday. A few days later, with "shocking suddenness" and in puzzling

circumstances, he died of "acute indigestion." The rumors began to fly. The Hearst press ran a false report that Ince had been a guest on the publisher's ranch, not the yacht. **Elinor Glyn**, who was on the yacht, reported that the guests were sworn to secrecy—including a gossip columnist who would claim she wasn't even there but subsequently became a power in the Hearst organization. The district attorney of San Diego where Ince was taken ashore declined to investigate the likeliest possibility—illegal drinking on board (it was then Prohibition), which would have aggravated Ince's ulcers—and Ince's body was soon cremated. Over the years the story has become as persistent as the unproved tale of **Fatty Arbuckle** and the champagne bottle, that Hearst shot Ince in a fit of jealous rage, mistaking him in the dark for Charlie Chaplin who was paying rather too much attention to mistress

Marion Davies. Ince's widow is said to have received a "trust fund" from Hearst, plus $625,000 from **Carl Laemmle**, who bought Días Doradas in 1927. Under the terms of Ince's will, his family was prohibited from investing any of the money in films. A former actor, Ince had produced (or "supervised") the first Westerns at his ranch in Culver City, which later grew into MGM. He had also discovered some of Hollywood's first stars, including Tom Mix and **William S. Hart**.

Irvine Family

The largest piece of Southern California land to survive essentially intact from the Spanish era to the Second World War was the Irvine Ranch in Orange County. James Irvine Sr. (1827-1886) was a 49er of Scots-Irish ancestry who invested the profits from his San Francisco grocery business in real estate. During the drought of the 1860s he acquired at distress prices about 100,000 acres in the south, much of which formerly belonged to the **Sepulveda** and Yorba families. Replacing cattle with sheep, Irvine prospered as an absentee rancher. His son James (1867-1947), born and raised in San Francisco, once rode his bicycle 450 miles south to visit the property he would inherit in 1893. The ranch was incorporated in 1894 and diversified into agriculture. James, Jr., and his family continued to reside primarily in San Francisco until the 1906 earthquake, when they moved into the white frame ranch house more or less permanently. Something of a despot, James, Jr., found that his wealth enabled him to get away with antisocial excesses, even cruelty. His overriding passion was his estate, which remained intact except for 160 acres donated for a county park in 1867, townsites sold for Santa Ana and Tustin, 2,300 acres requisitioned by the government for El Toro Marine Air Station during World War II, and the right-of-way for two interstate highways. On his death he left 82,000 acres, about a quarter of all the land in Orange County, including the prime beachfront between Newport and Laguna, to the Irvine Foundation. Two of James's children predeceased him, and his son Myford died a reported suicide in 1959, leaving three females in the fourth generation of California Irvines. Her grandfather's favorite and, with 22 percent of the foundation stock, his largest beneficiary, Joan Irvine Smith (1933-   ) spearheaded the transition from farming to urban development. Under her prodding, the foundation donated the land for a new University of California campus and launched affluent new housing and shopping developments. When the foundation threatened to sell out to Mobil Oil in the mid-1970s, she blocked the sale in court and participated in the creation of a new Irvine company in 1977. Said to take after her grandfather for stubborn wilfulness, she has continued to argue over the future of the patrimony with the new regime she helped create.

Robert Glass Cleland wrote The Irvine Ranch of Orange County, 1810-1950 *(San Marino, 1952). For the juicer details of Irvine family history, see Stephen Birmingham's* California Rich *(New York, 1980).*

William Irwin (1827-1886). California's thirteenth governor (1875-80), Irwin was born in Ohio and graduated from Marietta College (1848). In Northern California after 1852 he went into the lumber business, ran a livery stable, and founded a country newspaper, the *Yreka Union*, which he edited until his election as a Democrat for governor in 1875. A contemporary described Irwin as "gentlemanly in appearance, courteous in demeanor, and particularly kind to visiting strangers." Former Governor **Frederick Low** remarked that Irwin made his reputation by "looking wise and keeping his mouth shut." As the state's chief executive during a period of economic distress and labor activism, he signed a gag law directed against **Kearney**ism, vetoed a relief bill for the destitute ("the State is not a grand insurance company") and was inclined to blame the economic crisis on Chinese labor. On the other hand, he appointed **Henry George** to a government sinecure, thus subsidizing the preparation of *Progress and Poverty* (1879). Irwin opposed the 1879 Constitution, largely drafted by **Kearney**'s Workingmen's party, which when adopted extended his term an extra year to 1880.

Ishi (1862?-1916). Thirty-five years after Custer's last stand and 25 years after Geronimo's Apaches laid down their arms, a lone survivor of a stone-age California Indian tribe stumbled into the twentieth century town of Oroville. It

was 1911 and Ishi, the last of the Yahi living in the foothills of Lassen Peak, had come to the end of his resources. Naked, filthy, and frightened, he was locked up in the local jail, an object of curiosity for tourists with Graflex cameras and of potential profit ("See the Wild Man of Oroville!") for enterprising vaudeville impresarios. He was fortunate to find his way into the sensitive and understanding custody of University of California anthropologist Alfred Kroeber and his colleagues, who possessed a knowledge of local Indian languages and were able to establish communication. Ishi eventually took up residence in the university's Museum of Anthropology on San Francisco's Parnassus Heights, where he came to terms cheerfully with the modern world. According to a beautiful memoir later composed by Theodora Kracaw Kroeber, wife of the anthropologist, Ishi preferred trolley cars to autos, had great respect for glue, and rated matches as "one of civilization's true delights. . . far above gas and electricity." For the rest, he considered buildings inferior to mountains and the early airplane less splendid than a bird. Ishi rated his new American friends as clever but lacking in reserve and respect for the power of nature. "He looked upon us as sophisticated children," remarked a university professor with whom Ishi returned on a camping trip to the Lassen foothills, where pupil and teacher exchanged roles. Ishi's new life lasted only four and a half years.

Lacking immunities, he suffered from respiratory infections and succumbed to tuberculosis. He was cremated—an Anglo approximation of a Yahi funeral pyre—and his ashes placed in a Pueblo Indian jar at Mount Olivet Cemetery.

Ishi in Two Worlds by Theodora Kroeber (Berkeley and L.A., 1961) is a rare pleasure.

George Lester Jackson (1941-1971). Jackson was a chronic delinquent from L.A. who at the age of eighteen, after robbing a gas station, pulled one of California's old indeterminant sentences of one-year-to-life. For eleven years in state prisons his was a busy life, devoted to the militant improvement of everything from his muscles to his mind. A graduate of "Dayview High School" (San Quentin), Jackson evolved his own personal concept of neoslavery, attributing all black crime to the social order. Transferred to Soledad, he found the racial situation there tense. As **Timothy Leary** put it, "when you check in there they issue you a sword and a garbage can lid." Many Soledad guards were unreconstructed southerners, Jackson found, unwilling to do farm labor and unqualified to sell insurance. Under the terms of his indeterminant sentence, he came up for review every year, and every year his hope of freedom was disappointed. In 1969, after three black inmates were killed, Jackson and two other Soledad "brothers" were charged with the retaliation murder of a guard. While attempting to "liberate" the Soledad Brothers from a Marin County courtroom in 1970, Jackson's younger brother Jonathan and a judge were killed. Also implicated in the Marin escape was **Angela Davis** who went underground, was eventually caught, and later acquitted. In the midst of these grim life-and-death struggles, Jackson conducted an ardent love life by correspondence. "No one, no one at all, can love like I," he wrote to Angela Davis, but she wasn't the only one; other correspondents included an upperclass, middle-aged white woman. Appointed an honorary field marshal in the Black Panther Party by **Huey Newton**, Jackson came close to living out Newton's concept of revolutionary suicide. Transferred back to San Quentin, he and five others died in an alleged escape attempt, the prison's bloodiest ever.

Jean Genet wrote the introduction to Soledad Brother; The Prison Letters of George Jackson *(New York, 1970).*

Helen Hunt Jackson
(1830-1885). She once

referred to herself as the "Indian Mrs. Stowe," and her romantic recreation of Indian life ranks as the *Uncle Tom's Cabin* of Southern California. A writer of sentimental fiction and poetry from Amherst, Massachusetts, Jackson had remained indifferent to the issue of abolition and actively disapproved of woman suffrage, the two great causes of her day. In 1879 she was roused by the dispossession of Oklahoma's Ponca tribe to take up the white woman's burden, writing a series of articles on the American Indian (published in 1881 as *A Century of Dishonor*). That same year she arrived in Los Angeles with an assignment from *Century Magazine* to write about the California missions. In the course of her research, she visited the Camulos Rancho on former mission land in the San Fernando Valley, and Indian settlements at Temecula and Saboba, locales later enshrined in legend. A woman of tenacious

purpose, she wangled a commission out of the government to do a report on California Indian problems with associate and translator **Abbot Kinney**. The report was soon pigeonholed, so Mrs. Jackson decided to dramatize her subject in novel form, weaving a plot out of real and imagined events and places. *Ramona* (1884), the love story of a half-breed señorita and her Indian husband, held great "pathetic" interest for *fin de siècle* readers.

Dispossessed by the Yankees and doomed to wander, the heroine yearns for olden days when the missions were palaces full of happy Indians. Shortly after publication, Mrs. Jackson died of cancer in San Francisco, where she had sought homeopathic treatment. But *Ramona* achieved commercial immortality, selling 600,000 books in 60 years. The first

novel about Southern California, it soon led to tourist exploitation of the region's sorry Indian past. Excursion trains made special stops at the Camulos Rancho ("Where Ramona Slept"), and "Ramona's Marriage Place" in San Diego became a sentimental shrine. An annual spring pageant of the Indian passion play was mounted in Hemet, while a town in the San Pasqual Valley was named after the Indian heroine. No less than three Hollywood movies were made of Ramona's life. Writer **Carey McWilliams** even suggested a monument to Jackson in Cajon Pass, the eastern gateway to "Ramonaland."

George Wharton James's Through Ramona's Country *(Boston, 1908) is considered a classic. Evelyn Banning wrote the most recent biography of Helen Hunt Jackson (New York, 1973).* Ramona *itself has survived twenty-nine printings and numerous editions.*

George Wharton James
(1858-1923). If one were

asked to invent an archetypal California eccentric, James

would help fill the bill. He was a defrocked and disgraced preacher, a former Methodist who helped make a new religion out of Californiana. Born in England, he arrived in Southern California in 1881 alone. His wife arrived later, only to accuse him loudly of adultery with virtually every woman in sight. After losing his Long Beach ministry in the scandal, the "Irreverend James," as the *L.A. Times* called him, launched a Pasadena literary salon where he expounded his ideas of nature worship, health faddism, and the glorification of Indian culture. James was also an amateur astronomer, the manufacturer of a snakebite kit, an outdoorsman and desert explorer, and a prolific, tireless publicist of California, an activity which brought him into competition with **Charles Lummis**, who dismissed him as a charlatan. James became social director of the Mount Lowe Hotel and editor of its tourist newspaper, finding time on the side to write over 40 volumes on the Southwest and to undertake extensive lecture tours.

James's books include a spiritual biography, The Radiant Life *(Pasadena, 1917); a biography of his pet bird,* The Story of Scraggles *(Pasadena, 1906);* Indian Basketry *(1901), a moderate success in its day; and* California, Romantic and Beautiful *(Boston, 1914).*

Arthur Janov

(1924-   ). The name sounds Central European, but Janov, guru of feel-good psychotherapy, was strictly a hometown boy from Los Angeles. He earned a B.A. at UCLA (1949) and a Ph.D. from Claremont Graduate School, did an internship in music therapy at the Sawtelle Veterans Hospital, and specialized in treating disturbed children. One day in the 1960s Janov observed a formerly withdrawn patient reenact a kicking, screaming childish tantrum, and "primal therapy" was born. All neurosis results from denial of need in childhood, he decided, and conventional psychotherapy does only a patch-up job on the symptoms. Using props such as baby bottles and cribs, he took his adult patients back to infancy to reexperience and empty the accumulated "pool of pain." As primal therapy evolved, Janov would start by leaving the patient alone in a hotel room for 24 hours, followed by three weeks of intensive daily therapy (the patient often spreadeagled to maximize his feeling of vulnerability), and seven or eight months of group sessions. In *Primal Scream* (1970) Janov described this treatment as 100 percent successful, the most important discovery of the twentieth century, the first psychotherapy for the masses. John Lennon and Yoko Ono moved to the West Coast to undergo primal therapy, and the handsome, curly-haired doctor became an instant celebrity. In his books, he claimed great success in treating perverts, alcoholics, and drug addicts. Patients wrote testimonials describing how their voice dropped an octave or their breats grew or they achieved relief from arthritis after undergoing primal therapy. Unable to keep up with the demand for his services, Janov began training therapists who started as patients, experiencing the orgasmic primal tantrum along with everyone else. (In the Janov universe, even the receptionist has "primals.") Continually expanding his reach, he founded a *Journal of Primal Therapy*, registered "primal therapy" with the U.S. Patent Office, and opened a Primal Institute in New York City.

Howard Arnold Jarvis

(1903?-   ). Jarvis was a minor gadfly on the California Republican circuit for 40 years before achieving celebrity as the chief curmudgeon of tax reform. Born poor and hardworking in Mormon Utah, he went all the way through school there without drinking, smoking, or ever laying eyes on a pregnant classmate. After graduating from the University of Utah (1925) and earning a law degree (1926), he put together a smalltown Utah newspaper chain to collect national advertising fees from Madison Avenue. At a 1934 Republican National Committee meeting, Jarvis shared quarters with a delegate from California, **Earl Warren**, who convinced him to move to the ultimate West. He earned a "shitful" of money during the Depression and World War II, buying land cheaper per square foot than linoleum, manufacturing garbage disposals and gas heaters, and degaussing ships for the military. Politically starstruck, he claimed to have discovered **Richard Nixon** in 1945 and even to have contributed to Nixon's slush fund. In 1962 Jarvis retired from business and took up

the cause of tax reform. For fifteen years he traveled up and down the state arguing that a man's home is his castle and should not be taxed to support surfing bums, permissive teachers, and food stamps. He tried and failed three times to get enough signatures to put his property tax limitation proposal on the ballot. With paid assistance from Paul Gann, a Northern California tax reform advocate, he finally got his measure qualified for the June 1978 election as Proposition 13. P.-13 won 64 percent voter approval, cutting state property taxes in half, and Jarvis made the cover of *Time* magazine as a national folk hero. A star at last, he went on talk shows to suggest trashing the Social Security system and pulling the U.S. out of the U.N. Meanwhile, doomsday predictions of the effects of P.-13—bankruptcy of schools, curtailment of police and fire services, and elimination of welfare—did not materialize, thanks largely to distribution of surplus state tax dollars. A proposal to cut state income taxes by 50 percent (''Jarvis II''), thus really tightening the tax screws in California, was defeated at the polls in 1980.

Jarvis claimed to have dictated his memoirs. I'm Mad as Hell *(New York, 1979), while fly-fishing.*

Robinson Jeffers (John Robinson Jeffers, 1887-1962).

Alone of California's major literary figures, Jeffers seems to have lived a life of pure mind. The son of a stern classical scholar and Presbyterian minister, he was educated at home in western Pennsylvania and in Europe before the family moved to Southern California in 1903 for the climate. At sixteen Jeffers became a junior at Occidental College, earning his B.A. in 1905 and enrolling

in graduate school at USC. There he met his future wife, Una Kuster, with whom he would carve a life on the Carmel seashore straight out of the ancient sagas. Jeffers did not actually build Tor House, his stone castle at Mission Point in Carmel, but he learned enough by observing its construction to build the adjacent tower. Theirs was a spartan lifestyle without unnecessary accretions, rooted in absorbed concern for trees, animals, nature. Just as the poet cemented stones from all over the world into his tower, he distilled his classical and Christian education into verse, creating a mythical landscape of strife, death, and doom on the craggy north California shore. He first won critical acclaim with *Tamar and Other Poems* (1924) and *Roan Stallion* (1925). In addition to verse, Jeffers also wrote a modern adaptation of Euripides' *Medea* (1946) for Judith Anderson, who made a great success of it on the stage. Since Jeffers's death his twin sons and other admirers have struggled to maintain Tor House as a literary shrine.

Melba Bennett, author of Stone Mason of Tor House; The Life and Times of Robinson Jeffers *(Los Angeles, 1966). is a devotee.*

James Jackson Jeffries (1875-1953).

In a strictly California context, the world heavyweight title matches between Jeffries and **James Corbett** in 1900 and 1903 were a battle of north against south, brain against brawn. Jeffries, a huge former boilermaker, son of a Los Angeles streetcorner

preacher, seemed the very antithesis of ''Gentleman Jim'' Corbett, the slender, nattily dressed San Franciscan. When the southerner ventured into the precincts of San Francisco's Palace Hotel before one fight, he was thoroughly snubbed for reasons of geography as well as class. But in addition to his size, Jeffries was also fast, a natural left-hander, and had the advantage of youth over Corbett, whom he twice defeated, southern brawn over northern brains. Retiring undefeated in 1905, Jeffries opened a saloon on L.A.'s Spring Street which became a hangout for the emerging movie colony. He made an ill-advised comeback as the ''great white hope'' against Jack Johnson in Reno in 1910, was kayoed, then retired for good. When

Prohibition put his saloon out of business, Jeffries repaired to his ranch in Burbank. For years, weekly amateur fights were held there, until local authorities put a stop to them, too. Rather a sad figure in his later years, Jeffries had little left at his death except the rights to his life story, in which no one seemed interested.

Hiram Warren Johnson (1866-1945).

The first major national politician spawned by California, Johnson started out as a progressive reform leader and ended up as a self-righteous and cantankerous old reactionary. He first rose to public prominence in 1908 when he replaced the injured **Francis Heney** as prosecutor of the San Francisco graft trials. Nominated for governor as a reform Republican in 1910, he toured the state for four months in a bright red ''Locomobile,'' preaching the expulsion of the moneychangers (the railroad) from the temple. This platform involved him and his brother Albert, both lawyers, in an epic confrontation with their father, a Sacramento attorney-politician and ''wheelhorse'' of the Southern Pacific. Once elected, he called for a whole slate of reforms, from utility regulation to worker's compensation and woman suffrage. As governor (1911-1917) Johnson drastically changed state politics with the enactment of initiative, referendum, and recall measures, all calculated to strip power from such bosses as his father and return it to the people. Having eliminated the bosses,

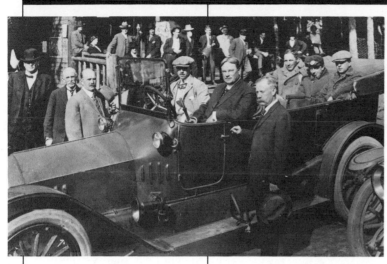

however, Johnson's progressives found they had opened the door to special interest lobbyists. As a minority party they were able to maintain themselves and their high intentions only by the expediency of cross-filing, another Johnson innovation. Californians dominated the 1912 national Progressive party convention of Republican dissidents, who nominated Johnson as Theodore Roosevelt's running mate in their third-party bid for the U.S. presidency. (The experience reinforced Johnson's innate inability to defer to anyone and probably cost him the presidency. In 1920 he declined to become Harding's running mate; Coolidge, who accepted, soon became president.) Johnson was elected to the U.S. Senate in 1916 and remained there until his death. Unable to dominate Congress, he became its leading obstructionist. Having opposed U.S. entry into World War I, he became a leading foe of the League of Nations, which he considered a giant plot to sell out to the British. He also opposed reciprocal trade agreements, supporting sky-high tariff protection for the corporations he had once pushed out of California politics. He supported FDR in 1932 but later turned against him. A lifelong isolationist, given to ill-tempered fulminations against the "yellow peril," he made his last great stand against the drafting of teenagers to fight in World War II. Shortly before his death—ironically, the day the U.S. bombed Hiroshima—Johnson cast the only vote in the Senate Foreign Relations Committee against the U.N. charter.

Amazingly, there is no biography of this problematic, complex Californian. See George Mowry, The California Progressives *(Berkeley, 1951) and* California's Prodigal Sons, Hiram Johnson and the Progressives *by Spencer Olin (Berkeley, 1968).*

John Neeley Johnson

(1825-1872). The Know-Nothings were Anglo-Saxon nativists of the 1850s, opposed to the influx of "papist" immigrants; many were former Whigs who chose to join the racist American Party rather than the new antislavery Republican Party. In California, where the "yellow peril" gave Know-Nothingism a special animus, the faction actually elected a state governor in 1855. Described as "the most startled man in the state when informed that he had been elected," Johnson was a thirty-year-old lawyer and former Whig from the Midwest. As the state's fourth governor (1856-1858) he tried to deal with the ongoing problems of creating (and financing) such state institutions as prisons and hospitals. He also had to contend with the inexperience of his legislature, which was dominated by Know-Nothings; he actually vetoed bills for poor spelling, punctuation, and ambiguity (such as the failure to distinguish between public and private trees used by telephone companies). Johnson met his Waterloo in San Francisco's Second Vigilance Committee. Although sympathetic to law and order, he felt obliged to declare the city in a state of insurrection; later, finding himself powerless to enforce his authority, he vacillated. He was not nominated for reelection. Leaving California, he served a term on the Nevada State Supreme Court (1867-1871). He died in Utah after suffering sunstroke.

Jim Jones

(James Warren Jones, 1931-1978). In the early 1960s *Esquire* magazine ran an article on the safest places to sit out a nuclear holocaust, among which were Eureka, California, and Belo Horizonte, Brazil. Jones, an Indianapolis preacher who counted fallout among his many phobias, tried Brazil first, then moved with a thousand followers to Northern California in 1965. Ukiah, then Redwood Valley, served as staging areas for Jones's forays into the big leagues of San Francisco and Los Angeles, where the mod preacher with his dark glasses and sideburns expounded a mixture of "apostolic socialism," faith healing, and racial integration. By voting as a block, moreover, his church became a power to be reckoned with locally. In 1972 Jones bought a former San Francisco synagogue for his Peoples Temple. He consolidated his position there by energetic efforts in the 1975 mayoral campaign of George Moscone, who appointed Jones to the city housing authority in gratitude. Members of the Peoples Temple lived communally and frugally, enabling Jones to build a multi-million dollar financial empire on their Social Security and welfare checks and other assets. One of his investments was four thousand acres of jungle in Guyana, intended as the group's final refuge from fascist persecution or fallout. The hegira to Jonestown, Guyana, took place in 1977, sooner than anticipated, prompted by a magazine exposé of Jones's fake healings, sexual obsessions, and paranoid brutality. In Guyana he was able to consolidate his spiritual dictatorship thanks to complete control over outside communications. (The KKK was marching in the streets of Los Angeles, Jones told his followers, and drought and famine were widespread.) The regime at Jonestown was one of hard labor, poor rations, and "white nights" of rehearsal for mass suicide on the day of judgment. The tension was heightened by defections and by the legal efforts of former members to reclaim their children in Guyana. In 1978, Congressman Leo Ryan from San Mateo County, an accomplished political grandstander, decided to investigate for himself. The rest is gruesome history: Ryan became the first U.S. Congressman killed in the line of duty when Jones led some 900 of his followers in a jungle nightmare of suicide and murder.

The best of many recent books, most of them instant spinoffs from media coverage, are In My Father's House *(New York, 1981) by Min Yee and Thomas Layton, brother of Larry Layton, accused slayer of Ryan; and* Our Father Who Art in Hell, The Life and Death of Jim Jones *by James Reston (New York, 1981).*

John Percival Jones

(1829-1912). Jones was a Comstock millionaire who spent a reputed $500,000 to win election in 1873 as a Nevada "silver senator." During a relaxed 30 years in the U.S. Senate, he found time to boost the California beach city of Santa Monica as a rival to the metropolitan pretensions of Los Angeles. (L.A., for its part, sneered at "Jonesville.") Jones built a hotel and bathhouses, hired a silver-tongued auctioneer, and brought investors down from San Francisco by steamer for his 1875 sale of town lots equipped with scarlet-and-gold sunsets. According to the

senator's plans, Santa Monica was to be the ocean terminus for his Los Angeles and Independence Railroad, connecting his mining interests in the Panamint Mountains of Death Valley to a world market. The LA & IR beat the Southern Pacific through the Cajon Pass in 1875, but its future was sealed by the crash of Nevada silver the following year and by the failure of Jones's backers, the Temple and Workman Bank. The Southern Pacific took over the LA & IR and condemned Jones's wharf. Santa Monica reverted to a sleepy resort where the merchant classes of L.A. kept summer cottages. (Jones himself built a splendid mansion, The Miramar, at the corner of Ocean and Nevada, later Wilshire.) Ironically, the Southern Pacific revived Jones's dream of a world harbor at Santa Monica a generation later but lost out to Wilmington in the "free harbor" contest of 1899.

David Starr Jordan

(1851-1931). The first president of Stanford University was a naturalist, a pacifist, and something of a Social Darwinist, as well as a prolific writer and world traveler. A native of New York state who chose his own middle name in honor of minister **Thomas Starr King**, Jordan earned an M.S. at Cornell (1872). He first came to California to complete the ichthyological survey for the 1880 census. He was the president of the University of Indiana when Senator **Leland Stanford** arrived by private railroad car to discuss Jordan's belief that people

should found their own universities. Jordan hesitated at first to accept the presidency of the new school, wary of Stanford's personal control and of the "discordant individualism" which he believed rampant in California. But Jordan could not resist the temptation of a university "hallowed by no traditions and hampered by none"— something of an experiment in moral engineering—and in 1891 took up residence on campus in a cottage modeled after the Petit Trianon at Versailles. His first impression, he wrote was of being on an extended picnic in the beautiful Santa Clara Valley, but he was soon busy teaching a course on evolution and giving talks on morality in the style of a biblical patriarch. Jordan presided with tact and diplomacy over what he called Stanford's "Stone Age," the obsessive and excessive building campaign pushed by the widowed Mrs. Stanford. When most of the buildings came tumbling down in the 1906 earthquake, he accepted their loss

philosophically. Somehow he also found time to write prolifically and to explore odd corners of the earth, always looking for a moral lesson. (The subheadings in his voluminous memoirs read "On to Oberammergau," "Salvation of South Africa," etc.) Jordan was active on behalf of world peace, believing that war resulted in the survival of the unfit. Personally, he did his own part during 25 years at the new university to increase the number of the fit, sending out some 6,000 graduates with Stanford diplomas. Mount Jordan in Tulare County is named for him.

See Jordan's Days of a Man, Being Memories of a Naturalist, Teacher and Minor Prophet of Democracy *2 vols., (New York, 1922). Jordan also figures prominently in Kevin Starr's* Americans and the California Dream *(New York, 1973; Salt Lake City, 1981).*

Theodore Dehone Judah

(1826-1863). When Judah first tried to promote a railroad across the Sierra Nevada he was thought to be an impossible dreamer. Worse, many considered him a monomaniac and avoided his company. A graduate of Rensselaer Polytechnic with experience engineering the railroad bridges and grades at Niagara, Judah came to California in 1854 to work on the Sacramento Valley Railroad. When that line was completed as far as Folsom, he began to envisage a road east to link up with the transcontinental, a feat which he believed would bring the entire Pacific Coast, Hawaii, and even the Far East within the sphere of the California railroad. After eight years of promoting and two trips to

Washington, D.C., Judah finally recruited four Sacramento merchants, **C.P. Huntington, Hopkins, Stanford**, and **Crocker**. The Big Four, as they became known, were more interested in making a fortune than in the railroad itself and would do the minimum necessary to collect the generous subsidies voted by Congress in 1862. Judah refused to accept their scheme to "move" the Sierra foothills, with their higher subsidy per mile, several miles closer to Sacramento. He also objected to "polite embezzlement" by the Big Four in awarding construction

contracts to themselves, and complained loudly of the poor work being done by Crocker's crews. Judah was on his way back East in search of money to buy out the Sacramento merchants when he died of fever in Panama. The railroad proceeded just fine without him, giving the Big Four the predicted stranglehold on western commerce. Little remains today to recall Judah except a boulevard in San Francisco and a monument in Sacramento.

Helen Hinckley, Rails From the West, A Biography of Theodore Judah *(San Marino, n.d.) is adequate.*

Winnie Ruth Judd

(1905-   ). She was the sensation of Los Angeles for one banner-headline week in 1931. On October 20 local newspapers announced the "amazing and grewsome discovery" of the bodies of two women, one of them dismembered, in trunks which had been shipped by rail from Phoenix to L.A. The alleged perpetrator of the "fiendish" act (assumed at first to have been male) was revealed the following day to be an attractive 25-year-old doctor's wife, Mrs. Judd, still "evading one of the greatest criminal dragnets ever spread in the West." The *Los Angeles Times* got hold of a long, incoherent letter written by the fugitive to her husband, a disordered account of anger and jealousy involving the two dead women. By week's end, Mrs. Judd, who had walked some twenty miles to Altadena where she hid out in a tuberculosis sanitarium, had surrendered and the *Times* was running her personal memoirs. She was soon

extradited to Arizona, adjudged insane, and committed to the state hospital. There the story would have ended except that Mrs. Judd proved an accomplished escape artist. Over the years she went AWOL seven times, the last time remaining free for several years as housekeeper-companion to an elderly woman in Northern California. By then it was 1969, she had served 38 years for her "fiendish act," and was arguably rehabilitated. When she was apprehended, **Melvin Belli** rose to defend her, offering to hire Mrs. Judd as his own housekeeper. She was finally paroled in 1971.

Winnie Ruth Judd *(NY, 1973), by Dwight Dobkins and Robert J. Hendricks is largely from the Arizona point of view.*

C[ourtney] C[hauncey] Julian (1885-1934). It was one of the biggest scandals in Southern California history, leaving the leaders of Los Angeles business and society exposed as a gang of financial pirates. C.C. Julian, a Canadian-born huckster, arrived on the scene in 1921, set out to find oil, and struck four gushers in a row. A master of what was then called ballyhoo, he wrote his own advertising copy: "Hey! Redbloods!" he asked, "If you were given a tip on a racehorse that was a strong favorite at odds of 30 to 1, would you place $50 or $100 on him?" Needless to say, Julian "Pete" (Petroleum Company) never found another drop of oil, but pools of gamblers were formed, each enriching itself with the proceeds from the next.

Somewhere along the way Julian exited from the scam, leaving associates to issue some five million shares too many in his company. When the bubble burst in 1927, panic broke out at the Los Angeles Stock Exchange on Spring Street. Members of the original pool, having reaped $670,000 interest on a $1 million investment, were indicted for usury—including **L.B. Mayer** of MGM; **Harry Haldeman**, head of the Better America Federation; and **C.B. DeMille**, who had recently run the moneylenders out of the temple in his film *Kings of Kings*. Julian, ever an artful dodger, bought a local radio station to broadcast his opinion of current events— "applesauce," he concluded—and continued to promote a mineral venture in Inyo County and oil wells in Oklahoma. But high drama soon degenerated into soap opera. In 1928 Julian brought an insanity complaint against his wife, who promptly divorced him and had his L.A. mansion with all its contents—including a gold-lined bathtub—sold at auction. In 1933 he jumped bail on a mail fraud charge and turned up with a beautiful nineteen-year-old "secretary" in Shanghai, where he made his last headline by committing suicide after a party at the Astor Hotel.

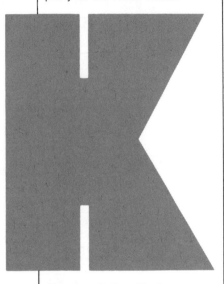

Henry John Kaiser

(1882-1967). He was a Paul Bunyan of American industry, a grade-school drop-out who built faster and bigger dams, bridges, and ships. Born in New York state, Kaiser was a road-builder in the Pacific Northwest before establishing his headquarters in Oakland in 1921. He soon acquired a reputation for accomplishing the impossible. He had no cement plant when he bid on his first dam contract and no shipyard when World War II broke out, but he managed to bring in Hoover Dam two years ahead of schedule and to turn out Liberty Ships in record time at his new

Richmond yard. A steel plant in Fontana, built to supply the shipyard, became the largest in the West; an aluminum plant, created to supply the Kaiser-Frazer Automobile Company, became the world's fourth largest. (The auto company, one of few Kaiser failures, was phased out after ten years.) Something of a health nut—he stoked his enormous energies with the new chemical vitamins and hormones—Kaiser established an important new prepaid health care program, his proudest accomplishment. In 1954 he retired to Hawaii, where he dredged, hauled, and built a resort complex at Waikiki. At the time of his death, there were 170 major Kaiser plants in 30 states and 40 countries, plus 29 hospitals and 42 clinics. *Fortune* magazine eulogized the founder as the most dynamic industrialist since Henry Ford and possibly the most versatile ever. But the legendary Kaiser energy began to dissipate in the second and third generations.

Kaiser Industries was liquidated in 1977, leaving under family control only the steel plant in Fontana, by now a white elephant and the largest single source of air pollution in Southern California.

The only book on Kaiser concerns his health plan: Kaiser Wakes the Doctors *by Paul DeKruif (New York, 1943).*

Isaac Smith Kalloch

(1831-1887). Kalloch, who had a meteoric career as mayor of San Francisco, was probably the most famous American preacher of his day after Henry Ward Beecher. Like Beecher, he too was involved in a major sex scandal, while head of his own parish, Boston's Tremaine Temple Baptist Church. (**R.H. Dana** successfully defended Kalloch in an 1857 trial, the transcript of which became a bestseller.) Later, during a decade in Kansas, the Reverend Mr. Kalloch branched out as a horsebreeder, railroad superintendent, and college president. Wherever he went, the "Sorrel Stallion," as the handsome, charismatic preacher was called, became embroiled in controversy. Moving suddenly to San

DE-YOUNG FIRING UPON KALLOCH FROM THE CARRIAGE

Francisco in 1875, he established the Metropolitan Temple, the largest Baptist church of the day, which provided him with a salary of $20,000 yearly and a twenty-room mansion on Mission Street. Kalloch soon went into politics as a champion of **Kearney**'s Workingmen's Party against the "millionaire monopolists." When *S.F. Chronicle* editor **Charles de Young** called him a "travelling mountebank" and a "burlesque divine," raking up his colorful past, Kalloch replied with comparable aspersions against the de Young family. The conflict escalated alarmingly: Charles de Young shot Kalloch twice; Kalloch survived to become mayor in 1879; and when authorities made no move to prosecute de Young, Kalloch's son shot and killed the editor, for which he was tried and acquitted. (Historian James Bryce remarked that Kalloch, Jr., "had only done what the customary law of primitive peoples requires. It survives in Albania and is scarcely extinct in Corsica.") As mayor, Kalloch was entirely preoccupied with self defense. The board of supervisors, dominated by Boss **Buckley**'s machine, tried to impeach him for encouraging "turbulent and vicious" parades and for accepting free railroad passes. His political base destroyed by bickering, Kalloch retired after his term was up and in 1883 left San Francisco for the (hopefully) greener pastures of Washington Territory.

M.M. Marberry obviously enjoyed writing his biography of Kalloch, The Golden Voice (New York, 1947)

Denis Kearney

(1847-1907). "Nowhere else," Karl Marx wrote of San Francisco in the late 1870s, "has the upheaval most shamelessly caused by capitalistic centralization taken place with such speed." Instead of a Lenin or a Stalin, however, San Francisco produced Kearney, a barely literate former sailor from Ireland, to lead the working class protest against the "bloated bondholders." Actually, Kearney got a lot more mileage out of attacking the other end of the economic spectrum, filling the sandlots with his harangues against the Chinese. The high point of his career came late in 1877, when he led crowds up to railroad baron **Crocker**'s Nob Hill mansion, separated by a spite fence from a despised Oriental neighbor—a graphic juxtaposition of the dual enemy, the rich and the Chinese. Kearney's Workingmen's Trade and Labor Union elected a third of the delegates to the 1878 state Constitutional Convention, but they were too

politically inexperienced for the most part to translate their beliefs into legal clauses. In the 1879 municipal election in San Francisco, the Workingmen's slate included a rabid Fenian for sheriff, a grade-school drop-out for school superintendent, a lottery vendor for tax collector, and **Isaac Kalloch**, the controversial Baptist preacher, for mayor. Kearney, meanwhile, went to jail briefly for calling **Claus Spreckels** a labor thief. (He lacked the wits to prove it, a rival labor leader jeered.) There was dissension in the workers' ranks and complaints that Kearney was keeping all the contributions for himself. He soon lost control of his party, for which he blamed the shiftlessness of the working class. Thanks to an inheritance which he multiplied on the stock market, Kearney moved up to Pacific Heights and a life of leisure. (It has been suggested, and the idea is not entirely implausible, that the "inheritance" was a bribe.) But he remained a troublemaker to the end. Shortly before his death in Alameda where he moved after the earthquake, Kearney tipped off San Francisco graft investigators to the existence of a double set of books kept by the Southern Pacific.

James Bryce devoted a chapter in his American Commonwealth (1889) to "Kearneyism in California," but a British peer could hardly be expected to do justice to an Irish labor rebel. Every U.S. history book devotes a paragraph to Kearney's "the Chinese must go," but so far no biographer has tackled the problematic Kearney himself.

Stephen Watts Kearny

(1794-1848). In the American conquest of California, Kearny represented sober authority as against mere adventurism. A career army officer from a prominent New Jersey Tory family, he became known as the father of the U.S. cavalry (or dragoons, as they were then called) during years of Indian fighting on the Great Plains. In 1846 Kearny was given command of an expedition to take possession of Upper California from Mexico, with the rank of General of the Army of the West. Having met **Kit Carson** en route with the news that California was already pacified, Kearny was therefore unprepared on arriving in December 1846 for his clash with the Californios at San Pasqual, described as the worst American defeat since 1812. (As horsemen, the cavalry general noted grimly, the Californios were all so skilled they could be circus daredevils.) Rankling over his losses and the fact that he had to be rescued by the U.S. Navy, Kearny was further aggrieved when Commodore **Stockton** named **Frémont** his successor as civil governor of California. Kearny's were indisputably the superior orders from the military point of view, and there was little doubt of the immediate outcome. But despite (or perhaps because of) his courtmartial for insubordination, Frémont emerged as the popular hero of the day. Kearny, posted to Mexico, soon died of yellow fever. There are California towns and schools named for both Frémont and Stockton, but there is only an army base named for Kearny. (The San Francisco street is named for Civil War hero Philip Kearny.)

Dwight Clarke's Kearny, Soldier of the West *(Norman, OK, 1961) is a staunch defense of the general. With his intimate knowledge of the facts, Clarke has some interesting comments to make on Irving Stone's fictionalized version of the same events in* Immortal Wife, *the life of Jessie Benton Frémont.*

William Keith

(1838-1911). A Scot who arrived in California in 1859 to do engravings for a *Harper's* magazine article, Keith became the premier artist of the state's bonanza era. He

possessed the facility to turn out a picture in a few hours, specializing in brooding landscapes pierced by rays of sunlight. A Swedenborgian who believed in mystic occurrences, Keith used to argue with his friend and fellow countryman **John Muir** about the accurate representation of nature. But there was no arguing with his success. Keith's canvases sold at fantastic prices for the day, between $1,000 and $2,000 apiece, to the railroad and Comstock magnates. "To have one of his dim meadows in the parlor," wrote historian

Oscar Lewis, "was as much a badge of social consequence as a summer at Del Monte." (Keith's work was also very popular in Boston, it should be pointed out.) Trading on his social contacts, he also did portraits in the style of Rembrandt of such worthy local burghers as **D. O. Mills**, **Joseph LeConte** and **Collis Huntington**. Keith lived in Berkeley for 25 years, commuting to a succession of studios in San Francisco where he held social and artistic court, an eminent Bohemian with his long shaggy mane. Thousands of his paintings were destroyed in the 1906 earthquake and fire, but Keith was so prolific that on his death five years later he left 400 canvases, which sold for an average of $1,500 apiece. (There are also a lot of phony Keiths, particularly in Southern California, it seems.) There are permanent displays of his work at the Oakland Art Museum and at Saint Mary's College in Moraga.

Brother Cornelius of Saint Mary's, author of Keith, Old Master of California, *two vols. (NY, 1942 and Fresno, 1956) was a leading member of the Society for Sanity in Art.*

Robert Walker Kenny

(1901-1976). Kenny was California's leading liberal jurist from the Depression through the McCarthy era. The son of a banker, he graduated from Harvard Military Academy in Los Angeles and drove up to Stanford (B.A., 1920) in his own Stutz Bearcat. Going first into journalism and then into law, he became a municipal court judge at 29 and a New Deal activist, afflicted with a strong case of what he called

"infracaninophilia"—love of the underdog. Elected to the state Senate as a Democrat (1939-1943), he introduced 46 bills on his first day, including a proposal to outlaw capital punishment. As state attorney general (1943-1947) Kenny investigated migrant labor conditions, restrictive housing covenants, and school segregation. Persuaded to run for governor in 1946, he was defeated in his own primary by Republican **Earl Warren**, who cross-filed as a Democrat. He spent the next decade defending constitutional liberties on a national scale. As attorney for the Hollywood Ten, Kenny devised what became known as the "Augmented" and "Diminished Fifth" defenses. He also fought against blacklisting and was one of the attorneys along with Ben Margolis who successfully fought Smith Act prosecution of California Communist leaders all the way to the Supreme Court in 1956. Previously, Communist party membership had been considered synonymous with sedition; Margolis and Kenny demanded proof of sedition, which broke the back of the Smith Act. Kenny spent his last years as an L.A. Superior Court judge, looking in his black robes like "a Gaelic version of one of the lesser Buddhas," his biographer remarked, dispensing good humor along with justice.

Janet Stevenson's The Undiminished Man; A Political Biography of Robert W. Kenny *(Novato, CA, 1980) is an appreciative account.*

Stan Kenton (Stanley

Newcombe Kenton, 1912-1979). It was the summer of 1941 when a tall,

gangly local boy, a graduate of Bell High School (1930), opened at the Rendezvous Ballroom in Balboa. With its sharp syncopation and screaming brass, the loudest ever, Kenton's band would provide the music for the coming of age of the World War II generation. The band moved up to Hollywood Palladium, the swankest ballroom of the day, in the fall of 1941, and began to tour cross-country. In New York, their music was considered undanceable, but in fact Kenton disdained "dance" music. "Our band is for creating moods and excitement," he explained. "Our band is built to thrill." In 1947 he moved into progressive jazz, and in the 1950s explored "third stream" music, trying to bridge the gap between classical and jazz. (His theme "Artistry in Rhythm" was based on Ravel's *Daphnis and Chloe*.) The Kenton sound would never again be so right as it was during the dawning days of World War II. In 1957,

Kenton bought the old Rendezvous in Balboa and found that you can't go home again. His old fans were tuning into Lawrence Welk while a new generation had been weaned on rock 'n' roll, which Kenton dismissed as "children's music." Personally, the years took a heavy toll on the constantly peripatetic bandleader, who suffered recurring bouts of alcoholism and depression. A convert to Freudian psychiatry, he always had a busful of musician-patients. Three marriages ended in divorce, and the problems were passed along to a second generation. Kenton's daughter Dana (1956-   ) had drug problems as a preteenager and social workers placed her at Synanon for therapy. Her brother Lance (1958-   ) joined her there and remained as one of **Chuck Dederich**'s trusted lieutenants. In 1978 Lance Kenton was charged with conspiracy to commit murder in connection with the rattlesnake attack against a Los Angeles lawyer fighting a custody suit against Synanon.

Carol Easton, Straight Ahead, The Story of Stan Kenton *(New York, 1973) is conventional biography. William F. Lee,* Stan Kenton: Artistry in Rhythm *(Los Angeles, 1980) is a collective sketch.*

Jack Kerouac (Jean Louis Kerouac, 1922-1969). A working-class writer of French-Canadian descent, Kerouac was a Columbia University dropout from Lowell, Massachusetts, a self-educated vagabond whose autobiographical novels became the holy writ of the generation he named "beat." Spawned on the streets of

New York, the Beat generation came of age in San Francisco, the lodestar of Kerouac's continuous wanderings during the 1950s. A refugee from suburban repression, he travelled light—hitching, or hopping freights, buses, "travel bureau" cars, and even stolen cars, the latter courtesy of **Neal Cassady**. Cassady was part of the magnetic pull of the West Coast, but there was also the mystique of the road, the pure experience of perpetual motion unlocking memory and desire. In 1951 Kerouac spent six months writing in Cassady's attic on Russian Hill. On other trips he worked as a Southern Pacific brakeman out of San Francisco. The lights of the downtown office buildings reminded him of Sam Spade, and the fog inspired him with an "end-of-the-continent sadness." People-wise, he thought everybody looked like "broken-down, handsome, decadent movie actors." On a bus trip south to L.A., coming down the Grapevine into the city's "great sprawls of light" he fell in love with a Chicana seatmate, but their love did not survive a few weeks of (north again) stoop labor in the San Joaquin Valley. Kerouac's travels were curtailed by celebrity when *On the Road* was finally published in 1957. There followed a rapid succession of remembrances-on-the-run by the American Proust, as he liked to think of himself. *Dharma Bums* (1958), inspired by a camping trip to Yosemite, includes an account of **Ginsberg** (Goldbook) reading "Howl"

("Wail"), while *Big Sur* (1962) is a chronicle of the author's nervous breakdown at **Ferlinghetti**'s cabin there. (That trip, he came west by crack train, and flew back.) Kerouac once tried to transplant his widowed mother to Berkeley, but the operation didn't take. California, the end of the road, was a dead end for him. He eventually returned to live in Lowell, Massachusetts, and then in Florida. Earthbound, he drank himself into an early grave.

There are several works on Kerouac, of which Dennis McNally's Desolate Angel; A Biography of Jack Kerouac, the Beat Generation and America *(New York, 1979) is the most comprehensive and up-to-date.*

Clark Kerr (1911-   ). More than any other state, California embraced the ideal of public higher education for all, a goal which Kerr was instrumental in promoting until it backfired on him. A Quaker from Pennsylvania with a Swarthmore B.A. (1932), he earned his Ph.D. in economics (1939) at the University of California, Berkeley. Appointed a Berkeley professor of industrial relations, Kerr gained a national reputation as a labor economist and arbitrator. He became chancellor at Berkeley in 1952 and president of the entire UC in 1958 in a calculated effort to restore good will after the McCarthy-era loyalty oath crisis. He also wrote a "Master Plan for Higher Education," forecasting advanced education for 50 percent of the state's college-age students. Kerr launched construction of three new UC campuses during his administration. Within the university he put an end to overt discrimination by fraternities and sororities, and supported student political activities. But despite his strong liberal credentials, he looked very uptight and bankerly and for all his efficiency was sometimes an indecisive administrator. Moreover, barely a year before the Free Speech crisis broke on him, he wrote the scenario for his own downfall in a lecture at Harvard University, describing the "multiversity" as a knowledge industry with students as potentially disaffected workers. (It was published in 1963 as *The Uses of the University*). In the fall of 1964 when students went on strike to protest curtailment of their "free speech," Kerr tried to play his usual conciliatory role, mediating

between the governor who wanted order restored and the students who of course did not. He survived the immediate crisis but two years later, only 17 days after the inauguration of Governor **Reagan**, Kerr was abruptly dismissed.

The Berkeley Student Revolt *(Garden City, N.Y., 1965), edited by Seymour Lipset and Sheldon Wolin, is a collection of readings on the end of the Kerr administration.*

Ken Elton Kesey

(1935-   ). Kesey was a graduate writing fellow at Stanford in 1958 when he volunteered for drug experiments at the local veterans' hospital. The hospital inspired his successful first novel, *One Flew Over the Cuckoo's Nest* (1962), and the drug experience launched him as a pathfinder in the psychedelic era. Exploring the parameters of permissible madness in contemporary society, Kesey became the center of a group called the Merry Pranksters, specialists in public put-ons. In 1964 the group set out on a stoned journey to the East, traveling across country in a highly-amplified, day-glo-painted schoolbus. Hitting all the high spots of the hippie era, they visited **Timothy**

Leary in Millbrook and **Fritz Perls** at Esalen, California; they attended the Beatles concert at San Francisco's Cow Palace, and invited the Hell's Angels to meet the hippies at Kesey's place in La Honda, California. Militantly apolitical, Kelsey played "Home on the Range" on his harmonica at a 1965 antiwar rally. Instead, of activism he sponsored public "acid tests" which expanded into "be-ins" and the mixed-media "Trips Festivals" at the Fillmore Auditorium in San Francisco, the convention center of hippiedom, where he presided as Captain Marvel. Busted for drug possession in 1965 and again in 1966, Kesey fled to Mexico. Society needs outlaws, he believed, but he got tired of the paranoia and returned to serve six months on a California work farm before retiring to the relative obscurity of an Oregon ranch.

Tom Wolfe's Electric Kool-Aid Acid Test *(New York, 1968) about Kesey and the Pranksters is prime reportage of the psychedelic era.*

Asa Keyes (1877?-1934).

As district attorney of Los Angeles County during the graft-ridden roaring Twenties, Keyes (rhymes with "tries") led a life of constant temptation. In 1925 Governor **Friend Richardson** accused him of leniency towards "arch-criminals," in particular a bunko artist named Big Hutch who was allowed to cop a plea and then escaped from a road camp. When **Aimee Semple McPherson** disappeared in 1926 and returned with an improbable story of kidnapping, Keyes charged her with perjury and false evidence, then dismissed the case on the

eve of trial amid rumors of a $30,000 bribe. A native of Los Angeles and long-time civil servant, he managed to buy a house on Rodeo Drive in Beverly Hills. It was the **Julian** petroleum case that proved his undoing. In 1928 a grand jury indicted the D.A. for allowing the Julian "Pete" swindlers to go free in exchange for a bribe from a Spring Street tailor and bootlegger. As the local press summarized, Keyes "acquired bad habits, neglected his work, fell in with evil companions. . . and at last his liquor-weakened moral fiber yielded under stress of temptation." He was tried, convicted, and sentenced to one to fourteen years in San Quentin, which posed something of a security problem since he was responsible for the presence there of fully a third of the current inmates. Continuing to protest his innocence, he was pardoned after nineteen months by Governor **James Rolph** and returned home to Beverly Hills to begin a second career as an automobile salesman.

Edward Kienholz

(1927-   ). "No giggles in the gallery," the press reported on Kienholz's 1966 show at the Los Angeles County Museum of Art, which the board of supervisors had tried to ban as obscene. Something of a cultural primitive from the backwoods of the Washington-Idaho border region, Kienholz arrived in Los Angeles in 1953. He was so poor that he scavanged materials for his constructions, or free-standing assemblages; and L.A., a city of incredible waste, seemed like a gold mine. His was an art of the streets, a gut commentary on such current events as school integration, or the execution of **Caryl Chessman**. ("If you believe in an eye for an eye," the artist inscribed on his piece, *Psycho-Vendetta*, ". . . stick out your tongue.") Kienholz had his first exhibit at the Cafe Galleria in Laurel Canyon in 1955. Avoiding the formal art establishment, he opened his own galleries, Now in 1956, and Ferus in 1957. Soon he became the leader of avant-garde art in L.A. A favorite hangout was Barney's Beanery, which Kienholz reproduced in a 1965 tableaux, conceiving the customers as clockheads. (A Beverly Hills stockbroker bought the construction for $25,000.) His most controversial piece, the one that offended the moral sensibilities of the county board of supervisors, was *Back Seat Dodge '38* (1964), a car he found in Santa Monica Canyon and fitted out with mannequin lovers in the back seat. (The door of the Dodge was opened for inspection 32 times on the first day of the 1966 exhibit, the press noted.) In 1973 Kienholz left Los Angeles for a year in Berlin. Finding a more congenial and receptive environment for artists there, he and his wife-and-collaborator, Nancy Reddin, the daughter of an L.A. police chief, subsequently divided their time between Europe and Hope, Idaho.

Billie Jean Moffitt King (1943-   ). As a tennis champion from the

public parks of Long Beach, King more than any other U.S. player helped transform the game from a stuffy country club exercise into a highly lucrative professional sport. She took her first lesson from a Recreation Department teacher at Houghton Park, with her mother selling Tupperware to help pay the expenses. Two days before graduation from Long Beach Polytechnic High School, the chubby seventeen-year-old left for Wimbledon, where she and Karen Hantze won a surprise doubles title. King won three consecutive Wimbledon singles titles (1966-1968) under the old amateur system

that provided only "expenses" to the top players. She would go on to win three more Wimbledon titles as a pro. Always outspoken on the subject of open tennis, or open money for all players, she signed one of the first pro contracts in 1968, then worked and played overtime to gain equal status and prize money for women players. Open tennis meant an endless succession of airports, motels, and fast food restaurants. In 1971 and 1972 she earned the top prize money in women's tennis, $100,000 a year. During these years she also had two knee operations, an abortion which became a subject of public

controversy when she signed a public petition, and rare reunions with her husband, a sports promoter with his own jet-set schedule. Later, there would be a media flap and a court case over the resolution of a lesbian affair. The high point of King's career was the night she beat **Bobby Riggs** at the Houston Astrodome in 1973. "Tennis finally got kicked out of the country clubs forever and into the world of real sports," the country's top female jock wrote of her victory. "Balloons, bands, noise, the works. . . I loved it." King's brother Randy Moffitt played baseball for the San Francisco Giants.

King has produced two as-told-to memoirs under the same title, Billie Jean *with Kim Chapin (New York, 1974) and* Billie Jean *with Frank Delford (New York, 1982), the latter to have the last word on her lesbian affair.*

James King of William (1822-1856). King stands dramatically in San Francisco history as the conscience of the city, the martyr who purchased public redemption with his life. Born in Washington, D.C., where the name King was so common he added the patronymic William after it, he set out for the West for his health just before the discovery of gold was broadcast. King established a successful banking operation in San Francisco but was ruined by an embezzling employee. Determined to pay his debts and reform the city in the process, he turned to journalism. As crusading editor of the *Bulletin*, established in 1855, "he was as the avenging fury to all corrupt judges, dishonest

officials, bought jurymen, and political hirelings." **Josiah Royce** credits him with a courage approaching desperation. Read today, his editorial diatribes convey a quality of hysteria and personal vengeance rather than public service. Not surprisingly, King made many enemies, including a newly elected city supervisor who shot him after having his past residence in Sing Sing exposed by King in the *Bulletin*. While King lingered between life and death for a week, San Francisco's second Vigilance Committee was formed, gave the culprit a rudimentary trial, and hanged him while the bells of the city were tolling King's death knell. A mile-long funeral procession, the most imposing in San Francisco history, bore the editor's body to Lone Mountain. As Royce wrote, "The deed aroused the greatest exhibition of popular excitement in the whole history of California."

Villains and Vigilantes by Stanley A. Coblentz (New York, 1936) is dated.

Thomas Starr King

(1824-1864). A highminded Unitarian minister from Boston, Starr King was considered a moral giant in Civil War San Francisco. Arriving in 1860 with a "providential intimation," he found the city "a vast struggle of houses over half a dozen sand hills," the streets "bilious with Chinamen." But he soon achieved a social stature unattainable by a self-educated preacher in Brahmin Boston, and he discovered the mountains and redwoods, which inspired his Yankee imagination with yearnings for "Yosemites of the soul." A stirring orator, Starr King is credited with almost singlehandedly swinging California to the Union cause. He lectured up and down the state, drawing inspiration from biblical and geographical themes: "The Choice Between Barabbas and Jesus," "The Treason of Judas Iscariot," "Lessons from the Sierra Nevada,"

"Living Waters from Lake Tahoe," etc. **Bancroft** described him as small of stature, with soft and luminous eyes and a gentle disposition, yet capable when aroused of swaying multitudes. By 1864 he had achieved financial security thanks to some silver investments, and had moved into a new Gothic-style church on Geary Street, the Union flag flying from the roof, when he died suddenly from pneumonia. As historian Kevin Starr points out, Starr King stands second only to Lincoln in state history as a martyr for the Union cause. There is a monument to him in Golden Gate Park, a mountain named for him in Yosemite, and a redwood in the Mariposa Grove. He is one of only two Californians represented in the Congressional Hall of Statuary, the other being **Junípero Serra.**

Arnold Crompton's Apostle of Liberty; Starr King in California *(Boston, 1950) is the most recent biography.*

The Kingston Trio.

The top-selling U.S. music group circa 1960 was the Kingston Trio, three Stanford-area college boys singing folk and calypso tunes in fraternity-house harmony. Pondering what to do after graduation, Bob Shane (Menlo College, 1957) and Dave Guard (Stanford, 1956), both from Hawaii, and Dave Reynolds (Menlo College, 1956) from California, put together an act and opened at San Francisco's Purple Onion in 1957. For a few brief shining years they enjoyed top billing at the hungry i in San Francisco, the Ash Grove in Los Angeles, and the Newport

Jazz Festival. With their West Coast preppie style—crew cuts and button-downs and cute wives in pedal-pushers—they were the last musical survival of the Eisenhower era, soon to be rendered as obsolete as dinosaurs by the rock music and hippie revolutions of the 1960s. Guard sold his share (for $300,000) in 1961, leaving a reconstituted trio which finally went into limbo in 1967.

Abbot Kinney

(1850-1920). Only scattered remnants remain today of the dream of Kinney, a modern Ozymandias who brought the canals of Venice to the Southern California coast. Born in New Jersey of good New England lineage (R.W. Emerson and O.W. Holmes were relatives), he studied in Europe before making his fortune as a cigarette manufacturer. Traveling the world in pursuit of health, he settled near Sierra Madre in the San Gabriel Valley in 1880. There **Helen Hunt Jackson** found him, master of an improbable snow-white hillside house called Kinneyloa staffed by Chinese servants and an army of gopher-hunting cats. Jackson (who later wrote a book called *The Hunter Cats of Connorloa*) drew on Kinney's knowledge of local Indian lore in her 1883 investigation of California's Mission Indians. A universal intellect, Kinney wrote books on sociology, metaphysics, child-rearing, and free trade, as well as a descriptive treatise on the beneficial properties of the eucalyptus. Having concluded that "for men of Anglo-Saxon

for Knowland's U.S. Senate seat, Knight was defeated, as was Knowland for governor. Back in L.A., Knight had his own TV show briefly, "Judge for Yourself," dispensing legal education to laymen, and accepted a comfortable sinecure as an insurance company executive.

The University of California, Berkeley, conducted extensive oral history interviews on the Knight administration.

Walter Knott (1889-1981). The great common man, California-style, survived a fatherless childhood and hard-scrabble years of farming to create the state's second largest amusement park. As a boy in Pomona, Knott was an enterprising backyard farmer. He tried cantaloupe picking in the Imperial Valley, raised beans in the Coachella Valley, and struggled unsuccessfully to farm a Mojave Desert Homestead. After years in the wilderness he joined a cousin in Buena Park. An Anaheim city park superintendent named Boysen had experimented nearby with a giant berry; Knott tracked down a few withered vines which he carefully husbanded into a successful farming operation during the Depression. To supplement their roadside berry stand, Cordelia Hornady Knott began serving chicken dinners, so good that they attracted long lines of customers. The amusement park evolved as entertainment for the overflow crowd from the restaurant. Knott built a ghost town in 1940, followed by a gold mine, more restaurants, other diversions, and most of them on pioneer themes of man vs. nature. Eventually three

or Teutonic descent, the climate of the foothills is used up in the course of three or four summers," he purchased coastal land near present-day Santa Monica. He apparently considered turning Santa Monica Canyon into the Nob Hill of L.A. and lined the streets of the palisades with the salubrious eucalyptus but eventually decided to bypass the bluffs in favor of the sand dunes. Kinney's approach to land development was to combine art with utility,

history with hygiene. To drain the marshy strip of coastline just below Santa Monica, he created a fifteen-mile network of canals suggestive of the Italian lagoon city. For culture, he constructed an auditorium at the foot of a pier and booked Sarah Bernhardt to appear in *Camille*. But visitors to Venice, California, preferred the beach to the lecture hall, side-shows replaced art on the pier, and new residents ignored the Doge's injunction

to build in the Venetian style. Some of the stagnant canals were filled in during the 1930s, but others survive, lined with the usual jumble of Southern California styles of architecture. Kinney's ranch in the San Gabriel Valley is now an expensive tract, Kinneyloa.

Venice, 1904-1930 (Venice, 1978) by Jeffrey Stanton and Annette Del Zoppo, and Fantasy by the Sea (Culver City, 1979, 1980) by Tom Moran and Tom Sewell are both illustrated histories of Kinney's dream.

Goodwin Jess Knight (1896-1970). At the age of fourteen, according to his campaign literature, Knight was already out on the hustings, handing out leaflets urging **Hiram Johnson's** election as governor. He graduated from Manual Arts High School in L.A., went on to Stanford (1919), was admitted to the bar in 1921, and served eleven years as a Superior Court judge in L.A. He also made a modest

fortune speculating in gold and commodities. But Knight's real love was politics. Elected lieutenant governor in 1946 and 1950, he even considered running against popular governor **Earl Warren**. When Warren was appointed to the U.S. Supreme Court, Knight replaced him in 1953. A middle-of-the-road Republican, "Goodie" Knight mobilized strong labor support to win his own term in the

governor's mansion in 1954. He was husky and hearty, given to a lot of convivial backslapping and sonorous speeches. A widower, he became the first governor to marry in office, choosing for his bride the composer of a campaign song entitled "Our Goodie." Knight's political career came to an abrupt end in 1958 when **William F. Knowland** elbowed him out of the gubernatorial nomination. Running instead

KNOTT'S BERRY FARM

BOYSENBERRIES 5¢ Box

generations of Knotts were involved in the do-it-yourself, pay-your-own-way (no bank loans) Berry Farm Park, which managed to thrive even in competition with nearby Disneyland. A replica of Independence Hall was completed in 1966 and in 1971 a theater named after **John Wayne** ("a true Berry Farm kind of man"). The Knotts continued to live frugally behind their berry market, American Gothic millionaires, but they now bought the berries from other farmers. A Goldwater supporter and contributor to conservative causes, Walter Knott became a popular after-dinner speaker on behalf of free enterprise and the American dream. He also returned to the desert to buy the real ghost town of Calico, where his uncle John King had worked the Silver King mine. Restored by the Knotts,

Calico became a county park.
Helen Kooiman, author of Walter Knott, Keeper of the Flame *(Fullerton, CA, n. 1973), makes no claim to objectivity.*

Knowland Family. They were as proper Californian as it is possible to be, pioneer stock, conservative Republican pillars of the community of Oakland for a century. Joseph Russell Knowland (1873-1966), born in Alameda and educated at the College of the Pacific, became a six-term U.S. Congressman (1904-15), publisher of the Oakland *Tribune* which he bought in 1915, and a charter member of the state historical society. His son William Fife Knowland (1908-1974) went into politics after graduating from the University of California in 1929. As a member of the state legislature W.F. led the campaign against **Tom Mooney**'s release and

supported his local D.A., **Earl Warren**, for state leadership. Locally, Knowland's influence was so strong that opponents once campaigned to "Take the Power out of the Tower," meaning the *Tribune* tower. In 1945, when he was still overseas during World War II, William Knowland was appointed by Governor Warren to fill out **Hiram Johnson**'s term as U.S. Senator. Twice reelected, he became known as the "Senator from Formosa" for his strident support of Chiang Kai-shek. His militant anti-Communism helped foster a Korean War climate of fear and anxiety, particularly on the West Coast. (Knowland talked about invading mainland China—what if China decided to invade mainland California?) Slow, deliberate, highly ambitious, Knowland became Senate majority leader and aspired to the U.S. presidency, calculating that his best bet was through the California governorship. He declared his candidacy in 1958 without consulting incumbent governor **Goodwin Knight**, who had to settle for a U.S. Senate nomination. Running on an open-shop platform with gratuitous references to Hungarian freedom fighters, Knowland was defeated (so was Knight), leaving the presidential field clear to another ambitious Californian, **Richard Nixon**. Reduced to the status of publisher in a depressed community rocked by black power militancy, Knowland tried belatedly to bring the *Tribune* into the twentieth century. His father had been so straitlaced that he had refused to call

Governor Brown "Pat"; William Knowland loosened things up, making space for what he called responsible black leadership, but community PR was not his strong suit. Shortly after the *Tribune*'s 100th anniversary celebration, he was found dead of self-inflicted gunshot wounds at his summer home on the Russian River. **Patty Hearst** had just been kidnapped, and Knowland was fearful of the Symbionese Liberation Army, relatives said.
Joseph Russell Knowland wrote (and published) California, a Landmark History *(Oakland, 1914).*

Jack Kramer (John Albert Kramer, 1921-   ). Kramer was a poor boy from the desert who was inspired by seeing his first tennis match at the Pomona County Fair to imitate the glamorous players in their long white flannels. His family moved to Montebello so he could commute daily by the red cars to the Los Angeles Tennis Club, *the* place for tennis in California after the decline of the Berkeley Tennis Club. The blond crewcut Kramer looked the part of the all-American boy athlete, but looks were nothing compared to his drive. Long white flannels may have appeared

The Spierton

glamorous, but they were cumbersome, so Kramer became the first man to win at Wimbledon (1947) in short pants. A proponent of the ''big game'' characterized by constant attack, he also played the percentages, coolly writing off a certain number of points to conserve his energy for those that counted. After winning his second consecutive singles title at Forest Hills in 1947, he turned professional and dominated the pro circuits until sidelined by arthritis in the 1950s. (His active career was probably extended a few years by the new wonder drug, cortisone.) Kramer then became the czar of pro tennis, organizing and promoting tours and tournaments all over the world. He supported open (professional) tennis, but had become identified with the authoritarianism of the old amateur regime under which top stars collected only ''expenses'' under the table. And when open tennis finally arrived, Kramer refused to offer equal prize money to women, arguing that they could not play as well as men or draw an equal share of the gate. To everyone's relief, he bowed out, with some philosophical remarks about player greed. An astute businessman, independently wealthy after years of taking 50 percent of the gross on the pro circuit, he acquired a Palos Verdes tennis club and the Los Serranos Country Club.

Kramer's The Game; My Forty Years in Tennis *(New York, 1979) has a rare sense of history for a tennis memoir.*

Heinrich Alfred Kreiser. *See* Henry Miller.

FREE LECTURE

KRISHNAMURTI
The World Teacher
''HAPPINESS THROUGH LIBERATION''
HOLLYWOOD BOWL
TUESDAY, MAY 15, 8:30 P. M.
Ensemble of Harps, 8:00 P. M.

Jiddu Krishnamurti (1895-   ). According to theosophist doctrine, California was to be the cradle of a new civilization, the special province of the new ''World Teacher.'' In 1909 sect leader Annie Besant discovered the latter in the person of a young East Indian boy, supposedly the reincarnation of spirtualist Helena Blavatsky who died a few years before his birth. Krishna and his brother Nitya were taken to Britain and raised on the model of proper young Englishmen. They had their teeth straightened, learned to play croquet and golf, and acquired upper-crust accents and haberdashery, including gray homburgs and malacca walking sticks. The World Teacher became a worldly and discontented young man, embarrassed to be considered the ''living flame'' by his friends. The turning point of his life came during a 1922 visit to Ojai (pronounced O-high, theosophists explained), California, selected by Mrs. Besant for its rich occult influences. There Krishna had an out-of-body experience that refocused his life on spiritual matters. Seeking treatment for the tuberculosis of which Nitya eventually died in Ojai, the brothers also visited Hollywood doctors of spiritualistic persuasion who prescribed the **Abrams** Oscilloclast. Krishna returned to Ojai every spring, accompanied in 1926 by Mrs. Besant, who acquired several hundred acres there. In 1928 he made his first U.S. public appearance at the Hollywood Bowl before a rapt audience of 16,000. But the years of preparation were aborted in 1929 when Krishna rejected the role of World Teacher and repudiated organized religion, proclaiming truth a ''pathless land.'' Liberally supported by aristocratic patrons, he continued to lecture, travel, and write as an independent spiritual force, maintaining a base in Ojai where he coexisted with the country club set, Mrs. Besant's successors (she died in 1933) at the Happy Valley School, and even a few resident Rosicrucians. Krishna's ''nondisciples,'' no longer permitted to worship him, might if they really wished present him with a Lincoln convertible or Mercedes Benz, rival guru **Alan Watts** used to say, with affectionate envy.

Krishnamurti's writings take up several inches in the card catalogue of any large library. An excellent account of his early life is given by Mary Luytens, herself a participant in the drama: Krishnamurti; The Years of Awakening *(New York, 1975).*

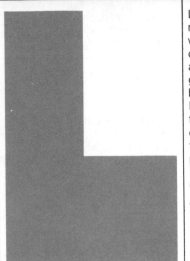

Carl Laemmle

(1867-1939). Laemmle seems the most human of the Hollywood moguls, a tiny patriarch (shorter than **Mary Pickford**) with a horde of hungry relatives and a reputation for penny-pinching. An immigrant from Germany, he first got into the nickelodeon business in the Midwest because he owned a long narrow drygoods store, just right for projecting the early "flickers" after hours; and from exhibition he moved into production. Laemmle is credited with inventing the star system to create a demand for his films, and he took great pride in his legal battle with the Trust which claimed a monopoly on motion picture patents. He took somewhat less pride in his product. He made a virtue out of necessity during the Trust-dodging years, shooting the first film on location abroad: *Ivanhoe* (1913), in England, of course. And when director Erich von Stroheim went ruinously over budget on *Foolish Wives* (1921),

Laemmle advertised the first million-dollar movie. But he was best known for quickie comedies, cheapie westerns, and salaries so small that the greatest talents in the business (**Mary Pickford** and **Irving Thalberg**) slipped through his fingers. He also established the only city in the world dedicated to movie production. Universal City, located in the historic Cahuenga Pass where **Andrés Pico** surrendered to **Frémont**, was a 230-acre principality with its own police and fire departments, a main thoroughfare named Laemmle Boulevard, and a poultry farm for Laemmle's prize leghorns. Uncle Carl picked up a little money on the side by admitting tourists for 25 cents each, and posted warnings to turn off the lights. Laemmle bought **Tom Ince**'s palatial Benedict Canyon estate, complete with private projection room (partially

deaf, he preferred the old silents), and made an annual pilgrimage home to Laupheim, Germany. After his death, 70 relatives were found on the studio payroll. (As Ogden Nash put it, "Uncle Carl Laemmle/Has a very large faemmle.") The Laemmle theatre chain was founded by Carl's cousins Max and Kurt. Universal was taken over in 1969 by Music Corporation of America (MCA). Admission to Uncle Carl's tour is now $9.75.

John Drinkwater's Life and Adventures of Carl Laemmle *(New York, 1931) is a commissioned biography.*

Louis L'Amour

(Louis Dearborn LaMoore, 1908-). California is full of record-holders for every category of novel ever sold. In the Western genre, **Zane Grey's** successor was L'Amour, a drifter from North Dakota who was a longshoreman, sailor, professional boxer, and lumberjack before publishing his first book—poetry—in 1939. In the early 1950s, under the pseudonym Tex Burns, he wrote the Hopalong Cassidy series which developed into a popular TV series. In 1953 L'Amour had his first *succès d'estime* with *Hondo*, which was made into a film the following year. He wrote *Shalako* (1962) and *Catlow* (1963), both of which also paid off as films. In the mass paperback market, L'Amour passes for something of a scholar of the old West, mining old pioneer journals and folk traditions to create authentic frontier drama. His novels, featuring stock characters like the lonely drifter and the mysterious villain, make a

distinction between builders and exploiters of the westward movement. They also convey reverence for nature, a concern with the cultural melting pot, and proud individualism. Included among L'Amour fans, mostly conservative nostalgia-buffs, are Dwight Eisenhower and **Ronald Reagan**.

Roger Dearborn Lapham

(1883-1966). A leading shipping executive and one-term mayor of San Francisco, Lapham possessed a rare quality verging on extinction: tolerance of dissent. Born into a Yankee clipper famiy and graduated from Harvard (1905), he inherited a fair amount of noblesse oblige along with the presidency of the family American-Hawaiian Steamship Company (better known by workers as "American Highwayman") with headquarters in San Francisco. During the 1936 waterfront strike Lapham alone accepted **Harry Bridges**'s challenge to shipowners to debate the issues before 10,000 striking workers, winning points for gumption if nothing else. A globetrotter by predilection as well as vocation, he had to surmount a court challenge by **Vincent Hallinan** over his legal residence before he could run for mayor of San Francisco in 1943. Once elected, he appointed a Communist to the city's committee on race, a labor radical to the UN committee, and an anarchist to the art commission. When a local gadfly challenged municipal acquisition of the Market Street Railway, Lapham personally signed a petition for his own recall to get the issue on the ballot. The big event of his administration was the 1945 conference on the United Nations, which the gregarious mayor hosted with gusto. He also tried to get San Francisco appointed permanent UN headquarters, but the Russians vetoed the city as too far away from world capitals. Lapham retired after a single term as mayor, going off on diplomatic assignments to China and Greece. A rare voice of moderation during the Cold War, he served as director of the anti-McCarthy Fund for the Republic.

Lapham's wife Helen Abbot Lapham wrote Roving with Roger *(San Francisco, 1971).*

Thomas Oliver Larkin

(1802-1858). A Yankee trader and diplomat in Mexican California, Larkin was probably the only man who enjoyed the confidence of both sides during the American conquest. Although he had been urged by Governor **Juan Alvarado** to

apply for Mexican citizenship and land grants, "Señor Larquin" remained loyal to his Massachusetts birthright, preferring to buy his land outright—bargaining shrewdly, of course. In Monterey, where he settled in 1833, he built California's first two-story house in a style subsequently called Monterey colonial, a gracious mixture of Spanish and Yankee traditions. In 1844, on being appointed U.S. consul in Alta California, he immediately sent back East for an elegant uniform with a generous supply of gilt buttons. His voluminous correspondence reveals political realism and wit, whatever the occasion. "I am decidedly a Government Upholder," he wrote during the 1845 revolution, "and will assist a new Government the same as I did the old one." A year later, with the arrival of **Frémont** and the revolt of the Bear Flaggers, Larkin noted that "the pear is near ripe for falling," all the while keeping up his ceaseless traffic in "callicos" and "brown Mantas." The American conquest brought a boom in

trade and also a final tug at the trader's loyalties. Trying to effect a peaceful transition, he found himself caught between Californios and Americans—"a fall of either appeared sad to me." After his consulship expired in 1848, Larkin traveled to Washington to lobby on behalf of his financial claims, including payment for a wharf built for the Mexicans plus various "exigencies of the war." Although most of his claim was disallowed, he remained a wealthy man, the owner of some 100,000 acres in California. In San Francisco where he settled in 1848, he at one time owned all the land extending from present-day Larkin Street to the sea.

Reuben Underhill wrote a Larkin biography, From Cowhides to Golden Fleece *(Stanford, 1939, 1946). George Hammond edited* The Larkin Papers, *10 vols. (Berkeley, 1951-1964). A smaller collection of Larkin's correspondence (*First and Last Counsel, *San Marino, 1962) was edited by John Hawgood, a British scholar who doesn't think local historians are up to snuff.*

Jesse Louis Lasky

(1880-1958). One of the founding fathers of Hollywood, Lasky grew up in the Bay Area. Moving from San Jose ("a city where you could take your time about dreaming") to San Francisco, he played the cornet for German-American picnics, cooch dancers, and traveling medicine shows. He tried the Alaska Gold Rush and the Hawaiian Islands, returning home broke. It was in vaudeville that he first found his stride, as a duo-cornet act with his sister Blanche and then as the entrepreneur of such improbable acts as the Lasky

Quintette—four girl cellists and a male bass playing Victor Herbert music from inside a giant sea shell. His brother-in-law Sam Goldfisch (later **Goldwyn**) came up with the idea of making movies. In 1913 they sent **Cecil B. DeMille** west to shoot *Squaw Man*, Hollywood's first feature film. In 1916 there was a merger with Adolph Zukor's Famous Players, which in the 1920s became Paramount. In charge of production from 1916 to 1932, Lasky alternated between a twenty-room apartment in New York and a 50-room Santa Monica beach house with two swimming pools. A street was named after him in Beverly Hills, on the site of a race-track of which he was a director. But Paramount ran into hard times—**Fatty Arbuckle**, who was tried for manslaughter, director **William Desmond Taylor** who was murdered, and actor Wallace Reid, who died young of dope addiction, were all under contract to the studio—and Lasky, something of a lamb among the Hollywood lions, took the heat. He continued to produce independently after 1932, functioning as executive idea man. One of his better ideas was a film about a simple war hero named *Sergeant York* (1941).

See Lasky's autobiography, I Blow My Own Horn *(Garden City, NY, 1957).*

Peter Lassen

(1800-1859). Lassen was a Danish-born blacksmith and trapper who found a paradise for the taking in Northern California before the American conquest. He arrived overland in 1839 and soon applied for

Mexican citizenship and for a 22,000-acre land grant within view of the volcano now bearing his name. Following the example of **John Sutter**, Lassen tried to create a self-sufficient community at his ranch, with his own blacksmith shop and a vineyard tended by Indians. In 1847 he went east with **Stockton**'s party, returning the following year with a group of settlers from Missouri, some of whom complained that the Lassen Trail did an unnecessary amount of meandering. Nor did they appreciate Lassen's Benton City, named for the Missouri senator, which soon lost its citizens to the Gold Rush and eventually slid into the river. A poor businessman, Lassen is said to have understood "the mountains, the rocks, the rushing streams, and even the wild Indians better than civilization." After losing his ranch in 1850 he dreamed of a 50,000-square mile territory called Nataqua extending from California into present-day Nevada, with himself as

president. And of course there was always the hope of striking it rich in the gold fields. It was while he was out prospecting that "Old Pete," as his cronies called him, was murdered by the Indians. A county, a national park, a forest, and a mountain were eventually named in his honor. Until the recent eruption of Mount Saint Helens, Lassen Peak, which underwent a period of activity from 1914 to 1921, was considered the only active volcano in the 48 states.

Ruby Swartzlow's, Lassen, His Life and Legacy (Mineral, CA 1964) is for local history buffs only.

Fermín Francisco de Lasuén (1736-1803).
Historically, Lasuén has suffered by comparison to **Junípero Serra,** whom he succeeded as president of California's missions. Where Serra was a dynamic trailblazer, Lasuen was a plump diplomat, according to biographer Francis Guest; and while Serra was driven by zeal, Lasuén was motivated primarily by obedience. In fact, after ten obligatory years

of mission work in Baja California, Lasuén had asked to return to Mexico City, consenting to remain in California only as a penance to obedience to his vows. Lasuén's apprenticeship in Alta California under Serra was admittedly difficult. First assigned to San Gabriel as a supernumerary, he received his own mission at San Juan Capistrano only to take refuge in San Diego after an Indian attack exposed the vulnerability of the Franciscans in outlying areas. Lasuén remained at San Diego, considered the most difficult mission in California, until his appointment to succeed Serra in 1785. His tenure as president of the missions (1785-1803) was a period of development and expansion, with the number of missions doubling to eighteen. In fact, instead of "withering away" as originally intended when the Indians achieved maturity, the missions were being consolidated as ends in themselves. The very picture of portly benevolence, Lasuén weathered a scandal over the ill-treatment of Indian neophytes and successfully countered charges by enemies of the missions. He was buried at Carmel Mission, and the headland at Los Angeles Harbor was named Point Fermin in his honor.

Francis Guest wrote Lasuén, A Biography (Washington, DC, 1973).

Milton Slocum Latham
(1827-1882). Latham served only five days as California's sixth governor, then resigned to fill a vacant seat in the U.S. Senate in 1860. A senator was considered to outrank a state governor in

those days, and Latham, an ambitious, aggressive young man, had an abiding interest in rank and all its trappings. Born in Ohio and graduated from Jefferson (Pennsylvania) College in 1845, he spent a few years in the South where he was recruited to the "chivalry," the pro-slavery wing of the Democratic party. Following the Gold Rush to California, he was elected a U.S. Congressman in 1852; three years later, he returned to San Francisco as collector of customs, a powerful patronage position. In the 1857 U.S. Senate elections Latham was outmaneuvered by **David Broderick**, but fell heir to the seat (1860-1863) after Broderick's death. His political ambitions buried in the Civil War, Latham returned to San Francisco to go into banking and investments. In 1874 he was charged with accepting a $250,000 bribe for delivering the California Pacific Railroad, of which he was director and treasurer, to the Southern Pacific, but the matter was apparently dropped. A key figure in fashionable society, Latham maintained a townhouse in Rincon Square and a palatial estate in Menlo Park, with a whole retinue of butlers and footmen. His second wife, Mollie McMullen, ordered two trousseaux yearly from Paris and was one of **Gump**'s largest customers for household ornamentation. **Gertrude Atherton** wittily describes how the Lathams once made elaborate preparations for the proper entertainment of an English duke, who turned up dressed as a cowboy.

Latham's papers in the Stanford

University Library have so far inspired two M.A. theses. He is not to be confused with a later Milton Latham, a Harvard graduate who established the Latham Foundation for the Promotion of Humane Education in Berkeley.

Annie Laurie (Winifred Black Bonfils, 1863-1936). The first women journalists were called sob sisters because they were supposed to make readers weep over homeless children, fallen women, and lost dogs. A handsome former chorus girl from Wisconsin whose primary qualification for journalism was sheer brass, she got a job in 1890 with **William Randolph Hearst** who promoted her as Annie Laurie, the *San Francisco Examiner*'s answer to Nellie Bly. Privately, she used her first husband's name, Black, even after her marriage to Bonfils. Her first assignment was to faint on Market Street in order to do an exposé of ambulance and

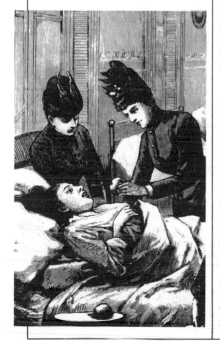

hospital services. Another of her stories, about the crippled son of a prostitute, led to the establishment of the Little Jim Fund for a children's hospital. She became a local fixture in San Francisco, leading the march at the Policeman's Ball, campaigning against the closure of streetcorner flower stands, and urging the preservation of the Palace of Fine Arts. Hearst transferred her for awhile to New York where she enjoyed the status of an international celebrity, making news as well as reporting it. She traveled to the South to expose child labor, to the South Pacific to visit a leper colony, to Paris for the 1919 Peace Conference, and to Utah to investigate Mormon polygamy ("Crush the Harem!"). There were also a few years in Denver, where her second husband was an editor, but she eventually returned to her Spanish-style home on Russian Hill. One of her last assignments, a measure of Hearst's confidence in her, was to write the authorized biography of his mother.

Ernest Orlando Lawrence (1901-1958). The prophet of big-machine, high-energy physics, Lawrence was a "can-do" scientist, an innovator who ignored the constraints of theory and tradition to improvise around the impossible. Some of his ideas did not work, of course, but the cyclotron did. Arriving at UC Berkeley in 1928, the Norwegian-American from South Dakota with a Yale Ph.D. (1925) took over an old wooden shack on campus and put together a team of

gung-ho assistants to man his first jerry-built cyclotron for accelerating particles in a circular magnetic field. By 1930 Lawrence had become the youngest full professor in UC history, and in 1938 he was awarded the Nobel Prize, the first winner from Cal (or any other state university, for that matter). He also became something of a celebrity, everybody's favorite physicist, with his picture on the cover of *Time* magazine.
Lawrence's cyclotrons, by first making possible the production of large amounts of fissionable material, led to the World War II Manhattan Project for the design and creation of the first atomic bombs at Los Alamos, New Mexico under the auspices of the University of California. During the Cold War, Lawrence's operations expanded to a former naval base in Livermore, where **Edward Teller** created the first thermonuclear device. The university also developed a sideline in nuclear medicine under Lawrence's brother

John, an M.D. and pioneer in radiation therapy for cancer. Essentially a promoter, Ernest Lawrence attracted talented scientists, energized them with his ideas and his optimism, and left them to do the work while he travelled in the innermost circles of the military-industrial complex. He became the personal friend of admirals, generals, regents, and just plain captains of industry, who considered the engaging inventor refreshingly normal for an "egghead," just one of the boys at the exclusive Bohemian Club. In keeping with his international stature, Lawrence enjoyed prerequisites somewhat beyond the means of most university professors: a ranch on Mount Diablo where he escaped to tinker with color-TV tubes, a beach house in Balboa, and a new Cadillac every year. He also enjoyed his own private endowment fund, made up of contributions from wealthy admirers, which he used to help like-minded physicists. Basically a conservative cold warrior, he had no patience with "bohemians" in the laboratory, even writing off his old friend **Oppenheimer** for less than true-blue Americanism. Thanks to Lawrence's genius and his tireless efforts, about a third of the entire UC budget at the time of his premature death consisted of funds earmarked for support of Los Alamos and the radiation labs.

An American Genius; The Life of Ernest Orlando Lawrence, Father of the Cyclotron (New York, 1900) by Herbert Childs is authorized and comprehensive. For a more controversial view, see Lawrence and Oppenheimer by Nuel Pharr Davis (New York, 1968).

Timothy Francis Leary (1920-   ). The prophet of LSD, Leary started out as a promising young Ph.D. (1950) from the University of California, Berkeley. As director of psychological research at the Kaiser Foundation Hospital in Oakland (1955-1958) he devised a widely used personality test—so widely used that it was administered to the author himself when he was later jailed on drug charges. Leary first took LSD around 1960 while teaching at Harvard, which fired him for his psychedelic experiments. Convinced of the drug's "redemptive" potential, he became an itinerant evangelist, proclaiming that LSD would cure even homosexuality. Back in hippie-generation Haight-Ashbury, he advised the faithful to "turn on, tune in, drop out." By California standards, Leary rated as something of a

square, a generation removed from the real action. While **Ken Kesey** and his Pranksters were exploring the great outdoors tripped out on acid, Leary was seated lotus-style on an Oriental carpet behind drawn bamboo-stick curtains, master of the controlled environment. While Kesey was capturing virgin Pepsi-generation minds, Leary's appeal was to the uptight adult world. But for sheer persistent outlawry, Leary outdid all rivals, graduating with dishonor from another basic California institution, the penal system. Busted in 1970 and sentenced to ten years on drug charges, he escaped that year from a minimum security "POW" prison camp near San Luis Obispo. (The Weatherman Underground took credit for arranging the escape, and the FBI later spread the word, possibly untrue, that Leary finked on them. Fleeing abroad, he was deported from "eleven backward nations," according to his counterculture *curriculum vitae*, and eventually returned to serve a total of four years in California prisons. Emerging cheerfully unrepentant in 1976, he developed a new specialty in the mildly provocative: lectures on "What Does Woman Want?", bumperstickers proclaiming intelligence the "Ultimate Aphrodisiac," and a 1982 debate tour with Watergate burglar Gordon Liddy.

Leary wrote Jail Notes *(New York, 1970) and* Confessions of a Hope Fiend *(New York, 1973).*

John LeConte (1818-1891) and **Joseph LeConte** (1823-1901). When the University of California opened in 1869 with eight professors, two of them were the brothers LeConte. Born in Georgia of French Huguenot descent, they grew up on a plantation where they were educated by their father, a passionate amateur scientist. Both John and Joseph earned medical degrees but preferred to study and teach the natural sciences, Joseph going to Harvard to do post-graduate work under Agassiz. Having lost their land and slaves in the Civil War, pessimistic about the future of the South under Reconstruction, they considered emigrating to Maximilian's Mexico before they were accepted by the new California university, of which John became president (1876-1881). For Joseph particularly, the move west was enormously stimulating, both intellectually and socially. Relieved of the burden of personal responsibility for his slaves, he was also thrilled by individual freedom from restraining influences. Both brothers were avid outdoorsmen and found much food for scientific thought in California. Always interested in optics, John wrote a study on the deep blue color of Tahoe and other high mountain lakes. Joseph, during long fruitful summers in the Sierra, developed his belief in evolutionary idealism, finding God immanent in the majestic Yosemite. An exceptionally popular teacher, he sometimes attracted so many students it took him a month to grade exams. Frank

Norris remembered his lecture on glaciers as such a masterpiece of analytical eloquence that students burst into applause. Joseph was also one of the founders of the Sierra Club, which erected a lodge in Yosemite in his honor. He continued to make pilgrimages into his beloved mountains well into his 80s, wondering each time, "Is this my last, my very last?" He died in camp at Glacier Point on a Sierra Club expedition.

The Autobiography of Joseph LeConte was published posthumously (New York, 1903).

Andrew Daulton Lee
See Christopher John **Boyce.**

Lotte Lehmann (1888-1976). In 1939, one of the world's leading sopranos retired to Santa Barbara to live out her remaining years in stately serenity. Prussian by birth but Viennese by warm personality, Lehmann was considered in her day a great operatic actress, a regal beauty with a voice of great "melancholy expressiveness." From such starring roles as the Marshallin in Strauss's *Rosenkavalier* she turned in her later years to *lieder*, less demanding on the voice. Lehmann gave her final concert in Santa Barbara in 1951, although she remained active as a teacher at the local Music Academy of the West. She chose an Austrian-style country house in Hope Ranch, but in other respects entered into the spirit of her new home. She became a naturalized citizen in a 1945 ceremony at the Santa Barbara courthouse. She appeared in a 1948 MGM movie, *Big City*, and is said to have coached actress-singer Jeanette MacDonald. (Her better-known pupils include Grace Bumbry and Shirley Verrett.) Santa Barbara designated her birthday as Lotte Lehmann Day and in 1968 presented her with a cake in the shape of the Vienna State Opera House. The concert hall at UC Santa Barbara was named in her honor; and she left her papers, including correspondence with Strauss, Puccini, and Toscanini, to the UCSB library.

Lehmann wrote two memoirs, Midway in My Song *(New York, 1938) and* My Many Lives *(New York, 1948), principally about her years as a diva.*

William Alexander Leidesdorff (1810-1848).

A major figure in early San Francisco history, Leidesdorff arrived in 1839 as captain of a schooner in the hide and tallow trade. Born in the West Indies of Danish and Creole parentage, he settled in Yerba Buena in 1841, became a naturalized Mexican citizen, and applied for a 35,000-acre land grant in the Sacramento Valley. The enterprising Leidesdorff also served as **Thomas Larkin**'s vice-consul,

ran a ship's chandlery, kept the books as treasurer of San Francisco, and imported a Russian sidewheel steamer that took eight days to travel from San Francisco Bay to Sacramento and later sank in a gale. Obviously distracted, he earned a reprimand from Larkin for failing to inform him of the Bear Flag revolt and the capture of the eminent **Mariano Vallejo**.) A bachelor, Leidesdorff possessed a romantic aura; there were rumors of a southern belle who died of a broken heart when her family rejected him as a mulatto. After his own premature death and burial at the Mission Dolores, his estate produced a hornet's nest of lawsuits. The downtown San Francisco street bearing his name, once located on the waterfront, receded with the generations to become the "paupers' alley" of the stock exchange district.

Leidesdorff's San Francisco Town Journal *(San Francisco, 1926) is a facsimile edition of the account book he kept as a city treasurer, showing total municipal assets of $4,476 in 1847.*

James Lick (1796-1876). Lick was the proverbial eccentric bachelor millionaire, a penny-pinching pianomaker who became one of the wealthiest men of his day, the Carnegie of California. Born in Pennsylvania of German farming stock, he apprenticed as a carpenter and left for South America some time after fathering an illegitimate son. It is said that the girl's father, a miller, rejected him, and that he left with a broken heart, but Lick was as sparing with basic information as with a dollar. After twenty years in Argentina and Peru he arrived in San Francisco in 1847 with a $30,000 nestegg and with 600 pounds of chocolate to sell for his Peruvian neighbor (and later San Franciscan) Domingo Ghirardelli. Everybody thought Lick was crazy to invest his money in sand dunes and mud holes, but with the Gold Rush the value of his property skyrocketed. During 30 years in California he built a series of monuments, starting with a mansion and a mahogany-lined flour mill (so much for the Pennsylvania miller!) in San Jose. In 1862 he opened the Lick House on Montgomery Street, San Francisco's first grand hotel. In Southern California, he acquired Catalina Island and the Los Feliz Rancho. "Of irritable and thoroughly disagreeable temperament," as historian **H.H. Bancroft** remarked, Lick ended his days in a small room at his hotel, working and reworking his will to make sure that the forlorn of the world would benefit from his fortune, later estimated at $1,750,000. For orphans, he willed an asylum;

for old ladies, a home; for the great unwashed, a public bathhouse; for poor boys, a vocational school; for dumb animals, a gift to the SPCA. His greatest benefaction was the Lick Observatory, opened on Mount Hamilton in 1888 with the largest of the nineteenth century telescopes, under which Lick lies buried. (Scientist **George Davidson** suggested cremation, to which Lick replied, "No, sir! I intend to rot like a gentleman.") Besides the observatory, other contemporary survivals of the miserly millionaire are the Lick Freeway (Highway 101) linking San Francisco and San Jose, and the Lick-Wilmerding Vocational School, where the former pianomaker's workbench is prominently displayed.

The Generous Miser (Pasadena, 1967) is a cursory biography by a great-grandniece, Rosemary Lick.

José Yves Limantour

(?-1885). The largest and most audacious land fraud in state history was attempted by a French resident of Mexico, who was a shipping magnate and soldier of fortune. Limantour had curried favor with Governor **Manuel Micheltorena** during the 1840s in order to get a land grant, the borders of which he later altered to take in half of San Francisco, including Alcatraz and the Farallon Islands. His expanded claim was pronounced valid by the Board of Land Commissioners in 1856, causing widespread consternation among inhabitants of the area in question, some of whom paid a total of $300,000 for quit-claims. Limantour was brought to trial in 1858 and convicted of fraud. To escape imprisonment he fled to Mexico, where his son and namesake became a minister of finance and his grandson a symphony conductor.

Kenneth Johnson, José Yves Limantour v. The United States (Los Angeles, 1961).

Malcolm Lockheed (1887-1958) and Allan Haines Lockheed

1889-1969). They were aviation pioneers who gave their youth and their Scots name (originally spelled Loughead), to a firm that would grow into the nation's largest defense contractor. Their mother, Flora Haines Apponyi Loughead (1855-194?), was a daring woman for her day, a novelist (*The Abandoned Claim*, 1891) and journalist in San Francisco and Santa Barbara. Their older half-brother Victor, who spelled his name Lougheed, was an engineer who published early books on aviation (*Vehicles of the Air*, 1909). Allan taught himself to fly and in 1916, he and Malcolm set up shop in Santa Barbara as Loughead Aircraft. (Pronounced Lockheed, the

family name was changed to the phonetic version in 1919.) The company first produced the F-1 Flyboat, the largest seaplane of its day. After a trip by F-1 to the channel islands in 1919, the king and queen of Belgium awarded the brothers the Order of the Golden Crown. Despite the success of the Lockheed Vega, in which Wiley Post and **Howard Hughes** set records, the aircraft company went through various vicissitudes—Malcolm leaving to work on hydraulic brakes in Detroit, Allan selling real estate in the San Fernando Valley on the side—before it was sold in 1929 to the management that made it a leader in aviation and defense contracting. When Allan Lockheed returned to aviation after World War II with a twin-engine monoplane, he had to resume the Loughead trademark.

Jack London (John Griffith London, 1876-1916).

London burst on the American literary scene in the year 1900 with his powerful tales of man against nature. The illegitimate son of an astrologist and a spiritualist,

he grew up in the Bay Area where his stepfather John London made several unsuccessful attempts at farming. A school dropout at thirteen, at fifteen he was carousing with oyster pirates on the Bay, at eighteen he rode the rails across the U.S. and back, and at 21 he was a veteran of the Alaska Gold Rush. London's thirst for knowledge led him to consume Spencer, Huxley, and Darwin; his experience of poverty turned him to Marxism. Thanks to enormous perseverance, the "Boy Socialist" of the Bay Area evolved into the "father of proletarian literature" in the U.S., his sheer crude vitality making Victorian sentimental mannerism seem insipid by comparision. The best of his books are *Call of the Wild* (1903), *Martin Eden* (1909), and *John Barleycorn* (1913). Unabashedly materialistic, London was a prodigal and profligate son who turned out novels at the rate of two or

three a year and made enormous sums for the day but always spent more than he earned. In 1910, after two years in the South Seas, he returned to settle in the Valley of the Moon, where he planned to farm his 1,500 acres scientifically and to build a redwood and stone castle. Wolf House burned before it was finished and London, deep in debt and subject to black moods, committed suicide soon thereafter. He is buried near the ruins of Wolf House, now Jack London Historical Park. Biographer **Irving Stone** considers him an archetypal Californian: a man of strong physical appetites, pagan and iconoclastic, antipathetic to tradition, spontaneous, enthusiastic, reckless—a prince of good fellows who worked, played, and lived to the utmost. California's first native literary genius was also a white Anglo-Saxon chauvinist and an eternal child whose photos at the age

of 40 reveal a bloated boyishness.

See Irving Stone, Sailor on Horseback (Boston, 1938) and for a more critical, even Freudian assessment, chapter 7 of Kevin Starr, Americans and the California Dream (New York, 1973; Salt Lake City, 1981).

Anita Loos (1888-1981). A Northern Californian by birth, Loos, who began writing scripts for **D.W. Griffith** when she was a teenager, held the southern part of the state in low esteem. Northerners were descended from argonauts, she maintained (her maternal grandmother, Cleopatra Fairbrother Smith, arrived by clipper via Panama with a grand piano in her baggage), while southerners waited, lazily, for the railroad. In the early days of the century, the Loos family drifted south, where her brother Clifford became a pioneer in group medicine (Ross-Loos) and Anita was soon the prolific author of jaunty-jolly, charmingly impudent scripts. The ease of her accomplishment added to her cynicism about Hollywood, where former chambermaids and chauffeurs were enjoying overnight celebrity, instant wealth, and unlimited power in the most costly form of entertainment ever devised. Loos, a tiny (four foot eleven inch, 90-pound) vampish brunette with China-doll looks and a taste for elegant couture, became a celebrity in her own right: the "Soubrette of Satire," fan magazines called her. From two-reelers for Griffith she moved on to custom tailor projects for Douglas Fairbanks, Sr. and Constance Talmadge. But she yearned for the sophistication of New

York and would spend eight days of a two-week layover between pictures making the round trip in the elegant Santa Fe Super Chief and the Twentieth Century Limited, all mahogany panelling and lace antimacassars. On one of these trips, inspired by a would-be actress whose admirers included H.L. Mencken, she scribbled down a story about a dumb ingènue named Lorelei Lee. Published in 1925, *Gentlemen Prefer Blondes* would eventually go through 45 editions, establishing Loos as the Colette of American sexual comedy. Personally, as befitting a daughter of argonauts, she had a weakness for rogues and brigands, among whom she included her husband John Emerson and her great pal **Wilson Mizner**. She modeled the Clark Gable role in her screenplay of *San Francisco* (1936) after Mizner.

Loos wrote two charming memoirs, A Girl Like I (New York, 1966) and Kiss Hollywood Goodbye (New York, 1974). Cast of Thousands (New York, 1977) is an illustrated, coffee-table enlargement of the first two.

Loud Family. At first glance they seemed ideal candidates for a TV documentary on family life: an affluent, handsome, energetic family of seven, living out the American dream in a Santa Barbara ranch-style house with view, pool, three-car garage. "A lovely family commercial," Pat Russell Loud (1926-)thought it would be, although she knew better. Producer Craig Gilbert, who chose Santa Barbara after reading local writer **Ross MacDonald**'s detective novels about man's search for family, was then undergoing a divorce and had his own gloomy thoughts on the subject of The Family. His ambitious, aggressive film crew, all easterners, just reeled it all in, sure they were on to a good thing. In fact, each side of the camera was exploiting the other, a perfect symbiosis of exhibitionist and voyeur. Beyond the plastic California facade, the camera revealed Bill Loud (1921-), successful salesman and apparently unfaithful husband, overwhelmed by his five teenagers and their hordes of friends; and his slender, long-suffering wife, tolerant of her children (particularly of their eldest son, camping it up as a drag queen) but not of her husband. The camera seemed to exaggerate fault lines and catalyze tensions, culminating in the break-up of both marriage and family. The twelve-part series first ran on public TV in 1973, arousing particular interest in the East, which congratulated itself on its superiority to western mindlessness. Anthropologist Margaret Mead called the documentary the most

important event in human thought since the invention of the novel, while the *New York Times Magazine* compared Bill Loud to Willie Loman, a modern everyman. The Louds felt exploited at first but moved quickly to cash in as talk-show guests. Pat Loud even found her midlife identity crisis eased by celebrity: "Apparently I've acquired a real self just by being on Channel 13." A defector from the California dream, she left stuffy Santa Barbara to join the opposition. At last report she was living in New York, and four of her five children were seeking careers in show business.

Pat Loud wrote A Woman's Story, prime soap opera, with Nora Johnson (New York, 1974).

Frederick Ferdinand Low (1828-1894). California's ninth governor, a former shipping clerk from Maine, Low arrived in 1849 on the same ship from Panama with **William Gwin**, **Hall McAllister**, and Jessie Benton **Frémont**. Going into business in Marysville with two brothers, he branched out into banking and inland steamship operations. Low was a practical, common-sense Yankee who regarded Yankee who regarded business as his life's work but consented to accept election to Congress in 1861. Returning to California in 1863 as collector of the port of San Francisco (he accepted the job out of patriotic duty, he said, considering it not particularly remunerative), he was soon elected as the candidate of the Union (Republican) party to the first four-year term as governor (1863-1867). Low later led a faction called, for some forgotten reason, the Short-hairs. He opposed special legislation favoring private enterprise, refused to encumber the state with debt for railway construction, and spoke out courageously against the persecution of Orientals, although he favored immigration restrictions. A supporter of public education, he laid the groundwork for the establishment of the University of California which dedicated a library to him in gratitude. President Ulysses S. Grant sent Low to China and Korea as U.S. Minister (1869-73), after which he returned to San Francisco as manager of the Anglo-California Bank (1874-1891).

Thaddeus Sobieski Coulincourt Lowe

(1832-1913). Lowe started out as a balloonist, an explorer of "the great easterly river of the sky," serving during the Civil War as an aerial spy for the North. At the age of 56, independently wealthy from his water-gas process and appliance business, he moved to California for a change of pace. From his manorial residence on Orange Grove Avenue in Pasadena, he pondered the majestic wall of the San Gabriel Mountains, and conceived the idea of a "railway to the stars." Others said it couldn't be done, but Lowe found a way, using cable supported by an electric trolley system. The Mount Lowe Railway, the steepest line of its day, was completed to Echo Mountain (3,000 feet) in 1893 and to 5,000 feet in 1895. (The peak named after Lowe extended to 6,100 feet.) With its bridges

NEW-YORK, JULY, 1866.

seemingly suspended in air and its dramatic route through yawning precipices, the railway was a major tourist attraction for 25 years. ("Switzerland and Italy combined," ads promised. "From Roses and Orange Groves to Snow in Two Hours' Time.") Lowe built hotels and an observatory and installed a searchlight with a beacon visible 150 miles away at sea. His plans also

called for a vast underground temple and an institute where scientists could meditate in the quiet, clear atmosphere. A better inventor than a businessman, he lost his mountain empire to bankruptcy in 1898. The railroad was taken over by Pacific Electric and continued to run until 1938, when the mountain was allowed to reclaim its course. Lowe's many descendants include his

son Thaddeus, Jr., who managed the Grand Opera Block in Pasadena, and a granddaughter Florence Barnes McKendry, who gained some notoriety during the interwar period as a society aviatrix.

Eugene Block, Above the Civil War; The Story of Thaddeus Lowe *(Berkeley, 1966).*

Charles Fletcher Lummis (1859-1928).

Lummis was a man of grand affectations, a professional character who worked the gray area between showmanship and scholarship in turn-of-the-century Los Angeles. Born in New England and educated at Harvard, he threw off traditional Yankee inhibitions to go native Californian, calling himself Don Carlos, dressing picturesquely in a green suit, red sash, and Indian jewelry, and acquiring considerable attention as a result of his womanizing and drinking. His very arrival in 1885 was an act of grandstanding: Lummis walked to Los Angeles from Cincinatti, 3,705 roundabout miles in four and a half months, heralded by bulletins to **Harrison Gray Otis** of the *L.A. Times.* Otis even met him at the San Gabriel Mission and accompanied him the last ten miles into town. Lummis went to work for Otis as city editor the following day, but theirs was not an entirely congenial collaboration. (When Lummis proceeded to expose wrongdoing by a police chief Otis supported, the publisher replied, "This is contrary to the policy of the *Times.*") Lummis worked himself into a nervous collapse in 1887, retired to the wilderness for a dramatic recovery, and returned in 1894 as editor of *Land of Sunshine*, a Chamber of Commerce publication renamed *Out West* in 1902. He used his magazine to promote local culture and launched crusades to restore the missions, canonize Father Serra, save the redwoods, protect the Indians, and above all to extol the Spanish heritage. ("Though my conscience was Puritan, my whole imagination and sympathy and feeling were Latin.") Incidentally, he also promoted tourism, inventing the slogan "See America First." As city librarian of Los Angeles (1905-1910) Lummis was shockingly unconventional, sponsoring

groups like the "Bibliosmiles" with their lectures on "The Six Best Smellers" and branding books like cows. He also wrote prolifically: ads, ballads, brochures, travel books, 2,500 letters yearly and a diary that grew to 40 volumes. (His wife divorced him when she found one volume detailing his love affairs—written in Spanish and Greek.) If this were not enough, he built his own rock castle using boulders from the Arroyo Seco ("Any fool can write a book. . . It takes brains to build a house"). El Alisal, named for the sycamore tree, became a mecca for visiting celebrities. Nearby, Lummis founded the Southwest Museum, but lost control of it in 1915 to a more

conventional group of trustees. The eccentric editor, an anachronism even in his own time, was buried at El Alisal, which survives as an historical landmark.

Lummis's many works include A Tramp Across the Continent *(New York, 1892) and* The Land of Poco Tiempo *(New York, 1893). Edwin Bingham's* Charles F. Lummis, Editor of the Southwest *(San Marino, 1955) is considered the best of the biographies.*

William Gibbs McAdoo

(1863-1941). Woodrow Wilson's secretary of the treasury, his son-in-law, and his heir apparent, McAdoo retired from Wilson's cabinet in 1918 to establish an

independent political base in California. For the next twenty years the Georgia-born lawyer who had made a fortune building New York's Hudson River tunnels would be the storm center of California Democratic politics. In partnership with other politically ambitious attorneys, he had a clientele that included actor Douglas Fairbanks, Sr. who consulted him about the establishment of United Artists, and oilman E.L. Doheny, who kept him on a $100,000-a-year retainer. But McAdoo's consuming interest was politics, into which he plunged as soon as he had established legal residency. By 1924 he had become a "favorite adopted son" with national support for his presidential candidacy. That year McAdoo deadlocked with Al Smith, losing the Democratic nomination on the 103rd ballot to John W. Davis; four years later, McAdoo lost to Smith outright. In 1932 McAdoo threw the California delegation and the nomination

to FDR, while he ran successfully for U.S. Senator, whistlestopping the state in a new Lockheed Vega. Not quite in sympathy with the New Deal, he was nonetheless a loyal party man who built up his own machine with federal patronage. But time and place never came together for McAdoo. He lost control of the state Democratic party to **Upton Sinclair** in 1934 and in 1938 to **Culbert Olson**, suffering a personal defeat for reelection by Ham 'n' Eggs candidate **Sheridan Downey**. That year he was appointed head of the American President Line when the government reorganized **Robert Dollar**'s former company. Political to the end, McAdoo died of a heart attack while in Washington attending Roosevelt's third inaugural.

McAdoo's autobiography, Crowded Years *(Boston, 1931) and J. Broesamle's biography* William Gibbs McAdoo, A Passion for Change *(Port Washington, New York, 1973) both end with the move to California.*

Hall McAllister

(1826-1888). The brother of New York social arbiter Ward McAllister, Hall McAllister was a lawyer and leader of San Francisco society in its first generation. Born to the manor in Savannah and educated at Yale, he represented the epitome of refinement and forensic excellence on the frontier. (His father, Matthew Hall McAllister, also came west and became the first U.S. circuit court judge in California.) A large man, always dressed with dignity in a black frock coat and top hat, Hall MacAllister was considered so eloquent that his court appearances rivalled

opening night at the opera. Having labored mightily to reduce a case to its crystal essence, he would hurl "thunderbolts of scorn, contempt and ridicule" upon his adversaries, (He also had a weakness for incorporating doggerel into his arguments. This endeared him to **Mark Twain**, who wrote an imaginary legal drama starring a Hall McCannister.) McAllister dominated the San Francisco bar from 1851, when he argued the case for the vigilantes against the

lawless "Hounds," until the next generation. His name appears constantly in the early reports of the California Supreme Court. He negotiated a settlement for **James Lick**'s illegitimate son, defended **Adolph Spreckels** for shooting **Michael de Young**, and represented the Big Four against Ellen Colton, **David Colton**'s widow who released **Collis Huntington**'s letters describing bribes and election influencing. And while he may not have been the arbiter of local society (a champagne salesman named Edward Greenaway, originator of the Friday night cotillion, was probably the Ward McAllister of San Francisco), he and his wife, a southern belle with the elegance of a French marquise, entertained judiciously. After the decline of South Park, they moved to a townhouse on Mason near Sutter, also maintaining a country home, Miramonte, near Mount Tamalpais in San Rafael.

McClatchy Family

. The longest-surviving newspaper dynasty in California was established in 1857 by James McClatchy (1824-1883), an Irish-born 49er and activist in the early squatters rights movement in Sacramento. Land monopoly was "the curse, the blight, the dark cloud upon California," according to McClatchy, who was actually indicted (but not tried) for murder when a squatters' riot resulted in fatalities. Such virulent militance would become characteristic of his *Sacramento Bee*, which favored labor and occasionally succumbed to

labor's meaner instincts, including prejudice and intolerance. James McClatchy was succeeded by his sons, V.S. (Valentine Stuart, 1857-1938) as publisher and C.K. (Charles Kenny, 1858-1936) as editor. In 1923 V.S. sold out to his brother for $1 million to devote himself fulltime to the California Joint Immigration Committee, writing tracts against the "yellow peril" and the "Oriental hegira." C.K. was an enlightened supporter of women's suffrage, public ownership of utilities, and labor arbitration but waxed exceedingly wroth over radicalism at home and abroad. He advised vigilance against the League of Nations, death to labor radicals **Tom Mooney** the **McNamara** brothers, and **Anita Whitney**, and the razing of the UC Berkeley campus as a hotbed of Communism, atheism, and free love. An amateur theater critic and biblical scholar, he specialized in weighty admonitions: "We build not our cities with walls. We build them with men . . . ." Under C.K. and his heirs, the McClatchy publishing empire expanded to include the *Fresno Bee* in 1922, the *Modesto Bee* in 1927, and eventually a string of country-western radio stations catering to the tastes of the predominantly agricultural San Joaquin Valley. C.K.'s son Carlos, described as "bibulous," died in 1935; his daughter, Grace Eleanor McClatchy (1895-1980), formerly an aspiring playwright, took over as publisher in 1936. She was something of a recluse who opposed any recognition or privilege for herself, gave away her father's mansion for a library, and moved into the guest house. "I am content to have people think I live in a cave and wear horns," she explained.

Private Thinks by C. K. (New York, 1936) is a collection of editorials.

Robert Paxton McCulloch (1911-1977).

McCulloch, a Stanford engineering graduate (1931) from a midwestern family of industrialists, was an inventor-entrepreneur of Wild West outdoor toys. His first great success was an automobile supercharger which became standard equipment on the souped-up low-riders of the 1950s. He sold the supercharger to Borg Warner in 1943 to concentrate on McCulloch Aviation, a 60-acre complex near Los Angeles Airport. After World War II McCulloch came out with the first one-man chainsaw, capturing 60 percent of the market before he sold it to Black and Decker. His interest in high-performance engines took him from go-karts to helicopters, and from outboard motors to a lake on which to race them. In the 1960s McCulloch developed a new recreational community at Lake Havasu across the Colorado River in Arizona, for which he acquired London Bridge in 1968 as a $7 million conversion piece. Fascinated by gimmicks, he equipped his Palm Desert home with electronic control panels and perhaps the ultimate Southern California **Rube Goldberg** device, a kingsize outdoor sunbathing platform geared to turn slowly for optimum

tanning. McCulloch's high-octane life ended with a lethal combination of alcohol and drugs in 1977.

Ross MacDonald
(Kenneth Millar, 1915-   ). Detective novelist Millar was born in California but uprooted at an early age and raised in Canada. Eventually he earned a Ph.D. in literature and returned in search of his origins, settling after World War II in Santa Barbara ("just the right size for a city—about the same as Athens in the time of Pericles"). Under the pseudonym of MacDonald, Millar created a private eye named Lew Archer, a loner, friendless and seemingly homeless, hard-boiled in the style of a **Raymond Chandler** or **Dashiell Hammett** anti-hero but with a greater capacity for empathy. Most of Archer's cases involve emotionally disinherited children searching for their roots, the

sins of the parents working themselves out in a coastal California landscape besieged by fire, oil spills, and fog. The first two Archer novels were sold to Hollywood and made into disappointing films. (The 1976 *The Drowning Pool* was even reset in Louisiana and rewritten in southern accents.) But Millar continued to write, exploring his own bedrock experiences during a year in psychotherapy. His plots became increasingly convoluted, logically improbable but viscerally satisfying, as he expanded the social, psychological and literary range of the detective form in the context of California's "rockslide culture." Some of the best Archer novels are *The Wycherly Woman* (1961), *The Far Side of the Dollar* (1965) and *Black Money* (1966). Sadly, Millar succumbed to a rare form of premature senility in his mid-sixties. His wife Margaret Sturm Millar also wrote mystery novels.

John McDougal
(1818-1866). California's second American governor was described by contemporaries as a rank opportunist, a dandy, and an alcoholic. Born in Ohio of Scots descent, he arrived in San Francisco on the first steamer from Panama in 1848 and joined a brother in Sacramento, where he participated in the despoiling of **Sutter**'s vast landholdings. Elected to the Constitutional Convention in 1849 as a highly partisan Democrat, he is said to have announced during nominations for lieutenant governor, "I reckon I'll take that—I don't believe

anyone else will have it." When Governor **Peter Burnett** resigned midway through his term, McDougal served a year (1851-1852) as governor. He had a weakness for ruffled shirts, for whisky, and for issuing proclamations beginning "I, John McDougal," for which he became known as "I, John." The major issues of his administration were San Francisco's First Vigilance Committee and the selection of a state capital. McDougal took a public stand against the vigilantes, although he was believed sympathetic to them, and the state capital remained in San Jose, despite efforts and expenditures of various parties on behalf of other sites. Defeated for re-election, McDougal tried to resign at the last minute in favor of political colleague **David Broderick**, apparently just to create a commotion. The former governor's subsequent career was checkered: he was involved in duels with two San Francisco journalists and in 1856 was charged with election fraud. He died age 48 from apoplexy.

John Steven McGroarty (1862-1944).
McGroarty was 40 years old when he arrived in California at the turn of the century, an Irish Catholic from Pennsylvania. He soon made up for lost time, becoming one of the state's all-time most energetic boosters in poetry, history, biography, journalism, and politics. In 1911 he wrote a book giving California equivalents of the Seven Wonders of the World: the missions, the railroad across the Sierra Nevada, the

Owens River Aqueduct, so on. He also wrote a "Mission Play," a California nativity pageant for which he was decorated by the pope and the king of Spain. Premiered in 1912 in San Gabriel with a cast of descendants of old Spanish families, the Mission Play was a regular tourist attraction for many years at Riverside's Mission Inn. Seeking authenticity in all things, McGroarty lived at the Rancho Chupa Rosa in Tujunga and for some twenty years wrote a *Los Angeles Times* Sunday newspaper column datelined "From the Green Verdugo Hills." He must have kept extensive clipping files, for he compiled a dozen large volumes of what were called "mug

books," laudatory biographical sketches of local personages. (One of his collections was immodestly entitled *The California Plutarch*.) In 1933 he was honored as poet laureate of California, and in 1934 he was elected to the U.S. House of Representatives as a Townsendite. The **Townsend** old-age revolving pension plan which he introduced to Congress in 1935 resulted only in ridicule and disappointment, so McGroarty retired to Tujunga to revive his Mission Play, to write a few poems, no doubt, and to collect more short lives of the lesser Californians.

John William Mackay

(1831-1902). The youngest, ablest, and most popular of the Irish Big Four, Mackay was also the only one of them to "give back" any appreciable part of the fabulous silver wealth extracted from the Comstock. Born poor in Ireland, which he left during the potato famine, he joined the Gold Rush to California and worked as a laborer for several years before his first big strike in 1866. Even as one of the world's richest men, he remained simple and unaffected with a preference for homely comforts like corned beef and cabbage. His wife and children on the other hand, preferred to live grandly in Europe. Mrs. Mackay wore more diamonds than the czarina of Russia, it was said, holding court in a four-story Renaissance mansion on the Champs Elysèes. (When she complained of the cold, **Lillie Coit** acidly suggested she put on some more diamonds.)

Bored by society, Mackay lived apart from his family most of the time in hotel suites in San Francisco and New York. He gradually liquidated his mining interests and went on to make a second fortune in the cable and wireless business, breaking Jay Gould's monopoly. A legendary soft touch, he dispensed up to $50 daily while walking from his Palace Hotel suite to his office in San Francisco. His lifetime gifts, including a mining school and a church in Nevada, totaled over $5 million.

Silver Kings by Oscar Lewis (New York, 1947, 1967) is the standard work on the subject.

Rod McKuen (Rodney

Hooper, 1933-   ). A spiritual orphan of Depression-era California, McKuen became history's best-selling poet with his autobiographical verse and lyrics about love and loneliness. He was born in a Salvation Army Hospital in Oakland, the son of a dance hall girl and an unknown father. Raised in WPA camps all over the West, he dreamed of running away to join the movies; instead he became a teenage cowboy and nomadic casual worker. After Korean War military service McKuen got a singing gig at the Purple Onion in San Francisco, moving up from there to a brief Hollywood career as a B-movie version of Tab Hunter. In 1966 he published his first book himself, *Stanyon Street and other Sorrows*, a collection of profoundly obvious, instantly accessible verse titled after the street where he lived in San Francisco. Poetry readings

with instrumental accompaniment led to songwriting, recording, and more books which sold three million copies in the late 1960s. At his peak, installed in a Beverly Hills mansion with enough money to live royally for the rest of his life, McKuen was turning out a song a day. His production dropped off rapidly, however, at about the same time he hired a detective agency to find the father he never knew. The results of the search were inconclusive. Among many other leads the agency turned up a photograph of a blond man with a name resembling McKuen's. The poet, who once told a reporter he didn't believe in history and was bored by learning, chose a dénouement in true Hollywood fashion. Without any proof that the man ever knew his (deceased) mother or was even in California at the time of his conception, McKuen identified the author of his being. He might have saved a lot of trouble and expense by asking his mother, who lived to middle age, but the real story might not have sold as many copies.

See McKuen's Finding My Father *(New York, 1976).*

John McLaren

(1846-1943). McLaren was a crusading gardener, a crusty Scot who ruled the public parks of San Francisco for 55 years—such a character that he was enshrined in *Reader's Digest* and *Saturday Evening Post*. Shrewd, tyrannical, and capricious, he numbered among his idiosyncracies a hatred of statues and "Keep Off the Grass" signs. He

maintained constant vigilance against political incursions into his domain (chiefly, Golden Gate Park), personally blocking trolley lines, paving projects, horseless carriages, and later cars. "Uncle John" McLaren lived in a lodge in Golden Gate Park, and his birthday was celebrated as an annual civic event. In his lifetime he is said to have planted two million trees, transforming the sand wastes of the Western Addition into beautiful parkland. In 1928, a $2 million bond issue was passed for the creation of McLaren Park in South San Francisco.

McLaren wrote Gardening in California *(San Francisco, 1909).*

John Joseph McNamara

(1880?-1941) and **James Barnabas McNamara** (1882-1941). The key event in the labor history of Los Angeles was the bombing of the *L.A. Times*, a bastion of anti-union reaction, on 1 October 1910. Twenty employees lost their lives in what the newspaper headlined as "the crime of the century." Six months later, a special investigating team under **William J. Burns**, using the latest detecting techniques as well as the "third degree" and illegal extradition, delivered two

suspects from the Midwest to L.A.—J.J. McNamara, secretary of the International Bridge and Structural Iron Worker's Union, and his younger brother J.B. Labor sympathizers charged a frame-up by *Times* publisher **Otis** and raised funds to engage distinguished defense attorney **Clarence Darrow**. On the eve of the trial, however, the brothers changed their plea to guilty, setting back the cause of organized labor at least a generation in Los Angeles. Why did they do it? According to social historian Louis Adamic, the McNamaras considered themselves "soldiers in the cause of labor, in the war between the haves and the have-nots; Jesuits in the labor movement, their ends justifying any means." J.J. McNamara, sentenced to

fifteen years for another dynamite incident, was paroled in 1921, while J.B., who confessed to bombing the *Times*, served out his life sentence, not even applying for parole. At San Quentin he was one of few inmates able to tolerate **Tom Mooney**, whom he jokingly enrolled as an honorary member of "Dynamiters Anonymous." They received visitors together, including the cape-swinging aesthete **Lincoln Steffens**, and read Dreiser's *American Tragedy* together. At Folsom Prison, where J.B. was transferred for medical reasons, he served as model for one of the figures in a prison version of *The Last Supper*, still hanging in the prison chapel.

The best source on the McNamaras is Louis Adamic's Dynamite *(New York, 1931; Gloucester, MA, 1960).*

Aimee Semple
McPherson (1890-1944).
Migrating populations, historians tell us, tend to develop religious deviations in the process of moving. Certainly Los Angeles, enjoying a tremendous population influx after World War I, offered receptive audiences for evangelists of every persuasion and pitch. There were cowboy evangelists, singing evangelists, evangelists promising salvation through the salt-free diet, even "brain-breathing" evangelists, touting the secret of the Aztecs. The gospel according to Aimee Semple McPherson, adapted from the Salvation Army Christianity of her Canadian childhood, differed chiefly in presentation. True, she emphasized a religion of love rather than fear and substituted promises for threats, but the quality that brought her fame and fortune was sheer theatricality: she brought show business to religion. Widowed by Semple who died as a missionary in China, divorced by McPherson who objected to the lifestyle of a "holy hobo," she set out for California in 1918 with her mother, two children, and a secretary in the "Gospel Auto," an Oldsmobile. (She claimed to be the first woman to drive coast to coast—dictating her memoirs, moreover, as she drove.) Opening in Echo Park in 1923 to a full house, the Angelus Temple of the Foursquare Gospel (Jesus as Savior, Baptizer, Healer, and Coming King) showcased Aimee on a red velvet throne, Aimee sprinkling rose petals into the baptismal pool, and

Aimee in nurse's uniform and cape, rebuking cancer and exhorting illness to "melt away like the snow before the sun." There were skits, pantomimes, and tableaux accompanied by three bands, two orchestras, six quartets, and a 200-voice choir. Aimee did a faith healing stunt with a lion in the zoo; advertised in the theater section of the newspapers; dropped leaflets from the sky; and entered floats in the annual Tournament of Roses parade, winning a sweepstakes prize in 1925. A skillful mistress of media, she established her own radio station, KFSG or Kalling Foursquare Gospel, the third station in L.A. Kenneth Ormiston, who answered her ad for a Christian radio engineer, was apparently the motivation for her disappearing act in 1926, the biggest news story in local history. On May 18 Aimee vanished from the beach at Ocean Park, presumably drowned; five

weeks later, she turned up in the Arizona desert with a curious tale of kidnapping. (The engineer and the evangelist had merely wanted to get away from it all for awhile, it seems.) There were allegations of fraud and perjury, but Aimee brazened it out, delighting her fans with the bald-faced improbability of her story. But after this she began to change—breaking with her mother, bobbing her hair, and dressing fashionably. She got the Temple into some disastrous business schemes—a cemetery in Glendale, a Tahoe Bible resort, a sacred film company. There was an unsuccessful marriage to an actor hired to perform in a biblical oratorio. But Aimee remained a folk heroine, seemingly untouched by it all. (According to one estimate, she made the front page of the Los Angeles Times three times a week for five years, with rumors of marriage, feuds with her mother and daughter, reports of being spirited away in a coffin, or of signalling from a window in code to a mystery limousine.) Not even the reality of her death from an overdose of Seconal diminished her appeal. Buried at Forest Lawn in a tomb fit for Cleopatra, she was succeeded as head of the International Church of the Foursquare Gospel by her son Rolf McPherson.

The standard biography is Storming Heaven *by Lately Thomas (New York, 1970); the most recent,* Least of all Saints *by Robert Bahr (Englewood Cliffs, N.J., 1979). McPherson narrates the story other own life,* From Milkpail to Pulpit, *available on record and tape from the Angelus Temple in Los Angeles.*

Carey McWilliams

(1905-1980). The foremost modern commentator on California social history, McWilliams moved west from Colorado in 1922. Working his way through USC and USC law school as a clerk in the *Los Angeles Times* business office, he had a ringside seat for the parade of such colorful, roaring-twenties characters as **Aimee Semple McPherson** and **C.C. Julian**. He also found time to interview **Gertrude Atherton** and **Fremont Older** for a biography of **Ambrose Bierce**, published in 1929. By then, he was working for a conservative ("Dickensian," he joked) L.A. law firm, which tolerantly allowed him to pursue his interest in civil libertarian and labor issues. Moving from observation to activism, McWilliams was appointed chief of the state division of immigration and housing (1932-42) by Governor **Culbert Olson**. Out of this experience came his classic *Factories in the Fields* (1939), a nonfiction *Grapes of Wrath*. As a public official McWilliams earned the undying enmity of the California right, which tried to pass a bill abolishing his job. (**Jack Tenney**, the McCarthy of California, would later call him a member of every "commie-front" organization on the coast.) After World War II McWilliams began writing about local issues for the progressive New York-based weekly, *The Nation*, also expanding his social commentary into books: *Prejudice* (1944), about the wartime internment of the Japanese; *Witchhunt* (1950), about the "Red scare"; and

two seminal works of interpretive history, *Southern California Country: An Island on the Land* (1946) and *California: The Great Exception* (1949). In 1951 McWilliams moved to New York where he edited *The Nation* for twenty years, an expatriate Californian.

The Education of Carey McWilliams *(New York, 1978) is his autobiography.*

Magnin Family

The swankest department store chain in the U.S. was founded by a German-Jewish family in San Francisco in 1876, catering to the Nob Hill carriage trade. The store was named I. Magnin but the real power behind the operation was not Isaac but his wife Mary Ann (1849-1943). (Isaac was a carpenter/idealist who peddled Marxist tracts by bicycle in Golden Gate Park.) Widowed in 1907, the redoubtable Mary Ann carried on from her apartment at the St. Francis Hotel with the help of her sons. Grover Magnin (1885-1969) was the youngest, but Mary Ann considered him the most capable and put him in charge. He hired top architects for the store's first branches (the distinctive white marble Magnin facades are not only elegant, but by sheer verticality they also eliminate the pigeon-dropping problem) and added designer clothes to the inventory. Also a resident of the St. Francis, Grover married a beautiful model and collected art in his penthouse apartment. Joseph Magnin (c. 1870-1953) broke away in 1913 to establish his own store, sentimentally referred to as "the store that love built," since his estrangement from the family dated to his marrying an employee against Mary Ann's wishes. In its third generation in California, the Magnin family produced a part-time actor and a leading American rabbi. I. Magnin was sold to the **Bullock**'s chain in 1944, and J. Magnin to a Hawaiian conglomerate in 1969, leaving Joseph's son Cyril (1899-   ) with time to moonlight as the pope in a 1971 film, *Foul Play.* A former president of the San Francisco Port Authority and ubiquitous man-about-town, Cyril Magnin also liked to pose as Mr. San Francisco. His cousin Edgar Fogel Magnin (1890-   ), son of Mary Ann's son Samuel and a graduate of Hebrew Union College (1914), was assigned in 1915 to L.A.'s Wilshire Boulevard Temple, at one time the largest and wealthiest Jewish congregation in the U.S. Complimented on his beautiful stained glass windows, he said: "I have always believed in quality, like the store." Rabbi Magnin became something of the token establishment rabbi, delivering the invocation at **Nixon**'s first inauguration.

Cyril Magnin wrote the only memoir in the family, Call Me Cyril *(New York, 1981) with Cynthia Robins.*

Tom Maguire (1820-1896). An illiterate former hack driver from New York, Maguire became the "Napoleon of the San Francisco stage", the title of a WPA biography, during the Gold Rush. He opened his first theater, the Jenny Lind, in Portsmouth Square in 1850; twice it burned down and twice he rebuilt it, adding elaborate frescoes, cupids,

and a drop curtain depicting the Grand Canal of Venice. The entertainment ranged from variety shows and Chinese tumblers to **Adah Menken** and Shakespeare. During intermissions Maguire, resplendent in a top hat, spats, diamond rings and stickpin, would invite his guests to repair to the gambling saloon next door, which he, of course, also owned. When he got into a financial pinch, he managed to sell the theater for $200,000 to San Francisco for a city hall ("the Jenny Lind juggle," it was called), thanks to his friendship with fellow Irishman **David Broderick** whose machine controlled San Francisco at the time. When the second Vigilance Committee put Broderick's machine out of business, Maguire was sentenced to banishment, but simply ignored the sentence. By 1858 Maguire had an eleven-theater circuit in the West, and a monopoly in all the large towns of California. The following year he built a minstrel theater in San Francisco and in 1865 an opera house. His weakness was for the grandiose—for example, a Passion Play with 80 singers and 400 extras—and he overextended himself. There were also legal difficulties, including a suit for slander brought by the **de Young** brothers, and an arrest in New York in 1880 for pirating plays. (On the West Coast with thousands of miles between himself and any living playwrights, he had simply dispensed with the formality of paying royalties.) Maguire died poor in New York after years of obscurity.

The Jenny Lind was destroyed in 1906, Maguire's Opera House was condemned for street improvements, and his Academy of Music ended up as a furniture store.

The best source on Maguire is Craig Timberlake's The Life and Work of David Belasco, The Bishop of Broadway *(New York, 1954). Belasco, a native of San Francisco, did his apprenticeship under Maguire.*

Alma Mahler. *See* Alma Mahler Gropius Werfel.

Thomas Mann (1875-1955). The most revered German writer of his generation, Mann arrived in Southern California in 1941, a highly conscientious objector to Nazism. At first it seemed

an artificial paradise to him, garishly unreal, so new, so clean, so seemingly untouched by the holocaust in Europe. Pondering the ocean view from his new home in Pacific Palisades, he considered whether this perpetually sunny strip of coast might one day become a light-opera outpost of the Mikado. Meanwhile, Mann would live as he had in the Old World, wearing a suit and tie to walk his dog, accepting as his due the homage of the growing community of émigré intellectuals (including Bruno Walter, Franz Werfel, **Arnold Schoenberg**, and Mann's brother Heinrich). He

continued to write in his native language. "Where I am is Germany," the Nobel prize-winning author explained. "My home is in the works I carry with me." In 1943 he began his last great work, *Dr. Faustus*, the parallel story of a composer and a country in the grip of demonic obsession. Published in 1948, the book was not particularly well received in the U.S., and there was some unpleasantness with Schoenberg, whose twelve-tone system Mann attributed to his fictional Faust. The California years were a period of physical decline for Mann. Many of the émigrés would die there—his sister-in-law, a suicide; his brother; Werfel; **Schoenberg**. Finally, it was a senator from Wisconsin and not the Mikado, who cast the shadow over lotus land. Sickened by the spectre of McCarthyism, Mann moved to Switzerland in 1952.

Charles Milles Manson

(1934-   ). Born illegitimate in Ohio, Manson, who turned the California dream into a nightmare, would have been a deviant personality wherever he drifted. But the "family" he first gathered around him in hippie-era Haight-Ashbury was recruited largely from the state's mainstream, post-war babies who grew up into perversions of the California girl. Patricia Krenwinkle was born in 1947 in Los Angeles, graduating from University High School; Susan Atkins from the Bay Area and Lynette Fromme from Santa Monica were born in 1948; and Leslie Van Houten, born in 1949, was homecoming queen at her San Gabriel

Valley high school. Psychiatrist Clara Livsey, studying the background of Manson's followers, reported that they were all "Daddy's girls" who regrouped around a new father in a caricature of the child-centered American family, acting out their infantile narcissism and their conception of life as a magical mystery tour. Manipulating them with drugs, sex, and a apocalyptic garble of Scientology and Nazism, Beatle lyrics and the Bible, Manson led his tribe into the deserts and valleys of Southern California. At the old Spahn movie ranch in Chatsworth and at the Barker Ranch in Death Valley they rehearsed for doomsday, psyching themselves up to the brink of Armageddon. It arrived on the night of 9 August 1969, when the Manson family invaded the "rich piggy" precincts of Beverly Hills, brutally murdering pregnant actress Sharon Tate and four others at her rented home on Cielo ("heaven") Drive; the following night, there was a repeat performance at the Los Feliz home of Leno and Rosemary La Bianca. Convicted of murder in 1970 and sentenced to life when the death penalty was overturned, Manson retreated into the institutional womb of prison, where he had spent most of his youth. But his California girls continued to make waves: convicted murderess Susan Atkins was born again as a Jesus freak in prison while Leslie Van Houten sought to escape her murder conviction through two expensive retrials. Lynette Fromme, not involved in the

1969 murders, made a grandstanding attempt to assassinate President Ford in Sacramento in 1975.

See Clara Livsey, The Manson Women, A "Family" Portrait *(New York, 1980); and Vincent Bugliosi with Curt Gentry,* Helter Skelter *(New York, 1974).*

Herbert Marcuse

(1898-1979). The distinguished German-born philosopher, a Jewish refugee from Hitler, chose to end his academic career in relative obscurity at UC San Diego because, he explained, of the great nearby zoo. Lecturing on Marx and Freud, revolution and sexuality ("the fight for Eros is a political fight"), he attracted standing-room-only crowds of students and the undying enmity of local conservatives. Marcuse's work became fashionable in the 1960s for most of the wrong reasons. Considered an advocate of permissiveness, he was actually criticizing the "desublimation" of sex into a marketable commodity in advanced industrial society. As for revolution, he found American workers too preoccupied with their hi-fis and barbecues to get on with the class struggle as conceived by Marx and predicted that other groups would supercede them in the vanguard. Marcuse was more often than not critical of the fuzzy-minded New Left but nonetheless fell under suspicion of inciting it to revolt against authority. The university terminated his contract when he turned 70, but he continued to teach informally and to write, pondering the problems of civilization while walking on

the beach near his La Jolla home.

Marcuse's best-known works are Eros and Civilization *(Boston, 1955) and* One-Dimensional Man *(Boston, 1964). His biography remains to be written. For background, see Paul Robinson,* The Freudian Left *(New York, 1969) and H. Stuart Hughes,* The Sea Change *(New York, 1975).*

Edwin Charles Markham

(1852-1940). Markham was an obscure 47-year-old school principal when he saw Millet's painting, *The Man with a Hoe*, owned by the Crocker family, and wrote one of the few poems in history to create a popular sensation. Raised by his mother in the East Bay, he had graduated from the State Normal School in 1872 and taught in the Mother Lode town of Coloma before his election as county superintendent of education (1879-1886). In the 1870s Markham began writing an opus on destiny ("Des," for short), expounding his theories on the pre-mortal existence and history of man. He also spent a decade editing *Remarkable Pages from Thomas Lake Harris*, the Santa Rosa spiritualist. With the publication by **Hearst**'s *San Francisco Examiner* in 1899 of his vaguely socialistic poem, Markham became an overnight celebrity. Leading figures of the day debated the poem: railroad magnate **Collis Huntington** said a man should be glad to have a hoe, critic **Ambrose Bierce** said the poem had all the "vitality of a sick fish," and someone wrote a parody about **Hearst**, "The Man With the Dough." But the public loved the poem, and it was reprinted so many times that

it earned Markham $200,000 in the next 30 years. To cash in on his fame he went on a national speaking tour and established a new base of operations in Staten Island, where he spent the rest of his life writing mildly exalted verse ("sublime bilge", some called it). Thanks partly to his venerable, Whitmanesque appearance, Markham enjoyed a public stature far beyond his meager literary gifts. He was chosen to speak at the 1922 dedication of the Lincoln Memorial in Washington, D.C. and enjoyed an 80th birthday celebration at New York's Carnegie Hall. Back home in California, his old residence in San Jose, known as the "Hoe Man House," became a local shrine. When Markham turned up to tout his book, *California the Wonderful*, at the 1915 Panama-Pacific Exposition, he was fêted as the state's gift to the world.

Louis Filler's The Unknown Edwin Markham, His Mystery and its Significance *(Yellow Springs, OH, 1966) is as pretentious as it sounds.*

Henry Harrison Markham (1840-1923).

California's eighteenth governor (1891-1895), Markham was a lawyer from New York who moved to Pasadena in 1878 for his health, poor ever since he had been wounded during the Civil War. As a member of the board of the National Home of Disabled Soldiers, he helped establish the historic Old Soldiers' Home (later Sawtelle Veteran's Hospital) in West L.A. In 1890 *Los Angeles Times* publisher **Otis** supported Markham as the first Republican gubernatorial candidate from Southern California. "The dashing colonel from Pasadena," who never missed an occasion to recount battle stories, was elected with the support of the Southern Pacific Railroad. To encourage immigration to California, which then had a population of only 1.2 million, Governor Markham prepared a brochure on the state for distribution at the 1893 World's Fair in Chicago. He took a strong stand against capital punishment. And he responded with force to the labor disturbances of 1893-1894, calling out the National Guard and the state militia. He was not nominated for reelection.

John Marsh (1799-1856).

Imposter, miser, misanthrope, traitor—Marsh is a curious and unsympathetic figure in early California. Born in Massachusetts and graduated from Harvard, he taught school and worked as an Indian agent in Wisconsin, where he took an Indian mistress and fathered a son. The woman died and Marsh left for the West in 1832 under suspicion of arming the Sioux. In Los Angeles he set himself up as a doctor with his Harvard diploma—in Latin, no one could read it. Considering Northern California more congenial to Yankee farming stock, he bought a rancho at the foot of Mount Diablo. That the Indians regarded Diablo with fear and superstition he only rated as an advantage. Extremely avaricious and for years the only doctor in the San Joaquin Valley, Marsh charged for his medical services in cattle, up to 200 depending on distance traveled. He wrote numerous letters back East encouraging Yankee settlement, but when settlers arrived he charged them dearly for his grudging hospitality. He was also

regarded as a traitor, having ridden south with **Manuel Micheltorena** in 1845 only to persuade the Anglos on both sides to avoid fighting. With the discovery of gold, Marsh made a valuable strike on the Yuba River, and the prices of his cattle and produce escalated handsomely. But his wealth, which he buried on his property, brought him no lasting happiness. He built a three-story sandstone mansion with gables and a tower from which he kept a lookout for cattle thieves. He married but soon lost his wife. He was plagued by squatters and cattle thieves. Finally he was murdered by Mexicans who may or may not have found the buried treasure. As a last melodramatic touch, Marsh's long-lost Indian son, who turned up at the end of his father's life, spent ten years tracking down the murderers.

George Lyman's John Marsh, Pioneer *(New York, 1930) is dated.*

James Wilson Marshall

(1810-1885). The precious metals in California's Mother Lode were thought to produce

particularly strong "emanations," according to nineteenth century spiritualists—who included the discoverer of the first nuggets of gold at **John Sutter**'s Mill in January 1848. Born in New Jersey, Marshall had come overland from Missouri in 1845 and found employment as a carpenter at Sutter's Fort. Sutter, none too sober-minded himself, considered his carpenter eccentric, "notional," but competent enough to supervise construction of the new sawmill on the South Fork of the American River. After finding gold in the millrace it was all downhill for Marshall (and Sutter too), as hordes of squatters descended on their holdings. Because of the special powers of divination he was believed to enjoy, Marshall was in great demand as a guide but never again made any mineral discovery of significance. On the contrary; he soon lost his half interest in the sawmill, saw his land at Butte Creek sold to satisfy a judgment, and remained for the rest of his life an embittered and paranoid crank. But he never gave up hope of striking it rich. When the spirits failed him, he tried to locate gold by the use of electrical current from a galvanic battery, which he also touted as a cure for rheumatism. In his spare time Marshall wrote (or rather translated from the spirits) a manuscript entitled *The Hierophant; or Gleanings from the Past. Being an Exposition of Biblical Astronomy, etc.* In 1870 he attempted to redress his fortunes by a lecture tour, got up like a miner in a

flannel shirt and pants tucked into his boots, but he was a poor speaker. The state of California gave him a pension in 1872 but failed to renew it, angered by reports of his drunken improvidence. After his death, however, Marshall became acceptable in the state pantheon as the pioneer of pioneers, the man whose discovery brought "the march of civilization to our western borders," a discovery so momentous the very crusades paled by comparison. . .

John Marshall, The Discoverer of California Gold *(Georgetown, 1967) by Theressa Gay is an exhaustive treatment of the man and the period.*

Glenn Luther Martin

(1886-1955). McFadden's pasture in Santa Ana, where Martin built his first plane out of sticks, wire, and cloth, occupies a special place in the archaeology of aviation. His first model self-destructed while taxiing but Martin would go on to become one of the great airplane builders of the era. Using intuition, imagination, and a textbook on bridgebuilding stress, he finally got off the ground in August 1909 in another homemade plane and taught himself to fly by trial and error. The young garage owner, who looked like a Sunday school teacher, tall and austere with rimless glasses, was soon barnstorming all over the West in black leather cap, jacket, and puttees. He earned $2,000 for an exhibition at Brawley in the Imperial Valley, a similar sum for a stunt flight across San Francisco Bay, and instant celebrity as **Mary Pickford**'s flying costar in *The Girl of Yesterday* (1915), although he

refused the director's orders to kiss his ringletted partner. He also set a record for over-water flight (to Catalina and back from Newport Beach) and helped a sheriff's posse chase desperadoes through Southern California canyons. After World War I, when Martin became the leading U.S. producer of bombers at his plants in Cleveland and later Baltimore, nervous bankers put an end to his barnstorming days. His company later produced the first China Clipper and, after World War II, diversified into satellite and spacecraft design. Martin died at his Chesapeake Bay farm where he had spent his retirement monitoring the flight of birds. He was buried with his parents in Santa Ana.

Henry Still's To Ride the Wind *(New York, 1964) is a biography of Martin.*

Xavier Martinez (Javier Timoteo Martinez y Orozco, 1869-1943). The Mexican-born painter Martinez seems himself to have been rather a work of art, with eyes like "great beads of jet" (**Arnold Genthe**), long hair like "a huge black chrysanthemum" (W.H. Wright), and a wardrobe of baggy corduroys and flowing ties straight from the Left Bank. He came by the wardrobe honestly, having studied at the École des Beaux Arts in Paris (1897-1899) where his foster father was Mexican consul general. Earlier, he had graduated from the Mark Hopkins Art Institute in San Francisco, where he returned after four years in Europe. A member of the city's Bohemian Club and of the bohemian summer colony on

the Carmel-Monterey shore, Martinez moved to Piedmont after the earthquake and taught at the California School (later College) of Arts and Crafts from 1908 to 1942. In his art, he aspired to unify the influences of the Aztecs, the Moors, and the Impressionists, but his surviving canvases lean rather to the style of Whistler and Velasquez. His most famous creation was probably the frieze of black cats around the ceiling of Giuseppe Coppa's restaurant in the old Montgomery Block where **George Sterling**, **Gelett Burgess**, and others hung out.

Xavier Martinez by George Neubert (Oakland, 1974) is the catalogue of an exhibit at the Oakland Museum.

Groucho Marx (Julius Marx, 1890-1977). The Marx Brothers were distinctly New York City characters, products of East 93rd Street at the turn of the century, but

they spent the latter half of their lives enjoying the good life in Southern California. It wasn't all good, but Groucho could make a joke out of anything, even anti-Semitism. When his children were refused permission to swim at a restricted country club, he publicly embarrassed the club by asking if they could go in up to their waists, since they were only half Jewish. Visiting his brothers who had retired to Palm Springs, he joked: "If the Jews in Israel can sleep in the sand surrounded by hostile Arabs, I'm sure I can slumber peacefully in the sands of Palm Springs surrounded by nothing but gentile golf clubs." (Harpo, Gummo, and Zeppo Marx would soon become founding members of their own golf club, the Tamarisk, next to which Harpo built his house, El Rancho Harpo.) Groucho, who established a solo career on TV after his brothers retired, preferred to live in Beverly Hills, where the number one social problem was probably boredom. When the Los Angeles director of civil defense, a guest on Groucho's "You Bet Your Life" quiz program, said that his primary job was to make sure that every one in L.A. was conscious of the problem, Groucho quipped: "It's tough enough just to see that every one in L.A. is conscious." For company, Groucho frequented the comedians' corner at the Hillcrest Country Club with George Burns, George Jessel, Jack Benny, and Danny Kaye. In his last years, he and some old cronies established a "Geezer's Club" which met every Friday for lunch at Nate 'n' Al's delicatessen.

Charlotte Chandler's Hello, I Must Be Going (Garden City, NY, 1978) and Hector Arce's Groucho (New York, 1979) are the best of the Groucho books.

Paul Masson (1859-1940). In 1878 he left the Burgundian vineyards of France, then under attack by the dreaded phylloxera plant lice, to prospect for a little piece of Burgundy in the soil of California. He found what he was seeking at Charles LeFranc's Almadén vineyard near Saratoga and sealed his possession by marrying LeFranc's daughter. Defying the conventional wisdom that grapes should have full sun all day, Masson began planting up the shady hillsides to produce fine quality wines and California's first prize-winning champagne. He also built a chalet in the hills, La Cresta, fitted out with the Romanesque portal of a twelfth-century European church where he dispensed

legendary hospitality. Guests, including Charlie Chaplin and voluptous actress Anna Held (who is widely believed to have bathed in her host's champagne), enjoyed great slabs of French bread with pâtè, roast turkey, and, of course, unexcelled wines. Appointed a state viticulture commissioner by Governor **Hiram Johnson**, Masson ranked as a high dignitary of California wine—the Duc de Cognac, his cronies called him. His fortunes depleted by Prohibition, he had to sell the original LeFranc property and in 1936 he lost ownership control of La Cresta. But he continued to preside over the chalet and vineyards during his lifetime, a venerable old Gallic character in pince-nez and striped pants. Seagram's eventually acquired the Paul Masson label. Wine from the original LeFranc property was for years distributed mostly by subscription, as if it were a gilt-edged bond issue.

Robert Balzer's This Uncommon Heritage (Los Angeles, 1970) is an illustrated history of the Paul Masson winery.

Bob Mathias (Robert Bruce Mathias, 1930-   ). "The San Joaquin Valley not only raises wonderful crops but also mighty fine people," Harry Truman remarked during a whistle-stop campaign tour in 1948. He was referring chiefly to Mathias, seventeen-year-old Olympic decathlon champion, the running-jumping-and-throwing proof that California grows its athletes bigger and better. Mathias was born in the valley town of Tulare, then known chiefly (if at all) as the birthplace of tularemia, an infectious disease transmitted by rabbits. The son of a doctor, he overcame adolescent anemia by ingesting massive quantities of protein, recovering sufficiently to go out for track, basketball, and football. Clean-cut and handsome, he was elected senior class president. When his coach suggested the decathlon, training had to be improvised; there wasn't a javelin in all of Tulare County. After Mathias's phenomenal victory at the Olympic games in London in 1948, he enrolled at Stanford where he was a football star and a big man on campus. In 1952, having grown three inches taller and added twelve pounds, he won his second decathlon gold medal at the games in Helsinki. (That year another Tulare boy, Sim Iness, won a gold medal in the discus.) The question was, what to do for an encore. The people of Tulare chipped in to finance an inspirational movie with their hero and his wife playing themselves in *The Bob Mathias Story* (1954). There were a few more forgettable movie appearances (*China Doll*, 1958, and *It Happened in Athens*, 1962, with Jayne Mansfield) and a failed TV series about hardhats. For a grown man with good looks and a place of honor in the hometown heart, politics seemed a logical prospect. Mathias was elected to Congress as a Republican in 1966 and reelected again and again and again. He might have kept his seat indefinitely if two unforeseen events had not spelled defeat in 1974—Watergate and congressional redistricting

that grafted Tulare onto Fresno County.

Bob Mathias, Champion of Champions (New York, 1952) by James Scott, later a radical sports writer, is highly adulatory.

William Matson

(1849-1917). A Swedish-born seaman who arrived in San Francisco in 1867, Matson was instrumental in transforming the South Seas into an extension of the California dream. Starting as skipper of a lumber schooner, he became a shipping magnate in his own right, making the transition from sails to steam in the 1890s. He played a key role in the acquisition of Hawaii in 1898. In 1890 Matson was appointed consul-general of Sweden in San Francisco, and when he died his funeral was attended by the local diplomatic corps in full regalia. William Philip Roth (1881-1963), a former shipping clerk who married Matson's daughter Lurline, became president of the Matson Navigation Company in 1927 and chairman of the board in 1962. It was Roth who built the famous White Fleet, including the *Lurline* and *Matsonia*, to carry a new

luxury tourist trade to the Pacific islands. He bought the former **Spreckels** shipping interests, and made a deal with his rival **Robert Dollar** to split the Pacific, then gradually absorbed all the competition. The Matson Company also built the Royal Hawaii Hotel in Waikiki, a resort to rival California's Del Monte, attracting the kind of tourists who brought their own valets and roadsters. At home, Roth developed a 750-acre estate near Woodside call Malolo, Hawaiian for "fidelity, love, and life." In the third generation, William Matson Roth (1916-   ) helped develop San Francisco's Ghirardelli Square.

Cliff May (1908-   ). May

began designing ranch-style houses in California during the 1930s, updating and anglicizing the traditional western hacienda. His long, sprawling residences with patios enclosed by wings, had a quality of low-key luxury, evoking in the words of critic Brendan Gill "the simplicities of an earlier, more hospitable, and (we may pretend) more affectionate time." After World War II, May's ranch house

created a new suburban vogue all over the U.S. He personally designed over 1,000 individual houses—plus the *Sunset* magazine headquarters in Menlo Park (1962) and the Mondavi Winery in Saint Helena (1966). He also licensed a low-cost prototype to builders during the 1950s. Over 18,000 copies were built in the U.S. and abroad, possibly making May the most "popular" architect in history. But his name appears nowhere in the literary annals of architecture because he never bothered to seek certification (nor did **Frank Lloyd Wright**) from the American Institute of Architects.

Bernard Ralph Maybeck (1862-1957). A

familiar figure around Berkeley for over 60 years, a short gnome-like man in a smock and beret, Maybeck was the architect of the university community's distinctively rustic lifestyle. Born in New York of German parentage, he came west after finishing his studies at the École des Beaux Arts in Paris (1881-1888), seeking an environment receptive to innovation. He became the first instructor of architecture at the University of California at Berkeley (1893-1903), where he was instrumental in developing the university master plan financed by **Phoebe Hearst**. Maybeck personally designed Hearst Hall, a palatial women's gymnasium and social center, and also Wyntoon, Mrs. Hearst's medieval castle in Northern California. In 1903 he left UCB to go into private practice, specializing in rustic-

modern hillside homes. In 1910 Maybeck completed what many consider his masterpiece, the Christian Science Church in Berkeley. Asked to design the centerpiece for the 1915 Panama-Pacific Exposition, he shifted genres completely, creating a romantic neo-Roman Palace of Fine Arts. Because Maybeck built so extensively in wood on California's chronically flammable hillsides, many of

his creations have not survived. Hearst Hall at UCB burned in 1922 and a brushfire in Berkeley the following year claimed Maybeck's own house and fifteen others he designed in the neighborhood. In 1933 Wyntoon was lost, in what one imagines as a truly Wagnerian conflagration.

Kenneth Cardwell, Bernard Maybeck, Artisan, Architect, Artist *(Salt Lake, 1977).*

Louis Burt Mayer

(1885?-1957). As head of MGM the Russian-born former scrap-metal dealer was the highest salaried man in the U.S., but he wanted more — acceptance by the establishment. While **Irving Thalberg** made the pictures, winning MGM a reputation as the Tiffany of the studios, Mayer made the deals and

the political contacts. Short, carefully tailored, and pugnacious (he got into public brawls with Charlie Chaplin, Erich von Stroheim, and **Sam Goldwyn**), he lived a lavish lifestyle in an elegant Santa Monica beach villa. He took up horseback riding as a sport consistant with his social aspirations and built the most successful western

horsebreeding operation of the day. ("The Jews had taken over the worship of horses as a symbol," **F. Scott Fitzgerald** wrote in *The Last Tycoon.* "For years it had been the Cossacks mounted and the Jews on foot.") An ardent Republican, Mayer actively supported **Herbert Hoover** and even hoped to make the presidential nominating speech at the 1928 convention. (He was passed over as a "new" Californian.) To defeat **Upton Sinclair**'s 1934 campaign for governor, he produced bogus newsreels showing bums arriving in the state for a free handout. Mayer was one of the founders of the Academy of Motion Picture Arts and Sciences (1927), conceived as a sort of producer-dominated company union to preempt the formation of craft guilds. (The crafts formed their own unions anyway — during the Depression when the producers tried to impose a 50 percent pay reduction.) Mayer extended his network of personal influence through his sons-in-law, **David O. Selznick** and William Goetz,

financing the creation of Twentieth Century-Fox as a sinecure for the latter. ("The sons-in-law also rise," according to ancient Hollywood wisdom.) One of the most notorious lotharios of the casting couch, he left his wife on their 40th wedding anniversary for greater freedom with young starlets. In 1951, after 24 years as head of MGM, Mayer was forced out. He spent his last years rooting for McCarthyism ("drive the bums back to Moscow") and plotting his return to power.

Gary Cary wrote All the Stars in Heaven: Louis B. Mayer's MGM *(New York, 1981) which supercedes Bosley Crowther's overblown* Holywood Rajah *(New York, 1960).*

Zubin Mehta (1936-   ). His first impression of Los Angeles when he arrived in 1961 to fill in as conductor with the L.A. Philharmonic, was of a boundless city, new and remarkably clean despite its orange penumbra of smog. Born in Bombay, India, of Parsi ancestry, he had studied music in Vienna and at 25 had just been appointed to his first major conducting position — the Montreal Symphony Orchestra. Mehta's concert in L.A. was such a success that Buff **Chandler,** head of the Symphony Association, hired him as associate conductor. Unconsulted, world-ranking conductor Georg Solti resigned in pique, leaving the field clear for the handsome young Indian. Mehta took a disparate group of musicians who were accustomed to moonlighting at studio recording sessions for easy money and by sheer force of personality galvanized them into a respected orchestra. If his style was flamboyant, conductors are, of course, the exhibitionists of music and music is, after all, entertainment. Within two years after Mehta's arrival, attendance at L.A. Philharmonic concerts doubled. In December 1964, a new era began with the opening of the Los Angeles Music Center, its ushers dressed for the occasion in red Nehru-style caps and jackets. Continuously seeking new challenges, Mehta experimented with rock and "switched-on" (electronic) music. He traveled constantly, a jet-set conductor with regular engagements in Montreal and in Israel. Southern California offered him adulation and everything that money could buy—a Rolls Royce, a Brentwood mountain-top home with a breathtaking view of Catalina, a blonde actress for a wife—but that wasn't enough to hold him. In 1978, after seventeen years as superstar of the only musical show in town, Mehta moved to the world mecca of music, New York, as director of its Philharmonic.

Martin Bookspan, Zubin *(New York, 1978).*

Adah Theodore Isaacs Menken (1835-1868).
Menken was an American version of **Lola Montez**, a Jezebel from Louisiana whose compulsive flamboyance made her an international stage star and sex symbol. In the sensational finale of Byron's *Mazeppa*, her star vehicle, she appeared in flesh-colored tights strapped to the back of a horse. A decade after Montez, she too

made the long trip west, lured by **Tom Maguire**'s promise of $1,500 a week to appear at his new Opera House in 1863. Some say she got only $500 a week, but whatever the amount, she worked hard for it, playing the title roles in *Three Fast Women* plus five male roles in the same play. *Mazeppa* inspired so many local imitations, a San Franciso Columnist joked, that livery horses were refusing to be mounted by

anyone fully clothed. Like Montez, Menken married repeatedly (her second husband was fighter Johnny Heenan, "the Benicia Boy"), but she was also a poetess with a keen respect for the life of the mind. In San Francisco she gathered around her a literary coterie including **Bret Harte**, Artemus Ward and **Joaquin Miller**, and published her verse in the *Golden Era*. She also seems to have had time left over to entertain silver tycoons privately, for which the women of San Francisco shunned her. Returning overland to New York, Menken gave the most memorable performance of her career in Virginia City, where appreciative miners

showered her with nuggets and silver shares conservatively estimated to be worth $100,000. Thenceforth, despite her southern birth and international acclaim, she was considered something of a westerner.

Paul Lewis, Queen of the Plaza; A Biography of Adah Isaacs Menken *(New York, 1964).*

Yehudi Menuhin
(1916-   ). By some accident of fate, geography, and genetics, San Francisco in the 1920s produced a succession of musical prodigies. First and foremost was Yehudi Menuhin, who, at the age of eight made his professional debut with the symphony. His sisters Hepzibah (born in 1920) and Yaltah (born in 1921), both talented pianists, also made their debuts in San Francisco—as did local violinists Ruggiero Ricci and Isaac Stern. His parents were Russian Jews who emigrated first to Palestine and then to New York, where Yehudi was born. But San Francisco remained their promised land, and in 1918 they scraped up the train fare to come west. Moshe Menuhin became a Hebrew teacher, later superintendent of Hebrew schools in the Bay Area, and the family moved up from an apartment on Hayes Street to a house on Steiner Street. They were soon able to buy a Chevrolet, in which to explore Lake Tahoe and Yosemite, and a violin for Yehudi, a chubby blonde boy who insisted on imitating Louis Persinger, concertmaster of the San Francisco Symphony. Persinger consented to

instruct him, and Sidney Ehrman, a local patron, enabled the Menuhins to move to Europe in 1926 for further study, launching a charmed life of international travel and performance for the prodigy in short pants. There would be only brief visits home to the Bay Area. In 1936 Yehudi took a year off from the concert stage to spend a sabbatical on his family's new five-acre farm in Los Gatos. He spent his first honeymoon in a nearby cottage, and after World War II returned there for summers with his second wife and family. But for all of his adult life Menuhin was essentially a citizen of the world, based in Switzerland and later in England, where he opened a health food store and a music school.

Menuhin wrote an autobiography, Unfinished Journey *(New York, 1977).*

Gaetano Merola
(1879?-1953). The founder of the San Francisco Opera was a paisano who decided that if destiny did not intend him to return to Italy, San Francisco would do just as well. He first came West as accompanist to a Metropolitan Opera star, later returning to work as conductor and Hollywood musical advisor. While attending a football game in 1921 at the Stanford Stadium, which reminded him of the Roman Baths of Caracalla, Merola conceived the idea of presenting *opera al fresco*. The first season was an operatic—but not a financial—success, the Bay Area climate falling somewhat short of Mediterranean. In

1932 the San Francisco Opera moved into its own War Memorial Opera House and Merola became a full-fledged impresario, juggling performances and commitments and vying for new talent. (One find was a Santa Rosa policeman billed as "the singing cop.") Courtly and continental rather than flamboyant, he was described as a master of the shrug. A lifelong Puccini aficionado, Merola was conducting excerpts from *Madama Butterfly* at an outdoor concert when he collapsed and died.

Frank Finley Merriam
(1865-1955). "The last of the nineteenth century Republican governors," Merriam was the lieutenant governor who succeeded on **James Rolph**'s death in 1934. A former school principal from Iowa, he moved to Long Beach in 1910, served five terms in the state assembly, and managed **Herbert Hoover**'s statewide presidential campaign. Running for election as governor in 1934, the portly, bald (nickname: Marbletop) midwesterner found himself cast as the political heavy against **Upton Sinclair**, the shining idealist. (Merriam had used the national guard to quell a San Francisco waterfront strike; later he would call out the highway patrol to suppress a Salinas lettuce strike.) Thanks to a media smear campaign against Sinclair, Merriam was elected and proceeded to deal with the Depression in the approved Hoover manner, invoking economy and efficiency. Neither a popular nor an effective governor, he

found himself stymied by lobbyist **Artie Samish**. Merriam, a confirmed prohibitionist, proposed a tax on alcohol to offset declining state revenues. Samish, lobbyist for the liquor industry and a power in his own right, could and did make legislative life difficult for the governor, who tried to retaliate by appointing an investigative committee on lobbying. The Philbrick Report had little effect on Samish, but Merriam was defeated for reelection by **Culbert Olson** in 1938.

Manuel Micheltorena
(c. 1810-?   ). The last Mexican governor of California, Micheltorena has been described as stately, urbane, handsome (the handsomest man of his day, according to **Irving Stone**), inclined to indolence, and something less than heroic. He arrived in 1842 with an army of *cholos* (irregulars) who assured his unpopularity "by reason of the necessity of feeding and the impossibility of controlling them". The new governor's first act, **H.H.**

Bancroft reports, was to make an ass of himself. Informed (mistakenly, it turned out) that American Commodore Thomas Catesby Jones had seized Monterey, Micheltorena proceeded to remain right where he was, safe in L.A. Later, installed in Monterey, he tried to give the missions back to the padres. The governor married his mistress to pacify the church and managed to calm north-south rivalries, but the very presence of the Mexican satrap deprived the Californios of their native-born right to a divison of the spoils. The breaking point came in late 1844 over the *cholos*. The governor marched south to meet his enemies at the Cahuenga Pass, engaging in one of the bloodless mock battles Mexican California was famous for. ("The final clash," historian J.P. Zollinger explained, "seldom amounted to more than a laying on the table of all the cards in order that it could be argued who would win if the game were really played.") The governor had superior forces, so he may simply have been looking for a way to exit graciously, consenting to remove himself to Mexico in 1845. Contemporaries like **Thomas Larkin** could never manage to spell his name correctly, and later generations of settlers mistook "Micheltorena" for an abbreviated designation for Irish leader Michael Torrance.

Harvey Bernard Milk

(1930-1978). Milk used to joke that Castro Street sounded like a Cuban tourist resort. In fact, it was the staging center of the new American mecca for gays, San Francisco. Milk arrived in 1972, a New York Jewish refugee from heterosexuality, making the transition from Wall Street financial analyst to gay-hippie entrepreneur. His Castro Street camera shop became a neighborhood hangout and Milk became a leading gay activist, first running for the county board of supervisors in 1973 as a renegade Democrat without the support of the **Alice B. Toklas** Club, the mainline gay Democratic faction. Milk ran again in 1975, getting a boost out of repeal of the state antisodomy statute, the main legal weapon against homosexuality. But it was not until 1977, amidst local furor over Anita Bryant's antigay ordinance in Dade County, Florida, that Milk finally translated gay support into political power. "It's not enough anymore to have friends represent us," he had argued. "The time has come when the gay community must not be judged by our criminals and myths. . . . We must be judged by our leaders." Milk's friends say he had a premonition of early death, even writing his own epitaph: "Let the bullets that rip through my brain smash through every closet door in the country." The bullets were fired by Dan White, a former policeman and fellow supervisor, who also shot and killed Mayor George Moscone, a liberal elected with gay support. When White got off with voluntary manslaughter, his lawyers having argued diminished capacity due to overconsumption of junk food, gays rioted in the streets of San Francisco.

The Mayor of Castro Street, The Life and Times of Harvey Milk *(New York, 1982) by Randy Shilts is good social history.*

Kenneth Millar. *See* Ross MacDonald.

Frank Augustus Miller

(1857-1935). Theodore Roosevelt slept there, as did William H. Taft, both as president of the U.S. Tom Mix was married there and so was **Richard Nixon**. **Ronald Reagan** and Nancy Davis were married elsewhere, but came to the Mission Inn in Riverside for their wedding night. Their host, master of the famous inn, was Miller, an imaginative entrepreneur who transformed some unremarkable tourist cottages into a national curiosity. "Dramatize your resources," Miller used to say, and he certainly knew how. On the side, for sixteen years, he was manager of the local opera house. It was the turn of the century when he hired architect Arthur Benton to remodel his cottages in the Mission Revival style, a stroke of genius, for the Inn would profit handsomely from the confusion of historical, religious, and commercial motifs. An incorrigible collector, Miller embellished his hotel with dozens of bells, crosses, and other curiosities. He also acquired an Indian hogan, some of **Lola Montez**'s furniture, and an eighteenth century Mexican altar. He played host to

peripatetic artistes (legend has it that **John McGroarty** enjoyed the hospitality of the Mission Inn while writing his "Mission Play") and himself portrayed Father **Serra** in an annual nativity play. As another sideline, Miller developed nearby Mount Rubidoux into a religious shrine, the site of an Easter sunrise service since 1909. Already past its prime, the Inn fell on hard times after Miller's death, losing antiques and curios with each change of ownership until the Riverside Redevelopment Authority took it over in 1976.

Zona Gale, Frank Miller of Mission Inn *(New York, 1938); Esther Klotz,* The Mission Inn, Its History and Artifacts *(Riverside, 1981).*

Henry Miller
(Heinrich Alfred Kreiser, 1827-1916). California's greatest land baron, owner of an empire stretching from Oregon to the Baja, was a former butcher boy from Germany who arrived penniless in San Francisco in 1850. Venturing into the San Joaquin Valley to buy cattle for resale on the city market, he developed a fierce passion and a shrewd eye for land. During the drought of the Civil War years Miller began acquiring pieces of fifteen former Spanish ranchos. In 1857 he went into partnership with Charles Lux, an Alsatian and a butcher by trade, to handle retail sales. Lux possessed the dignity and presence to deal with bankers, but Miller was unquestionably the dominant partner. (When Lux died in 1887, Miller spent a small fortune buying off his partner's heirs, then went on just as well alone.) In the 1870s, with a view to controlling local water rights, Miller acquired 100,000 acres along the Kern River by falsely representing it as swamp land. This land involved him in one of the great legal battles of the West, culminating in a Supreme Court decision upholding English riparian rights over the Spanish tradition of appropriation. In the end, Miller compromised by donating land for a common reservoir. He possessed the capacity for benevolence (perhaps it was just peasant prudence) and fed drifters and hoboes, wisely seeking gratitude rather than enmity. His ranches were known as the "dirty plate route," because indigents were served at a second sitting off the same plates to save dishwashing. Miller favored the growth of the Southern Pacific octopus out of convenience. ("Bismark got rid of all the little kings and princes in Germany," he once said, "and I would like to get rid of all the little bosses in California.") Judicious loans to country assessors helped keep his land taxes low, and dominance in the cattle business enabled him to practically fix the price of California meat. Of his string of ranches he preferred the Gilroy one, but he was basically a working rancher, never happier than when he was riding along behind fat cattle on a drive planned with all the precision of a military maneuver. When he died, a half-century legal battle was fought over disposition of his estate. The town of Gustine was named for his daughter Augustine. Another Miller ranch became the private home of two successive mayors of Los Banos.

Ed Treadwell, author of The Cattle King *(New York, 1931), was one of Miller's attorneys; along with an inevitable partisanship, he also acquired a lot of privileged information.*

Henry Valentine Miller
(1891-1980). In 1947, **Hearst's** *San Francisco Examiner* ran a series of articles on a colony of sex anarchists living down the coast in Big Sur, piping their "doctrine of doom" and "cult of hate" straight to the University of California at Berkeley. (The pipeline apparently detoured around Carmel, where the *Examiner* found the American Legion alert to the threat, and around Stanford.) Guru of this sex cult was the infamous literary gangster Henry Miller, whose autobiographical sex novels (*Tropic of Cancer*, 1943 and *Tropic of Capricorn*, 1939) were banned in the U.S. For years after the *Examiner* article, Miller reported, tourists came to his door looking for the sex anarchy cult. The reality was considerably less titillating. During World War II, 50 years old, alone and suffering from writer's block, he left Europe and settled on the Northern California coast, which seemed to him a majestic backdrop for primal conflicts of heart and soul. There, in rustic if not primitive conditions (no telephone, no garbage disposal, the nearest grocer 40 miles away), the writer fought his way back to productivity. He was somewhat less successful at resolving the eternal battle of the sexes in real life than on paper. Miller married twice during the years at Big Sur and fathered two children, but both marriages failed. In 1961, after a Supreme Court ruling allowed publication of his books in the U.S., the tourists finally became an impossible nuisance. Also, the Big Sur life was a little too strenuous for a 70-year-old. The retired elder statesman of sex spent his last twenty years in good old bourgeois Pacific Palisades but kept his Brooklyn accent to the end.

Even nonfans of Miller's novels may enjoy his memoir, Big Sur and the Oranges of Hieronymus Bosch *(New York, 1957), a digression on the heightened reality of life on the edge of the Pacific. For standard biography see Jay Martin's* Always Merry and Bright *(Santa Barbara, 1978).*

Joaquin Miller
(Cincinnatus Hiner Miller 1837-1913). Miller was a literary poseur of exceptionally barefaced brass. A congenial confabulator, he

claimed to have been born in a covered wagon as a descendant of Pocahontas and to have reigned as the Great White Father of a utopian Indian republic on Mount Shasta. Actually, he was born in the Midwest, came to California at seventeen and performed alternately as a judge and a horse thief before finding his true vocation as a writer. It was **Ina Coolbrith** who suggested that Miller change his name (after **Joaquin Murieta**) and pose as the "Byron of the Rockies" on an 1870 trip to England. He even decorated Byron's grave with a wreath of hay, it was said. The Wild West pose was a great success in London society and Miller gained status in California for having put one over on the British. He set out on a lecture tour of the West wearing boots reaching almost to his waist and hair dyed bright orange, singing Methodist hymns in a purported Indian dialect and telling apochryphal tales of his legendary past. In 1886 Miller settled on a 70-acre estate in the Oakland hills, the "Hights," where he planted holly trees, erected monuments to **John Frémont**, Robert Browning, and Moses, and installed sprinklers on the roof to impress visitors with his rain-making ability. In 1897 he made a tour to Alaska wearing mukluks and a gold-buttoned fur suit, reciting verse about the frozen North. He was a performer rather than a poet, although his ode to Christopher Columbus was a pop classic of the day. Only Miller's fierce dignity, his biographer believes,

distinguished him from a mere snake doctor. When he died, he left instructions for his ashes to be scattered at the Hights, which later became a public park.

Miller's memoir, My Life Among the Modocs, *an 1874 bestseller, is indexed by the New York Public Library as fiction.* Splendid Poseur, *a biography of Miller by M.M. Marberry (New York, 1953), is pure pleasure.*

Darius Ogden Mills

(1825-1910). Mills was a 49er from New York, a former bank clerk who as a merchant in Sacramento took in so much gold that he decided to open his own bank. The Bank of D.O. Mills was very successful, and its proprietor was planning to return to the "States" in 1864 when **William Ralston** persuaded him to stay on in San Francisco as head of the new Bank of California. Mills was Ralston's opposite — dignified, austere, so conservative that he often refused to go into a venture without a guarantee against loss and so respected that he often got it. The association with Ralston made him enormously wealthy, and he

built a baronial country retreat down the peninsula in what is now Millbrae. Mills retired in 1873, sold his Bank of California stock, and set out on a trip around the world. After Ralston's suicide and the threat of bank failure in 1875, he helped the Bank of California to reorganize and resume business. Mills returned to live permanently in New York in protest against California's "radical" 1879 state constitution but retained extensive business interests in California and continued to winter there. His grandson Ogden Mills (1884-1937), born in Newport, RI, and raised with all the advantages of wealth, served as **Herbert Hoover**'s Secretary of the Treasury.

Jessica Mitford

(1917-   ). A radical refugee from the British aristocracy (two of her sisters became notorious facists, while a third wrote the definitive work on snob social distinctions), Mitford arrived in San Francisco in 1943, a war widow, to work for the Office of Price Administration. She and her second husband, labor attorney Bob Treuhaft, joined the local Communist Party in 1944 and soon moved across the bay to Oakland, where the class struggle had greater need of recruits. Mitford raised funds for the cause (one means was a benefit dinner, catered by radical Petaluma chicken farmers) and campaigned against police brutality and restrictive housing covenants for the East Bay Civil Rights Congress (CRC). Within the party she was a nonconformist, occasionally

criticized for lack of seriousness, but by society at large she and her husband were considered dangerous subversives and were hauled up before the House Un-American Activities Committee. When the CRC disbanded in 1956 Mitford took a job with the *San Francisco Chronicle* circulation department, but soon lost it, thanks to FBI intervention. The Treuhafts left the Communist Party in 1958, convinced that it had become stagnant and ineffective if not tiresomely self-righteous. The party's loss soon became the literary world's gain. Unemployed, with no marketable skills except her upper-crust verbal facility and marvelous wit, Mitford took up the pen. *Daughters and Rebels* (1960) was a memoir of her eccentric British upbringing: her mother ordered new banknotes from Harrods — "so much fresher" — and taught the children to eat with their lips curled back to economize on laundering napkins. *The American Way of Death* (1963) arose out of Bob Treuhaft's interest in the funeral industry. As a child Mitford misunderstood the words of the Communist "Internationale," translating "the final conflict" as "a fine old conflict," the title of her bemused 1977 memoir of life in California's radical underground.

Addison Mizner

(1872-1933) and **Wilson Reynolds Mizner** (1876-1933). The youngest of several children of a 49er, Addison and Wilson Mizner were born in the San

regulars Charlie Chaplin, Douglas Fairbanks, Sr. **Darryl Zanuck** and any passing maharajah, is said to have rivalled New York's Algonquin Round Table. The character of Blackie Norton, played by Clark Gable in the 1936 film *San Francisco* written by **Anita Loos**, was modeled after Wilson Mizner.

Addison Mizner wrote The Many Mizners *(New York, 1932);* The Legendary Mizners *(New York, 1953) by Alva Johnston is a sophisticated appreciation.*

Helena Modjeska

(Helena Modrzejewska Chlapowski, Countess Borentz, 1840-1909). They arrived in Anaheim in 1876, having journeyed from Poland via the Philadelphia Centennial and Panama, in search

Francisco Bay town of Benicia, where their father was collector of the port until removed as a result of a report by **J. Ross Browne**. They enjoyed diplomatic immunity as teenagers in Central America (their father was now U.S. minister plenipotentiary) and took off to join the Klondike Gold Rush in 1897. After a further period of wandering in the South Seas, Addison went on to become a self-taught society architect, designing mansions out of *One Thousand and One Nights* for the elite of Palm Beach. He never learned to draw proper plans or specifications, occasionally omitting a trifling necessity such as a staircase, but left some enduring landmarks on the South Florida coast. Wilson Mizner was a Falstaffian figure who worked

variously as a sports promoter, confidence man, innkeeper ("no opium smoking in the elevator") and Broadway playwright (*Deep Purple*, 1910). Joining his brother during the Florida real-estate boom of the 1920s, he retained his celebrated wit even in bankruptcy. One outraged landowner claimed misrepresentation, having been promised that he could grow nuts on his property; he could *go* nuts, Wilson corrected. After the crash Wilson repaired to Hollywood, where he dictated dialogue for early talkies (*Little Caesar*, *Merry Wives of Reno*) and was part-owner and resident wit of the original hat-shaped Brown Derby Restaurant across from the Ambassador Hotel. Booth 50 of the Derby, where Wilson held court with

of utopia. "What joy," Modjeska remembered thinking, "to cook under the sapphire sky in the land of freedom, to bleach linen at the brook like the maidens of the *Iliad*." A celebrated actress in Poland, she was the leading figure of the "ill-fated artist colony," as it became known locally, which also included writer Henryk Sienkiewicz. They selected Anaheim because they could communicate with the colonists there in German. They spoke no English at first, and their knowledge of agriculture was only slightly more advanced. "There was no system among our idealists," Modjeska wrote. "They worked or not, they discussed a great deal, they sometimes even quarrelled and then made up. . . . " As the money ran out, the actress set out to learn English in six months and to conquer the American stage with her regal bearing, mysteriously hooded eyes, and voice that aroused tears. She played Dumas's Camille, Schiller's Mary Stuart, Dante's Beatrice, Shakespeare's Juliet, reigning over the international stage for 30 years. In 1885 Modjeska returned to Santiago Canyon, 23 miles from Santa Ana, to build a summer cottage. Designed by Stanford White, it was called Arden, after Shakespeare's forest in *As You Like It*. She spent her last years on Bay Island, off Newport, later renamed for her. After her death, the city of Anaheim erected a statue of her as Mary Stuart in Pearson Park.

Modjeska wrote Memories and Impression *(New York, 1910). See also*

Theodore Payne, Life on the Modjeska Ranch (Los Angeles, 1962) and Wanderers Twain by Arthur and Marion Coleman (Cheshire, CN, 1964).

William Money

(1807?-1880). The first offbeat sect in California was founded in the 1840s by "Bishop" Money (pronounced Mo-*nay*), a Scots-born savant who arrived in Los Angeles via Mexico. He also wrote the first book printed in the region, a 22-page treatise in Spanish and English on his Reformed New Testament Church (1854). Money's sermons and diatribes against Catholics, Jews, and Mormons managed to convert a dozen or so Californios but fell for the most part on a tolerantly indifferent public. Also a doctor or naturopath, he claimed to have treated 5,000 patients (all listed in his *California Family Medical Instructor*, unfortunately lost to posterity), with only four deaths. Above all he was a scribbler, whose weather predictions and letters—including an "epistolary impugnation" against polygamy—frequently found their way to the *Star*, L.A.'s first newspaper. "Professor" Money's most ambitious concoction was a complex drawing of the hemispheres showing San Francisco on the brink of being engulfed by gushing subterranean currents called "Kuro Siwo." The leading local eccentric for 40 years, Money lived in an oval house in San Gabriel flanked by two triangular structures, with Greek, Latin, and Hebrew inscriptions on the gates.

William B. Rice wrote a short appreciation of Money; A Southern California Savant (Los Angeles, 1943).

Mondavi Family.

Someone once wrote a novel about the Mondavis, but insiders agree that the reality is much more interesting than fiction. They were a closely-knit, traditional Italian family who worked hard to prosper in the California wine industry. Settling in Lodi in 1922, they produced grapes for homebrewing by the country's Italian-Americans during Prohibition, doing well enough to send both sons to Stanford University. In 1943 the Mondavis bought and revitalized the Napa Valley winery of Charles Krug. But after the death in 1959 of patriarch Cesare Mondavi, the family became bitterly divided by fraternal strife. The more flamboyant elder brother eventually broke away to establish his own Robert Mondavi winery in partnership with French viticulturist Baron Philippe de Rothschild. He also filed suit against his conservative, methodical younger brother Peter, who enjoyed the considerable support of their mother and of Krug board member **Joe Alioto**. In 1976 the court ruled that Mondavi fraternal differences were irreconcilable, and Krug must be sold. Only then was agreement reached whereby Peter Mondavi bought out his brother's share of the family business, henceforth marketing Charles Krug as C.K. Mondavi.

Marilyn Monroe (Norma

Jean Mortensen, 1926-1962). She was a quintessential child of Hollywood, a spiritual orphan with a heritage out of **Nathanael West**'s *Day of the Locust*. Born on the charity ward at Los Angeles County General and baptized in **Aimee Semple McPherson**'s Foursquare Gospel Church, she grew up in a succession of foster homes. Her father, an itinerant Norwegian-American, disappeared before her birth; her mother, a film cutter, was soon institutionalized for paranoid schizophrenia. From the grounds at the L.A. Children's Home Society she could see RKO studios; during recess at Selma Avenue School, she chattered about movies and their stars, and on Saturdays she attended matinees at **Sid Grauman**'s Chinese and Egyptian theaters, measuring her feet against movie-star imprints and filling her head with celluloid fantasies. Marilyn dropped out of school to get married but was soon bored with the role of housewife. Discovered by a photographer, she got divorced, won a studio contract on the basis of her "flesh impact," and began to see the dreams come true. Acting was like "the games you play when you're a child and pretend to be somebody else," she once said. **Groucho Marx**, whom she met while doing a walk-on in a Marx brothers film, was like a familiar character from a fairy tale. (He, in turn, considered her a mixture of Mae West and Little Bo Peep.) Ambitious and selectively promiscuous, she traded up to a campy cameo as the dippy Miss Caswell, graduate of the Copacabana School of Dramatic Art, in *All About Eve* (1950). Not quite overnight, she became Hollywood's reigning sex symbol, the all-American

dumb blonde superstar of *Gentlemen Prefer Blondes* (1953) and *How to Marry a Millionaire* (1950). She herself would marry culture heroes: alltime-great baseball star **Joe DiMaggio** and respected playwright Arthur Miller, who wrote *The Misfits* (1960) for her. Anxious to be taken seriously, she tried to fill the gaps in her emotional and intellectual makeup with psychoanalysis and method acting classes. She also took barbiturates to level out her mood swings from rage to depression, so it was not quite unexpected when she was found dead of an overdose at 36. The surprise was that she had probably received the lethal dose by injection, that Robert Kennedy, attorney general of the United States, was one of the last known people to see her alive, and that no proper inquest was held. On the twentieth anniversary of her death, the L.A. county board of supervisors voted an investigation, and **DiMaggio** cancelled his standing order for roses delivered to her grave.

The best source on Monroe's life is Norma Jean by Fred Guiles (1969); on her death, The Life and Curious Death of Marilyn Monroe by Robert Slatzer (1974).

Pierre Monteux

(1875-1964). Monteux, a chubby, walrus-moustached Frenchman, orchestrated San Francisco's love affair with culture for seventeen years. A graduate of the Paris Conservatory, he became conductor as a young man of the Ballets Russes de Monte Carlo, presenting the world premieres of works by **Stravinsky**, Debussy, and Ravel. In the U.S. after World War I, he was invited to conduct in Philadelphia but suffered by comparison with the tall, charismatic Leopold Stokowski, then on leave. Monteux looked more like a chef than a conductor, people joked, but for San Francisco he had just the right combination of musicianship and Gallic charm. When he arrived in 1935, the San Francisco Symphony was setting nonattendance records even with only four concerts a year. Monteux imposed new

standards of quality and quantity, extended the repertoire to include modern works, started theme festivals, and showcased young soloists to create a vibrant new cultural enterprise. In 1947 he gave civic pride a large boost with a grand national tour for which the state legislature voted him California ambassador-at-large. A familiar and beloved figure around town, he wintered every year with his wife and dog at the Fairmont Hotel. For his 75th birthday, 10,000 guests celebrated at San Francisco's Civic Auditorium. In 1952 Monteux left San Francisco in search of new worlds to conquer and conducted the London Symphony until his death at 89.

Everyone is Someone (New York, 1962), is a nonsense memoir by Fifi Monteux, the family poodle.

Lola Montez (Eliza Gilbert, 1818-1861).

She was 35 when she came to California, a mysterious adventuress with a long and celebrated list of sexual conquests including composer Franz Liszt and King Louis I of Bavaria. She claimed to be the daughter of a Spanish matador, but was in fact Irish-born and raised in colonial India. A poor actress and an erratic, impulsive dancer, she commanded attention by virtue of her beauty and her imperious exhibitionism, throwing tantrums and striking men with her whip at the slightest provocation. Montez arrived in San Francisco with a full complement of admirers. On the ship from Panama she had met U.S. Senator **William**

Gwin, promoter **Sam Brannan**, and Patrick Hull, a local journalist who would become her third husband. She received local notables with champagne and caviar in her hotel suite, opened on stage in *School for Scandal*, and two months later married Hull in the Mission Dolores with the governor in attendance. For their honeymoon, they toured Sacramento and the Mother Lode, finally settling in the mining town of Grass Valley. Montez's career was not

going well: her celebrated "Spider Dance" was caricatured in San Francisco as "Spy-Dear Dance," and as an actress she was not even convincing as herself in *Lola Montez in Bavaria*. So she remained in Grass Valley for eighteen months, refitting a former gambling house with mementos of her amours. She studied animal magnetism and ESP, affected a bear for a pet, and took an interest in a pretty young neighbor named **Lotta Crabtree**. But her marriage soon came to an end, and she became bored. Spoiling for a fight, she used her horsewhip on a local newspaper editor. There was an unsuccessful Australian tour and then Montez, clearly past her prime, returned to the East Coast, where she spent her last years lecturing on free love and selling rejuvenation cream. Her house in Grass Valley became a local tourist shrine, and a nearby hill was named Mount Lola.

A ghostwritten autobiography (New York, 1859) is now a collector's item. For a contemporary biography, see The Uncrowned Queen; Life of Lola Montez *(New York, 1972) by Ishbel Ross.*

John Berrien Montgomery (1794-1873).

For most of the U.S. soldiers and sailors who participated, the conquest of California was something of a spree. Montgomery, a navy captain who raised the first stars and stripes over San Francisco in July 1846, is one of the few participants to emerge with a measure of military dignity and human compassion. A pious Episcopalian from New Jersey, he joined the navy at seventeen and rose to command the sloop USS *Portsmouth* on its maiden voyage around the Horn, arriving in Monterey in September 1843. The *Portsmouth* was assigned to remain in the vicinity, to "afford countenance and all proper protection to our citizens and their interests," for most of the next dramatic five years. Montgomery was not immune to the rhetoric of Manifest Destiny. "I hold it to be the privilege of all men everywhere," he announced in California, to "resist

oppression in whatever form or manner." But from his ship in San Francisco harbor the captain remained polite, conciliatory, and solicitous of the welfare of California's Mexican citizens. For Montgomery personally, California was a tragedy. Two of his sons, both midshipmen, left by launch for the Sacramento garrison and were never seen again. Probably they were murdered for the payroll they carried. The *Portsmouth* returned to Boston in 1848 carrying the original Bear Flag and later saw service in Africa and the Orient. Montgomery became commander of the Pacific Squadron, guarding the waters between Panama and San Francisco during the Civil War.

Montgomery and the Portsmouth (San Francisco, 1958) by Fred Rogers is dignified and respectful.

Thomas Jeremiah Mooney (1882-1942).

The most famous U.S. prisoner in the interwar period was a cantankerous San Francisco labor leader who did 22 years in San Quentin on a demonstrably bum rap. Born Irish in Chicago and raised "on the bloody side of the American labor movement," Mooney rode the rails west at 25, an iron moulder with a dream of radical glory. He won a trip to a 1910 European Socialist Congress for collecting a record number of subscriptions to *Wilshire's Magazine*, but otherwise proved utterly lacking in the personal requisites for union leadership. After an unsuccessful attempt to lead a wildcat strike against the

powerful United Railroads (URR) in 1916, Mooney was marked as a dangerous subversive and was tried three times for possession of explosives, probably planted by the URR. When ten people were killed by a bomb at San Francisco's 1916 Preparedness Day Parade, Mooney was widely considered the only local radical rash enough to have planted the bomb. The URR helped make a case against Mooney and his friend **Warren Billings**, and a politically ambitious district attorney of San Francisco won their conviction. Mooney's wife Rena was eventually acquitted of the

same charges, and the prosecution's key witnesses were exposed as a prostitute, an addict, a syphilitic, a spiritualist, and a pathological liar. According to legal procedure, however, new evidence of perjury was not then admissible to appellate courts, leaving open only the recourse of pardon by the state governor. President Woodrow Wilson personally intervened on behalf of Mooney and Billings, but the post-World War I "red scare" was too strong and the governors of California too fainthearted. The U.S. Labor Department actually bugged the San Francisco D.A.'s office—with the same cavalier disregard of legal amenities that convicted the radicals — recording a good deal of obscene braggadoccio and reactionary good-old-boyism, but only inferential evidence of a frame-up. So for a generation Mooney stewed in his San Quentin cell, an international symbol of injustice. A Mooney Congress was held in Chicago in 1919. The Sacco-Vanzetti case, although later more famous, first became known as the "New England Mooney Case." There was a pro-Mooney demonstration at the 1932 Olympics in Los Angeles, for which the demonstrators received stiff nine-month sentences as disturbers of the peace. A habeas corpus hearing that dragged on for nearly two years in San Francisco helped establish the principle that a criminal conviction obtained by perjured testimony constitutes denial of due process. But it took the election of **Culbert Olson** as governor to effect Mooney's release. In January 1939, now a middle-aged man with a terminal case of ulcers but as obstreperous as ever, Mooney led his own victory procession up the same route taken by the original Preparedness Day Parade 22½ years earlier.

Of two major studies, The Mooney Case *by Robert Frost (Stanford, 1968) is the more scholarly but does not disagree in any significant respect with Curt Gentry's* Frame-Up *(New York, 1967), more partisan and infinitely more readable.*

Julia Morgan (1872-1957). After his mother and his mistress, the most important woman in the life of **William Randolph Hearst**, according to his biographer, was

probably Julia Morgan. Born in San Francisco, an engineering graduate of UC Berkeley (1894), she became the first woman graduate of the École des Beaux Arts in Paris (1902) and the first woman architect licensed in California. A small, schoolmarmish woman in round horn-rimmed glasses and old-fashioned hats, Morgan built a successful San Francisco firm on commissions from the wellbred women of her day. She designed half the YWCAs from Oakland to Long Beach, using every style from Mission Revival to Italian Renaissance. She also developed a sideline in shingle-style houses and created a jewel of a Berkeley chapel, Saint John's. But her most celebrated achievement was the Hearst Castle at San Simeon on which she labored from 1919 to 1947, incorporating architectural booty acquired by Hearst all over the world and accommodating the tycoon's every grandiose whim. It was said that the only style

Morgan couldn't handle was modern.

Richard W. Longstreth's Julia Morgan, Architect *(Berkeley, 1977) is handsomely illustrated.*

Marion Morrison. *See* John Wayne.

Norma Jean Mortensen. *See* Marilyn Monroe.

John Muir (1838-1914). Muir once expressed amazement that Thoreau was considered a hermit for his life at Walden Pond, only two miles from the nearest town. For years the Scottish-born naturalist wandered alone in the remote mountains of California, supplied only with bread and tea and a few books for companionship, looking with his tangled hair and startling blue eyes like John the Baptist in the wilderness. As a boy growing up in Wisconsin, Muir showed early signs of mechanical genius. He invented one contraption to guillotine gophers and another, called the "early rising machine," to dump him out of bed at the desired hour; later he devised a semi-automated lathe which, had he patented it, might have supported him for life. Instead, he chose to abandon machines for the "inventions of God." At the age of 29 he walked a thousand miles to the Gulf of Mexico, but did not find what he sought. The following year he sailed via Panama to California and waded through knee-deep wildflowers in the San Joaquin Valley to reach his new spiritual and temporal home, Yosemite. Muir's was an all-ecompassing love of nature, embracing everything

from mountains down to playful squirrels (except perhaps for sheep, which he considered "hoofed locusts"). He was exhilarated by storms, fascinated by glaciers. He found in the mountains of California a greater number of distinct species of trees to absorb his interest than available anywhere else on earth. He had the ability to translate his supremely transcendant love of nature into gorgeous prose, describing the Sierra Nevada, for example, as "the range of light," a "vast beviled wall of purest marble," like the rampart of some great celestial city. So extraordinary was Muir that the great savants of the day, men like Ralph Waldo Emerson, sought him out. Indifferent to material exigencies until his marriage late in life, he nonetheless earned a fair living writing for popular and scientific journals. His writings were later collected

in *The Mountains of California* (1894), *The Yosemite* (1912), and other books. Having become something of a celebrity, he was able to travel to Alaska to indulge his interest in the movement of glaciers, "rivers of ice," and to Africa and South America to satisfy a childhood dream. He worked for the creation of Yosemite National Park in 1890, and in 1892 became the first president of the Sierra Club. Many landmarks in California were named for him, including Muir Woods in San Rafael, a tribute from a perfect stranger to a man who reportedly could tell the genus of a tree merely by the sound of the wind through its leaves.

Linnie Marsh Wolfe's Son of the Wilderness *(New York, 1945) was authorized by Muir's daughters. For a more up-to-date biography, see James Mitchell Clarke's* The Life and Adventures of John Muir *(San Diego, 1979).*

William Mulholland

(1855-1935). He was a former sailor from Ireland, an

amateur engineer who as water czar of Southern California made possible its great twentieth-century population explosion. Mulholland begged, borrowed, and stole water, principally from the Owens River Valley east of the Sierra Nevada, to meet the constantly growing needs of the arid southland. He personally supervised construction of the 225-mile aqueduct, a truly Roman endeavor, to bring the Owens Valley water south—water to make the desert bloom, to provide every householder with a square of green lawn, and to make the fortunes of landowners whose property on the periphery of the city skyrocketed in value. When Mulholland's "purest snow water" arrived from the Sierra in 1913, supply temporarily exceeded demand, prompting L.A. to increase its territory to include the San Fernando Valley and other suburbs. While others got rich and while the Owens Valley was fighting a losing war against the water imperialism of the south, the visionary Mulholland was absorbed with the future, with tapping the motherlode of "white gold," the Rocky Mountains. (Eventually this would be accomplished by means of Hoover Dam and another aqueduct.) In a gesture of civic gratitude, L.A. named a highway after its water chief in 1923. When finally completed, Mulholland Drive would meander along the spine of the Santa Monica Mountains, the last frontier in the Los Angeles basin, from the sea to the Cahuenga Pass. But Mulholland's life ended sadly. In 1928 his Saint

Francis Dam broke, inundating the Santa Clara Valley and taking hundreds of lives. A coroner's jury blamed the unstable rock formation of the site, not the construction itself, but questioned the dictatorial chain of command which left all decisions in the Department of Water and Power in the hands of a self-taught engineer. (Mulholland's formal education, writer John Weaver remarked, was limited to the three R's and the Ten Commandments.) "If there is an error of human judgment, I am the human," admitted Mulholland, then 72 years old, with seven haunted years yet to live. He was reincarnated as Hollis Mulwray in the fictionalized film about water, power, and incest, *Chinatown* (1974).

See Robert W. Matson, William Mulholland, A Forgotten Forefather *(Stockton, CA, 1976) and Remi Nadeau,* The Water Seekers *(Salt Lake City, 1974).*

Joaquin Murieta

(?-1853). The archetypal Mexican outlaw-hero, apotheosized in folklore and film, Joaquin Murieta falls into the gray area between history and myth. According to the facts, a bandit variously named Murieta, Muliati, Muerto, Valenzuela, and Carillo, committed daring crimes, mostly against Chinese, in California's Mother Lode during the winter of 1852-1853. An expert escape artist, he often made his pursuers look foolish. Soon, however, a band of Texas-style rangers claimed the $1,000 reward for his head, adding for good measure the hand of an alleged confederate, Three-Fingered Jack. The pickled head of

"Joaquin" (blue-eyed and brown-haired, incidentally) went on public display, and tourists paid to see "where Joaquin slept" all over California. Contemporary artists pictured him as a wild-eyed creature, more devil than man. In 1854 a half-Cherokee journalist named John Rollin Ridge wrote a "biography" of Joaquin Murieta, an impassioned tale of injustice, persecution, and revenge. Cincinnatus **Miller** was inspired by the subject to compose a 30-page poem and to change his name to Joaquin. Ridge's story was pirated and further embellished, giving rise over the years to a religious revival by Joaquin's "widow" in 1883 and to a 1936 film starring Warner Baxter as *The Robin Hood of El Dorado*. (As late as 1967, Chilean Nobel Prize winner Pablo Neruda wrote a drama about Joaquin.) Dissenting from the popular view, San Francisco literary critic Joseph Henry Jackson claimed the Joaquin story was made up out of whole cloth. Contemporary social historians tend to view

Murieta as a collective representation of Californios dispossessed by the American conquest and the personification of growing racial enmity in a period when California led the nation in crime and violence.

Remi Nadeau, author of The Real Joaquin Murieta; Robin Hood Hero or Gold Rush Gangster? *(Corona del Mar, 1974), has a vested interest in the existence of a real Murieta.*

Richard Joseph Neutra

(1892-1970). Neutra was in Chicago, where he had traveled to meet architects Louis Sullivan and **Frank Lloyd Wright**, when he saw a travel poster—"California Calls You." So he came west, finding a people he described as "mentally footloose" and a cultural naiveté "bordering everywhere on mix-up." Neutra made his name as a Southern California architect with his first major commission, the machine-age modern Phillip Lovell house (1929) on a hillside of Los Angeles. (**Rudolf Schindler**, who sponsored his fellow Austrian and took him into his own home and office in 1925, made sketches for the Lovell

house but Neutra got the job.) He also designed the Channel Heights housing project in San Pedro (1942), a cluster of houses in Silverlake, and the L.A. Hall of Records (1961-1962). A great many of Neutra's commissions were for schools: an open-air school in Bell (1935), Emerson Junior High in West L.A. (1938), Palos Verdes High School (1961), and the Fine Arts building at Cal State Northridge (1961). The complete pedagogical architect, he wrote books about the social, physiological, and metaphysical dimensions of space. ("Certain desired INNER DISTRIBUTIONS OF FORCE AND STRESS within our nervous system are THE REAL AIM OF ALL OUTER DESIGN BALLISTICS.") One of his last designs was **Robert Schuller**'s drive-in church in Garden Grove (1967). Can destiny be designed, Neutra asked? In his own work he conveyed what architectural historian Reyner Banham called "a nervous feeling of creative angst," Central European in origin but not wholly inappropriate to the Southern California landscape.

See Neutra's, Life and Shape *(New York, 1962), also Tom Hines's* Richard Neutra and the Search for Modern Architecture *(New York, 1982).*

Henry Mayo Newhall

(1825-1882). A native of Massachusetts and an auctioneer by training, Newhall joined the Gold Rush to California but soon found business more profitable than mining. His auction, wholesale and insurance interests prospered, and during the 1860s he invested his profits

in building a railroad from San Francisco south to Gilroy. After selling his railroad interests to the Southern Pacific in 1870, he began to acquire large pieces of range land: the El Piojo, San Miguelito, and Santa Rita ranches in Monterey County; El Rancho Suey and Todos Santos north of Santa Barbara; and the Rancho San Francisco in the mountains between Los Angeles and Bakersfield. The latter became known as the Newhall Ranch, the center of the rancher's new activities. One nearby town was named after him, and another after his Massachusetts birthplace, Saugus. The hardworking and aggressive Newhall seems to have been gracious and charitable, foregoing repayment of a mortgage loan so that neighbor Ignacio Del Valle's widow and children could retain possession of their land. Newhall's five sons inherited a total of 143,000 acres or 220 square miles, which they began to liquidate. El Piojo was sold to **William Randolph Hearst** in 1922, and Todos Santos became a military base, Camp Cooke, while remaining holdings were consolidated into the Newhall Land and Farming Company with headquarters at Castaic Junction. The company narrowly escaped bankruptcy during the Depression, thanks to two acts of nature. After the collapse of the Saint Francis Dam in 1927, the Newhall Ranch, the largest single property in the path of the floodwaters, received damages of $737,000 from the city of Los Angeles. And in 1936 a major oil field was discovered on Newhall land in

Potrero Canyon. A later family development, the Magic Mountain amusement park, also proved lucrative.

Ruth W. Newhall's The Newhall Ranch *(San Marino, 1958) is family history.*

Harris Newmark

(1834-1916). Newmark was the premier diarist of ninteenth century L.A., the Samuel Pepys of his own obscure but colorful backwater. A German Jew, he arrived in 1853 and set up shop downtown, learning Spanish before English. Before the Civil War, Main Street was L.A.'s main residential thoroughfare, and everything west of Main was considered "across the plains." There were only two classes, respectable folks and "evil" elements. The former were tolerant enough to embrace a great variety of people, Newmark found, and so closely knit that every death was personally felt. He noted the introduction of plumbing in the 1860s (L.A. had to send to San Francisco for plumber's tools), the first

electric lights in 1882 (bad for the complexion, ladies said), and the real estate boom of 1887 ("Peerless Long Beach," and Whittier—"It will dwarf Monrovia and eclipse Pasadena"). With wealth Newmark acquired culture, ordering a piano sent around the Horn, introducing fingerbowls to local society, and sending his son Maurice to study under the Grand Rabbi of Paris. But he never lost his amused tolerance of Southern California provinciality. When U.S. Secretary of State William Seward passed through town in 1869, Newmark turned up for the customary banquet in swallowtails, the mayor of L.A. appeared in an ankle-length duster, and the **Pico** brothers wore blue coats with brass buttons. When it was proposed to name a street after Euclid, Newmark noted, someone asked what Mr. Euclid had ever done for the city. Leading citizens who preferred to forget their humble origins were said to be greatly annoyed when his memoirs went into a second and third edition.

Sixty Years in Southern California, 1853-1913, The Reminiscences of Harris Newmark *(New York, 1916) was reprinted in 1970.*

Huey Percy Newton

(1942-   ). A new generation of black American leaders came of age in Oakland in 1966, the sons of southerners attracted to the World War II shipyards. Unlike the rival Student Non-Violent Coordinating Committee, which was basically southern-rural in orientation, the Black Panther Party was dedicated to the aggressive defense of urban blacks—by force of

arms, legal self-help, and sheer brass. The latter two were the distinctive contribution of Newton, the youngest and nerviest of the Panther founders. Born in Louisiana and named after its governor, Huey Long, Newton grew up in Oakland and graduated illiterate, he said, from Oakland Technical High School. While educating himself to read the militant classics, he paid the rent by a life of petty crime, then studied law to help him beat the rap whenever he got caught. Newton's ideas on

burglary ("liberating property from the oppressor") were scarcely original, but talking back to the "pig" definitely was—"pig" being a Newton epithet for cop, almost as loaded as "nigger." Always conscious of his image, he had his picture taken in the Panther beret and black leather jacket, seated coolly in a tropical rattan chair with weapons in both hands. In the process of transforming burglars into revolutionaries, Newton as Panther Minister of Defense led armed confrontations with the police

in Oakland's ghettoes. The white establishment responded immediately in force, and Newton was wounded in a 1967 shootout (an urban variation on southern lynching, he called it) that left one policeman dead. He spent nearly two years in jail (uppity as ever, he refused to do prison work for less than minimum wage) before his manslaughter conviction was reversed on a judicial error. The Panthers backed off from confrontation to community work, offering free breakfasts and health testing, but Newton was arrested again in 1974 for the murder of a black prostitute and fled to Cuba. He returned three years later to face the charges which, after two mistrials, were finally dropped in 1979. In 1980 Newton earned a Ph.D. from the University of California, Santa Cruz with a thesis on the FBI war against the Panthers, written with the aid of FBI documents obtained under the Freedom of Information Act.

Newton wrote Revolutionary Suicide *(New York, 1974), a memoir.*

Richard Milhous Nixon

(1913-   ). Nixon's early life has been thoroughly plumbed for clues to the disaster. His would seem to have been a bucolic childhood in the rural Southern California hinterland. He was born in a plain white clapboard house, built by his father in the middle of a Yorba Linda lemon grove. Like his brothers, he was named after the kings of England. In 1922 the family moved to Whittier, a closely knit Quaker community built around college and church, where they ran a mom-and-pop general store and the only gas station for miles around. Historians playing amateur psychiatrist have made much of Nixon's parents, his pious Quaker mother, college-educated and quietly dominating, and his Irish father, subject to black rages and unable ever quite to succeed. Certainly the combination produced in their son Richard a priggish and repressed personality, ambitious and aggressive, constitutionally careless of consequences. Nixon made his first headline in the *Los Angeles Times* by winning a 1929 debate contest. At Whittier College he was student body president and graduated second in the class of 1934, winning a scholarship to Duke University Law School. Having acquired a full set of eastern establishment values, he really wanted to become a Wall Street lawyer but, failing to get a bid, returned to Whittier. According to

information uncovered by writer **Irving Wallace**, Nixon's first court case was a professional disaster, with the judge threatening to turn the matter over to the bar association. During World War II he traded his Quaker convictions for military service. Nixon's first good shot at the big time came in 1945 when he ran for Congress as a Republican against "Communist" **Jerry Voorhis**, the first of many casualties on his road to political ruin. The main events of his life would henceforth be acted out on a national stage with only a few incidental California exceptions. There was another local campaign characterized by smear tactics against **Helen Douglas** in 1950 for the U.S. Senate. The pivotal "Checkers" speech, in which vice-presidential nominee Nixon justified secret contributions from wealthy California backers, was delivered from an NBC

theater in Hollywood. After this, "home" began to seem hostile territory. Nixon played a role in setting up the 1958 state Republican party fiasco in which his two chief rivals, **William F. Knowland** and **Goodwin Knight**, were both defeated, but even with a clear field he was defeated for state governor in 1962. "You won't have Nixon to kick around any more," he announced and moved onto the fast track of New York corporate law, which took him all the way to the White House in 1969. During Nixon's presidential years, a tacky beach town on the San Diego Freeway, San Clemente, became the site of a Western White House. It was there that the 37th President of the United States returned after resigning in disgrace in 1974, later choosing the ultimate anonymity of exile in New York.

A sampling of the Nixon literature: (pro) Bela Kornitzer, The Real Nixon *(New York, 1960); (con) Garry Wills,* Nixon Agonistes; The Crisis of the Self-Made Man *(New York, 1969); (self-serving)* The Memoirs of Richard Nixon *(New York, 1978); (skeptical) Fawn Brodie,* Richard Nixon; The Shaping of His Character *(New York, 1981).*

Thomas Tsunetomi Noguchi (1927?-   ).

In many parts of the country the coroner is a political appointee and occasionally not even an M.D.; elsewhere, the office is controlled by local medical schools, insuring their access to "biological resources." Only in L.A. is the coroner an independent, highly skilled, and occasionally eccentric celebrity. The Japanese-born-and-educated son of a physician, Noguchi emigrated

to California in 1952, joined the L.A. coroner's office in 1961, and the following year handled his first famous victim, a "36-year-old well-developed, well-nourished Caucasian female" named **Marilyn Monroe**. (Years later, a Monroe biographer would piece together the elements of the supposed suicide, faulting Noguchi for making unsubstantiated assumptions which purposely or not abetted a high-level coverup.) Noguchi was appointed to head the office in 1967 with overall responsibility for 20,000 investigations annually. Some of his most famous cases, which he handled personally, were Sharon Tate, Janis Joplin, and Robert F. Kennedy. To forestall the sort of speculation that followed John Kennedy's assassination, Noguchi conducted an exhaustive six-hour autopsy of Robert Kennedy, filing a 40-page report. In 1969 critics tried to have the coroner removed from office for alleged drug use, erratic behavior, and improper administration; but during six weeks of hearings he was vindicated of everything but overwork and eccentric humor. He subsequently achieved international celebrity for his work as a death detective, consulting on cases all over the world and regaling journalists with tales of skill and little twists of his macabre trade. Coming under fire for his obvious relish in reporting the deaths of Natalie Wood and William Holden, Noguchi was demoted in 1982.

A chapter in Roger Rapoport's, Superdoctors *(Chicago, 1975) is devoted to Noguchi.*

Nordhoff Family

"California is our own; and it is the first tropical land which our race has mastered and made itself at home in." With these words in the introduction of his *California for Travellers and Settlers* (1872), Charles Nordhoff (1830-1901), a New York reporter, launched a tourist wave and a real estate boom in the new American paradise. Arriving by the newly completed transcontinental railroad, Nordhoff's travellers and settlers were a better class of citizen than the 49ers—"doubly picked men," he called them, emigrants first from the Old World and then from the crowded cities of the industrializing northeastern U.S. The German-born Nordhoff himself joined this Darwinian migration of the fittest, settling first in Santa Barbara. (The nearby town of Ojai was originally called Nordhoff.) In 1887 the Mexican government rewarded him for literary services rendered to tourism with a 50,000-acre ranch in the Baja. Nordhoff's son Walter (1858-1937) moved to the Baja ranch, where his son Charles Bernard Nordhoff (1887-1947) enjoyed the childhood of a tropical Tom Sawyer. Walter Nordhoff also kept a house in Redlands, maintained a summer place on L.A.'s Terminal Island, and sent his children to private school in Pasadena. But home remained the Baja ranch until the 1910 revolution in Mexico, when it became something of a paradise lost. Walter Nordhoff moved to San Diego, where he ran a glazed tile factory; he later retired to Santa Barbara and wrote a novel which became a minor classic of California literature, *The Journey of the Flame*, published in 1933 under a pseudonym to preserve the author's genteel privacy. Charles Nordhoff, meanwhile, graduated from Harvard (1909) and went to France as a World War I ambulance driver, later joining the Foreign Legion and receiving training as a pilot. Restless after the war, he and another American war pilot got an advance from *Harper's* magazine to explore and write about the real tropics. Nordhoff and James Hall both settled in Tahiti, married native women, and raised large families while collaborating on *Mutiny on the Bounty* (1932), *Botany Bay* (1941) and other adventure tales of men against the sea. In a joint biography by Paul Briand, Hall comes off rather better than the aloof and imperial Nordhoff, blond and icy-blue-eyed, who lapsed into sexual and alcoholic excesses his grandfather would have attributed to the enervating tropical climate. Nordhoff eventually divorced his Tahitian wife and returned to live in Santa Barbara, working on such Hollywood film scenarios as *The Tuttles of Tahiti*. His brother Franklin Nordhoff (1894-1956) also wrote a popular book, *Fruit of the Earth* (1955), about ranch life in the Southern California valleys.

See In Search of Paradise; The Nordhoff-Hall Story *by Paul Briand (New York, 1966). Charles Nordhoff's* California for Travellers and Settlers *was recently republished in a centennial (1972) edition by Ten Speed Press.*

Mabel Ethelreid Normand (1895-1930).

Most of her films have been lost, but Normand's spirit survives like a wild Irish rose in Hollywood history. Both beautiful and funny, she was loved by not one but two of the great producers; she was also a central character in *the* murder mystery of her day. Mack Sennett, who met her when she was a skinny French-Irish mavoureen from Staten Island, brought her to California to star in his silent screen comedies. In Hollywood she ate ice cream for breakfast, is believed to have thrown the first custard pie on screen, and helped a British vaudevillian named Charlie Chaplin make the transition from stage to screen. "When the clowns went home it was this girl who was important," wrote Sennett, who was in love with her. But "Nappy," as Normand called Sennett (short for Napoleon), was less than true-blue. Finding him with another woman shortly before their scheduled marriage, she tried to commit suicide by jumping from an L.A. pier into the ocean. Thereafter she led a life of hedonistic self-destruction, all flags flying. **Sam Goldwyn** signed Normand to a contract in 1917 and fell in love with her, but she made fun of him behind his back and disappeared in the middle of a picture to go on a spending binge in Paris. Always frail and consumptive, she reportedly recharged her energies with cocaine. She became involved with director **William Desmond Taylor**, and was the last person known to have seen him

before his murder in 1922. After Normand's death from tuberculosis, her casket was carried by Chaplin, **D.W. Griffith**, Douglas Fairbanks, Sr., and **Fatty Arbuckle**.

Sennett's autobiography, King of Comedy *(Garden City, NY, 1954) is a loving tribute to Normand. Betty H. Fussell,* Mabel, Hollywood's First I-Don't-Care Girl *(New Haven, CN, 1982).*

Frank Norris (Benjamin Franklin Norris, 1870-1902). The self-styled "boy Zola" of San Francisco, Norris in his too-brief life cut a stylish figure in local literary society. His father was a Chicago jeweler who brought the family west in 1884; his mother, strong-minded and culturally conscious, founded the San Francisco Browning Club. Well-educated for the day, Norris attended prep school at **Ralston**'s old mansion in Belmont, and tried the S.F. Art Association School before going to Paris to study art for two years. Enrolled at the University of California at Berkeley in 1890, he became a fraternity man, wrote the "pig" dinner ceremony celebrated by Fijis nationwide, and chartered a stagecoach for the 1892 Big Game against Stanford. He also spent a year at Harvard where he was considered something of a cowboy intellectual. Living on the East Coast, however, gave him a sense of perspective on the California experience. In 1899 Norris published *McTeague*, the naturalistic novel of a Polk Street dentist (later immortalized by Erich von Stroheim in a seven-hour film shot on location in San Francisco). *The Octopus* (1901) was conceived as the

first in a trilogy on the theme of man and nature vs. the railroad and the corporations, borrowing from the **Evans-Sontag** story and the 1880 Mussel Slough tragedy when several settlers were killed in a dispute over Southern Pacific land. The book seems terribly wordy today; but to generations of farmers in the Central Valley, historian George Mowry says, *The Octopus* was "more than a literary exercise; it was a part of their own biographies." The second volume in the trilogy, *The Pit* appeared just after Norris's death following an appendectomy.

Franklin Walker wrote Frank Norris, A Biography *(Garden City, NY, 1932).*

Kathleen Thompson Norris (1880-1966). One of the greatest sentimental storytellers of the first generation of mass women's magazines, Norris was the daughter of a San Francisco banker and Bohemian Club president. She was a local society columnist before her

marriage in 1909 to Charles Gilman Norris (1881-1945), younger brother of Frank. The newlyweds moved to New York because it was the thing for aspiring literati to do and also doubtless to get away from the senior Mrs. Norris, who had accompanied them on their honeymoon. Beginning in 1911 with the publication of *Mother*, Kathleen Norris turned out popular novels, many of them serialized in *Cosmopolitan* or *Women's Home Companion*, at the rate of two a year for 25 years. Charles Norris, meanwhile, labored to produce a total of seven naturalistic novels (*Salt*, 1917; *Seed*, 1930). With financial success they bought a ranch in California's Santa Cruz Mountains and a winter home in Palo Alto named Casa Abierta (later the Stanford University Newman Club). Something of a moral leader in her day, Norris supported the lost causes of Prohibition, the **Townsend** plan, and pacifism. America First, the antiwar organization of which she and Charles Lindbergh

were leading members, was discredited by fruitless approaches to fascist satraps during the 1930s. But the Women's International League for Peace and Freedom to which Norris also belonged would survive to oppose war in another generation.

Kathleen Norris wrote a memoir, Family Gathering *(Garden City, NY, 1959).*

John Knudsen Northrop (1895-1981). A self-taught pioneer of aviation, Northrop was a high school graduate from Santa Barbara who pestered the Lockheed (then Loughead) brothers into giving him a job as a draftsman. Soon he was living, breathing, eating, and sleeping aviation. "I would get up in the morning eager to see what we could do with the planes," he recalled at age 83, "and at night I would say, 'Tomorrow we'll see what we can do to make them fly better.' " An idea man with a genius for stress analysis, he is credited with devising the stressed-skin fuselage which reduced weight and drag and allowed significantly more cabin space. Northrop worked during his long career on the F-1 Flyboat, which was considered 40 years ahead of its time; on the Lockheed Vega which Wiley Post flew around the world in eight days in 1931; on other "crack ships" under his own name, such as the Northrop Alpha (the first plane with a reinforced metal fuselage), Beta, and Gamma in which **Howard Hughes** set a nine-hour cross-country record in 1936; and on the P-61 Black Widow, the first night fighter. For years, he experimented with an all-wing airplane, but lost a contract to produce it for the U.S. Air Force in a Pentagon power struggle. Restless, he worked for most of Southern California's aircraft companies: in 1923 he went to work for **Donald Douglas**; in 1927 he was back with the Lockheed brothers; he returned to Douglas during the Depression, then split off to form his own company in 1939. His real genius, however, was for design, not management. "There is a little bit of him in every airplane that flies," Douglas once remarked.

Emperor Norton (Joshua Abraham Norton, 1819?-1880). He was the reigning eccentric of El Dorado, a harmless madman who for nearly three decades enjoyed mock-

imperial privileges in the streets of San Francisco. An English Jew, raised in South Africa, Norton figured briefly as a prosperous gentleman merchant in Gold Rush California. He was said to have "seen the elephant," contemporary slang for risking everything on an elusive gold strike, and to have lost his mind after an attempt to corner the San Francisco rice market ended in bankruptcy. Norton issued his first imperial edict in 1856, affected a military uniform with sword and a plumed, cockaded hat, and imposed a modest system of tithing on sympathetic merchants—50 cents a month to help with court expenses. He lived in the same rooming house for seventeen years, the owner having declined his orders to seize the Palace Hotel as imperial headquarters. He printed up his own scrip in 50-cent denominations as well as manifestos and pronunciamentos on local and world affairs, in tones ranging from presumptuous dictation to tactful suggestion. Off with **Denis Kearney**'s head, the Emperor ordered during the anti-Chinese agitation, and death to Maximilian in Mexico for usurping Norton's prerogatives. But Norton also benevolently advocated a wage increase for local sailors and a bridge across the San Francisco Bay for general convenience. He made occasional trips into the interior to survey the general welfare. Once he turned up at a University of California reception for the Emperor of Brazil and quietly made his way to a seat on the platform,

where he was allowed to remain. He also attended legislative debates in Sacramento, although he disapproved of political parties and dissension. In death as in life, Emperor Norton was treated with dignity and affection by the city of San Francisco. He died, appropriately, in the streets, after which flags flew at half mast and the *Chronicle* announced that "Le Roi Est Mort." In 1934 his remains were moved from Lone Mountain to Woodlawn Cemetery with the mayor, the municipal band, and an infantry battalion in ceremonial attendance.

Allen Stanley Lane, Emperor Norton *(Caldwell, ID, 1939). William Kramer,* Emperor Norton of San Francisco *(Santa Monica, 1974).*

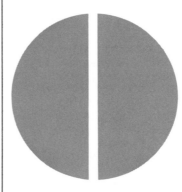

Jasper O'Farrell (1817-1875). The leading surveyor in late Mexican and early American California, O'Farrell was largely responsible for laying out and naming the famous streets of downtown San Francisco. Born and raised in Ireland, he is believed to have joined an English surveying expedition to South America in 1841 and to have arrived in California two years later. (Other accounts have him arriving as

a cooper on a whaler.) He surveyed a total of 21 land grants throughout Alta California, in payment for which he received a ranch in Marin County. (He later exchanged this for an estate in Sonoma County that he named Annaly, after his Gaelic home.) In 1845 O'Farrell accompanied **Manuel Micheltorena**'s forces south to the showdown in Los Angeles. He participated briefly in the Gold Rush and extracted a small fortune in three months from Bidwell's Bar. Appointed to survey San Francisco by the American military government, he discovered a divergence of a few degrees in existing intersections, the correction of which is known as "O'Farrell's Swing." He conceived of Market Street cutting across the city on a bias, and suggested the names—including his own, that of his assistant, Bush, and those of several town council members—for the streets north of Market. A sentimental tradition has it that O'Farrell named some of the streets south of Market for lady friends.

Fremont Older (1856-1935). He was a crusading editor of the old school, bellicose and sentimental, both actor and observer in San Francisco life for two generations. Named for Pathfinder **John Frémont**, he grew up in the Midwest in hardscrabble poverty after his father's death in the Civil War. A printer's apprentice at thirteen, Older was inspired by a biography of Horace Greeley to go west at sixteen. In the course of his career he

worked at nearly every newspaper in San Francisco, moving up from printer to reporter to, in 1895, managing editor of the *Evening Bulletin*. (Its motto: "The voice of the woman accused, the man oppressed, the child exploited.") Under his hand, circulation increased from 9,000 in 1895 to 111,000 twenty years later. Older specialized in screaming headlines, intimate stories about celebrities and outcasts, and sensational exposés. A large man who looked like a frontier marshal, he was "gregarious as a bartender," with friends and contacts everywhere, including the underworld. For years he and his wife lived at downtown hotels (first the Palace, later the Fairmont), always at the nerve center of city life. Older used the threat of exposure and even entrapment to get his way. After the 1906 earthquake he called in all his favors and used all his wiles to "get" the corrupt municipal government supported by the Southern

Pacific octopus. He and detective **William Burns** coerced a confession out of Boss **Ruef** ("Ruef Squeaks Like a Rat") but although the trials dragged on for years Ruef was the only malefactor to go to jail. Not satisfied with convicting Ruef, Older wanted to redeem him too, and campaigned for his release from prison. Later, the editor would repent of selling souls for headlines, trading character for circulation. The Olders spent their last years on a ranch in the Santa Cruz foothills, Woodhills, where the guest list was likely to include bankers and radicals, society matrons and reformed prostitutes. Commuting 90 miles daily to work, Older adopted a more contemplative lifestyle. He "got" literature in the sense that others get religion, running poems on the front page. He came to a parting of the ways with the *Bulletin*'s owner over the case of **Tom Mooney** whom he had convicted by headline and later sought, like Ruef, to redeem. Older spent his last years at **Hearst**'s *Call* writing a serialized memoir.

A better editor than writer, Older published My Own Story *(New York, 1926) and* Growing Up *(San Francisco, 1931). Evelyn Wells, a former reporter for Older, wrote a biography of her boss,* Fremont Older *(New York, 1936). His wife, Cora Baggerly Older, an "ardent Californiac," wrote* Love Stories of Old California *(New York, 1940).*

Culbert Levy Olson

(1876-1962). Elected in 1938 as California's first Democratic governor in 50 years, Olson was a tall, distinguished-looking attorney from Utah, a freethinker who was nonetheless impressed by Mormon concepts of

cooperative economics and social responsibility. Moving to Los Angeles in 1920, he became active in local Democratic politics as an opponent of **William Gibbs McAdoo** and was elected to the state Senate in 1934 with the endorsement of **Sinclair**'s EPIC (End Poverty in California) movement. A strong civil libertarian who favored public ownership of utilities, he opposed tidelands exploitation by the oil companies. As governor, his

first public act was to free labor martyr **Tom Mooney**, who had served twenty years since his controversial conviction for the Preparedness Day bombing in San Francisco. The Olson administration was chiefly preoccupied with the issue of relief. The governor favored "production-for-use" or self-help, but was forced by political realities—business on his right and the strong grassroots "Ham 'n' Eggs," or "Thirty-dollars-every-Thursday"

movement on his left—to run the conventional problem-ridden dole system. **Sam Yorty**, a former supporter of Olson, found an opportunity for political self-aggrandizement in investigating Communists in the state relief agency. In the end, Olson, who was a poor administrator and frequently lacking in diplomacy, lost control of his principles as well as his office. After switching from opposition to support of the U.S. Army-imposed evacuation of Japanese residents from coastal California, he was defeated for reelection by **Earl Warren** in 1942.

Robert E. Burke wrote Olson's New Deal for California (Berkeley, 1953), an academic view of the Olson administration.

Walter Francis O'Malley (1903-1979).

O'Malley changed the map of professional sports with his deal bringing the Brooklyn Dodgers to Los Angeles in 1957. Born in New York, educated in engineering and law, he replaced Wendell Willkie in 1943 as counsel to the Brooklyn team, gradually acquiring majority ownership. Frustrated in his efforts to build a new stadium for the popular, pennant-winning Dodgers, he picked up his marbles and moved west, also persuading the New York Giants to move to San Francisco, thus opening the whole continent to major-league baseball competition. Described as a "great horse trader" by L.A. mayor Norris Poulson, O'Malley negotiated a deal exchanging the derelict Wrigley Field in South L.A. for 300 tax-free acres in Chavez

Ravine, land originally scheduled for public housing. A municipal court judge ruled the deal illegal, but the Supreme Court disagreed and L.A. held a popular referendum, with a majority voting B for baseball. O'Malley's parsimony was legendary. His new ballpark contained no public drinking fountains, a small oversight which proved profitable to soda and beer concessionaires. He also tried diligently to get **Gene Autry**, whose California Angels shared the premises for a few years, to pay for a disproportionate share of the toilet paper. A genial patriarch with his Irish humor and double chins, he took a fatherly interest in the welfare of his players but never pretended to second-guess their professional ability. It was his business, and he definitely saw it as a business, to buy the best talent. "We must win," the Dodger owner explained. "We are not budgeted to field a club that just goes through the motions."

Cary S. Henderson, author of "Los Angeles and the Dodger War, 1957-1962," Southern California Quarterly (Fall 1980), considers O'Malley a gambler for moving to L.A. before the political and legal resolution of the Dodger deal.

Henry William O'Melveny (1859-1941).

The law firm established by O'Melveny is practically as old as Los Angeles, and its history, privately printed for members of the "office family," affords a rare view from inside the local establishment. The son of a judge from Illinois who arrived in Los Angeles in 1869,

O'Melveny was a member of the first graduating class of the old Los Angeles High School in 1875. He graduated from the University of California, Berkeley at age nineteen and read privately for admission to the bar two years later. There were few corporations in those days and no labor law; what L.A. did have in abundance was crime and land. O'Melveny chose to become an expert in land title and probate, preparing wills in English and Spanish which he personally read to the relatives after the funeral. In the case of client **Arcadia Bandini de Baker**, who died intestate in 1912, he spent four years helping to put together a settlement of her $7 million estate, contested by over 100 descendants. O'Melveny was also prominent in the development of hydroelectric power, representing power and electric companies all over the state. An outdoorsman, his favorite retreat was a ranch in the San Gabriel Canyon, where friends, colleagues, and clients frequently gathered, often in three-piece suits and bowlers, for fishing and good times. When the land was taken over for the Pasadena dam and reservoir in the 1930s, O'Melveny purchased twenty acres in Bel Air where he grew flowers "as widely known as his lawsuits." As Los Angeles continued to expand, so did the law firm of O'Melveny and Myers (Louis Myers, former chief justice of the California Supreme Court, joined O'Melveny in 1927), representing corporations whose presidents inclined to wear striped ties. O'Melveny's

son John branched out into the new field of entertainment law, representing the movie studios in libel, plagiarism, and bankruptcy suits. The patriarch himself, during the interwar years, took up some new special interests. He decided to defend **E.L. Doheny** in the matter of the Elk Hills leases, having satisfied himself as to the oilman's patriotic motives. (Although acquitted of bribery in Washington, D.C., Doheny lost his leases in California.) And he was active in the effort to defeat **Upton Sinclair**'s 1934 campaign for governor, considering Sinclair a threat to the development and prosperity of the state. The O'Melveny firm in 1981 became the first group of lawyers in the U.S. to erect its own skyscraper.

William W. Clary, who wrote the History of the Law Firm of O'Melveny and Myers, 1885-1965, 2 vols. (Los Angeles, 1966) was a senior member of the firm.

Carlotta Monterey O'Neill (Hazel Tharsing, 1888?-1970).

Eugene O'Neill's third wife (and the reason for his ten-year residence in California, where he wrote two of his most famous plays) was a celebrated beauty who happened to be from Oakland. In fact, she was Miss California of 1907 and placed second in that year's Miss USA contest. But she preferred to gloss over her origins in making the transformation from Hazel Tharsing into Carlotta Monterey (for the California town), Broadway actress and toast of sophisticated cafe society which is where O'Neill

met her. The O'Neills arrived on the West Coast in 1936 and decided to stay. They bought a 160-acre site near Danville and built a simulated adobe mansion with a view of the San Ramon Valley, called Tao House and furnished by *Gump*'s. The house was planned to hold 8,000 books and 300 pair of shoes, Carlotta's fetish. In California O'Neill enjoyed his last burst of creativity. Disheartened by isolation and the wartime difficulty in finding servants, the couple sold their house in 1944 and moved into a San Francisco hotel, returning east after the war. The last years before Eugene O'Neill's death in 1953 were plagued by medical and financial problems, the latter eased only by an annuity Carlotta claimed was from a California aunt. In fact, it was from a former lover, a Wall Street banker.

O'Neill, *a biography by Arthur and Barbara Gelb (New York, 1960), is* sympathetic to Carlotta; O'Neill, Son and Artist *(Boston, 1973) by Louis Shaeffer, is not.*

J[ulius] Robert Oppenheimer (1904-1967).

When Oppenheimer graduated from Harvard in 1925, the place for any aspiring physicist to do graduate work was Germany, so he earned his Ph.D. in Göttingen. As a professor, he made the University of California at Berkeley the mecca for theoretical physicists during the 1930s. Oppie, as his students called him, reigned over a smoke-filled room in LeConte Hall for a decade, with trips south every spring to teach at Cal Tech. A Promethean figure with enormous powers of comprehension and memory, equally at home in Dante, Dostoievsky, or Sanskrit poetry, he was insulated from everyday reality by his great intellect and by inherited wealth. He never read the newspapers, didn't bother to vote, and even remained unaware of the Depression, his friends joked. Suddenly awakened to social conscience, he became active in the late 1930s on behalf of migrant labor in California and other leftwing causes. His brother Frank, also a brilliant physicist who worked on **Ernest Lawrence**'s cyclotron, joined the Communist Party, but Oppie was too intolerant of boredom to sit through party meetings. Professionally, he was more interested in cosmic rays than in the secret of the atom, but he alone had the prestige and brilliance to lead the World War II Manhattan Project that created the bombs dropped on Hiroshima and Nagasaki. After unleashing the full measure of man's destruction, Oppenheimer seemed a tormented figure. Appointed head of Princeton's Institute for Advanced Study and a leading government consultant on atomic energy, he opposed development of the thermonuclear bomb on humanitarian grounds. A belated victim of McCarthyism, he was subjected to the ordeal of security hearings by the Atomic Energy Commission In 1954. Investigators seized on his political activities in Berkeley, particularly his relationship with **Haakon Chevalier**, and scientists who disagreed with his politics testified that he was a security risk. Oppenheimer's patriotism was never in doubt, but his authority was seriously discredited and his security clearance revoked, *ex post facto*, for access to "secrets" of his own invention.

See The Oppenheimer Case *(New York, 1969) by Philip Stern, and* Lawrence and Oppenheimer *(New York, 1968) by Nuel Pharr Davis. There was a resurgence of interest in the martyred physicist in 1982 with the televising of a fictionalized, English-made documentary.*

Edward Ortho Cresap Ord (1818?-1883).

In 1856, U.S. Army captain E.O.C. Ord was posted to Southern California to select the site for a military base in the San Bernardino area. A West Point graduate (1839), Ord was said to be the grandson of King George IV by his morganatic union with Maria Fitzherbert, a fact which may explain the glutinous grandness of Ord's given names. An old California hand, he arrived first in 1847, made a second trip west in 1850, returned in 1853 for six years, and was promoted to command the Department of the Pacific in 1868. On the 1856 trip, traveling south from Benicia by coastal steamer, Ord noted that the wharf at Monterey had fallen in and that the citizens looked sleepier than ever. Santa Barbara "I shall

hardly call a place," he wrote, and in L.A. he described tar dripping from the roofs "to the danger of careless pedestrians." Ord recommended against an army post in the San Bernardino area. Later, a base near Monterey—one of the country's largest—was named for this career officer who rose to the rank of general during the Civil War.

The City of the Angels and the City of the Saints (San Marino, 1978), edited by Neal Harlow, is Ord's report and diary of his 1856 trip.

Harrison Gray Otis

(1837-1917). As owner and publisher of the *Los Angeles Times* since the 1880s, Otis set himself up as the arbiter of civilization in Southern California. A former printer's apprentice from Ohio and editor of the *Grand Army Journal*, he rose to captain during the Civil War and acquired a taste for warfare.

During the Spanish American War, he took time out from publishing to serve as a brigadier general but was frustrated in his hopes for a top War Department post. He returned home to patrol Los Angeles in a limousine with a cannon mounted on the hood and had his newspaper headquarters designed like a medieval fortress complete with battlements. A self-proclaimed champion of industrial freedom, Otis fought a lifelong domestic war against trade unionism. In the 1890s he brought in scab labor from the Midwest at great expense rather than restore a twenty percent wage cut to his printers; in 1896, he formed the Merchants and Manufacturers Association to enforce his version of capitalism on the L.A. establishment. The local class struggle came to a head in 1910 with the dynamiting of the *Times* building by labor radicals. The publisher's reaction was so vituperative and vindictive that he aroused sympathy for the perpetrators. Theodore Roosevelt called Otis a "consistent enemy of every movement for social and economic betterment." **Hiram Johnson** described him as ruling Los Angeles in "senile dementia, with gangrened heart and rotting brain." To local historian Morrow Mayo, the publisher seemed a cross between Buffalo Bill and General Custer. When Otis wasn't manning the battlements against "anarchic scum," he was busy boosting civic development to his own personal advantage, creating a fundamental and enduring confusion in L.A. between

public service and private profit. In the 1890s the *Times* campaigned actively for a "free harbor" in San Pedro, as against the Southern Pacific-proposed "monopoly" harbor in Santa Monica; victory boosted family prestige, newspaper circulation, and real estate profits. So did the 1905 campaign to bring water from the Owens River Valley south to Los Angeles, or rather to the San Fernando Valley where Otis's son-in-law **Harry Chandler** put together a land syndicate which profited handsomely from such improvements at taxpayer expense. Otis's last hurrah was the Mexican Revolution of 1910-1911. Headquartered at the Oregon Hotel in El Centro, the bellicose publisher waved the flag and recruited an army of mercenaries to protect his extensive landholdings in Baja California. Under the terms of Otis's will, Chandler inherited the publishing empire and the county got the Otis mansion on Wilshire Boulevard, named The Bivouac, to be kept unchanged for an art institute. (The county quietly proceeded to remove from the grounds of the Otis Art Institute a fifteen-foot granite replica and monument to the martyred *Times* building, fallen in the class wars of 1910.)

Thinking Big by Bob Gottlieb and Irene Wolt (New York, 1977) interweaves family and civic history.

Richard Owens

(1812-1902?). Mapping the countryside on his transcontinental expeditions, **John Frémont** frequently gave the names of his men to rivers, valleys, mountains. **Kit Carson** was none too pleased

with the malodorous sink in Nevada that received his name; his friend and fellow trapper Owens came out much better with the river valley east of the Sierra. Carson and Owens had been farming together in New Mexico in 1845 when Frémont recruited them for his third and most eventful expedition. Arriving in time for the Bear Flag revolt, the expedition was reconstituted as the California Battalion of Mounted Riflemen with Owens as captain. Frémont considered Owens "a resourceful and energetic young man" who in Napoleon's France would have become a marshal. In fact, Owens distinguished himself in the California conquest chiefly for loyalty to Frémont, steadfastly refusing obedience to the regular army command. The conflict of authority culminated in Frémont's court-martial, which Owens crossed the continent to attend, although he did not testify. He returned to California at the head of a party of Gold Rush prospectors, then disappeared from history. There is no evidence that he ever saw the valley bearing his name.

Leroy Hafen, The Mountain Men, ten vols. (Glendale, 1968), 5: 283-90.

Romualdo Pacheco
(1831-1899). The only California governor ever to

lassoe a grizzly bear, Pacheco was the token Chicano in ninteenth-century California politics, the first "native son" to attain political leadership after statehood. Raised by a Yankee stepfather, a ship's captain, he went to school in Hawaii (where he learned French and forgot Spanish) and then went to sea with his own private tutor. Pacheco was handsome with cultivated manners and great personal charm. Presiding over the family rancho in San Luis Obispo, he impressed Anglos with old-style hacienda hospitality. In 1857 he was elected to the state Senate as a Democrat but switched to the Republican Party during the Civil War, also becoming a brigadier general of the native cavalry. Elected state treasurer in 1863 and lieutenant governor in 1871, he served out the last ten months of **Newton Booth**'s term as governor when Booth went to the U.S. Senate in 1875. Pacheco later went to Washington himself as a three-term congressman from Santa Clara (1876-1883) and to Central America as U.S. Minister (1890-1893). Having lost most of his personal fortune supporting his wife's theatrical ambitions, he died broke in San Francisco.

Peter Conmy wrote a short biographical pamphlet, Pacheco, Distinguished Californian (San Francisco, 1957).

Alexander Pantages
(c. 1870-1936). Pantages was a self-made man of Greek descent, largely illiterate but shrewd, who put together a chain of 68 ornate theaters. He was called the "lone wolf

of the theater" because he sold no stock and shared authority with no one. In the early years of the Depression, both Pantages and his wife, an accomplished musician, faced criminal charges. Lois Mendenhall Pantages was convicted of manslaughter when her car killed a pedestrian, the first legal decision recognizing the auto as a lethal weapon. (She was released on probation.) Alexander Pantages was convicted of raping a young actress in his downtown L.A. office. To compound his difficulties, he was also charged with contributing to the delinquency of minors in a San Diego "love nest." To appeal his conviction Pantages hired attorney **Jerry Giesler**, who got a ruling on the pertinence of the accuser's reputation in rape cases. At a second trial Giesler successfully argued that the young actress was indeed a very good actress. Before his death Pantages

sold all his theaters to RKO-Warner Brothers except one, the Hollywood flagship.

George Cooper Pardee
(1857-1941). Governor Pardee's father was an M.D. who became mayor of Oakland. Following in the paternal footsteps, George Pardee earned his M.D. in Leipzig (1885) and in 1893 was elected Oakland mayor. (Somewhere along the way, he also served as drum major of the University of California band.) Chosen governor of California (1903-1907) during the last years of Southern Pacific political dominance, he was a businesslike chief executive who urged economy, efficiency, and conservation. Pardee supported tax reform and gave attention to prisons and mental hospitals which, then as now, housed a disproportionate number of state citizens. He also advocated safe roads, out of consideration for horses, and

anticipated future state water needs. He became known nationally as the "earthquake governor," directing relief operations from Oakland for six weeks after the 1906 trembler. But he had a reputation for being anti-labor—"Pick-handle Pardee," the legacy of an 1894 railroad strike—and an enemy—San Francisco boss **Abe Ruef**. Ruef, who felt that the governor had welshed on a patronage deal, blocked his renomination. Pardee later served for many years as head of the East Bay Municipal Water District.

Pardee's unpublished reminiscences are in Stanford University's Borel Collection.

Dorothy Parker

(1893-1967). The sharp-witted Parker is credited with some of Hollywood's better putdowns. "The only 'ism' they really believe in is plagiarism," she said of the folks at "Metro-Goldwyn-Merde." A ranking member of New York's Algonquin Round Table, she moved west in 1933 after her marriage to Alan Campbell. As a writing team they commanded $5,200 a week during the Depression but found that movie money melted like snow in summer. (Some of it went for a colonial

mansion in Beverly Hills and a farm in Bucks County, Pennsylvania.) Except for *A Star is Born* (1937), their screen credits were so undistinguished that few blinked when Parker added to her resumé a nonexistent script for *Three Little Peppers and How They Grew*. During the McCarthy era Parker and Campbell were blacklisted for radical sympathies. They had to give up their mansion and farm for a little clapboard bungalow on Norma Place (named for Norma Talmadge) which Parker described as Peyton Place West. "You saw just as many celebrities as you would lunching at **Romanoff**'s," she said of her weekly visits to the unemployment office. After Campbell's death in 1963 from an overdose of sleeping pills, she returned to New York.

John Keats wrote a Parker biography, You Might as Well Live (New York, 1970).

William Henry Parker

(1902-1966). When appointed chief of police of Los Angeles in 1950, Parker announced his intention to personally prevent the city of angels from becoming a city of diablos. Born in South Dakota, the son of a congressman, he came to L.A. in 1923 and worked his way through night law school as a policeman. Finding that he could outscore his fellow cops on competitive exams, he decided to stay with law enforcement rather than law, rising steadily through the ranks. As chief, Parker made speeches about the moral decline of our times which he blamed on liberalism, the decisions of the U.S. Supreme Court, and working mothers. He also earned a reputation for unnecessarily rough treatment of suspects, minorities, and anyone considered a radical in McCarthy-era America. (Mobster **Mickey Cohen** once publicly called him a sadistic degenerate, for which Parker collected an out-of-court libel settlement.) All-powerful in his own domain, Parker personally thwarted Nikita Khrushchev's desire to visit Disneyland in 1959, claiming inadequate security. Diplomacy was never his strong suit. After the 1965 Watts Riots, which many blamed on his tough-cop ghetto policies, he issued the following explanation: "One person threw a rock and then, like monkeys in a zoo, others started throwing rocks." Parker was exonerated by the McCone Commission. He secretly aspired to become head of the FBI. When **Marilyn Monroe** died, according to her biographer Robert Slatzer, the police chief seized telephone records of her calls to U.S. Attorney General Robert Kennedy in hopes of furthering his ambitions. He died on the job, stricken at a Marine Corps testimonial banquet. The Parker tradition of law enforcement was maintained in Los Angeles by Edward Michael Davis (1916-), police-chief from 1969 to 1978, who suggested executing hijackers at the airport and advised citizens concerned about crime to "Bar your doors and pray." L.A.'s downtown police headquarters is named Parker Center.

Louella Oettinger Parsons (1881?-1972).

Born in **Ronald Reagan**'s hometown, Dixon, Illinois, she worked as a journalist in Chicago and New York before **Hearst** assigned her to cover Hollywood in the mid-1920s. Parsons created a new genre of personal reportage to chronicle the community and society of film, becoming a celebrity in her own right as the first nationally syndicated Hollywood columnist. She also had her own radio show, "Hollywood Hotel," delivering her scoops in a nervous, high-pitched voice. Never known for her accuracy or for her skill as a writer, she had instead a bulldog tenacity, a knack for discovering where the bodies were buried, and a taste for the lavish lifestyle of the movie colony. Living as she did in a Beverly Hills mansion with a Rolls Royce and a San Fernando Valley ranch, she treated moguls and stars as friends and peers as well as copy for her column. Parsons did a lot of PR for the industry, never hesitated to offer personal or professional advice, and assumed the prerogative of making and breaking careers. In the days when it mattered to get your name in the columns, she found that silence was often the best revenge. Her 35th anniversary in journalism was the occasion of a party at the Coconut Grove attended by everybody who was anybody, including the governor of California. Every Christmas she received a staggering amount of loot—pepper grinders shaped like the Eiffel Tower, spinning wheel lamps, etc.—from industry hopefuls

Increasingly lonely after the death of her third husband, "Docky" (Dr. Harry Martin), who had become head of the Twentieth Century-Fox medical department, she found consolation in contemplating an electrically lighted statue of the Virgin Mary in her Beverly Hills backyard.

Parsons wrote The Gay Illiterate *(Garden City, NY, 1944) and* Tell it to Louella *(New York, 1961).*

George Smith Patton, Jr. (1885-1945).

His grandfather was the first Anglo mayor of Los Angeles, his father was district attorney, and George Patton grew up privileged on the huge family ranch covering much of present-day Pasadena and San Marino, with summers on Catalina Island. Educated at home by oral readings from history and mythology, he never wanted to be anything but a warrior hero. The U.S. expedition into Mexico in 1916 provided young Lieutenant Patton with his first opportunity for martial glory. According to press clippings of the Battle of Rubio Ranch, which read suspiciously like Hollywood press agentry, he drove up to a "suspicious dobe" at the head of nine soldiers in three Dodge automobiles. Raising his ornamental six-shooters, he bagged three Villistas and returned to camp with their bodies strapped to the running boards. Patton's charisma and his genius as a tank commander took him to the top of the U.S. military command. He returned only briefly to California, training his Third Army for the African campaign in the desert sands near Palm Springs. And in 1945 he enjoyed a triumphal hometown victory parade, highlighted by a mock-battle of tanks before a cheering throng of 100,000 in the L.A. Coliseum.

Patton wrote an autobiography, War As I Knew It *(1947). The best of several popular biographies is Ladislas Farago's* Patton: Ordeal and Triumph *(New York, 1963).*

Edwin Wendell Pauley (1903-1981).

Pauley was an independent California oilman who became a controversial Democratic kingmaker. He first entered politics as an opponent of the 1931 Sharkey Bill which gave control of California production to the major oil companies. The bill was defeated by referendum, and Pauley went on to national politics as a rare businessman supporter of the New Deal. He did World War II service in lend-lease and petroleum administration and on the postwar Reparations Commission. His career in Washington came to an end in 1946, his nomination as Undersecretary of the Navy blocked by conflict of interest charges. (Interior Secretary Harold Ickes, who accused Pauley of abandoning federal claim to California tidelands in California tidelands in exchange for campaign contributions, also resigned in the controversy.) Back home in California, Pauley served for 32 years as a regent of the University of California, his alma mater, where he earned a varsity letter, a B.S. and an M.S. in the 1920s. He was generous with the university, donating over $2 million for a Pauley (sports) Pavilion at UCLA and a Pauley Nuclear Science Pavilion and ballroom at Berkeley. An ardent sportsman, he won a 1939 trans-Pacific yacht race and was part-owner for awhile of the Los Angeles Rams. In later years Pauley remained active as a "checkbook Democrat," a leading supporter of Governor **Pat Brown** and of L.A. Mayor **Sam Yorty**.

Linus Carl Pauling

(1901-   ). Pauling, with his combination of genius, idiosyncracy, and showmanship, could only be a westerner, the *New Yorker* once remarked. The first man ever to attain sole possession of two Nobel prizes, he was born in Oregon and graduated from the California Institute of Technology (Ph.D., 1925). He remained at Cal Tech for 40 years, a professor since 1931, doing formative research into the elementary grammar of chemical life. Pauling's theory of "resonating molecules" led to the development of various plastics, synthetics, and drugs, and in 1954 he was awarded his first Nobel for work on molecular structure. James Watson, who shared a later prize for deciphering the secret of DNA, feared at one time that Pauling was going to beat him to it, winning yet another prize. Pauling might have, had he not veered off into the social and medical dimensions of science. He was an early opponent of nuclear testing, warning of the dangers of fallout, for which McCarthy accused him of pro-Soviet leanings and the U.S. State Department denied him a passport. He got the passport in 1954 to attend the Nobel award ceremonies, and in 1962 won a second Nobel, the peace prize, for his stand against nuclear testing. In 1964, when the political climate at Cal Tech became too oppressive for him, Pauling moved to UC San Diego. Five years later, he took up residence at Stanford as director of his own Institute of Science and Medicine. There he set out to prove his hypothesis that vitamin C will cure everything from the common cold to cancer, the nearly unanimous opinion of the entire medical establishment notwithstanding.

William Leonard Pereira

(1909-   ). The premier architect of space-age California, Pereira won a succession of high-visibility prestige commissions. Reared in Chicago, he came west during the Depression as an art director for Paramount, at one time designing films for **Cecil B. DeMille** and **David Selznick**. (He shared a 1942 Oscar for special effects on DeMille's *Reap the Wild Wind*, and personally produced a 1945 George Raft melodrama, *Johnny Angel*.) In partnership with Charles Luckman during the 1950s, he designed the CBS building in Los Angeles, then went on to become master planner of the L.A. Airport and author of its flying saucer restaurant. He was also the master planner for Catalina Island and the Irvine Ranch, and designed at least one building on every major college campus in Southern California, most notably the futuristic Pepperdine-Malibu

complex. Pereira's work aroused strong feelings, both positive and negative. His UCSD library (1970), for example, was praised as a "stone flower of the freeway age," while his Los Angeles County Museum of Art (1964) was considered by many an aesthetic monstrosity. A whole community rose up to protest his most famous creation, the Transamerica Pyramid (1973) in San Francisco. A former member of the faculty at USC (1949-1957), Pereira worked for many years in a Los Angeles building designed by **Welton Becket**, another leading local architect.

George Clement Perkins

(1839-1923). California's fourteenth governor came west as a sailor before the mast and became a wealthy shipping magnate. His firm, Goodall, Perkins & Company, pioneered ferry operations on the Feather River and later established coastal connections from Alaska to Central America. An active Mason and a popular if bombastic speaker, Perkins was elected in 1868 as a Republican to the first of two terms in the state Senate. In 1879, with a campaign theme borrowed from Gilbert and Sullivan—"The Good Ship George C. Perkins"—he was elected governor. Under the new state constitution, which he opposed, his term was shortened to three years (1880-1883) to provide for subsequent elections in even-numbered years. In 1893 Perkins was appointed to the U.S. Senate to fill out the term of **Leland Stanford**, and won reelection three times. During 22 years in Washington he was active on behalf of U.S. naval power and adventurism abroad. He was considered such a stalwart supporter of the Southern Pacific and other vested interests that, according to a contemporary joke, a Standard Oil tanker would have rescued him if he ever got into deep water.

Fritz Perls (Frederick Salomon Perls, 1894-1970). A movement germinated on three continents, Gestalt therapy (from the German for "wholeness") found its time and place in Northern California during the 1960s. Perls was a German Jew who studied dramatics with Max Reinhardt, earned an M.D. (1920), and was analyzed by the Freudian *enfant terrible*, Wilhelm Reich, ideologist of the the orgasm. Fleeing from the Nazis, Perls became South Africa's first analyst but was bored by life there. After the war he moved to New York, where he developed Gestalt therapy in collaboration with his wife, also a psychologist, and with Paul Goodman. Laura Posner Perls considered her husband a mixture of bum and prophet, Goodman looked down on him intellectually, and Perls struck out on his own. His M.D. was never recognized in the U.S., so he built a practice based on freedom of speech. In L.A. during the 1950s he worked what he called the "freeway routes," driving out the Santa Ana or the San Bernardino to give consultations and lead therapy groups. Perls considered moving to Kyoto, Japan, and Elath, Israel,

before finding Big Sur, where he became resident guru at the Esalen Institute. A roly-poly jumpsuited figure, narcissistic, exhibitionistic, and egomaniacal, he became the class act of the human potential movement, thanks to his ability to engage people at first encounter. "My intermediate zone is less crowded than the average," he explained, enabling him to cut through layers of what he called bullshit, chickenshit, and elephantshit, to get down to essentials. Perls was reluctant to share his platform at Esalen with visiting swamis and gurus, and he became increasingly fearful of American fascism after the election of **Ronald Reagan** as governor and **Richard Nixon** as president. He spent the last year of his life on a Gestalt kibbutz in Canada.

Perls wrote and drew a memoir, In and Out the Garbage Pail *(Lafayette, CA, 1969). Martin Shepard's* Fritz *(New York, 1975) is a hip biography.*

Louis Petri (1912-1980). At the turn of the century, Petri's grandfather owned a hotel on Green Street in San Francisco, for which he bottled his own wine and made his own cigars. Going into wine production in a big way after the repeal of Prohibition, Louis Petri found it cheaper to buy grapes than to raise them, so he formed the Allied Grape Growers Cooperative to produce for the Petri label. Allied eventually acquired other vineyards and labels—notably Italian Swiss Colony in 1953—to become the largest wine marketing organization in the world before Gallo. Petri, high-powered San Francisco businessman,

essentially a deal-maker rather than a wine-maker, eventually sold out to Heublein in 1969. One of few local industry leaders to approve the takeover of California vineyards by absentee conglomerates, he cited the financial hardship of the long aging period for wine.

See The Petri Family in the Wine Industry *(University of California Oral History Office, 1971).*

James Duval Phelan (1861-1930). "Pericles could not have loved Athens more," according to a biographical pamphlet on Phelan, "than this man loved San Francisco." As reform mayor (1898-1902) of his native city, Phelan set a shining patrician example of civic virtue, particularly when compared to the blatant boss rule that preceded and followed. He supported a progressive new municipal constitution, promoted city beautification and culture, and laid the groundwork for a new city water supply. (Social peace was attained by repression of labor, his critics would say, and water at the expense of environmental protection.) Retiring after three terms, he emerged as a leader of earthquake reconstruction and provided significant moral and financial support for the 1906-1910 graft prosecutions. Phelan could afford a certain amount of altruism. The son of an Irish Catholic 49er who founded the First National Bank of San Francisco, he enjoyed a privileged upbringing. He was educated at the Jesuit college of Saint Ignatius (A.B., 1881) and went on for a law degree which he

never used, occupying himself instead with business, politics, philanthropy, and the arts. After the 1906 earthquake, he built a villa in the foothills of the Santa Clara Valley, named for Ordóñez de Montalvo, the nineteenth-century writer who first imagined a paradise called California. There, the bachelor millionaire's regular houseguests included writer **Gertrude Atherton** and tennis champion **Helen Wills** whom he called his "Olympian children of the California sun." As the only prominent California Democrat of independent means, Phelan was selected to lead the state campaign for Woodrow Wilson in 1912. In 1914 he defeated **Francis Heney** and **Joseph Knowland** to win California's first popular election for U.S. Senator. Phelan distinguished himself in Washington, as at home, as a discriminating host, a man of culture and refinement, but he failed to win reelection in 1920. In his will, the most absorbing document of its kind since **James Lick**'s, he left $20,000 each to Atherton and Wills, with a long list of smaller bequests to everyone from **Heney** to Conchitá **Sepúlveda** Pignatelli. Monalvo, bequeathed to the San Francisco Art Association, became a nonprofit center for the arts.

Mary Pickford (Gladys Smith, 1893-1979). A Canadian-born child actress with dewy eyes, a peaches-and-cream complexion and perfect golden ringlets, Pickford made her first film— *Her First Biscuits* (1909)—at a time when the "flickers" weren't quite respectable. She would fix that by becoming the world's first movie star with a salary of $10,000 a week, the object of idolatry worthy of the Virgin Mary. The reputation of "America's Sweetheart" was so firmly established that she survived her divorce from actor Owen

Moore and remarriage to Douglas Fairbanks, Sr. in 1920. Fairbanks (1883-1939) was a star in his own right, a swashbuckling athlete of silent costume epics. In private life, he was a physical fitness buff and sportsman who helped popularize the suntan. He liked to ride from his home, a former hunting lodge in rural Beverly Hills, all the way to the ocean, passing only a few other structures along the way. Expanded after the wedding into a large white country house with a green tile roof, Pickfair became the center of Hollywood high society, the Buckingham Palace of the film capital. A private screening room was installed, the first in the West (only the White House had one in 1920), and a pool with a white sand beach. For informal Sunday gatherings around the pool, male guests usually wore white flannels and a blazer; at formal dinner parties, there was a solid gold

service and a footman behind every chair. As king and queen of Hollywood, Pickford and Fairbanks reigned over premieres, issued statements on film policy issues, and laid cornerstones. Pickford was also an astute businesswoman ("It took longer to make Mary's contracts than it did her pictures," **Sam Goldwyn** said) who produced some of her own films, approved scripts, and selected cast and crew. In 1919 she and Fairbanks joined with Charlie Chaplin and **D.W. Griffith** to found United Artists, "a private golf club for us," they joked, while the moguls complained that the lunatics were taking over the asylum. Pickford, who continued to play sentimental adolescent heroines into her thirties (*Rebecca of Sunnybrook Farm*, *Tess of the Storm Country*, and *Little Annie Rooney*) cut off her curls in 1928 (two of them are said to be preserved at Pickfair, with two each at museums in San Diego and Los Angeles). She made her first talkie in the title role of *Coquette*, for which she won an Academy Award. She also began to experiment with spiritualism, ESP, astrology, and Christian Science while her husband was out conquering the world. Fairbanks and Pickford were divorced in 1935, and both married again, but it became an article of Hollywood faith that their love for one another was undying. Withdrawing behind the walls of her estate, Pickford wrote a novel, *The Demi-Widow* (1935), a book about spiritualism, *Why Not Try God?* (1934), and later dictated a memoir, *Sunshine*

and Shadow (1954). In 1937 she married again, to young Buddy Rogers who had given her her first screen kiss in *My Best Girl*. She multiplied her fortune through real estate, contributed graciously to charities, and spent the last thirteen years of her life in bed. Hollywood, which had grown old along with her, had become a disturbed and frightened place, she thought. Looking back, she was philosophical: "My career was planned. There was never anything accidental about it, it was painful, it was purposeful. I'm not exactly satisfied, but I'm grateful." After her death, Pickfair was sold for $5.4 million ("must be a fixer-upper," the probate judge quipped) to a basketball magnate.

See Robert Windeler, Sweetheart *(New York, 1974) and Booton Herndon,* Mary Pickford and Douglas Fairbanks *(New York, 1977).*

Andrés Pico (1810-1876). The younger brother of **Pío Pico**, the last Mexican governor, Andrés won the respect of the Americans for

defeating U.S. General **Stephen Watts Kearny** in their 1846 skirmish at San Pasqual. Elected to the state legislature in 1859, he introduced a bill for the secession of Southern California but the issue was swallowed up in the Civil War. He spent his last 30 years living at the San Fernando Mission, custodian of trunks full of memorabilia, and prospecting for brea or "tar" for axle grease in the hills north of the mission. Oil was later discovered in what is now called Pico Canyon.

Pío Pico (1801-1894). The last Mexican governor of California, Pico lived the second half of his life under U.S. statehood as an impoverished anachronism. Born at the Mission San Gabriel, son of a soldier, he was a revolutionary in his youth, participating in the 1831 revolt and in an unsuccessful coup d'état in 1838. In 1845 he stood off **Manuel Micheltorena**, then governor, at the Cahuenga Pass to become governor himself, a very hazardous position under the circumstances. Politics in the prestatehood era was characterized by constant feuds and intrigues, jealousy over rights and privileges, furious proclamations, and mock battles. Pico shifted the state capital to Los Angeles, leaving his arch-rival José Castro as commander-general in Northern California. He proceeded with the secularization of the missions, redistributing mission land in grants to his friends, including some Yankees who supported him against Micheltorena. (It

was charged but never proved that many of the grants were antedated after Pico left office.) The Yankees were skilled at a thousand tasks despised by Californios, Pico knew, wondering "Shall we become strangers in our own land?" Anticipating the results of Yankee encroachment, he considered annexation by France or England as alternatives. Unable to defend his territory against the Americans in 1846—Castro refused to even consult on the subject, fearful of being taken prisoner by his rival—Pico fled to Mexico, returning a few years later as a private citizen. A short, stocky figure with a white beard and a chivalrous manner, fond of dressing up in all his medals, the former

governor was an inveterate gambler who ultimately lost all his bets. En route into exile, he recalls in his memoir dictated for **H.H. Bancroft**, he won $2,000 in a game of monte; on his return trip to California he won even more. In 1852, however, in one of the great sporting events of the decade, he lost $25,000 and 300 head of cattle in a horse race against **José Sepúlveda**. Pico was in the habit of borrowing money and leaving notes scattered all over L.A., some of them cosigned by compadres who were ruined when Pico defaulted. (The moneylenders included his Yankee brother-in-law, whom he sued unsuccessfully.) In 1869 he sold his last major holding, his ranch in the San Fernando

Valley, for $115,000 which he used to build a downtown hotel. (Unlike most of the Californios, the former governor preferred city life to ranching.) The Pico House was the largest hotel of its day, featuring "water closets with convenient private access." But Pico eventually lost the hotel too, living the rest of his life on the charity of friends. The Pico House survives, restored, as does a home once inhabited by Pico in Whittier.

Don Pío Pico's Historical Narrative *(Glendale, 1973) is a recent translation by Arthur Botello of the memoir dictated for Bancroft.*

James Albert Pike (1913-1969). As Protestant Episcopal bishop of California the restless, hyperactive Pike was high priest of the new age. Born in Oklahoma, where he won the state-fair baby contest, he came to Los Angeles at eight with his widowed mother, graduated from Hollywood High School, and received a law degree from USC (1936). He then went back east to earn a doctorate in law from Yale and practice New Deal law before donning the cloth in 1942. Pike's religious progress was rapid. By 1952 he had become dean of New York's Cathedral of Saint John the Divine, a celebrity priest with a social conscience and his own television show. Returning "home" in 1958 as bishop of California, he led his church in search of "relevance," wore a peace cross during the Vietnam war, favored unionization of migrant farm workers, and ordained the first Episcopalian deaconess. He also challenged the dogmas of

virgin birth, incarnation, and resurrection, much to the distress of organized religion. Although eventually vindicated of charges of heresy, Pike left the high church in 1966 to become a "worker-priest" at Santa Barbara's Center for the Study of Democratic Institutions. Personally, he survived alcoholism, divorce, and finally, the suicide of a son. In his last years he experimented with parapsychology and went to Israel in search of the spirit of early Christianity. Equipped only with an Avis map and some Coca-Cola, Pike drove with his third wife into the Judean desert, where he perished of exposure. (She survived.)

William Stringfellow and Anthony Towne, friends of Pike, wrote The Death and Life of Bishop Pike *(Garden City, NY, 1976).*

Willis Jefferson Polk

(1867-1924). Polk was a leading architect, critic and aesthete in turn-of-the-century San Francisco. Born in the Midwest of genteel southern lineage, he came west in the late 1880s. Rejecting the excesses of bonanza-era building, he designed simple shingle houses (including one

for himself on Russian Hill) and sought the purity of classical forms in his public commissions. He also subjected the efforts of other architects to merciless ridicule in his writings in *The Wave* and elsewhere. **Sutro**'s Baths were designed to make the seals laugh, he wrote, while San Francisco's new City Hall was a monument to "the last degenerate epoch of architecture." Polk went into partnership with Daniel Burnham of Chicago and as the head of Burnham's West Coast branch in 1906 did a land-office business in earthquake reconstruction. Appointed head of the advisory committee for the 1915 Panama-Pacific Exposition, he conceived a plan for a new San Francisco Civic Center. Among his surviving constructions are a Petit Trianon designed for Charles Baldwin (now part of De Anza College in Cupertino); the Sunol Water Temple (after Tivoli's Temple of Vesta); and the glass-curtained Hallidie Building on Sutter Street. Polk also transformed the old Flood

House into the Pacific Union Club and worked on the rehabilitation of Mission Dolores.

Richard Longstreth edited A Matter of Taste; Willis Polk's Writings in The Wave *(San Francisco, 1979).*

Gaspar de Portolá

(1723?-1786). The first governor of California, Portolá is remembered chiefly for the fact that, unable to find Monterey, he inadvertently discovered San Francisco. After presiding over the expulsion of the Jesuits from Baja California, he sailed north with the Franciscan padre **Junípero Serra** in 1769 to claim Alta California, piercing the "aboriginal solitude," the "veil of mystery" shrouding the land since Sebastián Vizcaíno's last explorations in 1602. While Serra remained in San Diego, Portolá continued north in search of Monterey, which Vizcaíno had described in such glowing terms that he did not recognize it. ("Without being able to give the reason," he wrote, "we were all under hallucination, and none dared assert openly that the port was indeed Monterey.") The party pushed on and discovered San Francisco before turning back to San Diego. From Portolá's report, Serra recognized Monterey and returned there with the governor, holding a ceremony on 3 June 1770 to claim the land for God and country. Upstaged by the Franciscan, Portolá remained pessimistic about the future of California. His term as governor ended in 1771 and he returned first to Mexico and then to Spain, where he died.

Lawrence Clark Powell

(1906-   ). The son of a citrus marketing executive, Powell grew up in South Pasadena where he was the proud possessor of library card #3089. He enrolled at Occidental College, where his classmates included Ward Ritchie, later his publisher, but took time off from school for a round-the-world cruise as a saxophonist with a jazz band. Powell managed to write a doctoral thesis on **Robinson Jeffers** in the unlikely environs of Dijon, France. Back home he went to work for bookseller Jake Zeitlin and returned to school to earn a library degree. Powell joined the UCLA staff in 1938 and rose to head librarian, a controversial figure with cosmopolitan tastes. An outspoken critic of the proverbial dullness of most libraries, he was a witness for the defense at the trial of a Los Angeles bookseller who sold **Henry Miller**'s *Tropic of Cancer*. Working at a compulsive pace, Powell managed to find time between administrative duties and acquisition coups to become a leading authority on Southwestern history, culture, and bibliography. The Ward Ritchie Press published handsome editions of many of his works, ranging from several collections of essays to a personal memoir on the Malibu fire (*The Malibu*, Los Angeles, 1958, with W.W. Robinson) and a major study of the role of geography in literature (*California Classics*, Los Angeles, 1971). Among his other abilities, Powell was also a skillful academic diplomat who weathered a generation of university politics, including the McCarthy-era revelation of his own youthful fling with Communism.

Powell wrote a memoir, Fortune and Friendship *(New York, 1968).*

Nathan Pritikin

(1915-   ). In 1976, a college drop-out with no medical credentials whatsoever opened a Longevity Research Institute in Santa Barbara, affluent infirmary capital of Southern California. A former photographer and inventor, Pritikin had devised his own

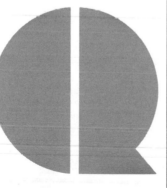

stringent low-cholesterol diet of grains and vegetables after a diagnosis of coronary insufficiency when he was in his 40s. Preaching the blessings of complex carbohydrates plus strenuous exercise, he moved from Santa Barbara south into an old Santa Monica beach club (former occupant: **Chuck Dederich**'s Synanon). Soon he was making the rounds of the TV talk shows, claiming "the most significant breakthrough in man's age-old quest for rejuvenation" and trading insults in *People* magazine with the rival guru of a high-fat regime. With celebrity Pritikin expanded beyond California, transforming former resort spas in Miami and Hawaii into residential Longevity Centers and establishing walk-in programs in major U.S. cities. He claimed testimonials from **Yehudi Menuhin**, Governor **Jerry Brown**, and **Cesar Chavez**. But his clientele was primarily the elderly affluent, those with the need and the means ($6,200-plus monthly) to seek a last-chance diet normally consumed only by the poor of the Third World.

Quentin (fl. 1830). California's first state prison

was named for an Indian who used to pilot a launch across San Francisco Bay. Quentin (pronounced Kayn-teen) was a Licatuit subchief who was himself taken prisoner by the Mexicans in 1824. He was converted to Catholicism, renamed for the third century Roman missionary and martyr Quentin, and put to work. The prison named for him ("San" was added by the Americans either for effect or by mistake) in 1853 was for years plagued by so many escapes that civilians avoided the neighborhood. Later, San Quentin developed an equally unhappy image as the site of the state's only gas chamber.

Max Rafferty (Maxwell Lewis Rafferty, Jr. 1917-1982). In 1935 an up-and-coming young college student published an article in the *Los Angeles Times* entitled "Communism Invades the Campus." Maxwell Lewis Rafferty, Jr., of the UCLA class of 1938 then proceeded to become a leading conservative educator of the post-Sputnik era, spearheading the politicization

of California's public school system. Rafferty climbed the educational hierarchy to superintendent of schools in Needles (1955) and La Cañada (1961) while earning his Ed.D. at USC (1956). In 1962, with right-wing financial backing,he was elected state superintendent of education, head of the largest public school system in the country. He also wrote a nationally syndicated column, often dealing with extracurricular matters like pornography (anti) and Vietnam (pro). Rafferty's educational ideal was the little red schoolhouse and a curriculum based on the McGuffey reader, "Hiawatha," *Ivanhoe*, and patriotism. He abhorred "leather-jacketed slobs" (the Sputnik era was the Beatnik era, remember) and described U.C. Berkeley as the "skid-row of higher education." He was reelected in 1966, but his political star went into rapid and permanent decline in 1968 when he ran unsuccessfully for U.S. Senator. Defeated for re-election as state Superintendent of Education in 1971, he moved to the Deep South as an educational school dean for eleven years before his death in an auto accident.

Rafferty's "Suffer, Little Children" (New York, 1962) is a collection of his polemics against progressive education. William O'Neill wrote Readin', Ritin' and Rafferty! A Study of Educational Fundamentalism *(Berkeley, 1969).*

William Chapman Ralston

(1826-1875). For a decade Ralston played a role in San Francisco life comparable to that of the Medici in Renaissance

Florence. The Bank of California, which he founded in 1864, funneled the enormous wealth of the Comstock into development of the city, its industry and culture. Generous to the affluent and the needy alike, Ralston brought the ruling elite in for a share of the profits and was famous for his benefactions to widows and orphans. Personally, he possessed a "truly Oriental imagination," according to his friend **Asbury Harpending**. For bank headquarters he built a marble palazzo at the corner of California and Sansome. For sheer amusement, he built a sumptuous villa, Belmont, with a ballroom worthy of Versailles and overnight accommodations for 120. He took pleasure in racing matched teams of black horses at breakneck speed to beat the railroad from San Francisco to Belmont. Fond of grand gestures, he named the town of Burlingame after a house guest, the U.S. Minister to China. (When cronies attempted to name a San Joaquin Valley town after the banker, he demurred, whereupon the town became Modesto, Spanish for modest.) During the construction of his Palace Hotel, Ralston bought a ranch to use its oak trees for inlaid floors, a foundry to forge nails, and a factory to make custom furniture. Unfortunately, these and other Ralston enterprises never paid off. In the early 1870s the new transcontinental railroad flooded the market with cheap goods, and the Comstock, once believed to

be inexhaustible, was nearing depletion. Ralston tried to recoup his fortunes by investing in a diamond mine, which in 1872 proved to be an expensive hoax, and in 1875 made an unsuccessful attempt to corner San Francisco's water supply. Faced with debts of $9.5 million and assets of only $4.5 million, he signed over his holdings, including Belmont and the Palace Hotel, to his associate **William Sharon**. While taking his daily swim at Black Point on the Bay, Ralston drowned; a coroner's jury blamed a cerebral attack. The Bank of California soon reopened, bailed out by stockholders, and Belmont served successively as a seminary, an asylum, and a convent. Sharon was popularly considered the villain of the piece while Ralston enjoyed the special historical indulgence reserved for men with a grand and generous vision of life.

George D. Lyman, Ralston's Ring *(New York, 1937, 1945). David Lavender, Nothing Seemed Impossible; William C. Ralston and Early San Francisco (Palo Alto, 1975).*

Ronald Wilson Reagan

(1911-   ). In the nineteenth century, retired California governors had a tendency to turn up as ambassadors to the world's banana republics; in the twentieth century they have become front-rank contendors for presidency of our very own banana republic. Having done his apprenticeship for politics in show business, Reagan defeated incumbent governor **Pat Brown** by a million votes in 1966. As a boy in the Midwest, he had been torn

between sports and acting, admitting that he just liked showing off. From radio sports announcing, Reagan got a contract with Warner Brothers to play ingenue roles, "good golly" beefcake. (Personally, he would have preferred cavalry-Indian movie roles.) After World War II, which he spent at "Fort Hal Roach" in Culver City, Reagan became determined to "bring about the regeneration of the world." During the McCarthy era he packed a pistol as president of the Screen Actors Guild; then as his acting career declined, he spent eight years as host of

General Electric TV Theater and traveling PR man for electrical progress and conservative Republicanism. In politics as in film, Reagan played the ingenue, selling himself as an American success story, a paragon of the simple virtues. As governor of California (1966-1975) he proved largely unable to practice what he preached about insidious state welfarism. Instead of cutting state spending, he was forced to accept the largest tax increase in state history. (In 1970, it was leaked to the press, he personally paid no taxes at all.) Refusing to live in the rickety governor's mansion, he had his wealthy backers buy him a new suburban villa (quoted at a million-four when the top price for a Sacramento home was $300,000). Back home in Southern California, he traded up from a Malibu ranch to a 688-acre spread in the Santa Ynez Mountains. Once elected, in 1980, to the big starring role, the presidency of the U.S., he used the Santa Ynez ranch as his home on the range. Gore Vidal described him jetting off into the sunset like a latter-day Tom Mix, accompanied by his wife, a designer version of Dale Evans.

Where's the Rest of Me (New York, 1965), taking the somewhat ambiguous title from his best film, King's Row *(1942).*

Hugo Reid

(1810?-1852). A Scot who left his homeland after an unhappy love affair, Reid wandered for six years before settling in Southern California in 1834. There he met and fell in love with an Indian woman, Doña Victoria, whom he married after the death of her first husband. The frontier had an ugly name for such bridegrooms—squawmen—but Reid cheerfully refused to conform to stereotype. For one thing, his wife owned two valuable San Gabriel Valley ranchos, later celebrated as Lake Vineyard and Santa Anita. According to the reports of houseguests who dropped by for two months at a time, the Reids were epicures who dispensed a most generous hospitality. Perhaps that is why Reid, a gentleman farmer, pioneer vintner, and aspiring writer, was always broke. An educated and cultivated man, his letters (mostly to **Abel Stearns**) reveal a wit and sensibility that speak across the century. When Stearns finally married in middle age, Reid wrote to wish the early arrival of children, "to wet your trousers when you are all dressed up, to remind you that you are the father of a family and that your friend esteems you." Reid himself raised his wife's four children as his own. Shortly before his death he finally found an appropriate literary outlet in a series of articles on Indian life and customs for the *Los Angeles Star*.

Susanna Bryant Dakin's A Scotch Paisano *(Berkeley, 1939) includes Reid's series on the Indians.*

Kenneth Rexroth

(1905-1982). The ultimate cultural cosmopolite of post-World War II California, Rexroth came of age in the Chicago literary renaissance of the 1920s. Orphaned as a boy, he enjoyed a special dispensation from his

guardian, later a governor of Illinois, to study art and literature in the streets and cafes of Chicago rather than in school. Self-educated in Japanese, Chinese, Greek, and Latin as well, he arrived in San Francisco around 1930. Despite the manifest provincialism of the city, it appealed to him as an "untouched Mediterranean village," with "none of the savage crowding at the trough that makes New York or Paris difficult." After the population influx of World War II, when San Francisco began to flourish culturally, throwing off artists, writers, and other creators, Rexroth came into his element. But the trough began to get a little crowded there too, with the arrival in the 1950s of literary carpetbaggers from New York. Rexroth served as the impresario of the epochal first reading of **Allan Ginsberg**'s "Howl" but soon fell out with the Beats, in particular with

Jack Kerouac who caricatured him as Rheinhold Cacoethes in *Dharma Bums*. Part of the problem was the extraordinary erudition of Rexroth, who was inclined to describe the redwoods as "a Karnak of purple Ionic columns" or to put down Mexican food as "only a slight improvement over Northern Ute cuisine." "I've lived in the kind of world Jack Kerouac imagines he has lived in," Rexroth told an interviewer, and the fact that it was true did not help overcome the generation gap. No matter. The Beats came and went but Rexroth survived, an expatriate in Santa Barbara during his last years.

In addition to the poetry for which he is chiefly known, Rexroth published a history of Communalism *(New York, 1974), collections of opinionated essays, and an absorbing account of his early years,* An Autobiographical Novel *(Garden City, NY, 1964, 1966), transcribed from talks over counterculture radio station KPFA in the Bay Area. A second installment of Rexroth's reminiscences was published in Santa Barbara in 1981, at the prohibitive price of $45.*

Malvina Milder Reynolds

(1901-1978). When songwriter Malvina Reynolds graduated from San Francisco's Lowell High School during World War I, she was denied a diploma because her parents were pacifists. An activist herself, she led a children's parade past the jail where **Tom Mooney**'s wife Rena was incarcerated, with placards reading "Set Our Music Teacher Free." She went on to study romance philology at UC Berkeley; but even as a Phi Beta Kappa and a Ph.D. (1939), she still found herself

discriminated against, as a woman, a Jew, and a radical. She married a union organizer and found employment during World War II as a steelworker. It was not until the 1950s that Reynolds found her own distinctive voice, husky and cracked, as a singer and songwriter about conformity, repression, and peace. She wrote the lyrics to Woody Guthrie's "Sally, Don't You Grieve" (1957) and collaborated on "Turn Around", later a Kodak commercial. Her "Little Boxes," a wry commentary on the row-house conformity of "ticky-tacky" South San Francisco, actually became a hit in 1964. A regular on the counterculture circuit for the last 25 years of her life, she also wrote fragments of an autobiography, issued to friends by newsletter, and the theme of her own wake: "Celebrate her death of whom it could be said / 'She was a working class woman and a Red!' "

Nikolai Petrovich Rezanov

(?-1807). The romantic saga of the Russians in California began in 1806 with the arrival of Rezanov on a touchy diplomatic mission. Formerly czarist ambassador to Japan, now head of the Alaska-based Russian American Fur Company, Rezanov ranked as the chief of a neighboring territory. The Russians needed food to sustain their trapping operations and generally desired to expand their trade and influence. "With the eye of a lover and a politician," as a contemporary European put it, Rezanov proceeded to disarm the suspicious Californios by courting sixteen-year-old Concepción Argüello, daughter of the commandante Buena. (He reported to Russian authorities that the romance "was not begun in hot passion, which is not becoming at my age, but arising under the pressure of conditions—remoteness, duties, responsibilities— perhaps also under the influence of remnants of feelings. . . .") After six weeks in San Francisco, Rezanov left for home to obtain czarist and papal dispension to marry. He died en route, leaving his Concha to pine away for periods variously reported as up to 40 years. (**Bret Harte** wrote a poem about the star-crossed lovers, and **Gertrude Atherton** a 1906 novel.) In 1812 another band of Russians arrived to establish Fort Ross, short for Rossiya, or Russia) as a fur-trading base on the Northern California coast. For a generation the Californios alternately worried about Russian encroachment and enjoyed the occasional society of such urbane Russian commanders as Alexander Rotscheff, a writer, translator and soldier of fortune. Fort Ross proved an expensive mistake and was sold, lock, stock, and barrel, to **Sutter** in 1841.

Thomas C. Russell translated and annotated The Rezanov Voyage to Nueva California in 1806 *(San Francisco, 1926).*

Friend William Richardson (1865-1943).

As governor and first lady of California (1923-27), Richardson and his wife were like Ma and Pa Kettle in the Capital, picturesque smalltown characters, just folks. Michigan-born and raised in San Bernardino, Richardson was a Quaker who had had his meetinghouse appellation legalized. In 1896 he bought the *San Bernardino Times-Index*, trading it in four years later for the *Berkeley Gazette*. Through the state press association, of which he was perennial president, Richardson came to know **Hiram Johnson** who appointed him state printer in 1911. Three years later he was elected state treasurer as a Progressive and in 1922 ran for governor, now a conservative Republican vowing to bury the Johnson machine. A stout, homely, frugal man, Richardson ran a no-frills administration, opposing unnecessary spending with single-minded determination. Favoring stringent law and order, he appointed his son-in-law warden of San Quentin. He set a record for use of the veto and left a surplus of $20 million in the state treasury when he was defeated for re-election. Richardson Grove State Park, 800 acres of redwoods in Humboldt County, was named for him.

Charles Francis Richter (1900-).

Richter experienced his first earthquake as a child in Los Angeles in 1910. After graduation from Stanford (1920), he earned a Ph.D. in theoretical physics from Cal Tech (1928) and joined the faculty there, remaining until his retirement as professor emeritus in 1971. During the 1930s seismology was a new field of scientific opportunity. Working with geologist Beno Gutenberg, Richter devised a logarithmic scale capable of measuring the intensity of an earthquake from any distance. In later years, he went to earthquake-prone Japan as a Fulbright scholar (1959-1960) and acquired a smattering of such languages as Russian to read international earthquake reports. Richter designed an earthquake-proof house in Pasadena, only to have it torn down in 1969 for a freeway. A *Star Trek* fan and devotee of science fiction, he preferred as a scientist to steer clear of earthquake prediction, concentrating instead on building and safety codes to minimize the dangers of earthquake impact.

Richter wrote Elementary Seismology *(San Francisco, 1958).*

Ridder Family.

Theirs is a family chronicle of sons begetting sons and newspapers, beginning with German-language and Catholic Church publications in New York and expanding into California in mid-twentieth century. The California papers became the personal fiefdom of Bernard Ridder (1883?-1975) and his sons Joseph and Daniel. (A third son, Bernard Jr., became president of Ridder Publications, which as of 1966 owned fifteen newspapers nationwide.) As publisher of the *San Jose Mercury*, Joseph Ridder (1920-) ran a tight Republican ship, refusing to print any criticism of politicians he favored, according to political analyst Lou Cannon. In Long Beach, Daniel Ridder (1922-), head of the *Independent Press-Telegram*, was also an active participant in municipal affairs—including some public affairs kept private from his own reporters, according to a 1976 exposé. Ridder Publications merged with the Knight chain in 1974, acquiring a certain national cachet in the process, but the California papers remained under strict and parochial family control.

Bobby Riggs (Robert Larimore Riggs, 1918-   ). The son of a fundamentalist preacher, Riggs grew up in L.A.'s Lincoln Heights, fifth of six brothers. Playing his first tennis tournament away from home, he boarded with the local Church of Christ minister. Riggs didn't look like much of a threat on the tennis court—short and skinny, with all the aplomb of Andy Hardy—but he played one of the shrewdest games of all time, strong on cunning and control. After taking his second U.S. singles title at Forest Hills in 1941 he turned pro, but there was little tennis activity during the war and his first major tour, during which he battled **Don Budge**, had to wait until 1945-1946. Riggs became known as a smart gambler (at Wimbledon in 1939 he claimed to have won $108,000 by betting on himself to win the singles and doubles titles) with a partiality for rich women. In the 1950s he neglected tennis for golf, a game recommended chiefly by its superior betting possibilities. After marrying into a wealthy eastern manufacturing family, he began playing tennis again on the roof of a New York City highrise. But he was more interested in winning a buck than in just being rich, and his wife's family didn't appreciate his outrageous gimmicks to liven up the odds, like playing in galoshes or chained to his doubles partner. So Riggs ended up back in California, an aging

pixie on the Newport Beach singles scene. With the advent of open tennis in 1968 he rose to the top of the 50-and-over age group. And he earned the undisputed title of male chauvinist pig by challenging first Margaret Court and then **Billy Jean King** to a "battle of the sexes," confident that even at his age he could easily defeat the best women players in the world. Riggs won the first round and lost the second, despite a $5,000 course of treatment from a Hollywood nutrition expert who prescribed a daily regimen of 400 pills.

Riggs wrote Court Hustler *(New York, 1973) with George McGann.*

Frederick Hastings Rindge (1857-1905) and **May Knight Rindge** (1865-1941). Theirs was one of the most beautiful ranches in California, twenty miles of prime coastline where the mountains run down to the sea, and they fought an epic twenty-year battle to keep it that way. The heir to a New England textile fortune, Rindge dropped out of Harvard in frail health and came west. A deeply religious man, he could only describe Rancho Topango Malibu Sequit, which he bought in 1891 for $133,150, as God's country. The sea with its gauzy veil of fog and glorious sunsets suggested eternity, the air seemed made for Ponce de Leon, and the seaside canyons with their spreading oaks brought Palestine to mind. Rindge believed his land had the potential to become the Riviera of California, but the prospect seemed too distant

for alarm—although trespassers were always a problem and a brush fire of uncertain origin in 1903 destroyed the family ranch house. (He did try, unsuccessfully, to close Santa Monica's saloons, a magnet for rowdies.) After Rindge's premature death, authorities moved to build the first highway through the ranch. May Rindge refused, personally patrolling the property on horseback. She even constructed her own railroad, becoming the only female railroad president in U.S. history, solely to keep the Southern Pacific out. Her husband's almost religious love for the land became in the mind of his widow an irrational obsession to preserve it at all cost. And the costs were enormous. Mrs. Rindge's legal battles were finally opposed even by her son, who saw his inheritance dissipated in lawyers' fees. In the end, the U.S. Supreme Court awarded the right-of-way to the state and $100,000 compensation to the family. Accepting the inevitable even before the completion of the Pacific Coast Highway in 1928, Mrs. Rindge began leasing beachfront lots—to movie stars, as it happened—with a reversion clause should the lessees indulge in alcohol consumption. But it was too late for her to control the terms of Malibu's future. Badly hurt in the crash, the Rindge interests went into bankruptcy in 1936. May's unfinished mansion was sold to the Franciscans for a retreat, and the rest of the ranch went on sale in 1941.

Frederick Rindge wrote Happy Days in

Southern California *(Cambridge, 1898); see* The Malibu *by W.W. Robinson and Lawrence C. Powell (Los Angeles, 1958).*

Robert Leroy Ripley (1893-1948). The leading American purveyor of the incredible truth, of tall and bizarre and sometimes apocryphal tales, was born humble in the small town of Santa Rosa, California. Dropping out of high school to help support his family, he became a cartoonist on the old *San Francisco Bulletin* while still in his teens. Moving up to the bigger leagues of New York, he once found himself short on material and submitted a set of oddities which evolved into the enormously successful "Believe It Or Not" business, a column with radio, TV, and even movie spinoffs, not to mention Ripley's traveling Odditorium of exhibits. He became a millionaire during the Depression, bought his own island in the Long Island Sound (renamed BION, an acronym for the column), and

"BELIEVE IT or NOT"

ran something of a traveling harem, voyaging restlessly all over the world in search of novelty. To meet the voracious demands of a column a day for 30 years, Ripley used research assistants, stringers, and frequently, unverified information. A difficult and somewhat disturbed personality, he was married only briefly and left his estate to his siblings. The town of Santa Rosa, where he was buried, erected a monument to him in the form of a church made—believe it or not—out of a single redwood tree. The church-museum contains a lifesize wax statue of Ripley plus his pith helmet, silk robe, and other curios.

Bob Considine wrote Ripley, The Modern Marco Polo *(Garden City, NY, 1961).*

Helen Wills Moody Roark

(1906-   ). The queen of women's tennis during the Roaring Twenties, Helen Wills was the daughter of a Berkeley doctor who gave her a tennis club membership for her fourteenth birthday. She won the national girls championship in 1921 and 1922, then moved up in 1923 to take the first of seven U.S. women's singles titles (1923-1925, 1927-1929, 1931). The press called her "little Miss Poker Face," "the Calvin Coolidge of tennis," but everyone admired her cool beauty, usually shaded by a white sun visor which became her trademark. Clearly a very well brought-up young lady, Wills studied art at the University of California, Berkeley. Before her graduation with honors in

1927 she took time off to play on the exclusive French Riviera circuit. It was there that she had her first and only encounter with the reigning star of European tennis, Suzanne Lenglen, losing to the older Frenchwoman. Lenglen retired in 1927 and Wills checked into the Claridge Hotel that year to win her first Wimbledon singles title. (Altogether she won eight Wimbledon singles titles: 1927-1930, 1932-1933,

1935, 1938.) Back home in San Francisco she married a tennis-playing stockbroker in 1929 and became a leading attraction in the salon of Senator **James D. Phelan**, who left her a Greek bust in his will. (Divorced, she married again.) It is of course impossible to know how she would stand up against today's players but **Jack Kramer** rates Helen Wills as one of the greatest of all time.

Wills wrote two memoirs, Tennis *(New York, 1928) and* Fifteen-Thirty *(1937) as well as a mystery novel,* Death Serves an Ace *(New York, 1939).*

Simon Rodia (Sam Rodilla, 1879-1965). The southeastern L.A. neighborhood of Watts is known for two things, the 1965 epidemic of destruction called the Watts Riots and the unique act of creative construction known as the Watts Towers. Rodia was a loner, an Italian-born tile setter and all-around handyman who lived in the mixed Chicano and black neighborhood. He is said to have possessed an

Encyclopaedia Britannica in which he read about Marco Polo, Columbus, and Galileo—Italian explorers of the world and the spirit—but that may be a fanciful bit of embroidery. What is known is that he spent 30 years constructing an elaborate structure out of the detritus of consumer society, scrap iron and metal, broken glass and crockery. Considered "highly significant" in the words of art history—"possibly the most significant structure ever created by one man alone"—the Watts Towers look something like an ornate oil derrick, a Gothic cathedral, and a jungle gym all in one. Rodia, a man whose acts spoke for themselves, deeded his property to a neighbor in 1954 and left. Five years later, the city of Los Angeles tried to demolish the towers as a public hazard. Then living in the Suisun Bay town of Martinez, Rodia remained silent while bureaucrats and activists, philistines and folk culturists marshalled their forces. The towers survived a stress test to become a remote outpost on the Los Angeles tourist circuit but were closed in 1978 for extensive restoration. Rodia died a month before the riots which spared his corner of the old neighborhood.

Earl Rogers (1870-1922). In the days before the advent of motion pictures, some of the celebrity and adulation later reserved for movie stars was lavished on great trial lawyers. Rogers, the son of a Methodist minister who rode circuit between Redlands and Pomona, built the largest criminal law practice in the

West in the early years of the twentieth century, thanks to painstaking preparation and consummate showmanship. Having done his apprenticeship in the Los Angeles law offices of **Stephen M. White**, he prevailed over White as defense counsel in the 1899 Alford murder case. Rogers clinched his reputation at the trial of Alfred Boyd for the 1902 murder of a card sharper called the Louisville Sport, shot during a night of drinking and gambling in Catalina. The defense attorney brought in the "death poker table" (what later attorneys would call demonstrative evidence) and so rattled the chief witness for the prosecution that he virtually admitted to the crime himself. As a local reporter remarked, "Rogers can ask a man his name in a tone that calls him a liar, perjurer, and a crawling reptile all at once." Considered a "howling swell," he wore custom-tailored suits, spats, and a Borsalino hat. In the courtroom, he affected a jewelled lorgnette, through which he peered at adversaries as if they were bugs under a microscope. Through these and other stunts he succeeded in throwing the most skilled of opposing counsel off balance. Rogers made big money ($100,000 alone for defending **Patrick Calhoun** at the San Francisco graft trials) and spent it liberally. But the strain of a high-stakes career and a weakness for alcohol began to tell on him in his early 40s. Soon it was said scornfully that Rogers would work for anybody. As a special prosecutor he helped

gather the evidence to bring the **McNamara** brothers to trial for the 1910 bombing of the *Los Angeles Times*, then turned around and defended the McNamara's lawyer, **Clarence Darrow**, at his first trial for suborning perjury. After that, his daughter **Adela Rogers St. Johns** remarked, he "started to drink up all the whiskey in California." Having gotten **Griffith J. Griffiths** off lightly by arguing the first alcoholic insanity defense, Rogers refused to admit that John Barleycorn had the same insidious effect on himself. He drank himself into an early grave.

Alfred Cohn and Joe Chisholm collaborated on Take the Witness! *(New York, 1934).* Final Verdict *(New York, 1962). Adela Rogers St. Johns' biography of her father, is thoroughly maudlin.*

Will Rogers (1879-1935). He was a former cowboy from Oklahoma's Indian Territory, a laconic lasso artist with a homespun philosophy and a yen for real estate. In 1919, already famous for his wit and wisdom, Rogers moved to Southern California to make silent movies. "Pleasant outdoor work," he called it, but the movie colony wasn't really his style. "Old Hollywood is just like a desert water hole in Africa," he quipped. "Hang around long enough and every kind of animal in the world will drift in." Contrary to his self-professed friendliness, he actively disliked some of the men he met in California and told them so. Rogers lived awhile in Beverly Hills, even serving as mayor, before moving to the wide open

spaces of the Pacific Palisades, where in the 1920s he bought 300 acres of land in the Santa Monica Mountains. There he created a nonworking version of the modern ranch, complete with barns, corrals, a eucalyptus-lined polo field, and "the house that jokes built." By now a national figure, syndicated newspaper columnist, and popular after-dinner speaker, he managed between traveling engagements to pick up two miles of prime beachfront at the foot of Santa Monica Canyon. But the state soon condemned the land to create Will Rogers State Beach, where whole generations of California teenagers would while away their summer vacations. After Rogers's death in an Alaska plane crash, the ranch too became a state park, a down-home sort of showplace where tourists could see what western ranching was never really like. There is also a Will Rogers Park in downtown Watts.

The most recent biography, Will Rogers, His Life and Times, *by Richard M. Ketchum (New York, 1973) is extensively illustrated. A Rogers* Autobiography *was published posthumously (Boston, 1949).*

James Rolph, Jr.

(1869-1934). Rolph was a popular five-term (1911-1930) mayor of San Francisco, a former shipping executive who lived all his life in the city's Mission District until his election as governor (1931-1934). He first came to statewide attention as the genial, gladhanding host of San Francisco's 1915 Panama-Pacific Exposition, proudly presiding over the city's reconstruction. A natty dresser, he favored special

blue four-in-hand ties, boutonnieres, and custom-made boots. He was called "Sunny Jim" and orchestras struck up "Smiles" on his arrival. Rolph ran for governor in 1918 but found himself in a unique dilemma under state cross-filing laws: he won the Democratic nomination but could not accept it, the Supreme Court ruled, because he lost his own Republican Party's nomination. Rolph's shipping company went bankrupt in 1921, which put something of a crimp into the mayor's legendary generosity (on a trip back East in 1919 to welcome the soldiers home, he took along a month's salary in change for tips) and increased his dependence on the corporate establishment. A consummate political showman, he attended cowmilking and frog-jumping contests, snow queen and bathing beauty pageants, even the "Rustler's Banquet," if he thought it would pay off in goodwill and votes. His gubernatorial administration has been called a "baroque interlude" in California politics. Rolph traded in his silk top-hat for a huge cowboy model, ordered whiskey for condemned prisoners, planted slogans on the Capitol lawn, and issued a record number of pardons. To counter the Depression, he suggested that everybody take a few extra weeks of vacation. He refused to sign a state income tax bill but did approve a sales tax ("pennies for Sunny Jim") which he spent liberally. There were complaints about cronies and relatives on the state payroll, and a nasty incident in 1933

when the governor publicly endorsed the lynching of kidnap-murderers by a San Jose mob. An invalid during his last five months, he died in office.

David Taylor's The Life of James Rolph, Jr. *(San Francisco, 1932) is a snow job.*

Michael Romanoff (Harry

Gerguson?, 1890?-1971). Where better than Hollywood for a creative con artist to work the lucrative line between fantasy and reality? During a long career as filmdom's favorite imposter, Romanoff, a purported survivor of the Russian royal family, left a trail of bad checks and broken hearts. Some said he was really a native of Ohio who had passed himself off as William Gladstone and as a lesser Rockefeller before becoming a Russian Grand Duke. Debonair and continental with his spats, malacca walking stick, and pencil moustache, he passed many tests of his aplomb. **Jack Warner**, who hired Romanoff as a technical advisor on a Foreign Legion film, found that he knew his stuff cold; but when Warner purposely gave him a difficult horse to ride, Romanoff ended up with a broken arm and general sympathy. (Visiting the convalescent, Warner was impressed by a skillfully doctored photo of the czar's family.) In the early Hollywood years, Romanoff "sat at your table and told stories." Later, he found his vocation as a Beverly Hills restaurateur and had his portrait painted as a beggar prince. The two Romanoff restaurants in Beverly Hills, founded in 1939 and 1951,

became famous for celebrity fist fights and extortionary prices. (Two others, in Palm Springs and San Francisco, were not successful.) In one of his last capers, Romanoff pulled strings in 1958 to have the U.S. House of Representatives grant him citizenship, whereupon he voluntarily renounced his claim to the Russian throne.

Frank Roney (1841-1925).

San Francisco labor leader Roney was an Irish rebel who immigrated to America in 1867 rather than spend the indefinite future in British prisons. Arriving in what he knew only as the "land of Lincoln," he was appalled at the desperate competition among laboring men to earn a living, particularly on the East Coast. In San Francisco where he settled in 1875, workers were somewhat better off, having started from a higher wage base during Gold Rush days of labor scarcity. With the completion of the transcontinental railroad in 1869, however, and the national economic crises of the 1870s, San Francisco was feeling the crunch too. Roney was **Denis Kearney**'s main rival and successor in the Workingmen's Party of California (WPC). Too recent an immigrant himself to feel comfortable with exclusionary policies, he opposed Kearney's racist demagoguery. When the WPC collapsed, Roney went on to found the Seaman's Protective Association and the San Francisco Trades Assembly (1881-1882). He also served as president of the League of Deliverance (1882), a "white labor movement," having reluctantly concluded that Oriental labor promoted slave wages for all. The league backed the Bay Area's first white laundry and devised the first union label to distinguish "free" from "slave-made" cigars. In 1886, after the Haymarket riot in Chicago, Roney organized San Francisco's first Labor Day parade, serving as grand marshal of a ten-mile-long procession in which 40 unions participated. A moderate, he opposed socialism as "soulless materialism" and the closed shop as an offense against his rebel pride; he also counseled arbitration and constructive action rather than strikes, political independence rather than "toadyism." Labor historian Ira Cross describes him as an intensely sympathetic figure, and idealist and a cynic at the same time, committed above all to the dignity of labor.

Roney wrote a lengthy Autobiography *(Berkeley, 1931).*

Josiah Royce (1855-1916).

The foremost American idealist philosopher was born in the quartz-mining town of Grass Valley. Later, it would seem a very backwoods beginning, but at the time Grass Valley was the home of **Lola Montez** and the sixth largest city in California. At age ten Royce went to school in San Francisco and at fourteen entered the preparatory class of the new University of California, then in Oakland. (By the time he received his B.A. in 1873, the campus had moved to Berkeley.) Royce returned to teach at UC Berkeley after studying in Europe and earning his Ph.D. at Johns

Hopkins (1878), but he felt himself an intellectual exile. If Berkeley were really the Athens of the Pacific, as some claimed, then it lacked not only a Pericles and a Socrates, Royce pointed out, but also common wisdom and ideals. For him, the most important reality was the life of the mind. He seized an opportunity to teach at Harvard and remained there for the rest of his life. (By Boston standards, he was considered something of a westerner in manners and dress.) Commissioned to write a book about California, Royce had occasion to ponder "the sad state where I had the odd fortune to be born." He visited **Bancroft's** library in San Francisco, interviewed **John C. Frémont**, and searched memory and literature for evidence of moral, social, and political growth on the frontier. California was born of individual ambition and greed, Royce decided, and baptized in the blood of the Bear Flag Revolt, an act of imperialistic conquest with racist overtones. He admired

the political facility of such new statesmen as **Broderick** and **Gwin**, if not their ideals, and found some small improvement in vigilante justice over mining-camp law. But the Californian, in the estimation of the expatriate idealist, was basically a wanderer with an inadequate sense of social responsibility, thirsty for life's pleasures but lacking interest in its vital relations.

Royce's 1886 study, California, *has been reprinted several times. He also wrote a Victorian novel set in California,* The Feud of Oakfield Creek *(Boston, 1887). Vincent Buranelli (New York, 1964) and Bruce Kuklick (Indianapolis, 1972) both wrote intellectual biographies of the philosopher. See also Kevin Starr,* Americans and the California Dream *(New York, 1973; Salt Lake, 1981).*

Abraham Ruef

(1864-1936). Ruef was a political boss worthy of cosmopolitan San Francisco at the turn of the century. Intelligent, cultured, fastidious, and vain, he ruled with finesse instead of muscle, arousing amusement rather than fear. Born in San Francisco, the son of a French-Jewish merchant, he graduated Phi Beta Kappa from UC Berkeley at eighteen, a classics major, and was admitted to the bar at 21. By age 23 he was the Republican boss of North Beach, but soon shifted to the new Union Labor Party which offered opportunity for faster advancement. A small, dapper figure with large mustaches, Ruef looked, a contemporary remarked, like the original flying trapeze artist—the "curly boss," they called him. What he needed was a tall, handsome, ethnically appealing candidate, whom

he found in the person of orchestra conductor **Eugene Schmitz**. With Schmitz groomed and promoted to mayor in 1901, Ruef's position seemed impregnable. As a lawyer and unofficial advisor to the mayor, he collected fees ranging as high as $200,000 from utilities, developers, and vice operators, for permits, franchises, and protection. Not selfish, he shared the money with the mayor and

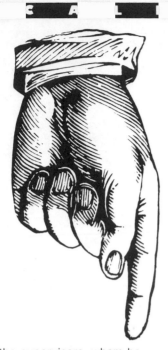

the supervisors, whom he would soon have opportunity to immortalize as the "paint-eaters," so greedy they would eat the paint off the walls. Ruef had the misfortune to live during the Muckraking era, of which he became California's primary object lesson. It took the earthquake and the combined energies of crusading editor **Fremont Older**, prosecutor **Francis Heney**, sleuth **William Burns** and millionaire **Rudolph Spreckels** to bring him to trial. Even then, Ruef had the wits to forestall his fate for nearly two years. He finally agreed to plead guilty but won sympathy for his refusal to implicate others. The original charges were dismissed on a technicality, but Ruef was retried and convicted in 1908 and sentenced to fourteen years in San Quentin, which he undoubtedly enlivened by his presence. While in prison he

wrote a memoir, "The Road I Traveled; An Autobiographic Account of My Career from University to Prison," which ran for three months in the newspapers. Released in 1915 after serving half his sentence, he spent his last twenty years dabbling in real estate. One of his ideas, a little before its time, was to turn Fisherman's Wharf into a tourist attraction.

Boss Ruef's San Francisco by Walton Bean (Berkeley, 1952) and Debonair Scoundrel by Lately Thomas (New York, 1962) are both excellent.

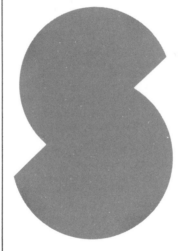

Ruth St. Denis (Ruth Dennis, 1878?-1968). She was a tall farm girl from New Jersey who studied Delsartean physical culture as a child and went on stage as a teenage Belasco actress. One day she saw the figure of Isis in an ad for Egyptian cigarettes and it struck her with a sense of destiny. St. Denis began creating dances around the persona of an exotic Eastern goddess, auditioning without success in New York. (Producer **Jesse Lasky** remembered her as an amateur dancer from Jersey

with a carload of scenery, weird music, and a cast of natives.) She eventually caught on in Europe with her repertoire of gypsy and Oriental dances. In 1915, Miss Ruth, as she was called, gravitated to Los Angeles, where she opened the first Denishawn School with her partner-husband Ted Shawn. The whole family came along: Miss Ruth's brother opened an Asian Bazaar on Sunset Boulevard, and her father joined the Civil War veterans at the Old Soldiers Home in West L.A. At first, California seemed a liberating influence, unleashing new ideas and "utopian longings of the human heart." Denishawn attracted among its first pupils the Gish sisters and a young dancer named Martha Graham, daughter of a Santa Barbara physician. Miss Ruth found no shortage of kindred spirits to join her Society of Spiritual Arts, which advocated dance as a religious ritual. But during the Depression, the dream began

to fade. The Denishawns separated, their school closed, and their world tours ceased. Miss Ruth returned alone to Los Angeles in 1942, working for a time during the war at Douglas Aircraft. She continued to make occasional public appearances into her eighties, a striking grande dame, and to hold court in small Hollywood studios cluttered with old costumes and memories, high priestess of her own cult.

Miss Ruth wrote An Unfinished Life (New York, 1939). See Walter Terry's biography, Miss Ruth (New York, 1969) and Divine Dancer (New York, 1981) by dance historian Suzanne Shelton.

Adela Rogers St. Johns (1894?-   ). Her father was California's top criminal lawyer, **Earl Rogers**, and she grew up in his office, rolling his cigarettes and kibbitzing on his cases—just one of the boys. At eighteen, unschooled but loyal, sentimental and 150 percent Irish, she joined the boys in the city room of **Hearst's** *San Francisco Examiner*. As successor to sob sister **Annie Laurie** she covered the Lindbergh kidnapping trial (*KEEP YOUR HANDS OFF OUR CHILDREN*, her headline screamed) and the abdication of Edward VIII (barely suppressing her tomboy antagonism to Wallis Simpson). A rooting, cheering fan, she attended the Dempsey-Tunney fight. Champion of the underdog and the celebrity, she led an ain't-we-got-fun life, complete with three husbands, an expense-account wardrobe by Hattie Carnegie, and houseparties at the Hearst ranch. Among her friends she counted Damon Runyan, Tom Mix, "my best friend Clark Gable," **Hearst** himself, and **Richard Nixon**, her former grocery delivery boy in Whittier, whose triumph over Communism she applauded. St. Johns also wrote Hollywood scenarios, public relations releases, women's magazine fiction, movie-star copy for *Photoplay*, a religious novel, and several gossipy memoirs, in addition to frequent appearances as a TV talk-show guest. Her life inspired two Hollywood movies: *A Free Soul* (1931), based on her relationship with her father, and *His Girl Friday* (1940) with Rosalind Russell as St. Johns.

Her books include Final Verdict *(1962) and* The Honeycomb *(1969).*

Mort Sahl (Morton Lyon Sahl, 1927-). In 1953, in the early middle ages of the Eisenhower era, a casually dressed young comedian opened at the hungry i (I for intellectual) in San Francisco. With the success of his bitterly iconoclastic political monologues lampooning comatose Republicanism and knee-jerk liberalism alike, Sahl won rare acclaim for an intellectual in show business. His credentials were strictly Southern California suburban: he grew up in South Gate, attended Compton College, and graduated from USC on the GI Bill, writing a thesis on city traffic. In 1960 he became the first comic to make the cover of *Time* magazine, which called him the "sweater comedian" for his dress preferences. He even wrote material for John F. Kennedy. After Kennedy's assassination Sahl got deeply into conspiracy theories, seemed to lose his sense of humor, and found his TV talk show replaced by wrestling telecasts. In the mid-1970s, however, he traded his sweater for a tux and opened in Las Vegas. (Despite his political pessimism, he also possessed an expensive taste for the sybaritic, as evidenced by his friendship with Hugh Hefner, his marriage to exotic China Lee and a Japanese-style home in Benedict Canyon.) It took 25 years after Sahl's San Francisco debut, but L.A. in the 1980s finally acquired enough sophistication for him to live and work (at the Comedy Store in Hollywood) in the same neighborhood.

Sahl wrote a polemical memoir, Heartland *(New York, 1976).*

Ruben Salazar

(1928-1970). Salazar became a Chicano culture hero when he was killed during a Vietnam-era Mexican-American antiwar demonstration. Ironically, in life he was sometimes called

a "Tío Taco," an Uncle Tom, for his success in the gringo world. Born in Mexico and raised in Texas, he joined the staff of the *Los Angeles Times* in 1959, married an Anglo woman, and eventually acquired a home with a pool in Orange County. Because of his behind-the-lines reports during the Dominican Republic intervention in 1965, he was sent as a foreign correspondent to Vietnam and Mexico City. Salazar returned to Los Angeles in 1969 to become news director of local TV station KMEX, and writer of a weekly column in the *Times*. Taking a deeper interest in the Chicano community, he pointed out that the Mexicans got here first, after all, but were still treated as a colonial population. The antiwar demonstration on 29 August 1970, the largest demonstration ever by Mexican-Americans in the U.S., was the local community's bloodiest confrontation since the World War II Zoot-Suit Riots. Taking refuge with his camera crew

in a neighborhood bar, Salazar was hit in the head by a tear gas canister and died instantly.

Salazar wrote Stranger in One's Land, *published by the U.S. Commission on Civil Rights in May 1970. The* Los Angeles Times *published a collection of his columns along with a eulogy by publisher* Otis Chandler.

Jonas Edward Salk

(1914-). Medical science is a thoroughly conservative profession, Salk biographer Richard Carter points out, one in which ambitious thinking is discouraged and individual celebrity is positively anathema. Few remember the names of the scientists who conquered typhoid and tetanus, and we do not call the rabies vaccine after Pasteur or the smallpox inoculation after Jenner. Then there is Jonas Salk, celebrated as the white knight of polio prevention who ended up, not inappropriately, as the head of his own research empire on the California seashore, beyond the scientific pale. A graduate

of City College of New York (B.S., 1934) and New York University (M.D., 1939), Salk was already a controversial figure at the University of Pittsburgh (1947-1963) where he developed his polio vaccine in defiance of the current orthodoxy that killed-virus vaccines don't work. Introduced in 1955, the Salk vaccine reduced the U.S. incidence of polio 61 percent in two years even without mass immunization, which was opposed by the American Medical Association and by rivals in the scientific establishment. Salk appeared, reluctantly to be sure, on Edward R. Murrow's "See It Now" and in the pages of *Life* magazine; a movie starring Marlon Brando was suggested, then mercifully forgotten. When defective Salk vaccine from a California pharmaceutical company caused an outbreak of polio, Salk's work itself was called into suspicion and his vaccine largely supplanted by the Sabin vaccine (named for Albert Sabin), which is more easily administered but which carries a greater risk of polio infection. What to do next? With a 27-acre gift of land and the support of renegade capitalist **Armand Hammer**, Salk built an interdisciplinary Institute for Biological Sciences, a center of cancer and immunology research, in La Jolla. Designed by architect Louis Kahn, the institute which opened in 1963, resembles a sci-fi mausoleum. For Salk, the move to California definitely qualified as life in the express lane. He became one of the few Jewish homeowners in exclusive La Jolla, and after

the breakup of his first marriage, married beautiful jet-setter Françoise Gilot, artist and former mistress of Pablo Picasso.

Richard Carter wrote Breakthrough: The Saga of Jonas Salk *(New York, 1965), a better-than-average biography.*

Arthur Henrietta Samish

(1897?-1974). He was like a character out of a Tennessee Williams play about the South, an overweight, garrulous old hell-raiser exuding a hint of evil intent. Samish grew up fatherless in San Francisco, raised by his mother whose name he added to his own in gratitude. He started as a page in the state legislature and learned the ropes, trading his way to political influence as California's most powerful lobbyist. From the Depression until the McCarthy era, Samish reigned in Sacramento as a political boss without a party. His office was in the Senator Hotel across from the Capitol, out of which he directed a staff of 25 "intelligence agents" and a clipping secretary who kept his little black book full of tips on candidates and incumbents. As lobbyist for the brewing industry, Samish had the funds to "select and elect" sympathetic legislators. Because of the cross-filing system under which most candidates for the state legislature used to be elected in the primaries, and by a judicious use of money, he was able to significantly influence future alignments. He operated on the simple principles of revenge and reward. Loyal to his friends,

he was vindictive when crossed. Samish claimed to have drafted John Pelletier right off L.A.'s skid row and elected him to the state legislature just to spite an enemy. He also took credit for throwing the 1940 state Republican delegation to Willkie, out of pique with his old enemy **Frank Merriam** who as governor had levied a state tax against liquor. He took pride in being named in the 1939 Philbrick Legislative Investigative Report as the "prototype of a lobbyist" and in *Collier*'s magazine in 1949 as "The Secret Boss of California." Samish's power remained essentially unchecked until the Kefauver hearings in 1951, after which the IRS spent two and a half years delving into his personal and business affairs. Charged with tax evasion, he served 26 months in federal prison. Released to retire on a pension from the Brewers Institute, he told the story of his life to writer Bob Thomas and sat back, unrepentant, to enjoy the flap.

Samish liked the title of the 1949 Collier's *article so much that he used it for his own memoir,* The Secret Boss of California *(New York, 1971).*

William Saroyan

(1908-1981). When Saroyan was growing up fatherless in World War I Fresno, about a fifth of the city's population was Armenian, attracted by the vineyards and by some mystical quality in the land. As a boy, he admired impoverished ethnic poets, sneaked into the Bijou (pronounced by-joe) Theater to see Saturday matinees, sold newspapers on the street, and went to work for

the telegraph company owned by the **Mackay**s. Later, he would recreate himself as Ulysses Macauley, telegraph boy in *The Human Comedy* (1943), a loving, life-affirming tribute to the child in man set in melting-pot California. Writing came easy to him: he dashed off *The Time of Your Life* (1939), his Pulitzer Prize-winning play, in six days, with time out for drinking, gambling, and wenching. With his cousin Ross Bagdasarian he made up a hollering Armenian-style song that went to the top of the hit parade, "Come On-a My House." Saroyan went to Hollywood in 1936 for a salary of $3,000 a week, which he made little pretense of earning. ("No Jew can ever cheat an Armenian," he said of his negotiations with MGM chief **Louis B. Mayer**.) Loud and proud, with a big black moustache like an Italian fruit vendor, he bragged and laughed and caroused his way through life, divorcing twice, a loving if negligent father. In 1964 Saroyan finally got serious. He returned to Fresno,

planted a forest around his house, bought the next-door house for privacy, and astonished local children with his bicycle-riding prowess. He also started writing again, mostly amusing memoirs, all the while insisting that his real work was simply being.

Saroyan's memoirs, all charming, include The Bicycle Rider in Beverly Hills *(New York, 1952),* Places Where I've Done Time *(New York, 1972), and* Sons Come and Go, Mothers Hang in Forever *(New York, 1976).*

Mario Savio (1943?-   ). With 27,000 students in 1964, the University of California at Berkeley was the home of DO NOT FOLD SPINDLE OR MUTILATE, a school where it was possible to get a B.A. without ever speaking to a professor. Having spent the previous summer agitating for civil rights in the South, Savio, a street-smart New Yorker, was manning a table for the Student Non-Violent Coordinating Committee at Sather Gate when the university authorities decided to restrict student political activities. By a combination of accident, training, and grandstanding, he became a leader of the Free Speech Movement that nearly took over the university that fall. A philosophy major, Savio had studied the concepts of alienation and civil disobedience. In practice, he went beyond passive resistance. he was charged with assault for biting a police officer in October, and made the front page of the *San Francisco Chronicle* on being forceably removed from the spotlight at a Greek Theater convocation. At the climax of the revolution, the December 1964 Sproul Hall sit-in, Savio

made a passionate plea for bringing the university to a grinding halt, and was arrested along with 761 others. The mood in student strike headquarters, the *New York Times* reported, was "*Waiting for Lefty* done off-Broadway," and Lefty never quite seemed to arrive. The Free Speech Movement degenerated into the "filthy speech movement," and Savio dropped out of school to become a full time protestor. Like countless other Berkeley students, unable to cut the university umbilical cord, he drifted in and out of local consciousness, chalking up a series of defeats in the back pages of the newspaper: the loss of his appeal (1967), an unsuccessful campaign as a Peace and Freedom Party candidate for the state Senate (1968), another for mayor of Berkeley (1971), and divorce from his wife (1977).

Joseph M. Schenck (1878-1961). Among the Hollywood moguls Schenck was something of a genial godfather, a man who got things done and took care of his friends. A short Russian-Jewish immigrant who never lost his gutteral accent, he was the owner of the Palisades Amusement Park in New Jersey when he fell in love with and married aspiring actress Norma Talmadge. "Together they looked like Snow White and an overgrown dwarf," **Anita Loos** thought, but she conceded that Schenck had the "subtle masculine allure which so often accompanies power." Schenck moved to Hollywood to further his wife's career, although he would

always miss New York, and took it stoically when she left him for Gilbert Roland. (She actually ended up marrying entertainer George Jessel.) In 1924 Schenck became chairman of United Artists, which he ran "mostly over a gold telephone and with the aid of a violent temper." In 1933 he went into partnership with **Darryl Zanuck** to establish Twentieth Century-Fox. An inveterate but shrewd gambler, he owned a share of the Agua Caliente casino in Tijuana, and his Beverly Hills home, according to Harpo Marx, was "a combination gym, sanitarium, harem, and gambling casino." When **Willie Bioff**'s union racketeers began exacting payoffs from the studios for "labor peace" in the late 1930s, Schenck and his brother Nicholas, then head of MGM, were delegated to deal with the extortionists. The payoffs were concealed by studio accounting, along

with such personal Schenck expenditures as a yacht and a masseuse. A subsequent government investigation of Bioff led to Schenck's conviction for income tax evasion. He served four months of a one-year sentence and was later pardoned by Harry Truman. Widely considered to have taken the rap for all the studios, Schenck was rewarded with an Oscar in 1952 for "services to the industry." He spent his last years telling old battle stories to aspiring young actresses such as **Marilyn Monroe**, who knew little and cared less about ancient Hollywood history.

Anita Loos describes Schenck in The Talmadge Girls *(New York, 1978).*

Rudolph Michael Schindler (1887-1953). The landscape of Southern California, from Catalina to Glendale and Newport Beach to Studio City, is dotted with

Schindler's small cubist experiments in form and space. The Vienna-born and-trained architect moved to Los Angeles in 1920 after a few years in Chicago, to work for **Frank Lloyd Wright** on the construction of **Aline Barnsdall's** Hollyhock House. The first fulltime modern architect in L.A., he created his greatest masterpieces in the early 1920 s. The first was his own home on Kings Road in Hollywood (1921-1922), a unique fusion of shelter and nature, office and residence, permanent cave and lightweight tent. His Newport Beach house (1922-1926) for medical columnist Dr. Phillip M. Lovell is considered one of the key works of twentieth century architecture, comparable to the best European work of the day. (A connoisseur of progressive design, Lovell also had a Schindler-designed cabin in Wrightwood and a **Neutra** house in L.A.) Subscribing to all the architecture journals, Schindler synthesized the currents of Expressionism, Zigzag Moderne, and *de Stijl* ("the style", a Dutch movement favoring rectangular forms in asymmetric balance) for California consumption. In his middy shirt and sandals, he was considered something of a Bohemian, says architectural historian Esther McCoy. Clients had difficulty getting mortgages for their modernistic houses, and few corporate commissions came his way. Neutra, who joined Schindler in L.A. in 1925, built a more successful local practice and national reputation. But Schindler's hillside homes, many of them

cliffhangers in the Hollywood and Silverlake districts, represent the ultimate fusion of art with the Southern California environment—"Californiated European architecture going with the flow of the California dream," in the words of another architectural historian, Reyner Banham.

See David Gebhard's, Schindler *(New York, 1971; Salt Lake City, 1980).*

Eugene Edwards Schmitz (1864?-1928).

A former violinist and later conductor at San Francisco's fashionable Columbia Theater, Schmitz was discovered by Boss **Abe Ruef** who groomed him for political superstardom. His primary qualifications for office were

his operatic good looks, his stage presence, and his Irish-German ancestry. Elected mayor of San Francisco in 1901 on the Union Labor ticket thanks solely to Ruef, he began to develop delusions of grandeur. He moved into a mansion and became preoccupied with his new social standing to the point that he exempted wealthy socialites from the customary payoffs for doing business with Ruef's machine. Schmitz was reelected in 1903 and 1905, despite growing evidence of municipal malfeasance. After the earthquake he assumed the role of tireless savior, which he brought off so well that he thought he was ready to run for governor. When **Francis Heney**'s graft prosecution

began to close in around him, he set off on a grand European tour on the pretext of persuading German insurance companies to make good on earthquake claims. Charged with extortion on his return, the mayor arrived in court "as pompous as a drum major," continuing to protest his innocence even during sentencing. Schmitz's first conviction was set aside on technicalities—among other things, the indictment failed to identify him as mayor—and he escaped along with everyone else except Ruef when the graft prosecution ran out of steam. He later tried oil, mining, and light opera (*The Maid of San Joaquin*), without success. Undaunted by widespread knowledge of the intimate details of his derelictions, he ran for mayor again in 1915 but lost to **James Rolph**. As a consolation prize, Schmitz was elected a San Francisco supervisor in 1917 and 1921.

Schmitz has only a supporting role in the two excellent histories of the era, Debonair Scoundrel *by Lately Thomas (New York, 1962) and* Boss Ruef's San Francisco *by Walton Bean (Berkeley, 1952).*

Arnold Schoenberg

(1874-1951). One of Hollywood's better anecdotes features **Irving Thalberg** and Schoenberg, creator of the arcane twelve-tone system of composition and one of the giants of twentieth-century music. An Austrian refugee from Nazism, Schoenberg settled in Los Angeles in 1934, suffering from asthma, culture shock, and recurring attacks of misanthropy. Thalberg, so impressed by an

early romantic piece of Schoenberg's that he was only twenty minutes late, was trying to interest the composer in writing the background music for Pearl Buck's *The Good Earth*: "Imagine . . . a terrific storm is going on . . . in the midst of an earthquake, Oo-Lan gives birth to a baby . . . ." According to one version, Schoenberg replied, "With so much going on, why do you need music?" Another version has the composer demanding $50,000 and complete control of the film's sound track, including dialogue, to be delivered in tempo with the music. Needless to say, Schoenberg spent his California years teaching at USC and UCLA instead of working on films. He was disappointed in the overall quality of his students, who included more than one film composer in search of "tips." (Asked for advice about an airplane movie, the professor suggested "music for big bees, only louder," thereafter referring to film scores as "big bee music.") Creatively, he considered Los Angeles "a completely blank page, as far as my music is concerned," and became embroiled in feuds with other émigrés. He once refused to attend a banquet for conductor Otto Klemperer ("I consider it unspeakable that these people, who have been suppressing my works in this part of the world for the last 25 years, now want to use me as a decoration.") and publicly accused **Thomas Mann** after the publication of *Dr. Faustus* (1948) of pirating his "intellectual property rights" to the twelve-tone system. As for the natives, Schoenberg considered them "mostly inferior, although often very kindly." Virtually the only aspect of Southern California life meriting his unqualified approval was tennis. Pictures of the family at their Brentwood home often show them all in tennis whites, which the composer was known to wear even to dinner parties. Schoenberg would have been infuriated that both USC and UCLA, which treated him in life with something less than the respect due to him, erected campus buildings in his honor after his death. Or then again, perhaps not. Through USC's Schoenberg Institute (repository of his scores and memorabilia, including plans for a musical typewriter) the composer finally achieved the recognition he deserved during his life in Los Angeles.

The Schoenberg family and friends take exception to the most recent and accessible biography, that by H.H. Stuckenschmidt, Arnold Schoenberg *(New York, 1977).*

Budd Wilson Schulberg (1914-).

Southern California was going through a tropical craze when Schulberg arrived in 1922, son of B.P. Shulberg, the 28-year-old tycoon of Paramount Pictures. He would long remember the caged monkeys and tropical birds in the Beverly Hills Hotel lobby, and the ostrich and alligator farms near his father's studio. Budd grew up in Windsor Square, the Bel Air of its day, and attended the city's melting-pot secondary school, L.A. High. After school, the family chauffeur would deliver him to a midtown corner where he sold the *Saturday Evening Post*. The chauffeur made off with the family jewels one fine day, and B.P. Schulberg was overthrown in a studio coup, indelible lessons in the vicissitudes of fortune. Budd went to the Soviet Union at seventeen, graduated from Dartmouth, and took a job as a junior writer for **David Selznick**, son of another has-been. (Schulberg's mother became, like Selznick's brother, a top agent.) Selznick assigned him to write an Ivy League college screenplay with **F. Scott Fitzgerald**, then in advanced stages of alcoholism. The family chauffeur turned up later in a short story Schulberg wrote for *Playboy*, Fitzgerald's collapse was the kernel of a novel called *The Disenchanted* (1950), and the whole Hollywood experience went into his classic *What Makes Sammy Run?* (1941), about a little ferret of a kid named Sammy Glick who begs, wheedles, cons, and steals his way to studio success. Producer **Louis B.** Mayer was so angry over *Sammy* that he told Schulberg's father, "It's an outrage, and he ought to be deported." B.P. Schulberg laughed. "Where to? He's one of the few kids who came out of this place. Where are we going to deport him to? Catalina?" Budd, who elected to live back East after World War II except for a period in the mid-sixties when he conducted a writers workshop in Watts, also wrote a highly acclaimed screenplay for *On the Waterfront* (1954). In 1951 he appeared before the House Un-American Activities Committee to name fellow former members of the Communist party, earning the undying enmity of the Hollywood Left.

Schulberg's Moving Pictures; Memories of a Hollywood Prince *(New York, 1981) is largely about his father who, at his peak, smoked $175 worth of cigars a week.*

Robert Harold Schuller (1926-).

When Schuller arrived in California in 1955, a former

Iowa farm boy ordained in the Reformed Church in America, (founded in 1628) his first church was an Anaheim drive-in movie. "Worship as you are, In the family car," he advertised. In 1961 he moved his Garden Grove Community Church into a **Neutra**-designed building with seating for 1,700 plus parking for 1,600 vehicles, all tuned in to the service by local radio. A Republican and Rotarian with a Mickey Mouse Club smile, Schuller described himself as the head retailer of his "shopping center for Christ," merchandizer of an upbeat version of Christianity—"spiritual tuneups," to extend the auto analogy. He went electronic with a nationally syndicated "Hour of Power," which claimed a TV audience of three million. Since 1970, over 20,000 pastors, lay people, and professors have "graduated" from his Robert Schuller Institute for Successful Church Leadership. Prosperous,

thanks to the media collection plate, Schuller achieved the ultimate apotheosis of California car culture and corporate religion with the unveiling in 1980 of his $14 million Crystal Cathedral, designed by Philip Johnson and John Burgee to accommodate 4,000 worshippers inside and 2,000 cars outside. Bigger than Notre Dame, the futuristic drive-in church featured 10,000 windows, a fourteen-story neon cross, and a highly touted million-dollar organ.

Michael and Donna Nason worked with Schuller closely for eight years before writing Robert Schuller: the Inside Story *(New York, 1982)*

Charles Monroe Schulz

(1922-   ). The creator of the Peanuts cartoon strip was born and raised in Saint Paul, Minnesota, the son (like his friend Charlie Brown) of a barber. He studied drawing by correspondence, became a cartoonist because he didn't

have the patience for "art," and in 1950 sold Peanuts to the United Feature Syndicate. With popular and financial success Schulz moved west, settling in Sebastopol in the early 1960s because it reminded him of Minnesota. The only thing missing was winter, so he built a public skating rink, the Redwood Empire Ice Arena, for consolation. On his 28-acre estate he had everything else a body could possibly want: golf course, baseball diamond, tennis court, riding stable, redwood grove, and a whole Noah's Ark of kids and

animals. To help pay the overhead, Schulz developed Peanuts into a multi-million-dollar conglomerate, with film, book, and merchandising spinoffs. At one point, a Peanuts version of Disneyland was even anticipated. But happiness, its seems, is considerably more complicated than a warm puppy. Schulz and his wife divorced in the late 1970s and their Sebastopol estate became a religious center. Soon remarried, the cartoonist relocated to the former diocesan residence of the bishop of Santa Rosa.

Death Valley Scotty

(Walter Scott 1872?-1954). Scotty's is an endearing variation on the strike-it-rich theme, a harmless high-life

fantasy that lightened the spirits of the times. Born in Kentucky, he arrived in Death Valley around 1884 as a water boy with a surveying

team. After a dozen years with the Buffalo Bill Wild West Show he returned there to discover gold, or so he said. This touched off a scramble of prospectors and a mock Battle of Wingate Pass, later the subject of a play starring Laurette Taylor. "Always play to the gallery and never mind the dress circle," maintained Scotty, a pudgy figure of a man in a red tie and stetson. Newspapers called him "the cowboy Croesus," or "King of the Desert Mine." His most famous stunt was to hire a train in 1905, stock it with champagne which he drank out of beer steins and dash across the desert to break the LA-Chicago speed record. Later, inspired by a Rhine palace he had seen on tour with Buffalo Bill, he built a dream castle in the improbable setting of Death Valley. (When the valley became a national monument, Scotty was allowed by special act of Congress to buy the castle grounds.) In 1930, he announced that he was going broke—"Millionaires aren't popular any more." He had a benefactor named Albert Johnson, whom he had restored to good spirits after a crippling accident. The true story of Scotty's riches was revealed in court in 1941 when a former prospecting partner sued for a share of the alleged wealth. Johnson was his gold mine, Scotty testified, and Johnson took the stand to affirm that Scotty's friendship "was his real gold." Johnson left Scotty's Castle to a religious foundation which in 1970 sold it to the National Park Service.

Hank Johnson's Death Valley Scotty *(Corona del Mar, 1974) is an informative picture book.*

Edward Wyllis Scripps

(1854-1926). At the age of 36 Scripps retired from his midwestern newspaper interests to develop his Miramar ranch north of the broken-down boomtown of San Diego. A cartoon of the day shows the profits of journalism being shipped west to the ranch where the absentee lord of the press lived for 30 years. The Scrippses were a large and contentious family of journalists, so numerous that middle initials were a necessity rather than a formality. The youngest of his father's thirteen children, E.W. grew up on an Illinois farm, discovering at an early age that he could use his brains to put other men's hands to work. He started out working on his brother's *Detroit Evening News*, but soon split off to establish his own *Cleveland Penny Press*, notable for avoiding the rabid political partisanship of contemporary journalism. Scripps was bold, imaginative, and restless, something of a radical, a social Darwinist, and a hypochondriac. At Miramar, which he expanded from 400 to 2,000 acres, he experimented with crops and with his children, directing their education and turning management of ranch personnel over to his sons as each in turn reached fifteen. He also expanded his newspaper network (then the Scripps-McRae League, later Scripps-Howard) into California, founding or buying the *San Diego Sun* in 1893, the *Los Angeles Record* in 1895, the *San Francisco News* in 1903, the *Sacramento Star* in 1904, the *Berkeley Independent* in 1907, the *Oakland Mail* in 1909. The advertisement-less San Francisco paper was an experiment which Scripps later repealed with the *Chicago Day Book*, for he believed in the primacy of the editorial department over business as well as politics. His other acquisitions were classified as "cheap afternoon papers for the masses," for Scripps was prolabor in an era when other newspapers were still writing about "the servant problem." Pessimistic and altruistic at the same time, he liked to say that he wanted "to make it harder for the rich to grow richer and easier for the poor to keep from growing poorer." Practicing what he preached, he would put up the capital for his newspapers, take 51 percent of the stock, and endow a hand-picked staff with the remaining 49 percent to sink or swim by their own efforts. Scripps discovered early that eccentricity was useful in evading antagonism. He said that he lived at his remote ranch to avoid the society of other rich men. (Miramar, by the way, was named after the Adriatic palace of the Archduke Maximilian, whose dreams of Mexican empire ended before a firing squad.) It was certainly remote (Scripps built his own road into San Diego, which later became the public highway) but unquestionably a working ranch. **Lincoln Steffens**, who dropped in for a visit with **Clarence Darrow**, really trying to raise money for the **McNamara** defense, described the ranch as "a good place to rest, except that E.W. Scripps did not care for rest." His wide-ranging intellectual inquiries gave rise to the Scripps Institution on Biological Research which in 1924 became the Scripps Institution of Oceanography. In 1920, after breaking with his eldest son James, who retained control of the Scripps Pacific Coast papers (later the Scripps-Canfield League), E.W. took to his yacht for the rest of his life. Almost as remarkable as E.W., her half-brother whom she called Eddy, was **Ellen Browning Scripps** (1836-1932), teacher, confidante, and banker. A working journalist for 21 years, she loaned him the money to buy Miramar, invested in his papers, and helped endow the Scripps Institution. Her other many benefactions included Scripps College in Claremont, which opened in 1927, the first U.S. college teaching ancient history to freshmen and working up to modern history for seniors. Like E.W., who was buried at sea after his death off the west coast of Africa, Ellen Scripps had her ashes scattered over the Pacific Ocean.

A selection of disquisitions by E.W. Scripps was published posthumously as Damned Old Crank *(1951). See also Negley Cochran's biography,* E.W. Scripps *(New York, 1933) and Albert Britt's biography of* Ellen B. Scripps *(Oxford, 1960).*

Glenn Theodore Seaborg

(1912-   ). Born in Michigan of Swedish ancestry, the Nobel prize-winning chemist grew up in the L.A. subdivision of South Gate. He worked his way through UCLA as a summer chemist for Firestone Tire and Rubber, then earned his Ph.D. at UC Berkeley (1937), remaining there to study radio isotopes created by **Ernest Lawrence**'s cyclotrons. On 23 February 1941 in Gilman Hall (later a National Historic Landmark), Seaborg officially discovered the element plutonium. He is also credited with codiscovering several more transuranium elements (including berkelium, element number 97, and californium, 98) for which he and Edwin McMillan shared the 1951 Nobel Prize. In the politics of science Seaborg was a moderate. He was considered a protegé of the conservative Lawrence but avoided open confrontation with **J. Robert Oppenheimer** and the liberal conscience. Thanks to the new international prestige and importance of atomic science, he was promoted in 1958 to chancellor of the university where he had earned his doctorate. And in 1961 Seaborg began a decade as chairman of the Atomic Energy Commission. In the early days of the New Frontier, when nuclear energy seemed to promise a new era of human achievement, Seaborg was the white knight of atoms for peace. Later, when disenchantment set in, it would be recalled that during World War II he developed the plutonium separation process yielding fissionable material for the bomb dropped on Nagasaki.

Man and Atom, *which Seaborg coauthored with William Corliss (New York, 1971), is a basic primer for the brave new world of nuclear energy.*

Bobby Seale (Robert George Seale, 1937-   ). Seale grew up in a government project building in Oakland, dreaming of a life of freedom in the Berkeley hills. He went through a period of infatuation with Indian lore, tramping the countryside in moccasins, armed with a tomahawk made in shop class. Trying to run away to the Pine Ridge (South Dakota) Indian reservation, "Nigger Tarzan," as the neighborhood kids called him, got only as far as the Sierra Nevada. Later, the U.S. Air Force sent him to South Dakota, curing him forever of that fantasy. In his autobiography, Seale described the murderous rages that were to earn him a bad-conduct discharge from the service. Back at Merritt Junior College in Oakland, he met **Huey Newton** and in 1966 cofounded the Black Panther Party, acting out his fury in armed confrontations with the white oppressor. ("A pig was downed, another wounded," he wrote. "It was our signal that shot around the country: Oakland, California, was on the map for sure.") He also seems to have enjoyed the favors of many Panther sisters, who vied with one another to sexually service their leaders. Arrested as one of the Chicago 7 at the 1968 Democratic

Convention, Seale turned the courtroom into a psychodrama, provoking Judge Julius Hoffman to have him bound and gagged. The ultimate status, however, was his trial in Connecticut for murdering an informer. The Chicago and Connecticut charges were eventually dismissed. In 1973 Seale ran for mayor of Oakland on a neo-Harding platform of a chicken in every pot, giving away free groceries and health tests. Defeated, he drifted out of the limelight, a sometime jazz musician and suicide-prevention therapist.

A Lonely Rage; The Autobiography of Bobby Seale *(New York, 1978).*

David O[liver] Selznick (1902-1965). In the dynastic scheme of twentieth-century Hollywood, the marriage of David Selznick to **Louis B. Mayer**'s daughter Irene in 1930 was the equivalent of a union of Montagues and Capulets. Selznick was the son of a dispossessed and exiled satrap, Lewis J. Selznick, who as a studio executive had been considered so unpredictable and erratic that he was forced out of power by such cronies as Mayer. Nurtured on a stab-in-the-back legend, David and his older brother Myron both grew up to lead irregular, obsessive, hedonistic lives. Myron Selznick became Hollywood's first cutthroat agent, holding his father's enemies to ransom for the services of star clients. David Selznick (he added the "O" for euphony, then extended it to Oliver) became a custom manufacturer of highly polished film projects. After

making such film classics as *A Star is Born* (1937) and *Gone With the Wind* (1939) he became obsessed with fear that he had passed his peak. This became a self-fulfilling prophecy. Selznick produced *Rebecca* (1940) and *Spellbound* (1945) during the war, then spent his last years liquidating his assets to acquire vehicles for his second wife, Jennifer Jones, whom he married in 1949. The plump, bespectacled producer was known around town for his grandiose lifestyle (servants on duty around the clock) and for his verbose memos. Art Buchwald called him the greatest memo writer in the industry.

Rudy Behlmer edited *Memo from David O. Selznick (New York, 1972) and Bob Thomas wrote a biography,* Selznick *(Garden City, NY, 1970).* David O. Selznick's Hollywood, *written and "produced" by Ronald Haver (London, 1980) is a high-gloss, expensive picture book.*

Sepúlveda Family. From the Spanish land barons down through the generations to a **Hearst** gossip columnist, theirs is a name intimately bound up with the history and geography of Southern California. José Andrés Sepúlveda (1803-1875), the third generation of his family in California, presided over the 48,000-acre Rancho San Joaquin stretching from the hills to the sea at San Juan Capistrano. One of the richest Californios of his day, he was a romantic, picturesque figure, elegantly dressed and generous to the point of recklessness. During the 1830s he became known as "Defender of the Faith" for his opposition to interfaith

Verdes Sepúlvedas managed to keep their rancho largely intact until the Depression, but eventually all the Sepúlveda land was subdivided and the descendants assimilated, their name remembered chiefly for the boulevard stretching thirty miles from San Fernando to San Pedro. A latter-day Sepúlveda, Ygnacio's daughter Conchita, married into the Italian nobility and became a Hearst gossip columnist, enjoying the hospitality of her boss at San Simeon as Princess Pignatelli.

The Pacific Coast Archaeological Society issued a Special Sepulveda Rancho Number, Vol. 5 (July 1969).

Junípero Serra (Miguel José Serra, 1713-1784). Serra was a Franciscan friar and scholar from Majorca, a small but indomitable missionary who traveled to Mexico in 1749 in search of new spiritual worlds to conquer. During twenty years in Mexico he dreamed of a string of missions extending into Alta (Northern) California, little enclaves of Christianity and agriculture. The expulsion of the Jesuits from Baja California in 1767 opened the way. Pushing north into "virgin" territory, Serra founded the Mission San Diego in 1769. The following year, after Governor **Gaspar de Portolá** failed to locate Monterey (first identified by Vizcaíno in 1602), Serra with his sure instinct for the new land guided the party there to establish a second mission (later moved to Carmel). During seventeen years in California the Franciscan leader had to contend with hunger, Indian attacks, and

marriage, but in 1846 he supported the American conquest. José Andrés was above all a passionate horseman who kept his mounts separated by color— blacks in one corral, sorrel in another—and won the most famous horse race of the day, defeating **Pío Pico's** Sarco with his Black Swan in 1852 for a prize of $25,000 in gold. The Sepúlvedas were numerous and well-connected. José Andrés's brother Fernando married into the Verdugo family, and two of his cousins owned the 31,000-acre Palos Verdes Rancho, operating a stage line from San Pedro to L.A. on the side. José Andrés's daughters all married Yankees and his sons, educated in the East, rose to prominence under the new regime. Andronico Sepúlveda became L.A. county auditor, while Ygnacio (1842-1916), a lawyer and judge, was appointed American chargé d'affaires in Mexico City. After José Andrés lost his Rancho San Joaquin to debt (it was sold in 1864 for $18,000), he set off on a last cattle drive to join his son in Mexico, where he died. The Palos the recalcitrance of Spanish military commanders who failed to share his dream. (Nor did he share theirs: when the Spanish crown imposed a tax to finance war against England, Serra remarked wryly on the astonishment of his Indians, who "themselves had such good and such frequent success in killing one another without any pesos.") Matters came to a head in 1772, when Serra returned to Mexico to petition for the removal of military commander Pedro Fages. It should be noted that Serra also feuded with Fages's successors and that he also had difficulties ("pious machinations") with less dedicated Franciscan brothers. Serra's greatest accomplishment, according to biographer Omen Englebert, "was to have made his fellow workers heroes in spite of themselves." Unquestionably a zealot, Serra was given to scourging and other forms of self-abnegation. He insisted on walking great distances despite a seriously ulcerated leg, the result of a scorpion bite in Mexico. From his headquarters at Carmel, he limped up and down El Camino Real, bringing cattle and bells to celebrate the creation of each new link in the chain of missions. The ninth and last mission personally consecrated by Serra was San Buenaventura, in 1779. After his death and burial at Carmel Mission he became an object of great veneration to latter-day Californians, some of whom campaigned for his canonization.

Works on Serra are so extensive as to merit a bibliography, California's Serrano Literature *(n.p., 1969) by Francis Weber, according to whom* The Last of the Conquistadores, Junípero Serra *(New York, 1956) by Omer Englebert is authoritative despite some errors in translation.*

John Serrano, Jr.

(1960-   ). The most significant U.S. educational ruling since the 1954 prohibition of school segregation was handed down by the California Supreme Court in 1971 in response to an East Los Angeles social worker seeking a better education for his son. John Serrano filed suit in 1968, charging that Baldwin Park where his son, John, Jr., was in the second grade, had a budget of only $600 per student per year, compared to $1200 in affluent Beverly Hills. Such a disparity, caused by variations in the property tax base, gave an unfair educational advantage to children living in wealthy neighborhoods, Serrano argued. The state Supreme Court agreed, ruling the property-tax basis of school financing to be unconstitutional. In 1976 the U.S. Supreme Court upheld the ruling with significant implications for property-tax-financed school districts all over the U.S. (Because funds to equalize educational spending would have to come from the state, New Jersey, for one, was prompted to institute its first state income tax.) In California, the governor signed a "Serrano compliance package" in 1977, establishing formulae to equalize school district expenditures. In the decade after the filing of the Serrano case, however, the focus of

educational protest shifted radically. In 1978 John Serrano, Sr. made the news as an antibusing advocate, while John, Jr., a six-foot four-inch letterman and honors graduate of Wilson High School, was enrolling at UC San Diego.

William Sharon

(1820?-1885). Sharon was a villain of the Comstock era, a daring investor who ruined others by his stock market manipulations, bought his way into the U.S. Senate, and got his just deserts at the hands of a southern belle who sued him for adultery. Born in Ohio and graduated from Athens College, he studied law before joining the Gold Rush to San Francisco. He made and lost one fortune in the Comstock, whereupon **William Ralston** gave him a chance to recoup as Virginia City agent of the Bank of California. Under Sharon's shrewd management, the Bank proceeded to extract millions of dollars worth of ore from the mountains. In 1872 Sharon ran against **John Jones** for Nevada's U.S. Senate seat, hoping to win by ruining Jones financially. Jones survived and won, so Sharon tried again in 1874 (against **Adolf Sutro**), recouping his enormous campaign expenses by further stock manipulations. He was elected but chalked up a new absentee record for the U.S. Senate, failing to attend sessions five of his six years (1875-1881) in office. Sharon sold Ralston short, too, then picked up the spoils after Ralston's suicide. It was with a certain vicarious pleasure, therefore, that San Francisco

observed Sharon's trials at the hands of Sarah Althea Hill, who in 1883 charged him with adulterous violations of an alleged secret marriage contract. After a six-month trial, during which Hill's attorney branded Sharon a financial and erotic giant but an intellectual and moral pygmy, the judge ruled the marriage contract valid. The ruling was eventually overturned after Sharon's death and after years in the courts and a host of subsidiary suits. Her hopes destroyed and her "second" husband, **David Terry**, killed in the act of defending her honor, Sarah Hill spent her last years in the Stockton asylum. But her legal trials against Sharon left an enduring body of precedent, later cited in such disparate events as **Harry Bridges**'s World War II citizenship difficulties and President Harry Truman's 1952 seizure of steel mills.

Robert Kroninger's Sarah and the Senator *(Berkeley, 1964) has an immortal opening: "On Saturday, September 8, 1883, former U.S. Senator William Sharon's accustomed afternoon repose was interrupted by his arrest on a charge of adultery."*

Frank Shaw (1877-1958). The recall movement originated in Los Angeles, the first major U.S. city to remove its mayor from office. Arthur C. Harper resigned in 1909 in the midst of recall proceedings (prompted by allegations of vice protection) and Shaw was recalled in 1938. Elected in 1933 over the opposition of the *Los Angeles Times*, which cast aspersions on his citizenship because he was born in Canada, "the mysterious Mr. Shaw" was a former wholesale grocery salesman with a crippled arm. Safely ensconced in his $10,000-a-year office during the depths of the Depression, "Hizzoner"

handed out keys to the city, put his brother Joe on the payroll as "private secretary," and generally watched out for his friends. He also reappointed a *Times* favorite as police chief and acquired for L.A.'s civic center a piece of *Times* property at four times its assessed valuation. Reform-minded citizens soon banded together in CIVIC—Citizens' Independent Vice Investigating Committee—to uncover graft in hospital administration, on the harbor commission, and elsewhere in the Shaw administration. The chief crusader for clean government was Clifford Clinton, a cafeteria owner of Salvation Army parentage. Clinton's revelations of mayoral corruption aroused little concern until a 1938 bombing attack on his home and another against his chief investigator, in which the police were implicated. Shaw, who had been re-elected in 1937 with *Times* support, was recalled a year later. He and his police chief went into early retirement, although his brother Joe continued to figure prominently in graft investigations for years. It has long been an article of faith among local historians that the overthrow of the Shaw machine drove the mob to abandon L.A. for Las Vegas. A revisionist historian now claims that the good guys were the bad guys and vice versa—that Clinton staged those bomb attacks and was financed by the mob, while Shaw was a benevolent New Deal supporter who brought the city $100 million in federal funds. To be continued, for sure.

Fred Viehe argues the revisionist case

in "The Los Angeles Political Machine," California History, *(Winter 1980-81).*

Millard Sheets (1907-   ). If the Masonic temples of California seem to look like banks and the banks like Masonic temples, it could be because the same man designed both in the same style. Sheets, a member of a Pomona ranching family, was a precocious and enterprising artist who by the age of 24 was already in charge of the art exhibit at the L.A. County Fair (itself started by one of his uncles). In 1929 he had his first exhibit in Los Angeles, showing paintings of California as seen by a native rather than a tourist, with a little help stylistically from Franz Marc and Paul Gauguin. Educator as well as artist, he became the head of the Scripps College art department (1931-1954) and director of the **Otis** Art Institute in L.A. (1954-1962). As a young man Sheets did sketches for architects. He also experimented with wall murals, the idea being to render the austere International style of architecture more palatable to the masses by embellishing it. In the 1950s banker **Howard Ahmanson** invited him to design first an office building and eventually 40 branches for Home Savings & Loan, all in the same monolithic style featuring grand and gaudy mosaic murals. (A political and economic conservative, the architect found some comfort in the fact that his new bank buildings soon paid for themselves in increased deposits.) Sheets's other creations include the official

seal of Los Angeles County and Scottish-rite Masonic temples in Los Angeles and San Francisco. In 1960 he moved north to Mendocino County.

Sheets is the subject of a two-volume study by the UCLA Oral History Program, The Los Angeles Art Community: Group Portrait *(Los Angeles, 1977).*

Moses Hazeltine Sherman (1853-1932). "The street-railway magnate of Los Angeles," Sherman was primarily interested in railroads as a means to sell land. He was a New Englander who moved to Arizona for his health in 1873 and rose to superintendent of public instruction and adjutant general of the sparsely populated territory before moving on to the Pacific Coast in 1889. Buying up existing franchises and fragments of electric railway lines, "General" Sherman put together the first interurban network in the L.A. basin along lines that prefigure the development of the freeway

system. He ran his first trolley to Santa Monica in 1896, then completed a line to Pasadena, linking the mountains with the sea. He also bought and subdivided land along the way, delivering prospective customers by rail into the hands of real estate promoters. After selling his railroads to **Henry Huntington** in 1901, Sherman participated with **Harry Chandler** and the local Republican old guard in several ventures: the Los Angeles Steamship Company, the Yosemite tourist concession, the Tejon Ranch, and extensive ranching interests in the Imperial Valley and Baja California. Their biggest coup took place in L.A.'s San Fernando Valley. Taking advantage of inside information acquired by Sherman as a member of L.A.'s Board of Water Commissioners about the planned Owens River aqueduct which would greatly enhance land values at its southern terminus, they bought and later sold the land at great profit. Personally, Sherman has been described as a "minor regional capitalist," loud, commanding, and somewhat eccentric. Divorced, he lived in the Westminster Hotel for 35 years, a familiar downtown figure in the full-length greatcoats he wore to ward off drafts. He left his name on the landscape (Sherman Oaks, Sherman Way, and Hazeltine Avenue named for his daughter); his multi-million-dollar fortune to USC, Pomona College, and Cal Tech; and his papers to a personal foundation in Corona del Mar.

William Tecumseh Sherman (1820-1891).

The Civil War general who declared that war is hell got an early experience of it in San Francisco during the reign of the second Vigilance Committee. Then an adjutant, Sherman arrived in 1847 during the American conquest, saw action chiefly as a surveyor, and observed enough of the country to realize that an ambitious young man lacking independent means might do well here. He therefore resigned from the army in 1853 to settle in San Francisco as a partner in a banking firm. When civic disturbances broke out three years later, Governor **J. Neely Johnson** appointed Sherman major-general in charge of the state militia in hopes of putting an end to vigilante rule. But the governor had little stature or means of enforcing his authority, the militia lacked arms and credibility, and the Vigilance Committee did pretty well as it pleased. Sherman was not notably

successful as a banker and his wife loathed San Francisco, so the Civil War offered him a welcome respite from civilian life. Considered one of the greatest generals of the war, he was later mentioned as a possible presidential candidate. Having also acquired in California a lifelong hatred of politics, Sherman declined emphatically and memorably: "If nominated I will not accept; if elected I will not serve." On a trip west during the 1870s he was fêted as a long-lost native son at a Palace Hotel banquet.

Sherman's Memoirs *(New York, 1957) contain picturesque glimpses of old California. See also Dwight L. Clarke,* William T. Sherman, Gold Rush Banker *(San Francisco, 1969) and Robert Athearn,* William T. Sherman and the Settlement of the West *(Norman, OK, 1956).*

Robert Pierce Shuler (1880-1965).

A radio preacher in Roaring Twenties L.A., "Fighting Bob" Shuler became a holy terror to the establishment, unseating a mayor, a D.A., and a police chief. Transferred in 1920 from the rural Midwest to Trinity Methodist Church in downtown Los Angeles, he upheld smalltown pieties against big-city sin. Jealous of his religious authority, he fulminated against the teaching of evolution at Cal Tech and acted as a self-appointed bowdlerizing Anthony Comstock in policing the morals of his clerical rivals, **Aimee Semple McPherson** in particular. (Other targets included the Automobile Club of Southern California and the Uplifters Club.) Shuler owned his own

radio station, KGEF, a gift from a wealthy admirer, which at its peak claimed 600,000 listeners. He enlisted a corps of "sin-spies," private detectives in the Lord's service, and broadcast their findings on the **Asa Keyes** payoff and other scandals. Making a bid for national influence, Shuler wrote a pamphlet on *The Un-American Activities of Al Smith*, and in 1932 was nearly elected to the U.S. Senate. But that year he lost his appeal for renewal of his radio license, which the old Federal Radio Commission had revoked on charges of sensationalism and the broadcasting of erroneous information. Shuler ran again for Congress in 1942, this time losing to **Jerry Voorhis**. He remained head of Trinity Methodist until his retirement in 1953, when he was succeeded by his son.

Bugsy Siegel (Benjamin Siegel, 1906-1947). The day after his death, Siegel became the feature attraction on the Beverly Hills movie-star-map circuit: "See Where the Crown Prince of the Mafia was Murdered!" A racketeer from New York's "Jewish mob," he arrived in California after the repeal of Prohibition to assume a new lifestyle. He built a white brick mansion in Beverly Hills, joined the Hillcrest Country Club, and was seen around town with the Countess Dorothy Taylor DiFrasso, a society thrill-seeker. So vain over his good looks that he slept with a chin strap, he used to visit his friend George Raft at the studios, flirting with the idea of being "discovered." The pretense of respectability evaporated in 1940 when Siegel was jailed in connection with a gangland murder. He was treated as a celebrity prisoner, however, enjoying frequent outside excursions, ostensibly to the dentist, before the indictment was dropped. During World War II he branched out from bookmaking to salvage metal; after the war, he became obsessed with the idea of erecting a Hollywood-style gambling paradise in a little desert town just over the Nevada line. Siegel's Flamingo Hotel opened in December 1946, the first of the glittering gambling dens to put Las Vegas on the map. But it was built at great cost, and there was an initial run of gambling losses. Siegel was visiting L.A. to placate the money men when he was assassinated in his girlfriend Virginia Hill's rented house on Linden Drive in Beverly Hills

We Only Kill Each Other (Englewood Cliffs, N.J, 1967) by Dean Jennings is the only biography available, and Jennings's sources in the underworld are not well known for veracity.

Norton Winfred Simon

(1907-   ). Simon represents a variation on the eccentric California millionaire industrialist, a businessman on the model of megalomaniac **W.R. Hearst** or loner **Howard Hughes** rather than Carnegie or Rockefeller. Born in Oregon and raised in San Francisco, he dropped out of the University of California, bored with professorial pedantry, to go into business. In 1931 he bought a bankrupt bottling company in Fullerton, built it up to annual sales of $9 million, sold it to Hunt Brothers Packing Company, then turned around and took over Hunt in his first major coup. Over the years Simon's industrial empire came to include such brand names as Wesson, Canada Dry, Johnny Walker, and *McCall's*. Appointed in 1960 to the UC Board of Regents by his old classmate **Pat Brown**, Simon began to diversify his intellectual interests. In 1964 he bought the famous Duveen collection of old masters which became the basis of an impressive art collection. Divorced in the late 1960s, retired at 62, and saddened by the suicide of a son, he went through a delayed and highly public midlife crisis. In 1970 he spent an estimated $2 million in a fruitless grab for the Republican U.S. Senate nomination. Remarried in 1971 to actress Jennifer Jones and installed in a luxurious Malibu beachhouse, he began wheeling and dealing in the art world as he once had in business, revealing the full force of an abrasive personality hitherto confined to board rooms.

Simon had earlier withdrawn his art collection from the Los Angeles County Museum of Art because he felt it was handled improperly. In 1974 he acquired his own private showcase, the financially troubled Pasadena Art Museum, by assuming a large indebtedness which was still only a fraction of the museum's worth. Complaints immediately began to fly: Simon was neglecting the museum's modern collection, its *raison d'être*, in favor of

his old masters; Simon couldn't get along with his curators; Simon refused to loan pieces from the Pasadena collection, and was selling works donated by artists or collectors. In other words, Simon was playing the market, and the art public be damned. At last report, the controversy in Pasadena was so intense that Simon was threatening to pack up his canvases and move them to San Francisco.

Upton Beall Sinclair

(1878-1968). Author of *The Jungle* (1906) and several score other novels on socio-economic themes, Sinclair moved to Pasadena in 1916 for the climate. Described by H.L. Mencken as a "sunkist utopian," he favored women's rights, followed fad diets, vacationed in single-tax colonies, and flirted with

psychic phenomena. During 50 years in California he was a member of the Pasadena local of the U.S. Socialist Party, a founder of the California branch of the ACLU, and several times a candidate for state office. Pasadena's seventh-ranking tennis player, Sinclair was an enthusiastic Californian, perennially boyish and

optimistic. After the Bolshevik Revolution, he recommended exile of the czar to Catalina Island—because of its salubrious climate and population of sheep, he explained, "proper subjects for autocracy." He set one of his best novels in California, *Oil!* (1927), inspired by the Signal Hill strike. (When *Oil!* was banned in Boston for sexual explicitness, the enterprising author printed a "fig-leaf edition" and sold the book on the streets wearing a figleaf-shaped sandwich board.) Another novel inspired by local events, *The Story of a Patriot*, about the **Mooney** case, seems to have vanished. In 1934 he campaigned to "End Poverty in California" (EPIC) as the Democratic candidate for governor. Sheridan Downey was the EPIC candidate for lieutenant governor, making a team known as "Uppie" and "Downie." An estimated $10 million was spent to defeat Sinclair as a radical revolutionary threat to the established order. "This is not politics," a Republican newspaper announced. "It is war." Hollywood in particular took Sinclair very seriously, warning that his tax theories would kill the movie industry. Thanks to propaganda photos and film of hoboes (actually movie extras) flocking to the new poverty-free paradise, Sinclair lost the bitterly contested election.

See Sinclair's Autobiography *(New York, 1962) and Leon Harris,* Upton Sinclair; American Rebel *(New York, 1973). Education professor Robert Hahn publishes an* Upton Sinclair Quarterly, *"Uppie Speaks," in L.A.*

Sirhan Bishara Sirhan
(1944-   ). "Mama, are we going to be blonde very soon?" thirteen-year-old Sirhan asked when his family settled in Pasadena in 1957, their emigration from Palestine sponsored by the local First Nazarene Church. Sirhan's father soon returned to the Middle East after a dispute over his paternal authority, leaving his wife and six children to fend for themselves. Within the pleasant white frame house on East Howard Street, theirs was an old-world family life; outside, however, was a whole exciting but confusing society. One brother was arrested for the attempted murder of his girlfriend who had broken up with him; another spent nine months in juvenile correction for possession and sale of marijuana; Aida, the only sister, died a painful death of leukemia in 1965. Sirhan, who lost two grades in emigrating, graduated from John Muir High School at nineteen, a quiet, polite, well-read boy who did odd jobs to help his family. He enrolled in Pasadena City College but was dismissed for poor grades and erratic attendance. He tried to become a jockey but was injured in a fall while working as an exercise boy. Small and dark, he was frequently mistaken for a Chicano, which didn't improve his job prospects. Inwardly seething with frustrated ambition and anger, unable to secure the status that even a high school education would have guaranteed in the Middle East, he began to explore political and spiritual alternatives. The Black Muslims turned him away for not being dark enough; the Rosicrucians were more gracious but a little too esoteric. Torn between two worlds, Sirhan remained an Arab nationalist while consuming Big Boy hamburgers, Tom Collins cocktails and Muriel Perfectas. He had his first girl at a drive-in movie in the backseat of his 1958 De Soto, which he longed to trade in for a new Mustang, but he kept his Jordanian nationality. Then he saw a *Pasadena Independent* photograph of Robert F. Kennedy in a yarmulke addressing a Jewish congregation and heard on the radio (KFWB, the "All News") that Kennedy wanted to send 50 bombers to Israel. The rest is history. On the night of 5 June 1968 Sirhan shot and mortally wounded Kennedy, also wounding five bystanders with his bullets, in the pantry of the Ambassador Hotel, where a victory party was being held after the California presidential primary. At his trial, while his lawyers tried to argue a defense of diminished (mental) responsibility, Sirhan clung to the dignity of political assassination and dreamed of making a deal with the U.S. State Department to return home to Palestine as a hero. Convicted of first-degree murder, he was reprieved by the abolition of the death penalty in California. A scheduled 1984 parole date was cancelled after 1982 hearings.

"R.F.K. Must Die!" by Robert Blair Kaiser (New York, 1970) is a detailed account of the assassination by a writer who worked on Sirhan's defense team. Why Robert Kennedy Was Killed (New York, 1970) by Godfrey Jansen is a view from the third world. Truman Capote's suggestion that Sirhan was a Manchurian candidate, programmed to kill, is developed in fiction form in Donald Freed's The Killing of RFK (New York, 1975).

C[onrad] Arnholt Smith
(1899-   ). Smith was a hometown good old boy—a member of the Florence School baseball team and the San Diego High School rowing team—a free-wheeling entrepreneur whose financial empire collapsed spectacularly in 1973. In 1933, with a down payment of only $10, he took over the financially distressed U.S. National Bank of San Diego, which became the centerpiece of his Westgate-California conglomerate. Later he acquired National Iron Works, which built tuna clippers, plus a prestige canning label under which to market the catch. In the 1950s Smith switched from shipbuilding to pro sports, picking up the San Diego Padres baseball team. Along the way he also bought a radio station, cab companies, real estate, and agribusiness interests. Ever onward and

upward, he erected a 25-story bank building in 1963 and in 1970 opened the Westgate Plaza Hotel. He enjoyed a luxurious lifestyle in La Jolla and Palm Springs, and sampled the hospitality of **Nixon**'s White House. The *Wall Street Journal* had indicated flaws in his empire as early as 1969, and in 1973, USNB became the biggest bank failure in U.S. history, with $400 million outstanding in questionable loans to Smith companies. *Penthouse* magazine ran an exposé of Smith's ties with the Teamsters and *Forbes* nominated him for swindler of the century. Adding injury to insult, the IRS hit the former "Mr. San Diego" with its largest claim ever against an individual, and he was convicted of illegal campaign contributions to his friend **Richard Nixon**. In 1979 he was sentenced to three years for state income tax evasion but remained free on appeal.

Gladys Smith. *See* Mary Pickford.

Jedediah Strong Smith (1799-1831). The first American to reach California overland from the East, Smith created instant consternation when he arrived at Mission San Gabriel in late 1826. A trapper and trader who during eight years in the West "paid his way in beaver," he was also seeking the Buenaventura River, a nonexistent route from the Rockies to the Pacific Ocean. Although Spanish authorities were becoming accustomed to Yankee trading ships, they sensed instinctively that the

bearded trappers posed a threat to the Californio way of life. (Happily oblivious to the profit motive, unable to comprehend the hunt for beaver, the Spaniards translated Smith's occupation as "fishing.") Smith was refused permission to continue north from San Gabriel, but he went anyway. He even left a group of his men camped on the Stanislaus River for a season while he crossed the Sierra Nevada to rendezvous with his partners at Bear Lake on the present Utah-Idaho border. On his return trip to California Smith was detained while Governor José María Echeandía pondered what to do with him. As there were no ships convenient to take the trapper to trial in Mexico, he was finally allowed to sell his beaver and outfit his men for an overland exit. At the end of 1827 Smith's party made its way through the San Joaquin Valley and along the

Northern California coast, where a stand of redwoods was later named for him, to the Columbia River. Not long afterwards, the intrepid trapper was killed by Indians on the Santa Fe Trail.
Dale Morgan's Jedediah Smith and the Opening of the West *(New York, 1953) is practically ancient history by California standards.*

Francisco Solano (?-1858). He was a chieftain of the Soscol and Suisun tribes, at six-feet-seven-inches, a monument of a man. Defeated in battle by **Mariano Vallejo**, he was converted to Christianity and his name was changed from Sem Yeto (mighty arm) to Solano after a Catholic saint. He became Vallejo's ally and chief lieutenant in pacifying the northern frontier. Prince Solano, as Vallejo called him, once accompanied his master to Monterey, arousing awe and fear in the populace there. He learned to speak Spanish well and was considered a skillful debater. The Suisunes were hit by a smallpox epidemic in 1838, leaving only 200 survivors out of 40,000 and Solano a prince without a people. Soon after the Bear Flag Revolt and Vallejo's capture by the Yankees, Solano disappeared. He wandered through Oregon and Washington north to British Columbia for twelve years, returning home only to die. A monument at his grave in Fairfield was later moved to the city of Suisun.

John Sontag (John Contant, 1862-1893). *See* **Christopher Evans**.

Phil Spector (1940-   ). Spector was a Los Angeles boy who broke into the

recording industry at eighteen by writing a hit song about his father, "To Know Him Is to Love Him." By the time he was 21, the "first tycoon of teen," as pop historian Tom Wolfe labeled him, had made his first million and created his own record company to produce, record, and distribute rock 'n' roll. Spector's trademark was a heavily overdubbed, almost Wagnerian "wall of sound" behind his vocal groups, the Crystals, the Ronettes, and the Righteous Brothers. Their biggest hits include "Spanish Harlem" (1960) and "You've Lost That Lovin' Feeling" (1964). A rebel against the corporate recording establishment, Spector became the archetype of the music producer as a Hollywood-type celebrity. In the late 1960s, when rock 'n' roll began to wane, he dropped out for a few years, returning as a producer on Beatles projects. He played a cameo role as a drug dealer in the film *Easy Rider* (1969)

and inspired the electronic maestro of *Phantom of the Paradise* (1974). Temperamental and reclusive, he acquired a highly fortified 40-room Spanish mansion in the Hollywood Hills.

See Tom Wolfe's Kandy-Kolored Tangerine-Flake Streamline Baby *(New York, 1963) and* Out of his Head; The Sound of Phil Spector *(New York, 1972) by Richard Williams.*

Spreckels Family. The founder of one of the liveliest dynasties in California history, Claus Spreckels (1828-1908) was a Prussian immigrant who opened a grocery store in San Francisco in 1856. Sugar brought around the Horn from New York was very expensive, so he built a refinery in the Salinas Valley to process local sugar beets. (The Salinas facility later became the largest of its kind in the world.) In 1876, when the annexation of Hawaii threatened to cut into his business there, Claus Spreckels went out to the islands and returned with the

Hawaiian king, it was said, in his pocket. Later, a deal with his principal East Coast sugar rival gave him a monopoly on the West Coast. Claus Spreckels had four sons, three of whom figured importantly in California history. John Diedrich Spreckels (1853-1926) was a dapper yachtsman who on an 1887 cruise "discovered" San Diego and set up his own little fiefdom there. In addition to a sugar refinery he built wharves, dams, the Hotel Coronado, and the city's transcontinental railroad link. His holdings also included two newspapers, the *San Diego Union* and the *San Francisco Call* (the latter acquired in John's name by his father to fight the annexation of Hawaii). Adolph Spreckels (1857-1924), the second son, ran the family business in San Francisco, building himself a block-long "sugar palace" in Pacific Heights. Late in life he married the free-spirited Alma de Bretteville (1881-1968), who claimed to have posed as a junoesque young art student for the Dewey Monument in Union Square. She gave San Francisco its Palace of the Legion of Honor, and for long years after her husband's death presided over his sugar palace and over local society, a salty old grande dame. The baby and rebel of the family, Rudolph Spreckels (1872-1958) made a fortune of his own in competition with his father. Tall and handsome in the florid family manner, he had a rather tiresome tendency to self-righteousness when it served his purposes. (He once testified in court that his parents were not

legally married.) After Claus Spreckels's death, John and Adolph contested his will and succeeded in having their younger brother largely disinherited. For the time being at least, Rudolph had enough money of his own to help finance (with **James Phelan**) the San Francisco graft investigations. For this his family and friends considered him a traitor to his class, and the local press caricatured him as "Emperor Rudolph" and "Rudolph Pickles." Something of a political faddist, he warned during the muckraking era of a day of reckoning for the rich; during World War I he declared himself a pacifist; and during the Depression, having lost his wealth, he became a follower of Father Charles Coughlin's cryptofascist National Union for Social Justice. When a local reporter found him living in an apartment in San Jose a few years before his death Rudolph Spreckels said that he preferred to think of himself as a "Mugwump."

*Three books which tell part of the Spreckels story—*Claus Spreckels, The Sugar King in Hawaii *by Jacob Adler (Honolulu, 1966);* The Man John D. Spreckels *by Austin Adams (San Diego, 1924); and* Rails of the Silver Gate *by Richard Dodge (San Marino, 1960)—are difficult to find. The family figures prominently in Stephen Birmingham's* California Rich *(New York, 1980)—at least as far as the third generation which chalked up twenty marriages, nineteen divorces, and not a single heir named Spreckels in the state.*

Robert Gordon Sproul
(1891-1975). As president of the University of California for 28 years, Sproul navigated through financial and political crises to achieve national academic recognition. Born in

San Francisco of Scots ancestry, he enrolled at UC Berkeley in 1909, joined a fraternity, became a drum major, and was elected president of his junior class. A year after graduating in engineering (1913), he returned as a cashier in the comptroller's office and advanced rapidly through the nonacademic ranks to become president in 1930. Sproul's first crisis was precipitated by legislature budget cutbacks during the Depression. An effective public speaker with the charm and looks of actor Robert Young, he campaigned up and down the state to get budget funds restored. Under Sproul the UC expanded from three to six campuses. To counter the separatist tendencies of the new southern branches, he brought statewide faculty together for annual "academic bonfire rallies." He also spent half his time on the road, a visible, personable symbol of the university. The major crisis of Sproul's administration was the McCarthy-era loyalty oath (suggested in California by **Jack Tenney**) that regents tried to impose on faculty in 1949. Outvoted by the regents and strenuously opposed by the faculty, Sproul sought a compromise to maintain university peace. There were resignations and lawsuits over the oath, declared unconstitutional in 1951, but Sproul's prestige kept the university intact. As the dean of American university presidents he enjoyed national standing. In 1948 he nominated former classmate **Earl Warren** as the

Republican presidential candidate. Several times during his long tenure Sproul turned down lucrative business and academic job offers to remain at the university, where he spent his entire life. During his presidency, UC enrollment increased from 19,000 to 47,000 annually. Among the growing body of alumni were Sproul's three children.

George A. Pettitt wrote 28 Years in the Life of a University President *(Berkeley, 1966).*

Leland Stanford (Amasa Leland Stanford, 1824-1893). At 268 pounds Stanford was the biggest and also the most politically prominent of the Big Four railroad barons. Born in New York and educated as a lawyer, he followed his five brothers west to Gold Rush California, where he opened a store and cofounded the state Republican Party in 1855. He ran unsuccessfully for governor in 1859 but was elected two years later on a Civil War platform of loyalty to the Union and Oriental exclusion. The state's first Republican chief executive, Stanford seemed completely oblivious to the conflict of interest involved in promoting government loans and land grants for his Southern Pacific Railroad (built, moreover, primarily by the despised Chinese coolies). Defeated for renomination, he retired to a life of conspicuous consumption as squire of a medieval fortress atop Nob Hill, a 9,000-acre thoroughbred ranch in Menlo Park, and a 55,000-acre vineyard in Northern California. (A pious Methodist, Stanford did not bet on his

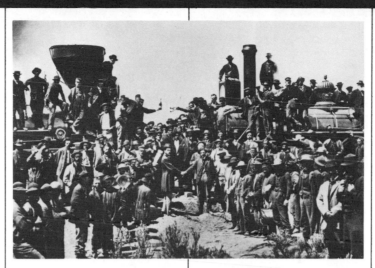

horses and claimed the wine would be used for medicinal purposes. The vineyard's product never rated high among connoisseurs anyway.) When their only son died on a grand tour of Europe in 1884, he and his wife, Jane Lathrop Stanford decided to endow a university in his name at the Menlo Park ranch, reasoning that any place so good for horses would also be good for students. At the time, with the new University of California just across the bay, there seemed about as much need for another school as for an asylum for sea captains in Switzerland, a New York editor remarked. Stanford was elected U.S. Senator in 1885 and in 1891, thanks to railroad connections, but devoted most of this time to establishing the Leland Stanford Junior University, which opened in 1891. Annoyed by his political presumption and by his obvious extravagance (impolitic in view of the railroad's campaign for relief from its debts), **Collis Huntington** brusquely

removed Stanford from the figurehead position of Southern Pacific president he had held for 28 years. When Stanford died in 1893, the railroad debt question was still unresolved, pending which the government seized all his assets. Jane Stanford sold her jewels to keep the new university going, and the probate court obliged by ruling that the faculty as "personal servants" could be paid. Six years later the U.S. Supreme Court released Stanford's $30 million fortune.

Norman Tutorow, Leland Stanford, Man of Many Careers *(Menlo Park, 1971), is the most recent biography.*

Sally Stanford (Mabel Marcia Busby Goodan Fansler Bayham Spagnoli Rapp Gump Kenna, 1903-1982). San Francisco's alltime best businesswoman, and after Alma **Spreckels** the city's wealthiest woman, was probably Stanford, the lady of a number of "houses" during the 1930s and 1940s. Born in Oregon, she married early to get away from home, and by

an unfortunate sequence of events was left with a felony record at sixteen. She married again and again. She admitted to "six to eight" husbands, trading up each time. But she doesn't seem to have needed her husbands. Alone, she possessed all the guts and drive and ingenuity to get what she really craved—class. She took her name from headlines of the Bay Area's annual Big Game one football season ("Stanford Wins"), and acquired a legendary chateau on Russian Hill on the eve of World War II. Originally built by Robert Hanford in 1907 for his inamorata, the house was transformed by Stanford into a bordello catering to the carriage trade. Her memoirs are conveniently vague about the specific nature of her business but quite insistent about having the best of everything, from colored maids in uniform and Beauty Rest mattresses to gourmet snacks. Her most famous house (also built by Hanford but for another mistress), at 1144 Pine on Nob Hill,

featured a glass-roofed Pompeian court, one whole floor designed as a hunting lodge, others decorated in period antiques, and a celebrated marble bathtub. Stanford went through a lot of San Francisco real estate: at one time she was running four houses, including one in Chinatown, as well as more conventional residences and apartment buildings. During World War II the Office of Price Administration got on her case for exceeding permissible rent ceilings in an elegant apartment house. She was also charged repeatedly with petty infractions related to her primary line of business. When she wasn't in trouble herself, the soft-hearted Stanford was going to bat for someone who was. She campaigned against the death penalty for red-light bandit **Caryl Chessman** and convicted murderess Barbara Graham, and opposed the shooting of deer in California. In 1950 she opened a successful restaurant in Sausalito, the Valhalla, and the following year made *Life* magazine after eloping to Reno with Robert **Gump**, of the jade family. Stanford ran for Sausalito's city council four times before she was finally elected in 1972. In 1976, the former madam became Madame the Mayor of the former pirate port at the other end of the rainbow from San Francisco.

Stanford wrote The Lady of the House *(New York, 1966), the basis of a TV movie with Dyan Cannon in the leading role. Curt Gentry devoted the final chapter of his* Madams of San Francisco *(New York, 1964) to Stanford, pinning down some of the facts on which she was understandably vague in her book.*

Abel Stearns (1798-1871). The few Anglos who made their way to California before U.S. statehood found it necessary to take out Mexican citizenship in order to marry or acquire land. Stearns, a Yankee of Jewish descent who arrived in Los Angeles in 1829, did this and more. By virtue of sharp wits and a judicious marriage, he rose and prospered in Spanish California society, the richest man of his day. Starting out as a shopkeeper, he won appointment as the city's first collector of customs. There were accusations of illegal dealings in contraband and two Mexican governors tried to deport him during the 1830s, but Stearns knew which strings to pull. Not a handsome man, he was called *caro de caballo*—"horseface". (Actually he looked rather like George Washington.) It was to avoid ridicule that he requested exemption from the usual public bans when at 43 he married the beautiful fourteen-year-old **Arcadia Bandini** (later **de Baker**). They set up

housekeeping in El Palacio, L.A.'s most imposing residence of the day, and drove around town in the city's first proper carriage, ordered from Boston for the young bride. Soon after his marriage Stearns acquired the 28,500-acre Los Alamitos ranch, which became the center of a land and cattle empire. He also built the Arcadia Block in L.A., the largest business establishment south of San Francisco. Profiting from the decline of the old rancho regime after statehood, Stearns put together a total of 200,000 acres plus thousands of "cattle of the plain" and hundreds of "gentle horses" before he in turn went broke, wiped out by the drought of the Civil War years. By 1864 his holdings filled two whole pages on the county delinquent tax list. Too proud to rent his pasture out for sheep grazing, the last of the dons was forced to subdivide and sell. His Los Angeles and San Bernardino Land Company became one of California's first high-pressure real-estate operations.

Stearns is probably the best-documented California person of his generation. His papers at the Huntington Library served as the basis for a biography, Yankee in Mexican California *by Doris M. Wright (Santa Barbara, 1977) and for social history of the era, Robert Glass Cleland's* Cattle on a Thousand Hills *(San Marino, 1941).*

Lincoln Steffens (Joseph Lincoln Steffens, 1866-1936). Steffens, whose family acquired the ornate Victorian house which later served as the California governor's mansion, enjoyed a boyhood right out of Tom Sawyer, exploring the Sacramento

Valley on horseback. After graduation from the University of California at Berkeley (a poor school, in his opinion) and three years in Europe studying the scientific bases of moral behavior, he became a well-tailored Wall Street reporter. His Socratic style of questioning prompted some unexpected answers, and Steffens went on to author the muckraking classic about civic corruption, *Shame of the Cities* (1904). Semi-retired at 44 thanks to an independent income, he became a roving reporter on issues and events of social conscience and consequence: the San Francisco graft trials, the bombing of the *L.A. Times*, and revolution in Mexico and Russia. ("I have seen the future," he said "and it works.") A rather effete figure with his moustache, Van Dyke beard, bangs, and pince-nez, he spent his last years in the Bohemian community of Carmel, a resident guru of the early twentieth century Left.

The Autobiography of Lincoln Steffens (New York, 1931) was a best-seller in its day. Justin Kaplan wrote Lincoln Steffens; A Biography *(New York, 1974).*

Gertrude Stein

(1874-1946). In 1880 the Stein family took the new railroad across the country from Baltimore to Oakland, where they settled into the old Stratton House, a ten-acre property with an orchard and a cow. Orphaned in 1891, the five children moved into a San Francisco apartment with Michael (1865-1938), the eldest, assuming his father's position in the Omnibus Cable Company. One of the Stein brothers, Simon, remained a San Francisco cable car gripman his whole life. Michael Stein, who traded up to vice-president of the Market Street Railway Company in 1893, sold out the family interest after the labor difficulties of 1901-1902

and joined his brother Leo and sister Gertrude in Paris, where they all became celebrated art collectors and Gertrude a world-renowned writer. In those days it was chic to be an American abroad, something that Gertrude Stein explored in her autobiographical ramblings. "No one was conscious of a grandfather and not held responsible for a father," she said of her California upbringing, which somehow exonerated her from the study of history and the observance of tradition in literature as in life. As a writer, she tried to do with words what the cubists were doing with paint. After 30 years in Europe, she made a single visit home to Oakland with her lifelong companion ("my 'yes' ") Alice Toklas, whose "autobiography" was Stein's best seller. "There's no there there," she remarked, finding the city considerably less interesting than her memory of it.

Janet Hobhouse, Everybody Who Was Anybody, a Biography of Gertrude Stein (New York, 1965) covers Stein's California years only briefly.

John Ernest Steinbeck

(1902-1968). The first Californian to win a Nobel Prize for literature, Steinbeck had by the time of the award in 1962 long since become an expatriate New Yorker. He was born in Salinas—"Lettuceberg" he would later call it—where his father worked for the **Spreckels** Company and was Monterey County treasurer for a decade. The family was culture-conscious, high church, and deeply concerned when Steinbeck spent several years dropping in and out of

Stanford University. After an unsuccessful first novel about pirates in the Caribbean, he began to write about more familiar people and places. With the publication of *Tortilla Flat* (1935) Steinbeck first came up against the Chamber of Commerce mentality that rejected his work as detrimental to tourism. *Cannery Row* (1945) would also be repudiated locally, an insult to civic pride, and *The Grapes of Wrath* (1939), the saga of Depression-era Okies in the San Joaquin Valley, was considered to be positively beyond the pale. To be sure, Steinbeck could be irritable in public, and his humor was not improved by marital problems. In 1945 he

moved to New York, a move that was not accompanied by any upsurge in creativity. He subsequently concentrated mainly on journalistic commentary, abandoning his youthful preoccupation with naturalism, philosophy, and allegory, except perhaps for *East of Eden* (1952). Steinbeck returned to California on his *Travels with Charlie* (1962), his poodle, and left his papers to Stanford, but never really came to terms with his heritage. Only after his death did Salinas awaken to the commercial possibilities of a celebrity native son. The city library was renamed for Steinbeck in 1972, the house where Steinbeck was born became a restaurant, and a neighboring condo project was called Steinbeck Flats.

Thomas Kiernan wrote The Intricate Music, A Biography of John Steinbeck *(Boston, 1979) without the cooperation of the writer's widow.*

William Dennison Stephens (1859-1944). As

24th governor of California (1917-1923), Stephens found his Progressive Party beliefs rendered obsolete by World War I and the ensuing "red scare." He was a native of Ohio who had moved to Los Angeles in 1887 and worked his way up through the grocery business to become head of the local Chamber of Commerce in 1907 and mayor in 1909. An effective speaker of the hail-fellow-well-met genre, he apparently had a poor memory for outstanding personal loans. (**A.P. Giannini** once acquired a bank with a Stephens loan on the books and had the temerity to collect it.) Elected to Congress in 1910, Stephens was serving his third term when **Hiram Johnson** made a deal with

the Progressive Party leadership to appoint Stephens lieutenant governor and thus his successor when Johnson went to the U.S. Senate. Inaugurated governor in 1917, Stephens was primarily concerned with the war effort. The major issue of his 1918 reelection campaign was labor radicalism, in particular the case of **Tom Mooney**, convicted of the Preparedness Day bomb deaths. Stephens procrastinated, then (after winning the election) commuted Mooney's death sentence to life. He also approved the ratification of Prohibition, supported a major increase in corporate taxes, and favored such special observances as "Ripe Olive Day" and "Gauze Mask Use Day." The proposed corporate tax increase proved Stephens's undoing, for conservative business interests combined to defeat both it and his 1922 reelection campaign. Having been admitted to the California bar as governor, Stephens retired to practice law.

George Sterling

(1869-1926). The prodigal son of an old Long Island puritan family, Sterling was shipped off to work for an uncle in the Bay Area in 1890. His first efforts at writing poetry brought him to the attention of **Ambrose Bierce** whose protegé he became. (An early Sterling library card lists his occupation as "pupil of Ambrose Bierce.") Sterling looked and acted the part of a poet: handsome, a romantic posturer with great pride in his profile and in his sexual

conquests. He and **Jack London**, his "great Man-comrade," were legendary carousers. In 1905 Sterling moved to Carmel where he became the nucleus of a famous Bohemian colony. Neighbor **Mary Austin** considered him a high priest of "austere exoticism . . . ridden by restless impotencies of energy." He enjoyed great adulation for his sonorous, high-flown poetry, but personally and artistically proved incapable of growth beyond precious youth to maturity. His wife left him over his chronic

faithlessness, and later committed suicide. Sterling moved to New York for awhile and attempted screenwriting in Hollywood. Anxious about losing his youth, he tried **Gaylord Wilshire**'s I-on-a-co belt and **Albert Abrams**'s electronic medicine. He spent his last years as the poet laureate of San Francisco's Bohemian Club, where he lived, also keeping a studio painted robin's egg blue in the Montgomery Block, where he held court in a dressing gown. An aging Peter Pan, he committed suicide at 57. Of eighteen volumes of poetry,

little is remembered today except a few fragments about "the cool, grey city of love" — San Francisco, where for a generation he passed as the greatest poet since Dante. He deserves to be remembered for the quality of his acquaintanceship, it has been said, if not the quality of his achievement.

See Donald Fleming, George Sterling, The Last Bohemian (Orinda, CA, 1972). Franklin Walker's Seacoast of Bohemia (San Francisco, 1966) is an excellent account of the Carmel Colony.

Robert Louis Stevenson

(1850-1894). "It is a strange thing to lie awake in nineteenth century America and hear one of these old heartbreaking Spanish love songs mount into the night air," Stevenson wrote in Monterey in 1879. Where others came west for fortune and adventure, the Scots writer had come for love. Fanny Osbourne, whom he met in Europe, was ten years his senior, married, and the mother of two, but she impressed him with such a sense of destiny that he followed her halfway around the world to Oakland. Forced

to wait several months for Fanny to divorce, Stevenson went through a period of tubercular ill-health and despondency. Struck by the haunting presence of the sea and the melancholy fogs, he wrote his epitaph, "Home is the sailor, Home from the sea." On better days, he roused himself to write amused descriptions of his surroundings, including Simoneau's Inn at Monterey, "part bar and part barbershop" or to muse on the juxtaposition of old and new, Latin and Anglo, at land's end. Finally married, Robert, Fanny, and her son Sam traveled to Mount Saint Helena (the "Mont Blanc of Napa County") for a honeymoon of sorts in an abandoned silver mine. Here on the edge of civilization Stevenson encountered the newly devised telephone, observed the rustics ("an unknown quantity between the savage and the nobleman"), and above all the weather: the puffs of cloud emitted by the mountain "like a Lapland witch," the seas of fog stretching out at the mountain's midsection, summer rain less likely than an earthquake. The Stevensons left California in 1880, but California continued to live in the author's imagination. The scenery of *Treasure Island* (1883), he told a friend, was Californian, and a late novel *The Wrecker* (1892), was set in Boss **Buckley**'s San Francisco. Grateful for the attention, the state made a museum out of the house in Monterey where Stevenson lay awake listening to Spanish love songs, and a state park at Mount Saint

Helena, where there is a yearly festival complete with treasure hunt.

James D. Hart's From Scotland to Silverado (Cambridge, MA, 1966) includes a biographical essay with Stevenson's shorter American writings.

Lyman Stewart

(1840-1923). The founder of Union Oil was a Bible-minded wildcatter with a mysterious instinct for locating oil below ground. Born and raised in northwest Pennsylvania during the first generation of American oil exploration, Stewart arrived in Los Angeles in 1883 to mine for some of California's fabled "black gold." City land was too expensive, so he moved north into the mountains and canyons of Ventura County. Stewart and his partners eventually found oil and in 1890 created the Union Oil Company, pioneering in the development of pipelines, refineries, oil-powered rigs and tankers, and new-fangled service stations. By 1910 Union Oil (headquartered in L.A.) had acquired a total of 230,000 acres of promising oil land, making the company such an attractive target that it had to resist takeover attempts by Standard Oil and by a member of its own board of directors, **E.L. Doheny**. Pious and abstemious to the point of eccentricity, the Scots-Presbyterian Stewart gave credit to the Lord for keeping his company prosperous and built chapels in the field for his roughnecks to attend. He accepted only a nominal salary himself and donated much of his wealth to the promotion of temperance and morality. In 1907 the oil magnate founded

a Bible Institute to spread the good book among the heathen Chinese. In 1914, after hiring a religious zealot as Union Oil treasurer and signing over an option on all his stock to benefit the Bible Institute, he was forced out of company leadership. Biola (the Bible Institute of L.A.) survived, relocating from downtown to Downey.

The Black Bonanza by Earl Welty and Frank Taylor (New York, 1956) is a friendly history of Union Oil.

Robert Field Stockton

(1795-1866). When Stockton arrived in California at the helm of the USS *Congress* in July 1846, he was more than willing to relieve his superior and more cautious officer, Commodore John Sloat, of the problems posed by the Bear Flag Revolt. An adventurous and ambitious officer, he conceived a bold plan of attack, entirely without instructions, to complete the American conquest of the

state. Assuming military and civil command, Stockton created **Frémont's** California Battalion of **Mounted** Riflemen under naval authority and turned his own sailors into a rudimentary force of marines. They captured Los Angeles later that summer when José Castro's forces fled— fortunately, for the American sailors knew little more of basic land commands than "charge" and "halt." Stockton was in San Diego that fall when General **Stephen Watts Kearny** arrived overland with his dragoons to meet immediate and stunning defeat by the Californios at the battle of San Pasqual. The navy came to the army's rescue, and the commodore pulled rank on the general, setting the stage for future melodrama. Aside from the fact that Stockton got to California first and therefore considered it his world to conquer, his temperament and style of leadership differed from those of Kearny, the hard-bitten Indian fighter. The more elegant Stockton, for example, travelled with such conveniences of civilization as a bedstead, in which he dreamed of martial glory. ("If I live and the enemy will fight," he wrote in early 1847, "I will give the San Gabriel a name in history along with. . . the Bridge of Lodi.") Having had his share of adventure, he set out for the Atlantic Coast—overland, no doubt fancying himself a veteran trailblazer—leaving Frémont as civil governor to reach the ultimate clash of authority with Kearny. Frémont was courtmartialed for insubordination, and Stockton, coincidentally or

not, resigned from the navy in 1850. Like Frémont, he too went into politics, winning appointment as a U.S. Senator from New Jersey in 1851 and figuring briefly as a Know-Nothing candidate for the 1856 U.S. presidential nomination.

A Sketch of the Life of Commodore Robert F. Stockton *(New York, 1856)* by *S.J. Bayard will be found only in the rare book department.*

Irving Stone (Irving Tennenbaum, 1903-   ). A third generation San Franciscan, Stone spent his summers as a boy picking fruit in the San Joaquin Valley or working at Lake Tahoe hotels. In 1920 he entered the University of California, a land-grant college where a poor boy could get an education for $25 a semester. Eventually he got an M.A. at USC and taught economics (1924-1926) before dropping out of academia to become a writer. Stone pioneered a new genre of biohistory, novelized biography based on extensive research. For subjects he ransacked all of Western history and civilization— Michelangelo, Freud, Darwin—with a strong sideline in Californiana. A fan of **Jack London** since boyhood, he wrote *Sailor on Horseback* (1938). Intrigued by **Clarence Darrow**'s ambiguous role in the *Los Angeles Times* bombing case, he put the event in the perspective of the attorney's lifetime in *Clarence Darrow for the Defense* (1941). Admiring the strength and courage of pioneer women, he enshrined Jessie Benton **Frémont** as the *Immortal Wife* (1944) of the pathfinder. Stone also wrote a straight

biography of Governor **Earl Warren** (1948), produced a colorful tapestry of the opening of the West, *Men to Match My Mountains* (1956), and edited a collection of memoirs of Berkeley, *There Was Light; Autobiography of a University* (1968).

Joseph Henry Jackson wrote Irving Stone and the Biographical Novel *(Garden City, NY, 1954).*

George Stoneman (1822-1894). California's fifteenth governor (1883-1887), Stoneman was a West Point graduate (1846) from New York who first came west in 1847 as a non-Mormon officer of the Mormon Battalion. As a reward for services during the Civil War, during which he was promoted to general and became the subject of a Currier and Ives depiction of an 1863 cavalry raid, he was appointed head of the Department of Arizona in 1870. He resigned from that position somewhat prematurely the following year when it was revealed that he was actually living on his 400-acre ranch, Los Robles, in Southern California. A self-professed Jeffersonian Democrat, Stoneman ran for governor in 1882 on an anti-railroad platform with the support of labor demagogue **Denis Kearney**. Charging the railroad with tax delinquency, he called a special session of the legislature in 1884 but was unable to get any of his reform proposals enacted. Opponents called him weak and vacillating, even hinting at a secret understanding with the monopolists. Stoneman made labor happy by proclaiming an 1886

holiday for a peaceful San Francisco demonstration, by way of contrast to the bloody Haymarket riot in Chicago. He also pardoned a record number of criminals, an achievement memorialized in satiric verse by **Ambrose Bierce**.

Thomas More Storke (1876-1971). The publisher of a smalltown newspaper is usually a businessman, politician, and civic booster; rarely, he also comes equipped with a moral conscience. Storke came from an old California family. His father, a mayor of Santa Barbara and state assemblyman, had courageously opposed the stranglehold of the Southern Pacific Railroad over the state. After graduation from Stanford, young Tom Storke acquired his first newspaper in 1900, buying, selling, and merging with the competition to create the *Santa Barbara Daily News and Independent* in 1913 and the *News-Press* in 1938. (He also picked up a local radio station, using his initials for its call name.) Always an activist (benevolent tyrant, some would say) in local affairs, he became the city's top federal official—postmaster—during World War I. Between wars, Storke dabbled in politics as a protegé of **William Gibbs McAdoo**, the former U.S. Secretary of the Treasury who had retired to Santa Barbara. The McAdoo-Storke forces played a key role in swinging the 1932 Democratic presidential nomination to Franklin Roosevelt, on whose ticket McAdoo was elected to the U.S. Senate. Back home in Santa Barbara, Storke channeled New Deal patronage into a new armory, reservoir, sewage system, airport, and post office. (When McAdoo resigned in 1937, having been defeated for reelection, Storke was appointed to fill the last eight weeks of his Senate term.) Up until 1960 Storke measured his accomplishments literally in *concrete* terms: a dam constructed here, a baseball diamond there. Then he read a book by Robert Welch in which the John Birch Society leader branded former President Eisenhower and others as Communist conspirators. When "West was West and men were men," Storke responded in a front-page editorial, such slander would have invited tar and feathers. Failing that, he for one was going to stand up and be counted against the John Birch Society—for which he was awarded a Pulitzer Prize in 1962.

Storke wrote a 1958 memoir, California Editor *(Los Angeles, 1958)* *which he updated in an abbreviated form as* I Write for Freedom *(Fresno, 1962) after winning the Pulitzer Prize.*

Joseph Baermann Strauss (1870-1938).

They said it couldn't be done: the mouth of the Golden Gate was too wide, too deep, and the seas too heavy. San Francisco's city engineer threw up his hands, but Strauss, a Chicago-based innovator in bridge design, also a poet and a dreamer, believed he could build a bridge connecting San Francisco with Marin County to the north. Moreover, he would build a beautiful bridge, dispensing with unsightly cable networks. After all, he had designed the Arlington Memorial Bridge across the Potomac River to Washington and consulted on the George Washington Bridge in New York. For nineteen years Strauss planned and lobbied and fought in the courts for permission to try. Shipping interests opposed the project, arousing the bogy of "quicksand." Since both approaches were on military reservations, the War Department had to consent, which ate up another year. The Depression-era Reconstruction Finance Corporation gave its entire appropriation to complete the nearby Oakland-San Francisco Bay Bridge. Finally, banker **A.P. Giannini** agreed to underwrite Strauss's dream of building the world's longest suspension bridge. Construction began in 1933 and was completed in record time, exactly on budget at $27 million. On 27 May 1937 the bridge was opened to pedestrians, some 200,000 of whom strolled over the breathtaking new roadway. In honor of the occasion, Strauss waxed poetic: "At last the mighty task is done/Resplendent in the western sun/Launched midst a thousand hopes and fears/Damned by a thousand hostile sneers." A year later, the bridge-builder died in L.A.

Levi Strauss (1830-1902).

Closeness breeds familiarity, so it is not inappropriate that the West's most popular pants, snug-fitting Levi's, should be known by the first name of the San Francisco merchant who first brought them to the world. ("Jeans," by the way, are named for the Italian port city where "genoese cloth" was first made.) Strauss was a Bavarian-born Jew, a former successful dry-goods merchant in Gold Rush San Francisco. One of the customers to whom he sold cloth was a struggling tailor in Reno, Jacob Davis, who first conceived of riveting the pockets and seams of his trim-fitting work pants to keep them from splitting. Davis made a deal with Strauss to patent, mass-produce, and distribute his pants, which soon became a standard item

among miners, lumberjacks, and cowboys throughout the West. Strauss died in 1902, a bachelor, leaving his end of the business to four nephews surnamed Stern; Davis was succeeded in the production end after the earthquake by his son Simon, who added overalls to the line and set up a mini-factory at the 1915 Exposition to help popularize the Levi Strauss line. Over the years, the basic levi was improved with metal buttons, orange stitching, a leather label and a red pocket tab. Under the leadership of Stern son-in-law Walter Haas and his sons, the company broke through the regional market, skyrocketing after World War II into the largest clothing manufacturer in world history, its product a worldwide sociological phenomenon.

Levi's by Ed Cray (Boston, 1978) is a popular history of the patriarchal family business.

Igor Fedorovich Stravinsky (1882-1971).

While touring the U.S. during the 1930s, the Russian-born composer conducted concerts at L.A.'s Shrine Auditorium. He visited the movie studios, which he described as "separate principalities," and discovered that the climate was good for his lungs. In 1941, he and his wife Vera de

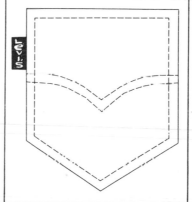

Bosset Sudeikina settled in Hollywood, carving out a little bit of home on Wetherly Drive, their victory garden planted with beets for borscht. During 29 years in California Stravinsky continued to experiment musically, moving from neoclassicism to serial techniques. Some of his short pieces were performed at the "Evenings on the Roof" concert series, but the Los Angeles Philharmonic managed to ignore the presence in its midst of one of the world's most honored living composers. Courted by the movie industry, Stravinsky sold options on some of his famous compositions to **Disney**, but was enraged by the use of his "Sacré du Printemps" in *Fantasia*. (He adored movies, particularly Westerns and comedies, but after a Hollywood party would come home to read Dostoievsky with his wife—"to remind ourselves about human beings.") A small man with a tendency to tuberculosis, he was an inveterate faddist of diets and exotic gymnastics. He was also something of a dandy, paying careful attention to local couture. For dining out informally, he favored a navy-surplus pea jacket and a blue-jean suit, which he wore with a silk scarf and sandals, recalled Marie **Huxley**, wife of Aldous.

Stravinsky in Pictures and Documents by Vera Stravinsky and Robert Craft (New York, 1978) is a delightful book. UCLA, competing with the University of Texas for Stravinsky's papers, offered to rename its Schoenberg Building as a Stravinsky Archive.

Robert Stroud

(1890-1963). Conceived as an American version of Devil's Island, the prison fortress of Alcatraz in San Francisco Bay was opened in the 1930s to house hard-case incorrigibles from the federal corrections system. The most famous of them was a third-grade dropout from Seattle who during 54 years in prison—including 42 in solitary—became an acknowledged expert on ornithology. A loner with a fierce code of personal justice, Stroud had killed a man in 1909 for beating up his girlfriend. He committed a second murder in 1916, stabbing a guard to death in front of 1,100 men in the dining hall at Leavenworth (Kansas) federal prison. (His death sentence was commuted to life in prison after his mother made a personal appeal to President Woodrow Wilson.) One day in the Leavenworth exercise yard, he found a nest of sparrows that he fed and nursed and even taught to perform tricks in his cell. Permitted to acquire a few canaries, he became totally absorbed in the drama of their courtship, nesting,

nurturing, and eventual death. Stroud began corresponding with bird lovers and experts, schooled himself to perform crude autopsies, and experimented with remedies for bird ailments, continually negotiating with prison authorities to expand his activities. Sublimating his aggressions into scholarship, he studied chemistry, bacteriology, and pharmacology to write *Stroud's Digest on the Diseases of Birds* (1933, 1942). In 1942 when he was transferred to Alcatraz, Stroud was forbidden to take his

birds along. After a major 1946 prison mutiny, he turned his attention to the study of men in cages but was denied permission to publish his two-volume study of the Federal penal system. Repeatedly refused parole, he spent his last years on the Rock learning French and Greek, a Promethean figure. A few years after Stroud's death Alcatraz was retired as a prison.

The Birdman of Alcatraz by Thomas E. Gaddis (New York, 1955) was made into a 1962 film starring Burt Lancaster as Stroud.

Adolph Sutro

(1830-1898). Sutro, later

mayor and benevolent patriarch of San Francisco,

made a fortune by accomplishing a largely useless but formidable feat of engineering. Born in Germany, he was a successful tobacco merchant in post-Gold-Rush San Francisco before becoming obsessed with the Comstock. Collaborating with a chemist to devise a better method of processing ore, he established a reducing mill. Then he conceived the idea of a tunnel under the Comstock, providing drainage and access to otherwise inaccessible ore deposits. Sutro lobbied, promoted, and juggled finances for fifteen years before the tunnel was completed in 1878. He sold out his tunnel holdings at their peak—fortunately, for the Comstock was nearing depletion and the tunnel proved an expensive irrelevance. Investing in San Francisco real estate, he acquired nearly ten percent of the city's area, including two of the city's seven hills: Mount Olympus, which he crowned with an enormous statue of "The Triumph of Light", and Mount Parnassus, which he donated to the University of California. Sutro moved into a simple cottage on the bluffs near Cliff House, filling his grounds (later Sutro Heights) full of plaster copies of European statuary purchased from a German stonecutter who decorated beer gardens. He battled the streetcar companies to get a cheap fare for the masses to the beach and in 1896 opened an enormous public bath house. (It closed in 1952 and burned down in 1966). And for the literati, Sutro collected books, amassing

one of the important libraries of California. Elected mayor in 1894 on a platform opposing the Southern Pacific octopus, he ruled the city like a small European duchy, opposing improvements that would tax the duke's extensive holdings. Sutro retired after one term, and soon lapsed into senility. (Sutro and Company, the stock brokerage, was founded by his cousins Gustav and Charles.)

Robert and Mary Stewart's Aldolph Sutro *(Berkeley, 1962) is bland biography.*

John Augustus Sutter (1803-1880). Sutter was a Rabelaisian figure, picturesque, adventurous, magnanimous, improvident, and dissolute. He was also a romantic, an imposter, and a dreamer whose dream coincidentally contained the key to U.S. statehood, the Gold Rush, and his own ruin. Having abandoned his wife, five children, and debts in Switzerland in 1834, he turned up five years later in California posing as a Swiss Guard officer forced to flee the French Revolution of 1830. A contemporary compared his uniform and grand manner to those of Cortez "in his palmiest days." By sheer force of personality and a shrewd appreciation of provincial intrigue, Sutter persuaded Governor **Juan Alvarado** to give him an eleven-league grant in the Sacramento Valley. There he established his New Helvetia, a self-sustained fortress community of pioneers, Indians, and a few Kanakas (Hawaiians), with himself as

benevolent patriarch. Being practically penniless, he expended rivers of colored ink ordering ("Please to send me. . .") supplies he could not pay for. The Russians departing from Fort Ross agreed to sell him their livestock and improvements in exchange for a note against Sutter's Fort. He also received a second land grant for his support of Governor **Manuel Micheltorena** at the comic-opera facedown in the Cahuenga Pass, even though Micheltorena capitulated. But each of Sutter's achievements or strokes of good fortune contained the seeds of later disaster. Thanks to its strategic position dominating California's Central Valley, Sutter's Fort proved the key to the American conquest. But military occupation proved costly, for **John Frémont** didn't pay his debts either, and statehood brought settlers to contest Sutter's title and revile him as a landhungry plutocrat. The discovery of gold at his lumber mill provided Sutter with the means of paying off

his mountainous debts but ultimately brought down on his possessions a horde of scoundrels and squatters. His family turned up from Switzerland in time for the final act of the farce, his dispossession at the hands of the courts (the Micheltorena grant was disallowed) and real estate sharpers. Publicly, Sutter was celebrated as the grand old man of California, appointed major general of the state militia (with a real and expensive uniform), and invited to preside over the new state's Constitutional Convention. Privately, however, he was approaching desperation and destitution. Some 49ers recall him playing himself in a theatrical extravaganza on the Gold Rush. In 1865, he moved east where he spent his last years seeking redress from Congress, if not for his lost land, then for expenses incurred during the conquest. A century later, alleged Sutter descendants were still suing the government for restitution.

The best of several biographies, both scholarly and impassioned, is J. Peter Zollinger's Sutter, The Man and His Empire *(New York, 1939), which was reprinted in 1967.*

May Sutton. *See* May Sutton Bundy.

John Swett (1830-1913). California's foremost nineteenth-century educator, Swett was fond of drawing an analogy between teaching and mining. The state's first teachers were, like everyone else, gamblers attracted by the Gold Rush; failing to find fortune in the mines, he said, they settled into the harder work of mining moral and intellectual riches. A Puritan

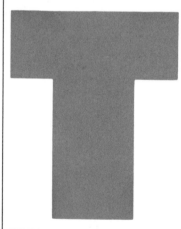

from New Hampshire, Swett held that the true wealth of a community lay in its educated citizens. These were the arguments he marshalled as state Superintendent of Public Education (1862-1867) to win passage of a new state school code and to secure funding through local property taxes. Swett also worked to raise standards of instruction. During one year alone, he traveled 3,000 miles by stagecoach to visit country schools, most of which he described as "meaner than pig pokes." On a trip to Southern California, he discovered that El Monte, a hotbed of secession, was unwilling to hire "loyal" teachers but unable to find literate rebels. Defeated for reelection in 1867, Swett returned to teaching and school administration in San Francisco, with particular attention to teacher training. One of his student teachers calculated that, over the years, she and a handful of classmates had taught over 500,000 San Franciscans.

Swett was a handsome man with a fighting spirit, a gift for rousing oratory, and a command of "forcible Anglo-Saxon." He was particularly incensed over the intrusion of politics into education. In 1889, under pressure from Boss **Buckley**'s flunkies, he resigned as principal of S.F.'s Girl's High School; years later he returned, vindicated, as city school superintendent. He retired to a farm near his friend **John Muir** in the Alhambra Valley. Muir, who acquired his property by marriage, was not fond of the valley but Swett loved it because it reminded him of New Hampshire.

Public Education in California (New York, 1911) is the title of Swett's autobiography.

William Desmond Taylor

(William Deane-Tanner, 1877-1922). The victim of Hollywood's most famous unsolved murder, he was a mystery in himself. At the time of his death, Taylor was a top director of silent films, a handsome, urbane bachelor enjoying the favors of not one but two well-known actresses. The last person to see him alive was **Mabel**

Normand, the madcap comedienne, who stopped by Taylor's bungalow court home on Alvarado (as fashionable a district in its day as the Sunset Strip 50 years later) for cocktails. The following day, as news spread of the death by shooting, the other woman turned up to claim her love letters. Mary Miles Minter told the police that Taylor was like "a beautiful white flame," embodying "all the glories of manhood in one private body." Investigation revealed, however, that Taylor was in fact a prosperous New York businessman who had abandoned his family and vanished in 1908. (His brother did a similar disappearing act in 1912 and may have been posing as the private secretary who robbed Taylor some months before his death.) To round out the picture, there were mysterious keys, pawn tickets which arrived by mail, and the suggestion of narcotics involvement by others in the director's circle. There were therefore quite a number of potential murderers, from unrequited lovers to "hop gangsters" (drug-pushers) not to mention 300 helpful individuals who confessed to the murder within a month.

Erle Stanley Gardner described the Taylor case in Los Angeles Murders *(New York, 1947). Samuel A. Peeples found the unsolved murder sufficiently compelling 50 years later to inspire a novel,* The Man Who Died Twice *(New York, 1976).*

Edward Teller

(1908-   ). One of several brilliant Hungarian physicists to emigrate to the U.S. in the interwar period, Teller became the Dr. Strangelove

of the thermonuclear era. The temperamental, beetle-browed scientist joined the World War II Manhattan Project at Los Alamos, where he stubbornly worked alone, generated constant ideas (most of them wrong) and twice walked out in protest. In the immediate aftermath of the war when most of his colleagues were tormented by the memory of Hiroshima, Teller forged ahead to design weapons of even greater destructive power. A leading critic of **J. Robert Oppenheimer**, he accused the former director of Los Alamos of holding the H-bomb back, thus giving the Russians time to catch up. In 1952 Teller was appointed professor of physics at the University of California and director of the Lawrence Livermore Laboratory, where he designed the first successful thermonuclear device. He also mobilized the political and scientific support to build it, arguing the case for U.S. nuclear superiority. During the Eisenhower era there were all-night lines on the Berkeley campus to register for Teller's Physics 10 course. But with his opposition to JFK's 1963 nuclear test ban treaty and the general polarization of the Vietnam era, became rather a campus archfiend. A radical Berkeley commune even held a war crimes tribunal to indict the "nuclear blackmailer," burning him in effigy outside his own house. Teller retired from the UC in 1975 to join Stanford's Hoover Institution as a senior research fellow.

Energy and Conflict; The Life and Times of Edward Teller by Stanley Blumberg and Gwin Owens (New York, 1976) is an affectionate account by friends of the physicist. Teller wrote The Legacy of Hiroshima *(Garden City, NY, 1962).*

Shirley Temple (Shirley Temple Black, 1928-   ). "What are we going to pretend today?" the world's most famous child would ask her mother on the way to the studio every morning. Born in Santa Monica, the daughter of a banker, she was discovered at the age of three in a dancing class and cast in one-reel *Baby Burlesks*, takeoffs on real films with kids as the stars. Soon she moved to the major studios, a bright and lively moppet with a preternatural ability to emote on cue. From small parts in grown-up films she advanced to her own custom-tailored vehicles: *The Little Colonel* (1935), *Curly Top*

(1935), *Rebecca of Sunnybrook Farm* (1938). (She was such a pro that director John Ford called her "One-Take Temple," while writer Graham Greene brought a calamitous lawsuit on himself by suggesting that she might really be a 30-year-old midget.) Her mother was paid $500 weekly to set Shirley's hair in 56 curls every night, go over lines with her, and remind her on the set to "sparkle." Her father, who had been promoted to branch manager for attracting a flood of children's savings accounts, retired to become an investment counselor, primarily for his daughter, who in 1938 at the age of ten had the seventh highest income in the United States. And the Temples moved from Santa Monica uptown to

Brentwood. Parents and producers were able to shield her from sophistication, but other than subtracting a year from her age they couldn't do much to forestall adolescence. At the age of twelve she enrolled in L.A.'s Westlake School for Girls, a socially-upscale prep school of the white-glove-and-cotillion genre, graduating five years later with a little time off for some forgettable films. She married well (the second time) and became a society matron in the posh Bay Area suburb of Woodside. **Richard Nixon** appointed her U.S. Ambassador to Ghana (1974-1976) and Gerald Ford made her his chief of protocol (1976-1978).

Robert Windeler's biography, Shirley Temple *(New York, 1976), comes in two sizes, with pictures and with more pictures.*

Irving Tennenbaum. *See* **Irving Stone**.

Jack Breckinridge Tenney (1898-1970). McCarthyism had a special preview in California thanks to Tenney, a state legislator who anticipated the national witchhunt by about five years. A resident of L.A. since childhood, he was a songwriter ("Mexicali Rose") and supporter of left-wing causes who travelled to the opposite end of the political spectrum after his defeat for reelection as head of the Hollywood musicians' union. First elected to the state assembly in 1936 and to the Senate in 1942, he used the legislature's Fact-Finding Committee on Un-American Activities (established in 1941) as a personal vehicle to crusade against subversive

"Commu-Nazism." With his wife as secretary and his L.A. office as headquarters of the committee, Chairman Tenney investigated the Communist "takeover" of labor, the German-American Bund, and the KKK, holding five days of hearings into possible fascist involvement in the Zoot-Suit Riots. After the war, Tenny's field of focus narrowed exclusively to Communists, who were taking over Hollywood, he claimed, and destroying the moral fiber of children with sex education in the schools. He wrote his own press releases, issued annual red-bound reports identifying "letterhead organizations," and staged hearings which "were not conducted in a manner calculated to permit rational findings of fact," as a Cornell University scholar tactfully put it. Few of his legislative proposals were enacted, but the University of California and the county of L.A., among others, adopted their own loyalty oaths to forestall state intervention. Eventually Tenney went too far. He was forced to resign from his committee in 1949 after imprudently accusing two state legislators of Communist ties. A vice presidential candidate on Gerald L.K. Smith's anti-Semitic Christian National Party ticket in 1952, Tenney retired from politics to practice law in Banning.

Edward Darrett wrote a responsible analysis of The Tenney Committee *(Ithaca, NY, 1951).*

David Smith Terry (1823-1889). The life story of Terry, the hot-tempered "dueling judge" from Texas, is a saga of chivalry, pride,

money, and violence. In 1855, then a state Supreme Court Justice, he ran afoul of the San Francisco Vigilance Committee through sheer truculence, barely escaping with his life after stabbing a vigilante with his bowie knife. A Southerner by birth and by fire-eating conviction, he provoked anti-slavery leader and U.S. Senator **David Broderick** to a duel in 1859 that proved fatal for Broderick and traumatic for the entire state. Terry served as a Confederate officer during the Civil War, then returned to private law practice in the San Joaquin Valley, gradually regaining respectability thanks to his unquestioned integrity and courage. He played a valuable role as a delegate to the 1878 state Constitutional Convention, helping to translate corporate responsibility into law. Terry seemed to be mellowing until, after the death of his first wife, he married a beautiful and exceedingly headstrong young woman. Sarah Althea

Hill was then at the climax of her "divorce" suit against Comstock millionaire **William Sharon**. When the case began to go against her, she made a scene in the courtroom of U.S. Supreme Court Justice **Stephen Field**, then riding circuit in California, who sentenced both Mr. and Mrs. Terry to jail for contempt. The final act of the melodrama took place in a San Joaquin Valley train station, where Terry unexpectedly ran into Field. Driven to the end by outmoded notions of personal honor, Terry purposely affronted the judge's dignity, whereupon Field's bodyguard shot and killed Terry.

A.R. Buchanan, David S. Terry, Dueling Judge *(San Marino, 1956).*

Luisa Tetrazzini

(1871-1940). Along with the temperament of the prima donna, Tetrazzini, the leading

Italian coloratura soprano at the turn of the century, also possessed a genius for self-advertisement. In 1910, locked in a contract dispute with impresario Oscar Hammerstein, she made a gesture which won her immortality in opera-loving San Francisco. To foil Hammerstein, who was trying to prevent her from appearing under any auspices but his own, the diva announced that she would sing for free in the streets of San Francisco. And so on Christmas Eve that year she appeared before a crowd estimated at a quarter million around Lotta's Fountain on Market Street, where she sang "The Last Rose of Summer." The spot was later marked by a bas-relief portrait and an inscription, "Here in 1910 Tetrazzini sang for the poor." Turkey, chicken, and especially ham served with pasta are called Tetrazzini after the coloratura.

Tetrazzini devoted two pages of her autobiography, My Life of Song *(New York, 1921), to "the greatest concert San Francisco or the world had ever seen."*

Irving Thalberg

(1899-1936). In Hollywood folklore Thalberg enjoys the role of the white knight, the creative genius who understood talent and appreciated quality, as distinct from the crude tyrants who extorted the credit and the profits. Contemporaries describe him as a "young Pope" whose name was uttered in cathedral whispers, a "Renaissance prince" and patron of artists. The legend was underscored by Thalberg's youth (at twenty he was head of production at Universal, at 24 creative

director at MGM), his well-mannered reserve, his devoted family life (his parents lived with him even after his marriage at 28), and his frail health. On the other side of the ledger, he helped perpetuate the autocratic, politically reactionary studio system, and he profited handsomely by it, both financially and emotionally. He was notorious for keeping employees waiting interminably, then commanding their appearance. **Anita Loos** once waited so long she was able to knit a scarf that, at $2,500 a week, cost MGM about $20,000. P.G. Wodehouse wrote several "Jeeves" stories while waiting a year for an assignment. The **Marx Brothers**, tired of waiting, lit a fire in Thalberg's office and roasted potatoes. Totally cut off from the real world, Thalberg put in a twelve-hour day at the studio, noon to midnight, then retired to his air-conditioned and sound-proofed Santa Monica beach mansion. His positive contribution to the art of film is hard to pinpoint. Certainly he fostered MGM's cinematic idealization of women, particularly the divine Garbo and the refined Norma Shearer, his wife. He was not a good writer and lacked the aggressive energy of a director, but he was said to have a strong story instinct and the ability to spot and overcome the problems in any film. He produced arguably better Tarzan and Marx brothers films than anyone else. His life and premature death of pneumonia inspired another culture hero, writer F. **Scott Fitzgerald**, to create *The Last Tycoon*. (When Norma Shearer read the book, she said, "But it's not a bit like Irving.")

Thalberg: Life and Legend (New York, 1969) is probably the least interesting of Bob Thomas's Hollywood biographies.

Hazel Tharsing. *See* Carlotta Monterey O'Neill.

Tex Thornton (Charles Bates Thornton, 1913-1981). The story is told that when Tex Thornton first visited a new Litton subsidiary, a punctilious telephone operator insisted on having his "Litt-Com" number before putting through a long distance call. "I guess it would be number one," replied Thornton, mild-mannered head of *the* glamor conglomerate of the 1960s. Born in Texas, the son of an oilfield firefighter, he earned a B.S. from George Washington University in 1937 and pioneered in the development of management sciences for the U.S. Air Force during World War II. After the war Thornton put together a management team of "whiz kids" (including Robert

McNamara) and sold their services to the Ford Motor Company. Finding his upward mobility blocked by the Ford bureaucracy, Thornton moved west to head the Hughes Aircraft Company (HAC) in 1948. There, under the eccentric **Howard Hughes**, the problem was, if anything, worse. Thornton and his assistant Roy Ash brought HAC into the highly lucrative field of military electronics but lacked the ultimate authority and the financial reward. In 1953 Thornton raised the money on Wall Street to buy his very own blue chip outfit, Litton, formerly a family-owned microwave tube company in Santa Clara. Over the years, using conservative financial principles and technological daring, he and Ash built Litton into a multi-billion dollar conglomerate, aesthetically pleasing to economists for the way all the pieces fit together. Litton acquired a Beverly Hills colonial mansion as headquarters and Thornton moved up to a Bel Air mansion. He also had a 200-acre ranch in Hidden Valley where he could ride horseback for hours on end. But—the common touch—he continued to drive to work in a Ford.

Beirne Lay's Someone Has to Make It Happen *(Englewood Cliffs, NJ, 1969) is almost obsequious.*

Lawrence Tibbett
(Lawrence Mervil Tibbett 1895-1960). California has spawned a lot of raw operatic talent, to be polished and refined in the great musical centers of New York and Europe. Jerome Hines and George London came from

Los Angeles, Marilyn Horne from Long Beach. The most Californian of them all was Tibbett (the final "t" started as a typo), a native of Bakersfield whose greataunt and uncle planted the state's first navel orange tree in Riverside. Tibbett's father, a Bakersfield sheriff, was shot and killed by notorious outlaw Wild Jim McKinney. Attracted by acting and singing both, Tibbett began performing in first-generation movie palaces as live entertainment between feature films. In 1923 he moved to New York, making his big breakthrough two years later when called upon to substitute as Ford in *Falstaff*. For a generation Tibbett was a leading baritone on the Metropolitan Opera stage, but he also remained

open to other possibilities. He was the first U.S. opera star to make sound films and was associated with an early radio hit parade. He was also a labor leader, serving from 1940 to 1952 as head of AGMA, a union of artists.

Katherine Augusta Tingley (1847-1929). At the age of 50 Tingley emerged from obscurity to command the American theosophical movement with her vision of a "white city" in California. The site of this city, revealed to her by **John Frémont** before his death, she said, was Point Loma, the headland north of San Diego. Thanks to contributions from wealthy benefactors, Tingley bought 132 acres of land there and erected glass-domed structures that were visible when lighted at night for miles at sea. Dedicated in 1897, the Point Loma community served as Tingley's headquarters until her death 30 years later. (A rival group of theosophists settled in Pismo Beach in 1903, and English leader Annie Besant later tried to create a colony in Ojai, on land also said to possess important spiritual properties.) Tingley, a handsome matriarchal woman with a taste for pageantry, was called the "Purple Mother" because of her fondness for that color. At Point Loma she presided over a school for the education of future generations of theosophists; a Greek theater where *The Eumenides* and other classics were performed; a publishing operation with the only Sanskrit press in the U.S.; and an extensive reforestation project. Wealthy followers built their own homes at Point Loma, while some 300 others, including skilled artists and craftsmen, lived communally. Inevitably, there were

problems in paradise. In the early years of the colony, the Society for the Prevention of Cruelty to Children investigated Tingley's progressive educational program for Cuban orphans, and the *Los Angeles Times* ran lurid accounts of theosophical life, prompting Tingley to file a libel suit that she won in 1903. Some years later, the wife of a benefactor sued the 70-year-old thrice-married Purple Mother for alienation of affections and won. But the most significant indictment against Tingley was that she drained the wealth and ability of the entire U.S. theosophy movement into her California Acropolis, leaving local groups to wither on the vine. Her death and the Depression sealed the fate of Point Loma: the land was sold, and the survivors retreated to worldly coexistence in the Pasadena area. After years of abandonment, its shattered glass domes a ruin of antique glory, Point Loma became the site of California Western University, now Point Loma College.

Emmitt Greenwalt's The Point Loma Community in California, 1897-1942 *(Berkeley, 1955) is a responsible, nonpartisan treatment.*

Dmitri Tiomkin

(1894-1979). With the advent of sound in motion pictures, composers were in great demand in Hollywood. One of the most successful was Tiomkin, a conservatory-trained pianist from Russia. At first he raided his youthful compositions for movie themes but soon learned to write in such commercially universal styles as jazz and country-western. Moreover,

Russia and the conservatory were better training for the movies than might be imagined. Prokofiev may have suffered under Stalin, Tiomkin pointed out, but Hollywood had its dictators too. One of Tiomkin's most difficult assignments was *Duel in the Sun* (1946) for **David Selznick**, who ordered eleven custom-tailored themes, including one "love" theme, one "desire" theme, and one "orgasm" theme, which Selznick made Tiomkin rewrite twice. (*Lust in the Dust,* the crew called the film.) He had less trouble writing an original cowboy theme for *High Noon* (1952), the Academy Award-winning "Do not forsake me, oh my darlin'." A master of the musical vernacular, he never spoke anything but fractured English punctuated by Russian expressions. He brought down the house when

collecting one of his three other Oscars, this one for *The High and the Mighty* (1954), by expressing his gratitude to Beethoven, Brahms, and Wagner.

Tiomkin's memoir Please Don't Hate Me *(Garden City, NY,1959) is as charmingly idiosyncratic as its title.*

Alice B[abette] Toklas

(1877-1967). Toklas was born in San Francisco, spent most of the first 30 years of her life there, and always considered herself an "ardent Californian." But after the 1906 earthquake she escaped her fate as housekeeper to her widowed father and went off to Paris, where she became amanuensis, gourmet chef, and lifelong companion to **Gertrude Stein**. Stein was a formidable figure, a medical school dropout with literary ambitions whose rue de Fleurus salon was filled with cubist canvases and such personal friends as Pablo Picasso, Henri Matisse, Ernest Hemingway and **F. Scott Fitzgerald**. Stein's rambling, unpunctuated manuscripts remained largely unpublished until she took on Toklas as subject. *The Autobiography of Alice B. Toklas* (1933), written as an experiment, was Stein's first critical and popular success. On a 1934-1935 U.S. lecture tour, Stein and Toklas spent a month in California hunting down their childhood memories (Stein grew up in Oakland), but otherwise lived out their lives in Europe. After Stein's death in 1946, Toklas, a tiny woman in bangs, baroque jewelry, and exotic costumes, launched a modest

literary career of her own, compiling two cookbooks interspersed with anecdotes. Her most famous recipe, however, for "Haschich Fudge," was actually contributed by an artist friend.

Toklas wrote The Alice B. Toklas Cookbook *(New York, 1954);* Aromas and Flavors of Past and Present *(New York, 1958); and* What is Remembered *(New York, 1963). Linda Simon's* The Biography of Alice B. Toklas *(Garden City, NY, 1977) is competent.*

Tokyo Rose (Iva Toguri D'Aquino, 1916-   ). She was born on the fourth of July in Los Angeles, where her family owned a grocery store on Wilmington Avenue. After working her way through UCLA's class of 1940, she went to visit relatives in Japan and was stranded there by the war. She found a job as a broadcaster at Radio Tokyo and married a Portuguese citizen but refused to give up her American citizenship. D'Aquino was only one of a dozen female disc jockeys for a popular hour of dance music and propaganda beamed to G.I.'s in the South Pacific. She called herself "Orphan Ann," not "Tokyo Rose," and sometimes addressed her chit-chat to fellow "orphans of the Pacific." Back home in California, her family was sent to an internment camp in Tulare, where her mother died. Forbidden to return to the West Coast, the remaining Toguris settled in Chicago in 1947. Arrested by American occupation forces in Yokohama in 1945, D'Aquino was held there a year without trial. Her persistent efforts to return "home" resulted in her trial for treason in San

Francisco in 1949. Local reporters described "Tokyo Rose" as "slight, neat, and poker-faced, with a harsh, rather than a seductive voice." The government went to great expense to convict her, flying in witnesses from Japan but denying the defense the same privilege. Iva D'Aquino's conviction (she was sentenced to ten years in prison, a $10,000 fine, and loss of her U.S. citizenship) was considered a surprise but few spoke out. "Tokyo Rose" faded into remote memory, an ill-starred cartoon character from the war. In 1976, the son of her original San Francisco attorney filed a petition for presidential pardon on her behalf, citing the government's use of perjured testimony and court pressure on the jury for conviction. On his last day in office, Gerald Ford pardoned D'Aquino.

A 1969 history of American Nisei does not even mention her. It took a mainland Japanese, Masayo Duus, to write her story: Tokyo Rose, Orphan of the Pacific *(Tokyo, 1979).*

Francis Everett Townsend (1867-1960). He was a family doctor from the Midwest who made Long Beach the capital of a great Depression-era crusade against poverty. The town was highly prosperous when he arrived after World War I, thanks to the pool of oil on which it was built, but when the economy went bust Townsend lost his job as a county welfare doctor. Depressed and in poor health at the age of 66, he came to the realization that "we might be too old to work, but we were not too old to vote." The

so-called Townsend Plan first appeared in the *vox populi* columns of the *Long Beach Press-Telegram* in 1933. Turn surplus workers into consumers, Townsend advised, by retiring everyone at 60 with a $200 monthly pension; the money would stimulate the economy. Townsend flew all over the country drumming up support for his "Old Age Revolving Pensions" (OARP Ltd.), sometimes called "the California Mathematical Miracle." He conducted open-air recitations of "give us this day our daily bread," collected six million signatures (thanks to the new chain-letter craze), and launched a national newspaper with a circulation of 500,000 to expose "stuffed shirts" and expound "the people's rights and privileges." (These included, in addition to the traditional four freedoms, freedom from poverty.) With the passage of the the Social Security Act of 1935, the Townsend Plan became obsolete. Its author was officially dismissed as a dangerous crank, the subject of a 1936 congressional investigation. Personally, Townsend attributed his popular success to California's climate and freedom from tradition. "California has been called the home of the crackpots," he wrote, "but that also connotes that it is the home of new ideas." Rejuvenated by his crusade against poverty, the doctor lived to be 93.

Townsend wrote a tedious memoir, New Horizons (Chicago, 1943). Luther Whiteman and Samuel Lewis, authors of Glory Roads (New York, 1936), consider the Townsend movement vaguely fascist.

Trader Vic (Victor Jules Bergeron, 1902-   ). San Francisco's leading restaurateur, an aficionado of exotic drinks and Polynesian barbecue, Bergeron grew up in the not very tropical climate of the Bay Area, French on both sides. His parents were salt-of-the-earth working class, poor but gifted with resilience and gusto. Bergeron lost a leg to tuberculosis at age four and spent two years in the French Hospital on Geary Street. He hobbled around on a crutch until he could earn his first wooden leg at eighteen but grew up to think of himself as "inconvenienced" rather than handicapped. In 1934 he opened Hinky Dink's restaurant at 65th and San Pablo in Oakland near his father's grocery store, serving a menu made up out of memory and fantasy. A breakfast his father used to prepare was renamed Ham and Eggs Hawaiian; the deviled crab was a recipe borrowed from Bernstein's Fish Grotto; and the rum

punches came out of a tropical daydream. (Bergeron claims to have invented the Mai-Tai.) The restaurant became a World War II hangout for navy fliers, attracting a growing clientele of sophisticated city slickers from across the Bay. In 1951 Bergeron opened the first Trader Vic's in San Francisco, expanding over the next 30 years to twenty branches in five countries, plus a chain of gourmet Mexican restaurants (Señor Pico) and a line of drink mixes. A sportsman, self-taught artist, and all-around bon vivant, he welcomed the elite of the Bay Area to his private dining room in the San Francisco restaurant and enjoyed a jet-set good life, including an African safari with the Bing Crosbys. He also found time to hound the Veterans Administration for its "inhumane" treatment of amputees, prescribing self-reliance and the work ethic with a little rum punch and Chinese food to fortify the resolve.

Bergeron wrote several books on food and drink preparation, including Frankly Speaking; Trader Vic's Life Story (Garden City, NY, 1973), a memoir interspersed with recipes.

Dalton Trumbo (James Dalton Trumbo, 1905-1976). The most successful of the radical Hollywood Ten screenwriters, Trumbo was the first of them to break through the blacklist. A WASP from Colorado and the only one of the Ten from a working class background, he supported his mother and sisters for years as a laborer in a downtown L.A. bakery before becoming a writer. Aggressive and energetic, he

became such a skillful smithy of scripts that he was able to command his own terms in Hollywood during the late 1930s and early 1940s. He was the only writer at MGM without the standard "morals" clause in his contract—he said he'd sign when **Louis B. Mayer** did—and he worked at home when he pleased, at a work table rigged up in his bathtub. He was also active in the film craft unions, took time out to write a pacifist novel, *Johnny Got His Gun* (1939), and somewhat casually joined what he called the "Red Cross" (Communist Party), a wartime gesture of concern for international social justice. Trumbo contributed some incisive social commentary to the *Nation*, and might have become a serious writer if he hadn't been dependent on

Hollywood-scale remuneration to support a lifestyle which included a mansion on Beverly Drive and a ranch in the Tehachapis—"swimming pool Communists," such leftists were called derisively. Subpoenaed to testify in 1947 before the House Un-American Activities Committee, he refused to name names, spent ten months in prison for contempt of Congress, and waited out the rest of the McCarthy era in Mexico. Back in Hollywood during the mid-1950s the blacklisted writers formed a tight little band of brothers, nourishing a cult of persecution—except for Trumbo, who was soon busy writing scripts under pseudonyms. As Robert Rich he won an Oscar in 1957 for *The Brave One*, and in 1960 he broke the blacklist when

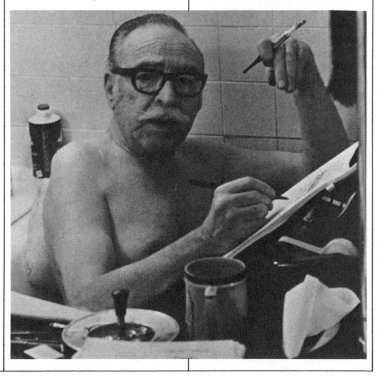

his name went on the screen for *Exodus.* Pugnacious to the end, he quarreled with some of his fellow radicals over their cult of martyrdom. Those who testified to save their careers, he argued, were also victims of a pernicious era.

Bruce Cook wrote a good biography, Dalton Trumbo *(New York, 1977). Trumbo wrote* Time of the Toad; Study of the Inquisition in America *(New York, 1972).*

Dick Tuck (Richard Tuck, 1923-   ). Tuck enlivened state and national political campaigns for a generation with his mischief-making, particularly at the expense of **Richard Nixon**. A one-time student at UC Santa Barbara and an active supporter of **Helen Gahagan Douglas** in the 1950 U.S. Senate race, he once hired a large auditorium for challenger Nixon, limited attendance to a handful, and called for a discussion of the International Monetary Fund. In 1962, when Nixon was campaigning for governor in L.A.'s Chinatown, Tuck planted a poster asking in ideograms about the loan Nixon's brother had received from **Howard Hughes**. Tuck himself ran unsuccessfully for the state senate in 1966. Walking Robert Kennedy's dog during the 1968 primary, he quipped, "To you it may be just a dog, but to me it's an ambassadorship." Describing himself as "independently poor," Tuck continued to crop up at all the conventions, writing and lecturing on humor in politics.

Lana Turner (Julia Jean Turner, 1920-   ). The heart of any small town is its drugstore. In Hollywood, that drugstore is called Schwab's and it is enshrined in legend

as the place where sweatergirl Lana Turner was discovered. Actually, it was about a mile east, in a now extinct soda shoppe across the street from Hollywood High School, that publisher Bud Wilkerson asked the fifteen-year-old sophomore if she wouldn't like to be in pictures. Her name was changed to Lana (as in "lah-de-dah," not "lady") and her mother, a beautician, died her brown hair so often it once came out green, but she demonstrated definite "screen impact" as the sexy girl-next-door in *They Won't Forget* (1937). She also retained the aura of a girl who might just hang out in a drugstore waiting to be

discovered. Lana finished her education at MGM, where she attended school with Mickey Rooney and Judy Garland and soon acquired a reputation as a good-time girl. ("If Lana Turner will behave herself," **Louella Parsons** warned in her column, "she is headed for a top spot. . . .") Lana managed to make it without behaving herself. Her film roles were tailored to capitalize on her quality of innocent notoriety—*Slightly Dangerous, The Merry Widow, The Bad and the Beautiful, Peyton Place, Imitation of Life,*etc. Her private live had always been public property and never more so than in 1958 when her thirteen-year-old daughter Cheryl Crane

fatally stabbed her lover, Johnny Stompanato, a smalltime hoodlum with a reputation for blackmailing lonely women. In Hollywood's biggest scandal since **Fatty Arbuckle**, the tabloids ran Lana's love letters to Stompanato. The death was ruled justifiable homicide, and Cheryl ended up in a home for delinquent girls from which she escaped twice. For Lana Turner, it was mostly downhill after that. Harold Robbins wrote a thinly disguised novel about the scandal, *Where Love Has Gone,* and the star's estranged sixth husband wrote a novel about an aging glamor queen, *The Body Brokers.* There was yet another unsuccessful marriage, after which Miss Turner occupied herself with preparing her memoirs.

In discussing her autobiography, Lana *(New York, 1982), a New York Times reviewer described her as a literary descendent of Louella Parsons.*

Mark Twain (Samuel Langhorne Clemens, 1835-1910). It was in San Francisco that Sam Clemens, a shrewd young scribbler from Missouri, became Mark Twain, highly beloved American writer. He arrived in

1864, age 28, after two and a half years observing the workings of the silver craze in Nevada, where his brother had been appointed secretary to the territorial governor. Clemens joined the literary circle around San Francisco's *Golden Era* and the *Californian*, got a job as a reporter for the *Daily Morning Call*, and began to experiment with style, humor, vernacular. Summing up the local weather, he wrote: "It has only snowed twice in San Francisco in nineteen years, and then it only remained on the ground long enough to astonish the children." Covering society, he observed that "Miss C.L.B. had her nose elegantly enameled, and the easy grace with which she blew it from time to time marked her as a cultivated and accomplished woman." He attended earthquakes, seances, and found the police an inexhaustible subject of serious fun. ("Ain't they spry? Ain't they energetic? Don't they make everybody nervous and dizzy with their frightful velocity?"). All the while Clemens was collecting material. At the Turkish baths he met a man named Tom Sawyer, who later hung a sign over his tavern at Third and Mission identifying himself as the original. The *Sacramento Union* sent Clemens to the Sandwich Islands, which on his return provided the subject for public lectures at one dollar a head admission ("the audacity of the proposition was charming") and the kernel of his first full-length book, *Innocents Abroad* (1869). By then, he was already famous as the author of the comic

masterpiece, "The Celebrated Jumping Frog of Calaveras County," written in 1865, while laying low in the country. When the Civil War ended, Clemens led the return of California writers to the American mainstream, saying of California: "It's a great place to live, but I wouldn't want to visit there."

The Autobiography of Mark Twain (New York, 1959) has gone through numerous editions. Roughing It (Hartford, CN, 1872) is Twain's semifictional account of the years in Nevada and California. Mark Twain's San Francisco (New York, 1963) has an excellent introduction by Bernard Taper and a selection of writings from the period, while Mark Twain in San Francisco, edited by Edgar Branch (Berkeley, 1969), includes all his writings for the Call, *daily reporting which he personally considered "sheer soulless drudgery."*

Luis Miguel Valdez
(1941-   ). The impresario of the Chicano cultural renaissance, Valdez was born to Mexican farm workers in Delano, capital of plantation California. (He grew up in the era of the Cisco Kid and the pachuco, Anglo contempt and noisy jukeboxes.) Valdez left the valley at fourteen, did his apprenticeship with the San Francisco Mime Troupe, and returned in the 1960s in the wake of farm worker

unionization by **Cesar Chavez**. For ten years on strike lines and street corners, Valdez's El Teatro Campesino performed mini-morality plays, variously described as "proletarian pantomime" and pure "agitprop." There was a hit play, *Zoot Suit*, based on Anglo-Chicano cultural conflict in World War II Los Angeles. (Thomas Sanchez wrote a 1978 novel on the same subject, entitled *Zoot-Suit Murders*.) Opened in 1978, Valdez's play moved to Broadway in 1979 where it was not a hit, and was made into a film, also not terribly successful. In 1981, El Teatro Campesino acquired its own theater, a converted packing shed in San Juan Bautista, thanks to a grant from the **Irvine** Foundation.

Rudy Vallee (Hubert Prior Vallee, 1901-   ). A popular early crooner with a Yale degree (1927) and a repertoire including his alma mater's "Whiffenpoof Song," Vallee made the transition from singing at tea-dances to performing on radio, film, and the stage. Whether cast as a *Vagabond Lover* (1929), as a stuffed shirt in *The Palm Beach Story* (1942), or as a singing businessman in Broadway's *How to Succeed in Business without Really Trying* (1961), he always seemed to be playing a caricature of himself. A New Englander by birth and by style, Vallee would rate mention here no more than generations of greater and lesser stars who passed through Hollywood, except that he tried to alter the landscape. Finding himself at

loose ends during the rock 'n' roll era, he flirted with the idea of running for mayor of Los Angeles in 1959 and again in 1967, imagining himself a Jimmy Walker, popular "hizzoner" of New York. When that image evaporated, Vallee tried to put his name on the map. Silvertop, his pseudo-Hitlerian castle in the Hollywood Hills, with a Catalina view and a championship tennis court atop a four-story bunker, is located on Pyramid Place. When Vallee tried to get his address changed to match his name, inspired by a French street sign for the rue de Vallée, he aroused a backlash highly unusual for a city where celebrity is nobility. "Why doesn't Vallee change his name to Pyramid Place?" a cynic suggested.

Vallee published two memoirs incorporating much of the same memorabilia: My Time Is Your Time *(New York, 1962) and* Let the Chips Fall *(Harrisburg, PA 1975).*

Mariano Guadalupe Vallejo (1808-1890). Vallejo was the Yankees' favorite Mexican, a progressive who favored American ideals, a

man of dignity with a stature superior to that of his temperamental and improvident compatriots. Born in California, the son of a soldier in **Junípero Serra's** guard, he claimed pure Spanish blood and nurtured the extravagant pride of the grandee. At nineteen he became a member of the territorial legislature, and at 27 was appointed military commander and "director of colonization" on California's northern frontier, stretching from San Francisco Bay to the Russian colony at Fort Ross. For ten years Vallejo ruled this territory like a feudal seigneur, personally acquiring 66,622 acres through two land grants. He pacified the Indians, founded the town of Sonora, and lived the life of a cultured country gentleman. He employed a Russian music teacher for his daughters and named his sons after the books in his library (Plutarcho, Platon, Napoleon). Vallejo remained aloof from the comic-opera coups of the late Mexican era, encouraged his sisters to marry Yankees, and gave land to new arrivals from the States. Despite his known sympathies, he was interned during the American conquest but submitted to the indignity calmly. He was also philosophical when the legislature refused his offer of land for a state capital (after he had incurred considerable expenditure), and when U.S. courts disallowed one of his land grants; certainly he had more than enough left. As a delegate to California's Constitutional Convention, Vallejo chaired the committee which translated the old Mexican districts into new California counties, to some of which he gave Spanish names. (*Solano* was named after his Indian satrap.) The last surviving leader of his generation, he took an ironic view of the changes occasioned by statehood. As he remarked to Abraham Lincoln on a visit to Washington, D.C., "The Yankees are wonderful people. . . Wherever they go, they make improvements. If they were to emigrate to hell itself, they would irrigate it, plant trees and flower gardens, build reservoirs and fountains and make everything beautiful and pleasant, so that by the time we get there, we can sit down at a marble-topped table and eat ice-cream." The land over which Vallejo once ruled is now covered with testimonial plaques to his achievements, including the Petaluma Adobe, which he built in 1834 and Lachryma Montes (Latin for "tear of the mountain"), his later American-style home. The town of Vallejo grew up on the land once offered for a state capital, while Benicia across the Suisun Bay was named after his wife.

Vallejo was the only member of his generation to inspire a full-scale Yankee-style biography, Vallejo, Son of California *(Portland, OR, 1944) by Myrtle McKittrick.*

S.S. Van Dine (Willard Huntington Wright, 1888-1939). Wright is best known as S.S. Van Dine, the creator of Philo Vance, a fictional detective in the author's own rather effete, East Coast image. Wright first achieved fame as "the boy iconoclast of Southern California," a cub reporter for the *Los Angeles Times* who wrote an artful exposé of Bohemian literary sexuality in Carmel ("Hotbed of Soulful Culture, Vortex of Erotic Erudition"). This 1910 article won him a promotion to literary editor of the *Times* at the age of 22 but Wright, who came from a genteel southern family, had his eye on the eastern mainline. In 1912 he left for New York and broke into the literary establishment with an anti-Los Angeles article for *Smart Set* that caused a furor, raised circulation overnight, and led to Wright's appointment as editor of the magazine. L.A., Wright wrote, was really a midwestern city run by transplanted village yokels with their predilection for corned beef, their smothering rural pieties, and their obsession with respectability. L.A. also offered "rare and glowing opportunities for faddists and mountebanks," "romantic scientists" dangling "the tinsel star of erudition before the eyes of the semi-educated. . . [and] infinite wisdom without the necessity of hard study." Wright, a Pomona College dropout who was expelled from Harvard

University for drinking absinthe in class (to wash the lectures down, of course), liked to think of himself as a linguist and a scholar. He tried composing music in the manner of Debussy and published a book on aesthetics in 1916 but soon found himself back in Los Angeles in disgrace, writing for movie magazines after an ill-conceived pro-German prank during World War I. While recovering from a nervous breakdown and drug addiction in 1923, he began to read detective novels and decided to try writing some. His first mystery, published in 1926 under the Van Dine pseudonym to protect his serious reputation, broke publishing records for the genre. Starring Philo Vance as the last of the upper-class house-party detectives, Wright's mysteries sold over a million books and were made into 27 movies with Basil Rathbone, Paul Lukas, and William Powell as the debonair, longwinded detective.

The best available source on Wright is Jon Tuska's The Detective in Hollywood *(Garden City, NY, 1978). Wright's article on Carmel is reprinted in Lawrence Ferlinghetti's* Literary San Francisco *(San Francisco, 1980).*

Isaac Newton Van Nuys

(1835-1912). In the 1870s, after cattle ranching had been wiped out by drought, California became the granary of the world thanks largely to Van Nuys. Born in New York of Dutch ancestry, he set out for California in 1865 because of his asthma. He opened up a store in Northern California and went into partnership with his future father-in-law, Isaac Lankershim, a German-born rancher with extensive holdings in Fresno and San Diego County. In 1869 Lankershim bought 60,000 acres in the San Fernando Valley and Van Nuys moved south to try to grow wheat there. Deeply ingrained with the farming ethic, he put off his children's requests for pocket money "until the rains come." The new land and climate seemed to favor wheat, and Van Nuys and Lankershim built a road south through Sepulveda Canyon to take their harvest to the primitive port at San Pedro, the first cargo ever shipped abroad (to Liverpool) from Los Angeles. Van Nuys also built a flour mill in downtown Los Angeles, eventually moved his family there, and began to invest his profits in commercial real estate, including the Van Nuys Hotel and the Van Nuys Building on Spring Street. (Lankershim, meanwhile, converted from Jew to Baptist and became the chief benefactor of **Isaac Kalloch**'s Metropolitan Temple in San Francisco.) The era of wheat cultivation in the San Fernando Valley lasted only as long as Van Nuy's lifetime. First, there was a rash of squatters contesting title to the old Spanish land grant. More serious was the shortage of water. The Lankershim-Van Nuys holdings were near the source of the Los Angeles River and under traditional riparian doctrine would have had first claim to the river's flow. In 1899, however, the Supreme Court ruled that the city of Los Angeles had prior claim to the river under Mexican and Spanish law. Ten years later Van Nuys auctioned off all his harvesters and threshers and sold most of his land in the valley to the **Chandler** syndicate, which would reap a bonanza with the completion of the aqueduct bringing water from the Owens River Valley.

James R. Page wrote a short biographical sketch, Isaac Newton Van Nuys *(Los Angeles, 1944).*

Tiburcio Vásquez

(1835-1875). The most famous bandito of his day, Vásquez spent twenty years robbing and rustling from Monterey County, where he was born, south to Los Angeles, motivated by general resentment of gringos—"I believed we were being unjustly deprived of the social rights that belonged to us." In 1857 he was caught for horse stealing and sent to San Quentin, where he was to return periodically. In 1873 Vásquez led his band of brigands in a holdup at Tres Piños near present-day Hollister, leaving three men dead. With a reward on his head, he went into hiding in the mountains and canyons of Southern California, then the best part of the country for hiding out, according to a San Francisco reporter named George Beers. (Two of his hiding places were named Vasquez Canyon and Vasquez Rocks.) Reporter Beers participated in the capture of Vásquez in the Hollywood Hills in May 1874, actually shooting Vásquez in the fracas. Over the next eight months, held in a San Jose cell awaiting trial, Vásquez became an object of curiosity and celebrity. He had a souvenir portrait taken for distribution to his many visitors, received flowers and

telegrams, and did not deny rumors of the Mexican Army arriving to prevent his execution. Through it all, observers noted, his "self-possession was supreme." A great crowd gathered to witness the bandit chief, "a man and a Californian," die with dignity on the gallows.

The California Outlaw Tiburcio Vásquez (Los Gatos, 1960), compiled by Robert Greenwood, includes the contemporary account by Beers.

Thorstein Bunde Veblen

(1857-1929). The trustees of Stanford University were pushing vocational education at the turn of the century when President **David Starr Jordan** hired economist Veblen to strengthen his academic hand. Author of *The Theory of the Leisure Class* (1899) with its critique of "conspicuous consumption," Veblen was an eccentric who had great difficulty in establishing a vocation himself. Born in Wisconsin of Norwegian parentage, he remained unemployed for years after earning his Ph.D. from Yale (1884). When the offer came from Stanford he had more or less been asked to leave the University of Chicago for fraternizing with the opposite sex. Women found some mysterious attraction in the professor and pursued him tenaciously, prompting his wife to leave him repeatedly. (She accompanied him to Palo Alto but soon left him for good.) Veblen's bachelor household at Cedro Cottage grew to include two needy students and their dying father, a Socialist housekeeper and her mother, and a little girl who thought the professor's initials stood for "Teddy Bear."

Veblen was not popular at Stanford which he considered too "country club." He discouraged students from enrolling in his classes by requiring excessive preparation, mumbling his lectures, and giving all C's. The trustees were antagonized by his pointed remarks about robber barons who purchased immortality for the price of a few classrooms and books. A decade earlier, liberal sociologist E. A. Ross had been fired because Mrs. Jane Stanford did not like his views. It therefore came as little surprise when Veblen was asked to leave Stanford in 1909, on the convenient grounds of "compulsive womanizing." After two more decades of academic wandering, he returned to Palo Alto to spend his last days alone and forgotten.

Joseph Dorfman wrote Thorstein Veblen and His America *(New York, 1934). Robert Duffus, who with his brother lived at Veblen's cottage, left an affectionate memoir,* Innocents at Cedro *(New York, 1941).*

August Vollmer

(1876-1955). Police science was pretty primitive at the turn of the century when Vollmer started out, an amateur among amateurs. A 29-year-old former mailman and Spanish American war veteran, he was elected police chief to clean up the town of Berkeley. On his first gambling raid, "the boy marshal" neglected to get enough evidence for conviction and had difficulty identifying his Chinese suspects. But Vollmer learned quickly and proved an enlightened innovator. His Berkeley police were the first in the U.S. to cover their

beats by bicycle, and in 1914, the first to become fully motorized. Vollmer kept files of fingerprints and modus operandi, experimented with communications systems and early lie detectors, and studied the causes and social dimensions of crime. Trying to improve the caliber of personnel, he instituted tests and recruited UC students as part-time "college cops." As Vollmer's fame spread, he was invited to help other cities beef up law enforcement. (At the end of a year in Los Angeles, his enemies—presumably criminals—ran billboards announcing that "The first of September will be the last of August.") The Berkeley chief with only a grade-school education became in 1929 the first professor of police administration in the U.S., at the University of Chicago. Three years later he retired from the Berkeley force to accept a similar professorship at the nearby University of California, devoting the rest of his life to teaching and writing

about progressive law enforcement. Methodical to the end, he escaped a protracted terminal illness by committing suicide, telling a servant to "call the police!" just before shooting himself.

Alfred Parker's Crime Fighter: August Vollmer *(New York, 1961) is a juvenile biography. Nathan Douthit's article in the* California Historical Society Quarterly *(Summer 1975) contains the same information in more adult form.*

Jerry Voorhis

(Horace Jeremiah Voorhis, 1901-   ). The California congressman whose career came to an end at the hands of **Richard Nixon**, Voorhis was a prototype for **Frank Capra's** *Mr. Smith Goes to Washington*, the earnest idealist in politics. Growing up affluent in Kansas, Voorhis worried about the inequality of wealth. As a Yale undergraduate he experienced a religious conversion and set out after graduation to practice what he preached, starting as an itinerant laborer. Voorhis found his vocation as teacher and surrogate father to homeless boys, using his inheritance to establish a school in the shadows of Southern California's San Dimas mountains. Moved by **Upton Sinclair**'s campaign to End Poverty in California, he first ran for Congress in 1934 and was elected in 1936 to represent the twelfth district, stretching from Pomona to San Gabriel. In Washington he earned the reputation of a rare saint in politics, compulsively mastering every issue and forming a principled opinion on every bill. He worked with almost religious zeal for school lunch programs, aid to migrant labor, and loans for small farmers, whom he considered the backbone of American life. He felt strongly about

Congress's failure to "break the stranglehold of monopoly," and was able by his alertness to head off a Standard Oil attempt to take over the same oil reserves that **E.L. Doheny** had relinquished twenty years earlier. In 1946 Voorhis with his earnest, boring speeches on serious issues was defeated for reelection by a sharp, ambitious young lawyer from Whittier, Richard Nixon, thanks to a telephone campaign suggesting Voorhis was a "Commie." Turning the other cheek, Voorhis settled in Chicago to spend the next twenty years working for the cooperative movement.

Voorhis wrote Confessions of a Congressman *(New York, 1947) and* The Christian in Politics *(New York, 1951).*

George Raymond Wagner. *See* Gorgeous George.

William Walker

(1824-1860). For most American adventurers of his generation, San Francisco was the El Dorado at land's end, but for Walker the city was only a springboard to greater glory. Born and raised in Nashville, nurtured on what **Twain** called the "Sir Walter [Scott] disease," he was a

knight in search of a quest. He tried medicine, law, and journalism, but these did not satisfy his need for Byronic grandeur. Arriving in San Francisco in 1850, he became the crusading editor of the *Herald*. Restless again, in 1853 he raised an expedition of 45 "colonists" to liberate Sonora and Baja California, posing as the advance guard of American democracy. This "filibustering" venture, financed by San Francisco capitalists with an eye on Sonora's mineral wealth, failed miserably. But Walker, tried and acquitted by a San Francisco jury of violating U.S. neutrality laws, emerged as something of a heroic figure. His biographer describes him as driven by ambition and idealism, "an addict of danger," a true and charismatic believer in his mission to civilize the

savages. In 1855 Walker raised another army of adventurers and poets, the type of men who could be heard arguing the relative merits of Aeschylus and Euripides over a campfire. They included **Joaquin Miller** (if we can take his word for anything), **Horace Bell**, and one of **John Sutter**'s sons, who eventually died of a tropical disease contracted on the venture. The destination this time was the troubled Central American republic of Nicaragua, which Walker invaded, conquered, and as its elected president set out to Americanize. Defeated in 1857 by a coalition of Central American states financed by Cornelius Vanderbilt, who had valuable interests in the country, he surrendered his powers and returned home, again a hero. There was a second expedition to Nicaragua later that year, a failure, after which the former president set down his memoirs in the style of Caesar's *Commentaries*. His final expedition, to liberate the Caribbean island of Roatán, ended in his execution by a Honduran firing squad.

Walker's memoirs were published as The War in Nicaragua *(Mobile, AL, 1860). Albert Z. Carr's* The World and William Walker *(New York, 1963) is good biography.*

Irving Wallace

(1916-   ). When **The Chapman Report** was published in 1960, *Los Angeles* magazine called its author the "Boccaccio of Brentwood." Banned in Italy, denounced by **Hedda Hopper** and **Louella Parsons**, barred from library shelves, *Chapman* was a fictionalized account of a Kinsey-type sex survey conducted in an affluent Southern California suburb resembling Brentwood, where Wallace lived. (Recognizing themselves in the novel's bored, frustrated, promiscuous housewives, some neighbors complained of invasion of privacy.) Wallace, who started writing magazine articles as a teenager in Wisconsin, moved to Hollywood at nineteen and wrote such movie scripts as *Jive Junction* (1943) and *Meet Me at the Fair* (1953). Thanks to a steady succession of his

extensively researched novels (*The Prize*, 1962; *The Seven Minutes*, 1967) he became one of the world's richest writers, reigning over a private library resembling a movie set and hosting in Brentwood the kind of parties Hollywood can no longer afford. Wallace also enterprised a new form of popular literary production, the collectively researched and written *People's Almanacs* and *Books of Lists*. Also prepared collectively, *The Intimate Sex Lives of Famous People* (1981) extended the sex circle begun with *Chapman* from Brentwood to the whole world.

Wallace cooperated with John Leverence in the preparation of A Writer's Profile *(Bowling Green, OH, 1974).*

Joseph Aloysius Wambaugh (1937-).

When Wambaugh bought his first Cadillac, he chose a black and white model, to ease the transition from police sergeant to celebrity novelist. A second-generation cop born in Pittsburgh of Irish-German ancestry, he joined the Los Angeles Police Department after earning a B.A. at Cal State L.A. in 1960. A decade later he published his first book, *The New Centurians*, depicting policemen as lonely, ordinary human beings, susceptible to corruption, violence, fear, and hope. Officially reprimanded for failing to get permission to publish, he nonetheless stayed on the force, turning out a second novel and a novelized account of a local cop-killing, *The Onion Field* (1973). With best sellerdom,

Wambaugh, a conservative Catholic family man, moved up from the Pomona Valley where he had lived since he was fourteen. He chose the exclusive enclave of San Marino in preference to Beverly Hills because the neighbors had brand names rather than screen credits, he joked—really, because it was more conservative and provincial than Beverly Hills. Wambaugh finally left the LAPD in 1974 with regret, for it was an unequaled source of drama and color as well as a way of life. But he continued to write about that life, most recently in *The Glitter Dome* (1981).

Jack L. Warner

(1892-1978). The Warners were a large, closely-knit tribe of immigrants from Poland who subscribed to the old-fashioned work ethic, the idea of everybody pulling together, the sanctity of contract. In the hedonistic world of Hollywood, therefore, Jack, who ran the family studio, was ill-equipped to deal with any contract actor who became a star. After all, he continued to pay the contract players who never made it at the box office—why should a contract become invalid simply because the studio made a hit movie? And so Warner Brothers became famous for its stars who refused to shine, actors who spent more time on suspension than at work at the "Buchenwald of Burbank"—Olivia de Havilland, Bogart, Bette Davis, Cagney. Davis complained the loudest, but it was de Havilland who went to

court and won a judgement that a contract longer than seven years constitutes involuntary servitude. Never mind that there was enough left after paying all the "help" for the brothers (Harry, Albert, Sam) and assorted relatives to live extremely well, including vacations on the French Riviera. (Jack preferred to host the French Riviera at his Beverly Hills mansion, which boasted its own golf course.) It was the principle of the thing. Everybody was on the make, greedy agents were ruining his actors, and Jack's only loyal friend in Hollywood was a Turkish masseur. (His popularity was not increased by his dropping a lot of names before the McCarthy-era witchhunting committees.) Nowhere in his autobiography does he say much about the movies that made Warner

Brothers' fame and fortune, the tightly integrated black-and-white social dramas: *Little Caesar, Casablanca, Streetcar Named Desire*. In Hollywood history, Warner Brothers ranks as the first studio to introduce sound and one of the last to hold out against the conglomerates. It was sold in 1966 to Seven Arts Corp.

Warner wrote My First Hundred Years in Hollywood *(New York, 1965).*

John Trumbell Warner

(Juan José Warner), 1807-1895). A Connecticut Yankee who came overland by the Santa Fe Trail on **Jedediah Smith**'s last trip, Warner changed his name and citizenship in order to qualify for a land grant in Mexican California. Warner's Ranch, where the Santa Fe Trail branched off to San Diego and Los Angeles, became an important waystation and trading post for 49ers and other new settlers. Many of them remembered the tall, blue-eyed trader, looking half Mexican and half sailor in his short jacket and bell-bottom trousers, as the first Californian they met. Warner's Ranch with its hot springs was also an important gathering place for local Indians, some of whom sacked and burned the trading post in 1851. Warner never rebuilt and eventually lost title under the new U.S. land laws. Elected to the state senate in 1850, he completed his term and settled in Los Angeles to found a newspaper. *The Southern Vineyard*, dedicated to harmony between Latin and Anglo, became embroiled in

Civil War-era conflicts. An ardent abolitionist, Warner was accused by southern sympathizers of treason during the Bear Flag Revolt and tried to defend himself in his newspaper. He was elected to the state legislature again in 1860 and became the first president of the Historical Society of Southern California in 1883. He also watched over living history in the person of **Pío Pico**, the indigent former governor of California, whom he supported in his old age.

Lorrin Morrison wrote Warner, The Man and the Ranch *(Los Angeles, 1962).*

Earl Warren (1891-1974). When Warren first went into California politics, a Republican party official urged him to claim descent from the Warrens of Virginia. In fact, his parents were born in Scandinavia, raised in the Midwest, and left all roots 2,000 miles behind to settle in the dusty valley town of Bakersfield, where any pretense at southern aristocracy would have been a joke. Warren's father, a hardworking railroad employee, insisted that his son attend college, so he enrolled at UC Berkeley, joined a fraternity and played clarinet in the band, and went on to the first class at Boalt Hall law school (J.D., 1914). Exhilarated by the cool breezes of the Bay Area after a childhood of dusty heat, he settled in Oakland where he was elected district attorney in 1914, making a reputation as a crimebuster. Elected state attorney general in 1939, he shut down dog-racing tracks in Northern

California and gambling ships in the south. Even-tempered, affable, with a quality of "friendly honesty," Warren was easily elected governor in 1942 and twice reelected. A Republican by registration, he sought and won bipartisan support, staffed his administration without regard to party, and pushed for progressive legislation including a medical insurance bill three times defeated by the American Medical Association lobby. Once a lawyer concerned with the strict observance of law and its enforcement, he broadened out to explore the concept of social justice. Warren and his large, attractive family occupied the Victorian governor's mansion in Sacramento for over ten years, the longest residence

of any first family in state history. In 1952 he played a pivotal role in the presidential nomination of Eisenhower, for which he was rewarded in 1953 by appointment as Chief Justice of the U.S. Supreme Court. There, the railroad man's son from Bakersfield, California, became known as a radical libertarian. In his first major decision, *Brown* v. *the Board of Education* (1954), he struck down segregation in education, later outlawing it in transportation and recreation as well. The Warren Court extended the substance of individual liberty under the Bill of Rights to include the right to free counsel, and protection against self-incrimination and unreasonable search and seizure. Warren also mandated legislative

reapportionment ("One man, one vote") which as governor he had resisted for reasons of political expediency. As Chief Justice for sixteen years, he was distinguished by his sense of fair play and basic tolerance rather than legal brilliance or moral superiority. He liked to think of himself as above politics, but in fact he had highly competitive partisan instincts. He once went to three football games in one weekend, and his memoirs (1977) are full of devastating asides about the stupidity and self-aggrandizement of political colleagues from Eisenhower to **Goodie Knight**.

California historian John Weaver wrote Warren: The Man, The Court, The Era *(Boston, 1967).*

Robert Whitney Waterman (1826-1891). California's seventeenth governor (1887-1891), Waterman first came west with the Gold Rush, then returned to Illinois where he was active in the new Republican Party. He came back to settle in San Bernardino in 1873, developing a silver mine in the Calico area. The nearby junction of the Santa Fe and California Southern railways was named first for him, then in 1886 renamed Barstow, to Waterman's pique. That year he shifted his base of operations south to Julian, where he bought the Stonewall (Jackson) Mine and an extensive cattle ranch. The mine, which was believed to be exhausted, yielded over a million dollars worth of ore in the next five years. Waterman was elected lieutenant governor as a Republican in 1886 and succeeded to the governorship when Washington Bartlett (a Democrat) died a few months into his term. "Old Honesty," as Waterman was called, planned to run the state just like a private business, announcing that he would not tolerate dishonesty or drunkenness. Failing to win nomination for a second term, he retired to San Diego. His ranch near Julian eventually became part of Cuyamaca State Park.

Alan Wilson Watts (1915-1973). For Watts, a student of Oriental religions who called himself a "spiritual entertainer," Marin County seemed the very edge of Western civilization. As a boy in England he had become interested in the Far East by reading Fu Manchu novels, a welcome escape from the culture of boiled beef and chilblains. He converted to Buddhism at fifteen, moved to the U.S. in 1940, and found a temporary spiritual home in the Episcopal Church. (As long as you accept the Book of Common Prayer, he remarked, you can be a theosophist or even a Marxist.) Watts left the Episcopal ministry in 1950 and completed his spiritual journey to the East by moving to the Bay Area, where he lived alternately on a converted ferryboat (the S.S. *Vallejo*) in Sausalito and at a retreat on Mount Tamalpais. He taught at San Francisco's American Academy of Asian Studies, lectured on KPFA radio, ran some of the first encounter groups at Esalen, and wrote literate books (*Psychotherapy East and West*, 1961; *The Joyous Cosmology*, 1962) full of suggestive insights. ("Isn't it possible that space itself is an amniotic fluid?") Watts was an unrepentant sensualist who preferred "active Zen" to "stone-Buddha" asceticism. Fond of wearing priestly robes, he saw himself in a sacerdotal role, keeper of the ancient magic. In this he remained eminently British, rejecting the artificial intimacy of the "Hi, Al" society and the humorless slovenliness of Beats and hippies in favor of style, ritual, and wit.

Watts wrote an intelligent autobiography, In My Own Way *(New York, 1972).*

John Wayne (Marion Morrison, 1907-1979). In the local order of things, the University of Southern California ranks as a party school and a football factory, in contrast to its more academic and democratic crosstown rival, UCLA. Wayne came from a financially and emotionally distressed suburban family, but membership on Glendale High School's undefeated 1925 football team became his ticket of admission to USC. (According to a popular variation on a school football song, the goal was to "Fight on for old S.C./The halfback wants his sal-a-ree.") Wayne pledged Sigma Chi and gained a reputation for prodigious alcohol consumption before dropping out to have a try at Hollywood. He started as a stuntman and only gradually settled into the role of a rawboned western hero, relying on a personal staff writer to cut all the "sissy" stuff from his dialogue. After a decade of quickie westerns, Wayne found a director who could capitalize on his personal authority and magnetism, John Ford, who starred him in *Stagecoach* (1939), *Fort Apache* (1948),

She Wore a Yellow Ribbon (1949), and *Rio Grande* (1950). Without Ford, Wayne went on to make *The Conqueror* (1955), *The Alamo* (1960), and *The Green Berets* (1968), all turkeys, but it didn't seem to matter as long as Wayne was the star. In life as in art, he stood for the traditional values of an idealized past. He was an early member of the Motion Picture Alliance for the Preservation of American Ideals, a group advocating vigilance against Communism. ("Wayne Calls for Delousing Film Reds," blared a 1950 headline.) He also personally licked another insidious "big C," cancer. In later years Wayne lived in Newport Beach in conservative Orange County, heartland of the John Birch Society. Orange County embraced him as a native son, named its airport after him and commissioned an eight-and-a-half foot statue of the actor to make the point. Another local reminder of his residence is Newport's John Wayne Tennis Club, where Declaration-of-Independence decor coexists with space-age electronic scoreboards.

See Maurice Zolotow's biography of Wayne, Shooting Star *(New York, 1974).*

Nathan Weinstein. *See* Nathanael West.

Johnnie Weissmuller (Peter John Weissmuller, 1904-   ). As a swimmer Weissmuller was the superman of his day, winning a total of five gold medals at the 1924 and 1928 Olympics. His world records would fall with the inevitable improvement of the new sport, but he remained unbeaten during his competitive career and held more records longer than any other swimmer. More than that, to a world just throwing off Victorian morals and physical inhibitions, the tall German-American boy from Chicago with his broad-muscled chest and long tapered limbs was a splendid sight in his swimming trunks. There was a certain natural inevitability in his casting as Tarzan, **Edgar Rice Burroughs**'s prince of the jungle, a role with few speaking lines to trip him up. (In fact, entering into the spirit of the thing, Weissmuller contributed an ancestral yodel to Tarzan's limited vocabulary.) Wearing nothing but a custom loincloth and gallons of liquid makeup over his bare skin (Douglas Fairbanks, Sr. had advised him to eliminate all body hair), he spent years on the backlots of Hollywood fighting jungle beasts, dangerous Hottentots,

and other assorted villains. Offscreen, he pursued the simple pleasures of the California lifestyle, moving to the rustic Uplifters ranch with his third wife and three children, surfing in Santa Monica Bay. As the years passed there were mounting marital problems (five wives in all), weight problems (Tarzan eventually put on some clothes as Jungle Jim) and financial problems, but Weissmuller gave it a good run for the money.

Water, World, and Weissmuller by Narda Onyx (L.A., 1964) is an authorized biography.

John B. Weller

(1812-1875). Weller was a professional politician from Ohio, a "chivalry" Democrat who struck political gold in California in the decade before the Civil War. Educated at Miami (Ohio) University and three times elected to Congress (1839-1845), he narrowly lost his campaign for governor of Ohio in 1848. President James K. Polk appointed him to lead the commission charged with setting the boundary between the U.S. and Mexico, but soon after his arrival in California Polk left office and Weller was replaced by **John C. Frémont**. Weller went into law practice and recouped his political fortunes by winning Frémont's U.S. Senate seat in 1851. Defeated for reelection by **David Broderick** in 1857, he again bounced back as governor of California (1858-1860). To relieve prison conditions and harsh sentences, Weller actually took personal charge of the state prison at San Quentin

during most of 1858 and made extensive use of the governor's pardon power. He also noted the overcrowding of state asylums, filled with human wreckage from the Gold Rush. On the eve of the Civil War, Weller signed a bill for the separation of Southern California into a territory called Colorado, but the measure died for lack of federal action. He was not nominated for reelection but, thanks to his pull in Washington, went off to Mexico as U.S. Minister (1860-1861). After the Civil War he settled in New Orleans.

Wente Family. In

viticulture terms, the Livermore Valley ranks as the Bordeaux of California, thanks to the Wentes. Carl Heinrich Wente (1851-1934), a simple, hardworking German, first settled in the valley in 1883 to make hundreds of thousands of gallons of *vin ordinaire*. Retailed under various labels, the Wente wine began winning prizes in the early years of this century. Carl Wente's eldest son, also Carl (1889-1971), became a banker and was so successful at rehabilitating foreclosed farms for resale during the Depression that he rose through the ranks at the Bank of America to the presidency in 1952. Herman Wente (1892-1961), a graduate of UC (1915), was the chemist and the promoter of the second generation, a popular member of the Bohemian Club, and director of California's Wine Institute. Ernest Wente (1890-1981), the farmer of the family, graduated from what

was then called the University Farm (now UC Davis). During Prohibition he switched the family holdings to livestock ranching but farsightedly kept his equipment in condition to resume winemaking after Repeal in 1934. Under the Wente Brothers label, first introduced that year, the state's finest quality dry white table wines were produced with great care and pride. Winemaking is the most intriguing form of agriculture, according to Ernest Wente— "to grow something and see what you can make of it." In the 1960s, alarmed by urbanization spilling over from the Bay Area, the family began expanding into the Salinas Valley, where the soil is said to resemble that of Reims, France, ideal for champagne.

See Ernest Wente, Winemaking in the Livermore Valley, from the University of California Oral History Office, 1971.

Alma Schindler Mahler Gropius Werfel

(1879-1964). It is difficult to tell from her photographs, which reveal a stout, unsmiling woman, or from her memoirs with their embarrassing sentimentality ("Amo . . . ergo sum"), what fatal attraction she possessed for the great Central European geniuses of her generation. For Alma Schindler, the daughter of an Austrian landscape painter, married in succession composer Gustav Mahler, architect Walter Gropius, and writer Franz Werfel, who was eleven years her junior. (In between marriages, she excited the admiration of artists Gustav Klimt and Oskar Kokoschka and countless others.) She and Werfel (1890-1945) fled the Nazis to Los Angeles in 1940, presumably attracted by the movie industry with its voracious appetite for books. (One of his novels, *The Forty Days of Musa Dagh*, was set to become an MGM movie, until the Turkisk government complained.) Werfel settled in to write his most famous book, *The Song of Bernadette* (1941), inspired by a visit to Lourdes during the exodus from Germany. Hollywood took his book, cast Jennifer Jones as Bernadette, and won five Oscars. Getting his bearings in the unaccustomed landscape, Werfel went on to write a utopian novel, *Star of the Unborn* (1946), variously described as a futuristic travelogue and a "Divine Comedy of our time." Alma, meanwhile, was trying to recreate her Vienna salon in Beverly Hills. The Werfels moved in a select circle of refugee geniuses including the **Mann** brothers and **Arnold Schoenberg**. A guest at Tusculum, as Alma called her house on North Bedford Drive, recalled the hostess as an overbearing woman with the bosom of a pouter pigeon and the voice of a barrack's bugle. Proposing endless toasts, she spiked them with malice against fellow émigrés. After Werfel's death in 1945 she stayed on alone in Beverly Hills but found the landscape increasingly empty and monotonous. (The natives had destroyed Indian culture, she explained, only to replace it with gas stations and beauty shops.) In 1952 she moved to New York. Her daughter **Anna Mahler** (1904-   ), who had come to

visit in 1950, remained to teach at UCLA. A sculptress with a European reputation, her specialty was busts of the great modern composers. Moving into a rustic cottage on Oletha Lane, she used an adjacent lot as an open-air studio while working on her fifteen foot *Tower of Masks* for UCLA's MacGowan Hall. Enjoying a unique entree into the world of music, Anna Mahler was commissioned to make portraits of conductors Otto Klemperer and Alfred Wallenstein for the Los Angeles Music Center. But her most striking creation was probably the mask she made at Arnold Schoenberg's death bed.

Alma Mahler Werfel wrote And the Bridge Is Love *(New York, 1958), an intellectually pretentious variation on the philosophy of fascinating femininity.*

Jessamyn West

(1902-   ). As a child in Yorba Linda, writer Jessamyn West was frightened but exhilarated by the Santa Ana winds sweeping from the desert to the sea, had nightmares about tidal waves, and shared the superstition that, as oil was pumped out, the ground would collapse. She learned to drive at twelve, made all-Southern California Girls Basketball Guard at Fullerton High School, and went on to Whittier College. A birthright Quaker, she attended a Sunday school class taught by her uncle, **Richard Nixon**'s father. As a writer, West is best known for *The Friendly Persuasion* (1945), tales of Quaker life in Civil War America. But it was only as an adult recuperating from

tuberculosis that she became absorbed in the Quaker ethos of her mother's Indiana girlhood. In her nonfiction and in some of her short stories, West explored the landscape of her personal experience, the archetypes of the collective Southern California experience. (The dusty Santa Ana, she was pleased to learn, ranks as one of the world's great winds.) A desert person, she preferred wind to rain, silence to sound, earth-tones to green. (The unnatural lushness of Palm Springs, she once said, is "like finding moss growing in the oven.") She and her husband, also a Quaker from Whittier and an educator, settled in the Napa Valley. But the epic experiences of West's life,

from tuberculosis convalescence to Hollywood screenwriting, all involved a return to Southern California.

West's beautifully written nonfiction works include To See the Dream *(New York, 1956),* Hide and Seek *(New York, 1973) and* The Woman Said Yes *(New York, 1976).*

Nathanael West (Nathan Weinstein, 1903-1940). For most screenwriters of his generation, Hollywood started out as a means to finance their "serious" efforts but soon became an end in itself. West was an exception, a writer who found the high life of the movie capital less interesting than its seamy underside, which he described in surrealistic detail in his novel *Day of the Locust* (1939). Born in New York of

Russian-Jewish ancestry, he entered Brown University on falsified credentials, changed his name, and affected a Brooks Brothers lifestyle. ("Tweedy Boy," **William Saroyan** would later call West.) After graduation he spent two years in Paris, returning to New York to manage a hotel where he put up his friends free of charge. The hotel was good "material," and the hours were good for a writer. In 1933, having published *Miss Lonelyhearts*, West moved to Hollywood to work for one of the second-class studios. The bright sunlight gave him headaches, and there were periods of financial and emotional desperation. Living in a cheap hotel on Ivar Street between studio jobs, he was depressed but fascinated by the tawdriness, the economic and religious cults, the fevered grasping for celluloid immortality — rendered in *Day of the Locust* as the siren song of an omnivorous insect. West was active on behalf of the radical causes of the day, from the Spanish Civil War to migrant labor. He was also an avid hunter, escaping from the "dream-dump" to more primeval preoccupations. He was returning from a hunting trip to Baja California with his wife when they were killed in an automobile crash outside El Centro.

Jay Martin wrote Nathanael West, The Art of His Life *(New York, 1970).*

Edward Weston

(1886-1958). Photographer Edward Weston hated Glendale, synonymous for him with middle-class boredom and conventionality. Married

at 23 to Flora **Chandler** of the newspaper family, he soon fathered four sons whose upbringing kept him shackled to a lifestyle he scorned in a place he loathed. Feeling hemmed in on all sides by real-estate sharks and "other despoilers of beauty," he established a portrait studio in a shack at 4120 Verdant Street and remained there, refusing to learn to drive and declining even to walk ("nothing but cheap ugliness to face"). Never mind that Weston lived within the sight of the wooded hillsides of **Griffith J. Griffith**'s Park; it simply was not where, or who, he wanted

to be. Affecting the cape of a European artist, he conducted affairs with women who came to the studio to pose in the aesthetic altogether. He also explored all the fashionable fads from naturopathy to astrology and the occult. In 1923 Weston decamped for the more congenial squalor of Mexico with artist Tina Modotti. Later he settled in Carmel, hung out his shingle ("Unretouched Portraits"), and became the center of the "f64" group, so-called after the smallest lens opening, the most sharply defined image. Weston found kindred souls in Carmel and a sense of place in the stark beachscapes of

Point Lobos. Novelist Harry Leon Wilson, for example, shared his distaste for Southern California. (Wilson called it "Sunny Cafeteria.") In 1937 Weston won the first Guggenheim fellowship in photography which enabled him to take a professional vacation from portraits. With his young second wife Charis (Wilson's daughter) at the wheel, he traveled the Southwest shooting landscapes almost totally devoid of people. These were printed in *Westways* magazine and collected in a popular book, *California and the West* (1940). Throughout his career, Weston sought abstract purity of form and texture in such objects as clouds, vegetables, sea shells, and the human body, which in his vision appears as impersonal as a vegetable or mineral. But nudes and philanderers remained unacceptable in any form to the babbitts of Southern California. When Weston died in Carmel, his in-laws the **Chandlers** couldn't find room in the massive "midwinter" edition of the *Los Angeles Times* to note the passing of one of the world's great photographers.

See Weston's Daybooks *(Rochester, NY, 1961 and 1966),* Edward Weston: Fifty Years *(1973) by his son Cole, also a photographer, and* Seventy Photographs *by Ben Maddow (Boston, 1973), which contains a biographical essay.*

Benjamin Ide Wheeler

(1854-1927). **Irving Stone** has left an unforgettable account of his first evening at UC Berkeley. The seventeen-year-old freshman was walking anxiously on campus when there appeared to him the apparition of a black-caped man on horseback, lifting his hat in dignified salutation. The equestrian was Wheeler, president of the university, out for his daily ride. A classics scholar from New England with a German Ph.D. (1885), Wheeler was teaching at Cornell in 1899 when the bid came from California. During the next twenty years he would preside over the transition of the small state college into a major university. To compensate for cultural isolation from the centers of American scholarship, he set out to make the UC an academic citadel unto itself. He was instrumental in acquiring the controversial **Bancroft** collection and reportedly recruited benefactors in the style of "Moses striking the rock." Although he was personally something of a benevolent autocrat, Wheeler helped establish the concept of student self-government. Ironically, in view of his efforts to establish institutional permanence, he suffered a major personal setback when a fire in the Berkeley Hills destroyed his own home and belongings. Wheeler Hall was named for him in 1916, despite his policy against naming buildings after living people.

Wheeler's The Abundant Life *(Berkeley, 1926) is a compilation of his articles and speeches.*

Clem Whitaker

(1899-1961) and **Leone Baxter** (1913?-   ). Because of the state's size and the weakness of political party organization in the era of cross-filing, California proved fertile ground for the

application of Madison Avenue techniques to politics. The son of a Baptist preacher, Whitaker was a former state capital reporter and lobbyist who teamed up in 1933 with (and married in 1938) Leone Baxter, head of the Redding Chamber of Commerce, to form a pioneering political campaign management firm. Whitaker and Baxter won their first campaign that year for Pacific Gas and Electric, a referendum against the federal Central Valley Water Project. In 1934 they helped defeat **Upton Sinclair** for governor by using his own radical rhetoric against him. (Is your church a fortress of capitalist graft, they asked voters, and is your marriage a form of prostitution?) Generally aligned with right-wing causes, they helped defeat single-tax and old age pension proposals during the 1930s, health insurance during the 1940s, and legislative reapportionment during the 1950s. For Republican party candidates they handled everything from campaign strategy and publicity to financial management. **Earl Warren** fired Whitaker and Baxter because he didn't like their techniques, which less forthright politicians all over the country were scrambling to imitate. In 1958 the team turned domestic campaigning over to their son and retired to a penthouse suite at San Francisco's Fairmont Hotel, headquarters of Whitaker and Baxter International.

Irwin Ross devotes a chapter of The Image Makers *(Garden City, NY, 1959) to Whitaker and Baxter.*

Stephen Mallory White

(1853-1901). Although Stephen White served only one term as a U.S. Senator from California (1893-1899), he was considered the most famous native son of his day, with a moral stature rare in the heyday of the robber barons. Born in San Francisco, the son of Irish Catholic 49ers, he moved to Los Angeles after graduating from Santa Clara College (1871) and passing the bar. Elected District Attorney of L.A. in 1882, he gained a reputation as a "terror to evil-doers." (He also secured a verdict, probably in private practice, for a girl seduced by **Lucky Baldwin**.) As the Democratic candidate for the U.S. Senate he won the endorsement of the staunchly Republican *L.A. Times*, which described "our Steve" as "a sturdy American boy, square, upright, true as steel, loyal, and brave." A stirring orator, White won his spurs in the Free Harbor fight of 1896, defeating the Southern Pacific campaign for a "monopoly harbor" in Santa Monica. He also opposed the American declaration of war against Spain in 1898 ("Remember the Maine") as "causeless and full of danger." U.S. Senators were elected by state legislature in those days, and White had no hope of reappointment by California's Republican-dominated legislature. After his premature death, the city of L.A., led by **Harrison Gray Otis** and **Harris Newmark**, erected a statue of White with arms outstretched over the civic center, memorializing "The virility of his repeated attacks, his freedom from all contaminating influence, and

his honesty of purpose." The only dissenting opinion is that of **Adela Rogers St. Johns**, who said White was a heavy drinker. The daughter of brilliant lawyer, **Earl Rogers**, whose own career foundered in alcoholism, she should know.

Stephen Mallory White—Californian, Citizen, Lawyer, Senator: His Life and Work *(Los Angeles, 1903), a two-volume compilation of his speeches, was published by the L.A. Times. Edith Dobie wrote* The Political Career of Stephen Mallory White *(Stanford, 1927).*

Charlotte Anita Whitney

(1867-1955). Bay Area socialite Whitney, a niece of U.S. Supreme Court justice **Stephen Field**, became a radical *cause célèbre* during the 1920s. A Wellesley College graduate (1889) of impeccable Mayflower ancestry, she wasn't satisfied with doing genteel "charity work." She became an Alameda County juvenile probation officer in 1903 and progressed through the prohibition and woman suffrage movements to embrace the causes of

socialism and pacifism during World War I. Inspired by the Bolshevik Revolution's promise of social justice, she followed the left wing of the U.S. Socialist Party into the Communist Labor Party in 1919. That year, after giving a speech on "the Negro Problem" for the California Civic League, Whitney was arrested in Oakland under California's new Criminal Syndicalism Act prohibiting, in effect, advocacy of political change. At her 1920 trial, half the spectators were fashionable clubwomen, the other half angry American Legionnaires, the press reported. She was convicted and appealed to the U.S. Supreme Court, which in 1927 ruled against her that constitutional liberties may be abrogated in cases of "clear and present danger of serious evil." Saved from prison by Governor **C.C. Young**'s unsolicited pardon, Whitney became a major figure on the left, serving as state chair and national committeewoman of the U.S. Communist Party and its candidate for the U.S. Senate

in 1940 and 1950. The Criminal Syndicalism Act was finally declared unconstitutional in 1968.

Native Daughter (San Francisco, 1942) by Al Richmond is a sympathetic portrait.

Josiah Dwight Whitney

(1819-1896). The author of a book on the mineral wealth of the U.S., Whitney was appointed state geologist of California in 1860, probably with an eye to the identification of lucrative new mining areas. A well-born New Englander, educated at Yale and in Europe, he arrived with a full set of eastern intellectual prejudices and fully intended to return to civilization as soon as he had filled in the blanks on the California map. Instead, he remained for fourteen years, ranging from topography as far afield as paleontology, often with controversial results. In 1866 his workmen found some skeletal remains which Whitney immediately identified as a great missing link, highly significant for human history. Unfortunately, the Calaveras skull proved of

doubtful antiquity. The state geologist also subscribed to the "cataclysmic theory" of the origin of Yosemite, but was corrected by the self-taught naturalist **John Muir** ("that shepherd," Whitney called him) who saw evidence of glacier formation with his own eyes. Whitney erred again in denying the existence of any oil reserves in California. Solicitous of his political base, he obliged Governor **Leland Stanford** with an official opinion placing the Sierra foothills fifteen miles closer to Sacramento than they actually were at a gain of $240,000 in government subsidies to the railroad-building Big Four. Finally, scholars complained that the state geologist was shipping valuable specimens to Harvard, and the California legislature failed to renew his appropriation. Whitney returned east, leaving his name behind on California's highest mountain.

See Edwin Brewster's Life and Letters of Josian D. Whitney *(Boston, 1909).*

Ray Lyman Wilbur

(1875-1945). Wilbur presided over Stanford University's coming of age, a period when the school's first graduates took over the faculty, the administration, and eventually the country. Born in Iowa, he spent his adolescence on a citrus ranch in Riverside. A tall, commanding, austere figure even as a youth, Wilbur said he chose to enroll at Stanford in 1892 because it had no ivy. He graduated as president of his senior class, earned an M.D. at Cooper Medical College (1899), and returned to Stanford as an

assistant professor of physiology. The only doctor on campus, he pitched in for medical emergencies like a smallpox epidemic and an outbreak of food poisoning at a sorority house. (Smallpox patients were quarantined to a hospital tent on a remote corner of the campus, and Wilbur and others at Stanford recorded a breakthrough in identifying the cause of botulism.) When Cooper became Stanford Medical School, Wilbur served as its first president (1911-1916), going on to the presidency of the university itself. He held the latter position from 1916 until 1943, with time out to work for former classmate **Herbert Hoover**'s World War I Food Administration and as President Hoover's Secretary of the Interior (1929-1933), a job he considered easier than running Stanford. When the subject of Colorado River water came up for discussion during the Hoover administration, neighboring states were convinced that Wilbur favored California at their expense. He continued to practice occasional medicine, consulting during President Warren G. Harding's fatal illness in San Francisco in 1923 and while Interior Secretary assisting at an emergency appendectomy on a wilderness trip. An advocate of rugged individualism, Wilbur opposed socialized medicine, federal aid to education, and "rah rah" school spirit, suggesting that students with trivial intellectual interests would do better at junior college.

See The Memoirs of Ray Lyman Wilbur *(Stanford, 1960).*

Esther Williams

(1923-   ). While hordes of aspiring young actresses were descending on Hollywood in hopes of being discovered, Williams accomplished this feat by leaving Los Angeles for San Francisco. Born and raised in the South L.A. suburb of Inglewood, she graduated from the neighborhood plunge to swim competitively for the L.A. Athletic Club at fifteen. She qualified for the 1940 Olympic Games and, when the games were cancelled because of war, joined Billy Rose's Aquacade at the San Francisco World's Fair, where she was discovered by talent scouts seeking an answer to ice-skater Sonja Henie. Williams is reported to have declined a movie contract because she couldn't act before being persuaded that it didn't matter. MGM constructed a permanent swimming pool set for her and filmed a series of **Busby Berkeley**-style water ballets—*Bathing Beauty* (1944), *Neptune's Daughter* (1949), *Million Dollar Mermaid* (1952)—that grossed $80 million for the studio in a decade. "Wet, she was a star," as one producer put it, but her few attempts at serious roles flopped. Williams moved uptown from Inglewood to Brentwood and invested her film earnings in various business ventures. The "mermaid tycoon," as *Life* magazine called her, became the proprietor of a West L.A. gas station, which opened with a lot of Hollywood hoopla, and a restaurant on Sepulveda Boulevard. She even had her own swimming pool business for awhile (a failure), and wrote a how-to book, *Get in the Swim* (1957.)

Thomas Williams. *See* Thomas Blythe.

Helen Wills. *See* Helen Wills Moody Roark.

Henry Gaylord Wilshire

(1861-1927). The great boulevard stretching from downtown Los Angeles to the sea was named after a millionaire socialist from Ohio, a Harvard graduate whose many interests included publishing, real estate, politics, and popular medicine. Wilshire arrived in L.A. in 1884, founded the first of several radical publications, and in 1890 ran unsuccessfully for Congress as a socialist. After a sojourn in London, where he ran for Parliament, also unsuccessfully, he returned to Southern California to develop his real-estate interests in Fullerton (where there is a Wilshire Avenue today) and downtown L.A. In 1900 he ran for Congress again, gathering more attention than votes. He was arrested that year for speaking publicly in a park (Pershing Square, then called Central Park), in violation of a city ordinance later declared unconstitutional. *Wilshire's*

Magazine, founded in L.A. in 1900 and devoted to coverage of strikes, monopolies, and nature cures, became something of a radical *cause célèbre* when the U.S. Postmaster General refused it second class mailing privileges. In 1903 Wilshire published one of **Jack London**'s early works, *People of the Abyss*. He spent his last two decades in New York, in Canada, and abroad, a "Champion International Peripatetic Office Seeker," publishing his magazine wherever he happened to be. He personally went through several fortunes, instead of practicing the wealth-sharing he preached. (On the contrary, friends and readers were continually being dunned to invest in, say, a Wilshire gold mine.) His last great venture was the "I-on-a-co health belt," advertised to cure cancer, paralysis and baldness by magnetizing the iron in the blood, for a consideration of only $60. *Ralph Hancock wrote* Fabulous

Boulevard *(New York, 1949). The entire run of Wilshire's Magazine is reprinted in* Radical Periodicals in the U.S., 1881-1961, *second series, vol.*

Benjamin Davis Wilson

(1811-1878). One of the first Anglo settlers in Southern California, Wilson arrived via the Santa Fe Trail in 1841, intending to go on to China. Instead he remained and married into the Mexican landowning elite. A trapper and trader from Tennessee, largely uneducated, he rose by force of character to play an important role in the early civic history of Los Angeles. "Don Benito" served briefly as the first Anglo alcalde of L.A. and in 1853 was appointed regional subagent for Indian affairs—the only honest Indian agent ever, it was said. He wrote a report on the neglect and oppression of local tribes, recommending that they be assigned reservations. An ardent Democrat, he served as a state senator (1856-1857 and 1869-1870) and campaigned actively for railroad and harbor development. But he was mainly a rancher, master

of an 1,800-acre estate called Lake Vineyard, site of present-day San Marino and Pasadena. (In addition to wine, Wilson produced a cactus brandy so strong it went down like an electric shock, a friend recalled.) Wilson's name survives on the mountain rising like a wall north of his ranch, where he cut a path seeking timber for wine casks. He also named Big Bear Lake, where he encountered numerous grizzlies while hunting. (His first wife, Ramona Yorba Wilson, lent her name to **Helen Hunt Jackson**'s Indian heroine.) Not much of a soldier himself—he was captured at the Battle of Chino during the Bear Flag Revolt—Wilson admired Robert E. Lee and Stonewall Jackson sufficiently to hang their portraits in his home, where his grandson **George Patton, Jr.** grew up aspiring to become a warrior.

Wilson wrote a brief memoir, included as an appendix to Robert Glass Cleland's The Pathfinders *(Los Angeles, 1929).*

Sarah Pardee Winchester

(1837?-1922). Like many another widow, Sarah Winchester moved to California after the death of her husband, seeking forgetfulness in a new environment. Her husband having been heir to the rifle fortune, she arrived in 1884 with an estimated $20 million to help assuage her grief. Mrs. Winchester bought an eight-room house in San Jose and decided to expand. She continued to build for nearly 40 years, improvising as she went along. Eventually, her house included 160 rooms,

five fully equipped kitchens, 48 fireplaces, three elevators, and miles of secret passageways. Some of the windows are fitted with latches designed like rifle trip-hammers, and some of the stairs lead to blank walls. Construction was interrupted only by the 1906 earthquake when the terrified Mrs. Winchester moved to a bayside barge for six months, and by her own death. Altogether, the house cost an estimated $5 million and resembles a small city. Locally, "Winchester Mystery House" is said to give off powerful emanations and to be haunted by the souls of all the dead killed with Winchesters, rumors undoubtedly calculated to increase the tourist traffic.

Ralph Rambro's Lady of Mystery *(San Jose, 1967) is strictly local history.*

Cal Worthington

(Calvin Coolidge Worthington, 1921-   ). In another time and place, he would have been a horsetrader or carney pitchman; in freeway-era TV-generation Southern California, he became the world's highest-volume salesman of used cars. A high school dropout and World War II veteran from Texas, Worthington went into the surplus business in Los Angeles after the war. With surplus running short, he bought an auto dealership. In the tradition of former owner "Mad Man" Muntz, he began pitching his wares on late-

night TV, producing, writing, and starring in his own commercials. Another car dealer appeared on TV with his dog Storm, so Worthington came up with a "dog" named Spot—alternately an elephant, a mountain lion, or a porpoise. A good ol' boy in a ranch suit, string tie, and urban cowboy hat, faintly reminiscent of Gary Cooper, he developed a cheerful, noisy hype ("I will stand upon my head," he sang, "until my ears turn red. . .") as the largest purchaser of local commercial time in Southern California. He even managed to maintain his good humor when the state sued him in 1978 for misleading advertising. "They don't like my singing," he explained. "Tell you the truth, I don't either." Worthington settled out of court in 1982 for $50,000 in penalties and costs—without, however, admitting any wrongdoing. A man you love to hate, he is even more aggravating by his absence than his presence, for absence means used car

sales are down and late movies become scarce.

Worthington's autobiography, My Dog Spot, *was not a best-seller.*

Frank Lloyd Wright

(1869-1959). Wright is responsible for the famous regional putdown, "It is as if you tipped the United States up so all the commonplace people slid down there into Southern California." An unconventional aesthete from Wisconsin, he believed people should strive for harmony ("usonia," he called it) with their natural environment. His rather grandiose idea of architectural usonia for Southern California was the Pre-Columbian concrete-block temple, two of which he built under conditions of soul-trying anguish for heiresses **Aline Barnsdall** and Alice Millard. During the construction of Barnsdall's Hollyhock House in Hollywood (1917-1920), Wright was also engaged on the Imperial Hotel in Tokyo, with all the attendant difficulties of remote-control construction; on the Millard house in Pasadena (1923), he came up against that universal enemy of aesthetics, the crooked contractor. (When it was all over, however, he said he would rather have built the small towerlike Millard House than Saint Peter's in Rome, a telling comparison.) Wright spent some time cultivating wealthy prospective clients but not enough of them were willing to live in Aztec temples (early Spanish, in a manner of speaking) to support a local practice. His son Lloyd Wright (1890-1978) enjoyed a more modest success. Originally trained as a landscape

architect, Lloyd Wright worked for Frederick Law Olmsted on the model industrial city of Torrance and on San Diego's Panama-California Exposition. During the 1920s he began designing concrete-block temples like his father's, economizing by adding temple motifs to stucco frames, as with his own house in West Hollywood (1928). Only his Swedenborgian Wayfarers' Chapel (1946) in Palos Verdes approaches his father's unrealized ideal of usonia in Southern California.

Frank Lloyd Wright wrote prolifically, including An Autobiography (London, 1932), *reissued in New York, 1977.*

Willard Huntington Wright. *See* S.S. Van Dine.

William Wrigley, Jr.

(1861-1932). Wrigley was an early twentieth century survival of the era when robber barons were men and not corporations. Starting as a traveling salesman for his father, a Philadelphia soap manufacturer, he launched chewing gum as a promotional gimmick to sell soap. Soon it was his primary product. Thanks to advertising stunts such as a mile-long sign in New Jersey, Wrigley captured 60 percent of the gum market to become one of the ten wealthiest Americans of his day. A baseball fan, he bought the Chicago Cubs and the Los Angeles Angels, constructed Wrigley fields for both teams, and injected the spirit of business (really, show business) into the world of sport. Wrigley acquired a palatial winter home in Pasadena in 1912, and in 1919 purchased Catalina

Island, a former pirate base across the channel from Los Angeles, where he built a $2 million casino, a summer home, and a baseball spring training camp. Promoting "the isle with a smile," the chewing gum magnate offered a prize of $25,000 for the first person to swim the channel, thus putting Catalina on the map. L.A.'s Wrigley Field was torn down in 1964 but Wrigley remains, buried near Catalina's Mount Ada (named after his wife, who died in 1958, having spent her last eleven years in a coma). Their island home is now a USC Conference Center, while their Pasadena mansion is the Tournament of Roses headquarters. Wrigley's most enduring legacy, however, is one of America's more obnoxious habits: gum-chewing.

An early authorized biography by William Zimmerman seems to have become extinct. Robert Hendrickson's The Great American Chewing Gum Book *(New York, 1976) contains background on Wrigley.*

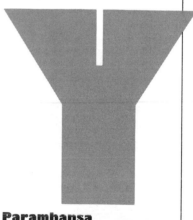

Paramhansa Yogananda (1893-1952).

Inspired by a vision of himself karmically linked to Christopher Columbus, who sought India but found

America, Yogananda left India for America in 1920. Eventually he found his way to Mount Washington in Los Angeles, where he founded his Self-Realization Fellowship (SRF) based on the mental and physical discipline of yoga. The long-haired guru with his beatific smile acquired a following of several hundred thousand disciples and some prime Southern California real estate. A "world brotherhood colony" was founded near Encinitas, on a bluff dramatically overlooking the Pacific, the gift of a businessman who is depicted meditating in a loincloth in Yogananda's memoirs. (His name was James Lynn, and he succeeded Yogananda briefly as SRF president.) The Encinitas facility bears a family resemblance to the Tijuana jai alai palace, but the SRF "lake shrine" in Pacific Palisades is more eclectic, featuring a Dutch windmill, a memorial to Gandhi, and a Mississippi houseboat (on

which the Yoga lived for a time). There was also a SRF center in Hollywood, a retreat in the Mojave Desert, and other churches in Southern California. Yogananda, who in life was able to slow the pulse in one wrist alone, dropped dead in the midst of a Biltmore Hotel banquet for the Indian Ambassador to the U.S. His disciples announced that the guru had made a conscious exit from his body, which was so devoid of "impurities" that it showed no sign of decay three weeks after death. This was confirmed by the director of Forest Lawn, where Yogananda was embalmed.

The Autobiography of a Yoga *(Los Angeles, 1956) is available in several editions, one of them bound in cushioned naugahyde.*

Sam Yorty (Samuel William Yorty, 1909-   ). When Yorty was elected mayor of Los Angeles in 1961, more than one old-timer vaguely recalled having voted for his father during the Depression. In fact, it was

one and the same Yorty, a miracle of political longevity. He left the Dust Bowl at seventeen for California, working his way slowly through Southwestern University and law school as a motion picture projectionist, shoe salesman and employee of L.A.'s Department of Water and Power. Having been endowed with an abnormally large set of vocal cords, he considered a career in opera but decided on politics instead. ("I would rather give a speech than eat," Yorty admitted.) He started out at the left end of the political spectrum with technocracy and **Townsend**ism, traveling steadily right after his election to the state assembly in 1936. He supported Governor **Culbert Olson** initially, then broke with him over the issue of Communists in government, bidding to succeed his friend **Jack Tenney** as the McCarthy of California. A perennial candidate, he ran unsuccessfully for the U.S. Senate in 1940 and for mayor of L.A. in 1945; won election to the state legislature again in 1949 and to Congress in 1950; then lost a 1954 bid for the U.S. Senate. Yorty endorsed **Nixon** for president in 1960 — a self-made man, he objected to the Kennedys "buying" the nomination — and ran for mayor of Los Angeles again in 1961 without his party's endorsement. He won as the candidate of the suburbs (he acquired Mickey Rooney's former home in Studio City) against downtown, the little man against the establishment, "Trash Barrel Sam" (his big campaign issue was

consolidation of garbage collection) vs. the tin can monopoly. He spent his first term feuding with the state Democratic establishment, travelling all over the world, and lumping his enemies together as "Communist dupes and demagogues." Yorty survived one electoral challenge by James Roosevelt, who campaigned against local government by tantrum, but was defeated in 1973 by black former policeman Tom Bradley. He returned to the limelight as host of his own TV talk show, sort of a crackerbarrel Johnny Carson.

Ed Ainsworth, Maverick Mayor *(Garden City, NY, 1966).*

Clement Calhoun Young (1869-1947). California's 26th governor, Young was a mild-mannered English teacher at San Francisco's Lowell High School and coauthor of a standard poetry text, before the earthquake disrupted everybody's lives. When the schools closed down pending reconstruction, he tried real estate, then politics, winning election as a progressive Republican to the state assembly. After ten years in the assembly (1908-18), the last six as Speaker, and two terms as lieutenant governor (1919-27), Young moved up to the governor's mansion in 1927. He enjoyed the backing of the Bank of America, which anticipated support for branch bank consolidation, and won the approval of lobbyist **Artie Samish** who praised him as "a fine man. . . he didn't fool around with politics". His opponents on the right, however, despised him as one of "**Hiram Johnson**'s hired gangsters," a reckless and extravagant administrator (he favored "mildly augmented" public works to combat unemployment. And at the other end of the political spectrum, Young was considered a middle-class babbitt (he pardoned **Anita Whitney** but did not oppose the Criminal Syndicalism Act under which she was convicted). A 1930 campaign poster photographed by **Ansel Adams** says "Elect C.C. Young, He left $31 million in the Treasury." Young was also a "dry" at the end of the Prohibition era. The more tolerant and openhanded **James Rolph** defeated him for the Republican gubernatorial nomination that year.

Darryl Francis Zanuck

(1902-1979). Of all the Hollywood moguls, Zanuck with his virility and playboy lifestyle was the most like a movie star himself. He was also the only WASP from middle America (Nebraska) to rise to the top of a profession dominated in its first generation by Central European Jews, a feat which he accomplished by sheer chutzpah. At fourteen he enlisted in the U.S. Army, serving in World War I France. As a struggling young postwar pulp-fiction writer, he joined the snobbish Los Angeles Athletic Club and took up polo. The film industry was then importing "name" authors, so Zanuck published his own first book (*Habit, A Thrilling Yarn That Starts Where Fiction Ends and Life Begins*, 1923) to get his foot in the door. He wrote Rin Tin Tin scenarios for Warner Brothers and advanced to head of production at Twentieth Century-Fox when he was 33. (Sixteenth Century-Fox, some called it, because the studio made so many historical epics.) Adopting an appropriately sporting lifestyle, Zanuck and family moved to a beach house in Santa Monica (polo) with weekends in Palm Springs (croquet) and winter vacations in Sun Valley (skiing). Exercising the proverbial absolute power of the mogul, he shaved off Robert Taylor's bushy eyebrows to create a matinee idol, made his ski instructor a producer, and bought a Cuban plantation to insure his supply of cigars. He went to North Africa with the army in World War II equipped with an Abercrombie & Fitch sleeping bag, prompting a Senate investigation of the "Hollywood colonels." After 21 years of high-energy Hollywood power, Zanuck quit to act out his own mid-life crisis, leaving his wife for a young Rumanian actress and forming his own production company. After a succession of disasters, both sexual and cinematic, he redeemed himself with *The Longest Day* (1962) and returned to head Twentieth Century-Fox. In 1970 he was ousted by his son.

Mel Gussow's Don't Say Yes Until I Finish Talking (Garden City, NY, 1971) is an almost-authorized biography.

Frank Zappa

(Francis Vincent Zappa, 1940-). Born in Maryland of Greek-Sicilian parentage, Zappa came of age in the Los Angeles hinterlands, graduating from Antelope Valley High School in 1958. An enthusiast of French composer Edgar Varèse, an

early experimenter with electronic music, Zappa wrote his first composition, a percussion piece, in junior high school. He and other local musicians performed together in various combinations and permutations (the Ramblers, the Blackouts) before the "Muthers" evolved in Pomona in the mid-1960s. Renamed the Mothers of Invention, they moved up to the Whisky à Go Go in West Hollywood and a double album, "Freak Out," in 1966. Under Zappa's leadership the group experimented with audience involvement, mixed media, symphonic forms, and bizarre lyrics made up of random syllables, clichés, and nostalgia. (Some Zappa song titles: "Memories of El Monte," "Brown Shoes Don't Make It," "Electric Aunt Jemima," and "Theme from Burnt Weenie Sandwich.") During years on the road Zappa filmed a surrealistic documentary on the rock 'n' roll lifestyle, *200 Motels*, his sprawling film score for which was performed by the Los Angeles Philharmonic in a 1970 series on contemporary music. The Mothers of Invention disbanded in the early 1970s and Zappa retreated to his own private recording studio in the basement of his (formerly Tom Mix's) log cabin in Lauren Canyon, where the "psychedelic **Stravinsky**" was said to be composing a sci-fi musical comedy. In 1982 he and his teenage daughter Moon Zappa scored a hit single with "Valley Girl," a satire on San Fernando Valley style.

David Walley's No Commercial Potential *(New York, 1972) is somewhat less sophisticated than its subject, Zappa.*

Index

Photo credits

The author and publisher wish to thank the following institutions and individuals who have made photographs available for this publication. Numbers and letters denote page number and position of the photographs on the page—t(top), b(bottom), l(left), r(right), and m(middle).

Academy of Motion Picture Arts and Sciences, 5, 7, 33r, 40b, 49, 52, 55, 73b, 74, 76, 78t, 85t, 88, 93, 94, 114b, 135b, 149, 150, 158, 159t, 162l, 166, 177, 201, 202tr, 203, 207t, 208, 213, 215, 216, 225t

Bancroft Library, University of California at Berkeley. 2, 9r, 15r, 22t, 31, 40t, 43, 59, 63, 69t, 70t, 71, 73t, 81, 85b, 89r, 97, 101, 104b, 117, 121, 139, 144, 145b, 151t, 152, 162r, 167, 173, 174, 176, 184, 186b, 189, 191, 193, 194t, 198, 205b, 209, 211, 214, 217, 220t

Welton Becket Associates, 13

Sara Holmes Boutelle, Julia Morgan Association, 145t

Tom Bradley, 21r

Edgar Rice Burroughs, Inc., 30

California Historical Society, 29l, 47b

California State Library. 6, 9l, 15l, 20, 21l, 22, 23b, 24, 25, 29r, 32b, 41, 42, 44, 46b, 47t, 48, 53, 55, 61b, 84, 89l, 90, 102, 103l, 105, 106, 110, 114t, 115, 119, 120, 131, 132t, 136, 137r, 140, 143, 146t, 151b, 153, 164, 169, 170l, 172, 190, 192t, 194b, 196, 199, 202tl, 207b, 210, 212t, 220b, 222

California State Supreme Court, 17

Center for Environmental Design, University of California, Berkeley, 135t

The Glen Fishback School of Photography, Inc., 218

Forest Lawn Memorial Park, 61t

The Gamble House (photo by Whittand Locke), 77t

Rudi Gernreich, (photo by James Ruebsamen), 70

Glotzer Management (photo by John Livzey), 225b

S.I. Hayakawa, 86b

Margaret Herrick Library, Academy Foundation, 33l

Billie Jean King, 109

Alfred Knopf, Inc., 148

Knott's Berry Farm, 112

Levi Strauss & Co., 197

Long Beach Independent, 205t

Los Angeles County Sheriff's Office, 18

Los Angeles Department of Water and Power, 12, 146b

Los Angeles Police Department, 50

McDonnell Douglas, 57

Paul Masson Vineyards, 133b

Yehudi Menuhin, 137r

Olympic Auditorium, 69b

Pasadena Tournament of Roses, 27b

Pritikin Longevity Center, 165

San Diego Historical Society, Title Insurance & Trust Collection, 35r, 188

Dr. Robert Schuller, 180t

Security Pacific National Bank Photograph Collection, Los Angeles Public Library. 3, 4, 8, 10, 11, 27r, 34, 36, 39, 46t, 56, 58, 67, 77b, 78b, 80, 87, 92, 95, 98t, 103r, 122, 123, 126, 127, 128, 141b, 147, 155b, 156, 157, 159b, 163, 171, 175t, 180b, 183, 192b, 219, 221t

Self Realization Fellowship, 28

Sunset Magazine, 86t, 178, 202b

Theosophical Society Archives, Pasadena, 204

Time, Inc., 35r

Transamerica Corporation, 160

Melissa Trumbo, 206

University of California, Los Angeles, 19, 37, 45, 98b, 100, 113, 129, 155t, 179, 185, 186t, 195

University of California, Riverside, 138

Flora Chavez-Wallechinsky, 212b

Cal Worthington, 223